INTRODUCTION TO COMPUTERS AND SOFTWARE

INTRODUCTION TO COMPUTERS AND SOFTWARE

Robert A. Szymanski

Donald P. Szymanski

Donna M. Pulschen

PRENTICE HALL, Upper Saddle River, New Jersey 07458

Library of Congress Cataloging-in-Publication Data

Szymanski, Robert A.
   Introduction to computers and software / Robert A. Szymanski,
Donald P. Szymanski, Donna M. Pulschen.
      p.   cm.
   Includes index.
   ISBN 0-02-418780-1
   1. Computers.   2.Computer software.   I.Szymanski, Donald P.
II. Pulschen, Donna M.   III. Title.
QA76.5.S993   1995
004--dc20   95-25227
                                                        CIP

Editor-in-Chief: Richard Wohl
Executive Editor: P. J. Boardman
Production Editor: Paul DiMaria
Managing Editor: Katherine Evancie
Interior Designer: Function Through Form
Design Director: Patricia Wosczyk
Copyeditor: Sally Ann Bailey
Proofreader: Joan Pokorny
Manufacturing Buyer: Paul Smolenski
Editorial Assistant: Jane Avery
Production Coordinator: Renée Pelletier
Cover Art and Profile Art: Marjory Dressler
Cover Designer: Julia Zonneveld Van Hook
Chapter Opening Artwork: Michael Miller, Head Spin Studio,
   except for chapter 3, courtesy of PIXAR and Darrel Anderson

©1996 by Prentice Hall, Inc.
A Simon & Schuster Company
Upper Saddle River, New Jersey 07458

Printed in the United States of America
10 9 8 7 6 5 4 3 2

ISBN 0-02-418780-1

Prentice-Hall International (UK) Limited, *London*
Prentice-Hall of Australia Pty. Limited, *Sydney*
Prentice-Hall Canada Inc., *Toronto*
Prentice-Hall Hispanoamericana, S. A., *Mexico*
Prentice-Hall of India Private Limited, *New Delhi*
Prentice-Hall of Japan, Inc., *Tokyo*
Simon & Schuster Asia Pte. Ltd., *Singapore*
Editora Prentice-Hall do Brasil, Ltda., *Rio de Janeiro*

For Laura and Eric, your love has brought true happiness and joy into my life

R.A.S.

For the truly meaningful part of my life, my wife Sue and children Paul, Stacy, and Michael

D.P.S.

For the Chip in my main memory and my dear Mother "bored"

D.M.P.

BRIEF CONTENTS

DETAILED CONTENTS

4 Computer Software: The Brains Behind the Brawn 106

● **INFOMODULE TWO**

LAYING A SOLID FOUNDATION FOR BUSINESS WITH INFORMATION SYSTEMS 126

PART III ■ Application Software

5 Document Preparation: Word Processing and Desktop Publishing 140

6 Data Management: Database Management Systems   168

7 Working with Numeric Data: The Spreadsheet and Other Useful Tools   190

8 Data Presentation: Graphics Software, Multimedia, and Hypertext 218

PART IV ■ Implications of the Information Age

10 Trends in Technology   294

PREFACE

This textbook presents a thorough, nontechnical guide for the practical use of computers. The novice and the non-computer major will see how computer hardware and software are used to acquire, manage, and use information vital to both personal and professional lives. We'll look at how technology works and describe how that technology is applied. Current examples are found throughout that illustrate these applications.

This textbook goes beyond the nuts and bolts approach to presenting computer concepts. In addition to learning the how's and why's of computers you will examine important issues such as ethical and legal considerations. We'll also look at the increasing global nature of computing and present an overview of the Internet. By combining these topics with traditional topics, the student will leave this class with a better understanding of the broad implications for the use of computers.

NOTE TO THE STUDENT

How does this book prepare you for the future? Using computers and information systems to achieve your information needs will be an important part of your personal and professional lives. Some experts think that if you do not know how to use a computer, you will be just as handicapped in performing your job as the person who cannot read.

It is important to be both information-literate and computer-literate. You must understand what information you need and how to use it effectively once it is acquired. To remain competitive in today's computerized world, you also need to know how and where computers and information systems are used to help you acquire the needed information. *Introduction to Computers and Software* is an interesting and informative guide on your journey. If you intend to become a computer professional, this book gives the broad-based background you need to pursue advanced course work.

Most of you will probably not be computer professionals. You may be in business, health, engineering, or one of the many other disciplines. Increasingly, these fields are incorporating new ways of using computers to gather and process data. The way you work will undoubtedly change as computer technology improves. Networking, multimedia, virtual reality, artificial intelligence, voice recognition, wireless communication, and telecommunication are a few technologies that your chosen occupation is using now, or may be using in the future. This textbook will inform you without overwhelming you with technical jargon. In each chapter, Highlight boxes relate an account of how technology affects nonprofessional computer users.

In day-to-day work, you will no doubt be required to use a word processor, data manager, spreadsheet, graphic, or communication software program. These are presented in generic terms; they are not tied to specific products. You concentrate on basic concepts rather than program-specific commands. After you have completed this course, your book will remain a handy reference.

Although computers played an important role in the preparation of this text, so did a talented group of publishing professionals. Computers and people working together made this book possible.

KEY FEATURES OF THE TEXT

To present thorough coverage of concepts, hardware, software, computer systems, information systems, communications, and related topics that educators have indicated are important, we have included these key features:

Unique organization through the use of subchapters, called Infomodules, which allow for flexibility and expandability in structuring a course.

Readability at the appropriate level, and a conversational writing style to hold the student's interest.

Sound and effective pedagogy designed to facilitate student understanding and interest in the subject matter.

Current examples of computer applications that relate concepts to actual situations.

Comprehensive coverage that includes discussions of contemporary issues such as

Information and its value

Ethics and legal issues

Artificial intelligence and related topics such as expert systems, neural networks, natural-language processing, speech recognition, computer vision, and robotics

Trends in technology, such as multimedia, storage technology, superconductors, parallel processing, optical computing, biochips, interoperability, visualization, pen-based computing, voice recognition, virtual reality, wireless computing, information superhighway, artificial intelligence, and green computing

Popular types of application software

Tips on document design, spreadsheet design, and business graph and chart design

Increasing use of communication technology

Increasing use of networks, commercial on-line services by professionals, organizations, businesses, and home users

The Internet and its basic services

Information about computer professions and about how computers are changing careers

Introduction to Computers and Software has been written for introductory-level students who may not be interested in continuing their study of computers and information systems, but who plan to pursue other career opportunities.

PEDAGOGY

The following pedagogical devices were chosen with both student and instructor in mind:

Infomodules provide significant coverage of special interest topics. These subchapters offer flexibility in structuring course content. They include key terms as well as review questions.

Chapter objectives alert students and instructor to the major points or concepts to be gleaned from the chapter.

Chapter outlines preview chapter topics and organization so students can see the relationships among the topics covered.

Profiles acquaint students with people who have made major contributions to the Information Age.

Highlight boxes focus on current computer uses and issues.

Sidebars, placed in the margin near relevant text, reiterate key points and serve as memory joggers.

Summaries review major concepts in the chapter.

Vocabulary self-tests spotlight words that are important to understanding the material. These key words are boldfaced where first defined in the text and listed alphabetically at the end of the chapter or Infomodule with text page numbers for reference and review. Key terms are also listed in the glossary.

Review questions check the student's understanding of the main topics in the chapter or Infomodule. They appear at the end of each chapter as a self-test comprised of 30 questions per chapter and 15 per Infomodule.

Issues for thought encourage discussion and group participation in problem solving.

Glossary, a handy reference at the end of the book, defines all of the key terms.

Index, a detailed guide to text topics.

Finally, full-color functional illustrations and 120 photographs clarify concepts, depict applications, and show equipment.

ORGANIZATION

The text is divided into four parts:

- Part One (Chapters 1 and 2 and Infomodule I) is an overview of computers, ethical considerations, and a historical perspective of computing.
- Part Two (Chapters 3, 4 and Infomodule II) describe computer hardware and software and information systems and their applications.
- Part Three (Chapters 5 through 9 and Infomodule III) describe microcomputer application software and introduce the Internet services.
- Part Four (Chapter 10) examines trends in technology.

Here is a quick look at the topics discussed in each chapter and Infomodule.

Chapter 1, "Computers in Your World," introduces students to the concept of information, how it is created, managed, and used. It describes the powerful tools of computers and information systems used in the creation and management of information. The chapter tells where computers are used and briefly explains how they work, what they can and cannot do, and the need to become computer and information literate.

Chapter 2, "Computer Ethics, Crime, and Privacy," defines ethics and looks at it in the context of corporate, individual, and government responsibility; it discusses crimes, legislation, and privacy issues.

Infomodule I, "A History of Computers," provides a summary of events, significant people, and their contributions throughout the history of computers and computing.

Chapter 3, "Computer Hardware: The Tools of the Trade," begins with discussions on why you need to know about hardware and an explanation of data representation. It continues with discussions of the central processing unit and main memory; input and input devices, including those used for physically-challenged users; output and hard and soft copy output devices; ports and device drivers; secondary storage media and devices; and it addresses common secondary storage problems and solutions.

Chapter 4, "Computer Software: The Brains Behind the Brawn," describes systems and application software. It examines operating systems and their importance. In addition, it defines computer programming and looks at different levels of computer programming languages.

Infomodule II, "Laying a Solid Foundation for Business with Information Systems," defines information systems and describes the different levels of management and the information needs of each, the basic types of information systems, the application of information systems in various functional areas of business and selected industries, and the system development life cycle.

Chapter 5, "Document Preparation: Word Processing and Desktop Publishing," describes the uses and features of a typical word processor and examines the features and benefits to using desktop publishing. It also describes elements to consider when designing a document for effectively communicating ideas.

Chapter 6, "Data Management: Database Management Systems," describes the uses and features of a typical database management system.

Chapter 7, "Working With Numeric Data: The Spreadsheet and Other Useful Tools," describes the uses and features of a typical electronic spreadsheet and prescribes some basic rules for designing effective spreadsheets. It also presents other popular numeric manipulation software programs such as accounting, personal finance managers, data analysis, and data modeling tools.

Chapter 8, "Data Presentation: Graphics Software, Multimedia, and Hypertext," defines computer graphics, the main types of graphics software and their uses, and examines the most popular types of graphs and charts used to represent data. Multimedia applications and hardware are presented followed by a discussion of hypertext.

Chapter 9, "Data Communication: Linking a World of Information," explains what data communication is and how data are transferred from one computer to another. The chapter introduces computer networks and covers some challenges presented by the use of data communication. It also describes applications including bulletin boards, commercial on-line services, electronic mail, facsimile, voice messaging, teleconferencing, telecommuting, electronic data interchange (EDI), electronic funds transfer (EFT), integrated services digital network (ISDN), and interactive TV. The chapter ends with a description of uses and features of typical communications software.

Infomodule III, "Introduction to the Internet," describes the Internet, its services and addresses. It also tells how to connect and gives etiquette tips for behavior on the "Net."

Chapter 10, "Trends in Technology," examines some technological trends: multimedia, storage technology, superconductors, parallel processing, optical computing, biochips, interoperability, visualization, pen-based computing, voice recognition, virtual reality, wireless computing, global communications, information superhighway, artificial intelligence, and robotics. Green computing and the effects of computers on careers are also discussed.

THE INSTRUCTIONAL PACKAGE

Instructor's Resource Manual contains chapter-by-chapter lecture outlines, answers to questions in the text, suggestions for using alternative instructional material, and a list of sources for additional reading.

Computerized Test Bank includes true/false, short answer, multiple choice, and fill-in questions. All questions are coded with the chapter number and organized by objective. This versatile test bank program allows the instructor to generate tests, edit existing questions, and add new questions.

Printed Test Item File is a hard-copy version of all questions in the computerized test bank.

Transparency Package consists of overhead transparencies that illustrate concepts presented in the text.

Electronic Transparency Package utilizing Powerpoint allows instructors to present transparencies in the classroom using their personal computer.

"Computer Chronicles" Video Library. Prentice Hall and "Computer Chronicles" have joined forces to provide a video library that offers a variety of documentary and feature-style stories on computers and applications of information technology.

The New York Times **"Themes of the Times."** Computers and information systems are constant themes in the news, both because of developments in the computer industry itself and because of the ways businesses use them on a day-to-day basis. To enhance access to important news items, the New York Times and Prentice Hall, through an exclusive agreement, are sponsoring "Themes of the Times." These complimentary copies of a "mini newspaper" containing reprints of selected Times articles are provided to instructors who use this book for their classes. "Themes of the Times" is an excellent way of keeping students abreast of the ever-changing world of computers and information systems.

IT Works. This interactive, multimedia tutorial CD-ROM accompanies *Introduction to Computers and Software.* It is designed to support the text through animations, photos, illustrations, and video clips. *IT Works* includes explorations, challenging interactive exercises, and quizzes. It is available at a discounted price when packaged with this book. More information is available from your PH sales representative.

ACKNOWLEDGMENTS

We wish to thank the following people who reviewed the manuscript and provided thoughtful and helpful suggestions for *Introduction to Computers and Software:*

Amanda M. Bounds, Florida Community College at Jacksonville; Eli B. Cohen, Wichita State University; William R. Cornette, Southwest Missouri State University; Timothy T. Gottleber, Northlake College; Patricia Nettnin, State University of New York–Brockport; Anthony J. Nowakowski, State University of New York–Buffalo; and David Van Over, University of Idaho.

So many people were involved in the development, production, and creative aspects of this project that the list of names would go on and on. Acknowledgment goes to A. J. Fuller at Bowling Green State University for some screen captures and special acknowledgment goes to the professionals at Prentice Hall who provided support, enthusiasm and helpful suggestions: P. J. Boardman, Executive Editor; Paul DiMaria, Production Editor; Paul Smolenski, Manufacturing Manager; and Patricia Wosczyk, Design Manager. Thanks also to Sally Ann Bailey for her copyediting.

R.A.S.
D.P.S.
D.M.P.

INTRODUCTION TO COMPUTERS AND SOFTWARE

COMPUTERS IN YOUR WORLD

OBJECTIVES

1.1 Describe several ways in which computer technology has changed the way you conduct your personal and professional business.

1.2 Differentiate between data and information, discuss the problem of information overload, explain what is meant by the value of information, and identify seven basic attributes of information used in determining its value.

1.3 Define the terms computer and information system.

1.4 Recognize the importance of possessing a basic level of knowledge, understanding, and skill in using computers and information systems.

1.5 Describe the three basic functions that computers perform, and explain the advantage of using a computer to accomplish them.

1.6 Identify the components that make up a computer.

1.7 Understand the purpose of software and describe the two main types.

1.8 Describe the steps involved in transforming data into information.

1.9 Identify four basic ways in which computers are used.

1.10 Understand the limitations of computers.

1.11 Define special-purpose computer, general-purpose computer, and embedded processor; specify the criteria used to categorize general-purpose computers and describe the major categories.

PROFILE

Raymond Kurzweil

Raymond Kurzweil, is an inventor, scientist, businessman, and author of the book *The Age of Intelligent Machines,* which examines human intelligence and suggests that machines can be built to imitate those abilities. Kurzweil was born in Queens, New York, in 1948. As a youngster he was a talented magician. But, as soon as he was introduced to computers at the age of 12, the true magic began. Kurzweil was interested in recognizing patterns, especially those involving music. He created a program that could compose new works just by matching the sounds of a particular composer. Later he would develop the Kurzweil 250, a keyboard synthesizer that can be programmed to sound like any instrument in its memory—even a concert grand piano. By the time Kurzweil was 15 he had written a program and sold it to IBM for distribution to its customers. Not your "average" teenager. Kurzweil's abilities with patterns is particularly important to the challenges of artificial intelligence (AI), where speech-pattern recognition is fundamental. AI was defined in 1956 by Marvin Minsky (one of Kurzweil's professors at MIT) as "the art of creating machines that perform functions that require intelligence when performed by people."

In 1976 Kurzweil came up with what would be called by some a machine as important to the blind as the development of Braille. The device could "read" and "speak" aloud in a robotlike voice. He went on the "Today Show" with the 350-pound Personal Reader. The apparatus caught the attention of Stevie Wonder, the blind singer, who wanted one. The $50,000 price tag did not deter Wonder, who took the unwieldy machine home and "read" all night. By 1991 the Personal Reader had become a briefcase-sized machine with a palm-size scanning device and a collection of nine "voices" that could even identify exclamation marks in the written word and read those passages with excitement.

Although machine intelligence is advancing rapidly and human intelligence is at a comparative standstill, human intelligence covers a broad expanse, while today's computer intelligence works in rather narrow areas of expertise. For example, Kurzweil's VoiceRAD machine, used by radiologists, can be programmed to recognize individual voices, and as a user utters specific words or terminology; the machine produces predetermined phrases and sentences that ultimately are compiled into written radiological reports. Using this machine saves doctors from the tedium of taking notes, dictating, and proofreading each report.

The future, according to Kurzweil, will likely include telephones that translate conversations into other languages, devices that give "voice" to persons with speech problems by recognizing voice patterns and printing the words, and robotic devices for paraplegics that would fit on their legs and permit them to walk. The future will tell us whether computers will ever "speak" for themselves. But whatever the future holds, it isn't hard to imagine more tricks up Kurzweil's sleeve.

I t is nearly impossible to escape the effects of computers and information systems today. From artist to zoologist, organizations and individuals, like you, are discovering the potential uses of computers and information systems to meet their information needs and reach their desired goals.

On a personal level, you may find them beneficial for tasks such as managing investments and finances, calculating taxes, preparing resumes, catching up at home on your school or office work, educating your children, and entertaining yourself and your family. Organizations, large and small, have long seen advantages in using computers and information systems. The pace of technological innovations and the pressures of competition keeps us searching for new and better ways to use computers and information systems.

This text lays the foundation for you to function in a world that makes extensive use of computers and information systems.

OBJECTIVE 1.1
Describe several ways in which computer technology has changed the way you conduct your personal and professional business.

HOW IS COMPUTER TECHNOLOGY CHANGING YOUR WORLD?

Even when you don't see them, computers and information systems are working behind the scenes—at school, at home, where you play, and where you shop, work, or transact business. Some computers are responsible for your leisure enjoyment and entertainment; others are found in government operations and most professions.

Computers Where You Work

Computers and information systems are used in business for many information processing tasks. These tasks include word processing, filing, and assembling numbers and facts associated with general office functions, such as accounting, payroll processing, personnel record keeping, and compliance with federal regulations.

The federal government is the largest user of computers and information systems and one of the largest funders of computer research. By one estimate, the federal government holds over 4 billion personal files on U.S. citizens. The U.S. Patent and Trademark Office receives over 20,000 documents every day, and the Securities and Exchange Commission receives more than 6 million pages of documents and reports a year. These agencies could not function efficiently without modern computers and information systems.

Computers and information systems simulate events such as automobile crashes or airplane emergency landings. These events involve a variety of factors that must be evaluated to locate weaknesses in new designs without risking human lives. NASA astronauts train by studying computer simulations of problems they could encounter during launch, in space, or upon return to Earth. The ability to simulate hazardous conditions without risk to humans has brought progress in space flight and Earth-bound vehicle safety testing (see Figure 1-1). The ability to compare and make inferences is important in many fields of study.

Advances in health care have been made possible through the ability of the computer to accumulate and store data. Hospitals use computers extensively, recording information on each patient's admission, prescribed medications, doctor visits, other hospital services, and of course the itemized bill. Computers and information systems are valuable as tools to diagnose and treat medical conditions (see Figure 1-2). Diagnostic equipment such as computer-aided tomography (CAT) and magnetic resonance imaging (MRI) rely on computers. Physicians compile the data they gather and visualize it graphically to

FIGURE 1-1
This body model is designed to simulate the mass and other characteristics of an actual human body to test a proposed seat belt design. Computer simulation aids engineers in identifying the most effective seat belt design to eliminate shoulder belt slack on impact.

(Courtesy of Daimler-Benz and Evans & Sutherland)

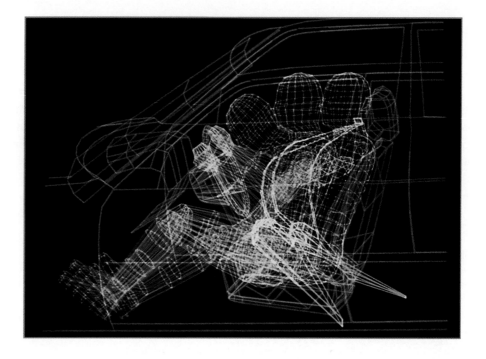

FIGURE 1-2
Physicians can access lab reports and other vital patient information during surgery with a computer placed in the operating room.

(Courtesy of Apple Computer, Inc.)

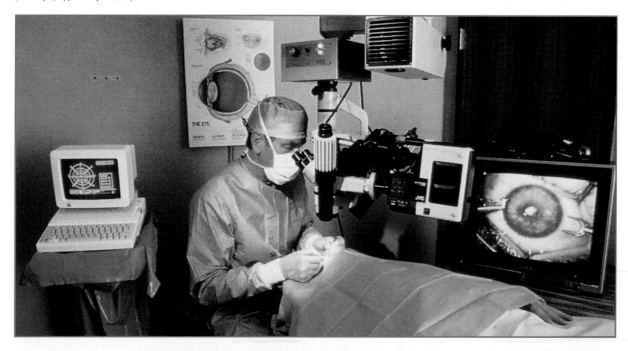

make it more understandable. Some medical students are learning anatomy and physiology by means of *The Electric Cadaver.* This "electronic book" displays text and images on the computer screen—even depictions of muscles and tendons at work—and gives students the ability to study the body's internal organs and skeletal structure.

Computers at Play

Our recreation and leisure-time pursuits, entertainment, and even our homes have been affected by computerization (see Figure 1-3). Some people stay in shape with

FIGURE 1-3
Representatives of Clairol use a computerized system that produces an image of the client. This image can then be modified to show the client how she would look with different combinations of makeup or hairstyles and colors without actually having to try them. The consumer can then use this information to choose the style she prefers.

(Courtesy of Clairol, Inc.)

computer-controlled monitoring devices that combine a microcomputer, a road bicycle, and an exerciser in a personally programmed course of exercise that simulates hills and lets you select speed, wind, and slope conditions. A screen simulation offers a panorama of the particular course you select.

In most professional sports, computers compile statistics, track ticket sales, create training programs and diets for athletes, and suggest strategies based on the past performance of competitors. The graphic art displays flashed on scoreboards also are generated by computers.

If you're a sports fan watching in an armchair, do computers affect you? Well, television networks use computers in the control room to bring you play-by-play action. With the help of a computer, a technician calls up replays of the action and inserts the commercial breaks on schedule. It is possible that the sport shoes you're wearing were designed using computers that checked stress points and then created a style and shape to offer maximum support for the foot.

A musical instrument digital interface (MIDI) links musical instruments to a personal computer, thereby enabling the computer to control a wide variety of instrument sounds (see Figure 1-4). The background music in many movies, television shows, and commercials is electronically generated. In addition, when you buy concert tickets, the ticket agency is probably part of a computerized network that registers the number of seats sold.

Computers have also gone Hollywood as seen in films like *Jurassic Park*. Computer-generated art lets designers create sets, special effects, and even imaginary characters in movies, videos, and commercials. Creatures, spaceships, and entire galaxies are created and manipulated by computers and then photographed by computer-driven cameras. Computer-controlled lighting systems on sound stages or in theaters produce a dramatic range of atmospheres.

Want to get away from it all? Computers help prepare your ticket, confirm your hotel room and rental car reservations, monitor the route of your train, or guide your plane to a safe landing (see Figure 1-5). Tulsa, Oklahoma, is the hub for American Airlines' reservation system, SABRE, the world's largest network of computers not used for military purposes. The system processes data at the rate of 1,400 messages per second. With the aid of over 700,000 miles of wires and circuits connecting five large computers, SABRE confirms your reservations while you wait.

One place you could "get away" to is Joyopolis, the Sega Enterprises theme park, in Yokohama, Japan. Here users enter virtual reality worlds where simulated "games" are played through the use of head gear and joysticks. These computerized video

FIGURE 1-4

Musician and entertainer Steve Loren of Columbus, Ohio, uses eight pieces of computerized equipment, a microcomputer, a keyboard, and a MIDI, such as "The Box," to make his synthesized music. With this equipment, he records demonstration tapes and gives live performances. Loren records all the instrumental music tracks himself, stores the sounds on disk, and plays them back as needed during his performances. As Loren sings, the system provides all the background music he needs (sometimes replicating the sounds of an entire orchestra), eliminating the need for other musicians to travel with him.

(Inset courtesy of Decillionix Co.)

arcade games won't be found in your home, but there are many other uses for computers and information system in your home.

Computers at Home

In more and more home offices, people use computers to continue their daytime work, organize personal informational needs, or conduct business for themselves. Microwaves, sewing machines, and coffee makers are among the standard computerized appliances in most homes. In addition, home automation systems with prices ranging from $1,500 to many thousands of dollars create so-called "smart" homes that maximize computer use. Lighting, heating, cooling, and security systems are among the computer-controlled functions. Sensors warn owners of fire or vandalism. Lawns are sprinkled automatically, hot tub temperatures are regulated, and motion sensors turn lights and heat on or off when a person enters or leaves a room.

The North Carolina Grandover Resort and Conference Center, an entire "smart" housing development, was ready for occupants in early 1995. Anything in the homes with an electrical signal is capable of being controlled and programmed by computers. Touch-screen computers offer communication with maid, laundry, yard, and courier services, too. These homes are also equipped with interactive video. Because these homes were built and networked together, the costs have been kept lower than if each home created its own system.

Volunteers for Medical Engineering built another kind of Future Home in Baltimore, Maryland. Not such a big deal, until you consider that the occupant of this "smart" house has the use of only one finger. The various computerized functions are activated either automatically, by voice commands, or by pressing a single button. The

FIGURE 1-5
A travel agent uses a computer network to access information stored on a remote computer. She can quickly identify availability and the price that suits a client's needs when booking airline flights, hotel rooms, and car rentals. She can also immediately update the information on the remote computer so that once a reservation is made it is no longer available to other agents.

whole-house sound system allows its owner to make phone calls from a microphone mounted on the wheelchair. This system can also be programmed to give reminders, such as "Take your pills."

Computers Go to School

Most schools in the United States have computers located in laboratories, classrooms, and registration offices. Many educators find computers to be valuable aids for instruction and tutoring (see Figure 1-6). Computer tutors are tireless and nonjudgmental when drilling students on mathematical facts or offering specialized lessons on particular subjects. Because many science laboratory experiments can be simulated by computer, young students become interested and excited by the interaction, the vivid color graphics, and the feeling of accomplishment gained from giving the right answers. The Boston Computer Society and Lotus Development Corp. sponsor a competition in search of our future programmers. Four-year-olds are not too young to learn about the computer mouse, and preteens develop computer games and create computer-generated artwork.

Many libraries, including those at Stanford, Harvard, and Yale, offer on-line searching capabilities. At Stanford, Socrates is an electronic card catalog system of 8 million books. Computers with on-line databases in the libraries allow easy and quick research. Librarians, staff, and visitors take advantage of the expanding computerized services. On campuses where computers are linked through networks, faculty members compile research data from their offices and students complete research projects and finalize term papers from their rooms. Many libraries have added scanning equipment designed to read articles directly into a user's computer. Scholars are particularly interested in bibliographic and abstracting services.

FIGURE 1-6
This instructor uses a computer to help motivate her students and make learning fun.

(Courtesy of Edmark Corporation.)

Museums and their curators have been using computers for years to manage their inventories. And now, they are availing themselves of the technology found in multimedia capabilities that give their visitors hands-on experience with their displays. The Michael C. Carlos Museum at Emory University offers a tour that allows its visitors to "play" a rare Costa Rican flute from one of its collections. This clearly would not be possible to do in person because of the potential for damaging the valuable collection. Many museums have addresses on the Internet, and you can "visit" and "view" their exhibits without leaving your computer screen.

Without doubt, computers are a part of your world. Surveys of recent college graduates indicate that the need is critical for more computer education and hands-on application training so you'll be prepared for real-world experiences. Developing the knowledge and skills to put them to work for you is essential to a well-rounded education in the information age in which you live. Turning to that education, let's discover the roles of data and information.

OBJECTIVE 1.2
Differentiate between data and information, discuss the problem of information overload, explain what is meant by the value of information, and identify seven basic attributes of information used in determining its value.

WHAT ARE DATA AND INFORMATION?

How can I track personal finances? How can I prepare an inventory of personal belongings and easily update it for insurance purposes? I have an idea for a novel, but the thought of a typewriter and having to make corrections and revisions prevents me from starting. What can I do?

How can my business keep track of and reduce the cost of inventory? We need a way to analyze our sales data so more cost-effective advertising decisions can be made. All my employees have computers on their desks, but nobody seems to be working with the same information. What can I do to remedy this?

You may have these and many other questions in your personal and professional lives. To make appropriate decisions and solve problems, you need to gather the data and turn them into information to help answer those questions.

You know there are many challenges to getting an education. Some are physical, some are mental, and some are emotional. But the computer has proved to be a great equalizer for students with any of these special challenges, giving the ability to express themselves through nonconventional devices.

Students who are not able to hold and manipulate a pen or pencil and paper input data through adapted keyboards, specialized pointing devices, or sip-and-puff switches. These devices mean that manual dexterity is not required. Blind or visually impaired students listen to their computers through speech synthesizers, where the computer "talks" to them. Voice recognition technology that allows users to enter commands through vocal commands is quite expensive and requires perfection before it becomes a common input method. But

there are software programs, called word prediction programs, whereby students only enter a single letter and the program offers choices of whole words from which to select. For example, merely entering the letter "C" prompts the program to offer common choices of words that start with that letter. The entire word does not have to be laboriously typed before it appears on the screen. This shorthand method speeds up data entry for special-needs students.

These special users focus attention on the thought process rather than the feat of creating each letter of every word in the document. And, once the written work has been saved, it can be easily revised or corrected where necessary. The final product is neat and legible.

This kind of education is indeed "special."

Data are raw facts (numbers, letters, special characters, or combinations thereof) that convey little meaning by themselves. Data are readily available to an organization. Every transaction that occurs supplies data. A **transaction** is a business activity or event. The receipt of an order or the sale of a product constitutes a transaction. **Information** is processed data that appears in context and conveys meaning to people. For example, data about each salesperson's performance can give a sales manager information about how well each individual is doing and how well the sales department as a whole is performing.

Strange as it may seem, one person's data may be another's information. For example, your first test grade of, say, 93 is information to you but is probably regarded only as data by your teacher.

Data
• Raw facts conveying little meaning

Information
• Processed data seen in context and conveying meaning

Information Overload

There typically is much more data available than needs to be collected for the decision-making, problem-solving, and control activities of most individuals. With computers and improved data communication, the problem is not the lack of data or the subsequent information that its processing can generate, but the fact that most people receive more information than they can possibly absorb. This condition is referred to as "information overload." The greatest difficulty is not in gathering data but in deciding what data need to be gathered to provide the necessary information and making sure the information gets distributed to the right people at the right time.

Determining the Value of Information

Also important is the ability to determine the value of information. Computers do not have the ability to "understand" what the data they process represents. Determining the value is up to you. Generally, people judge the **value of information,** that is, its meaningfulness and usefulness, based on the attributes of information. These attributes give the user a framework by which to judge meaningfulness and usefulness. Following are seven basic attributes of information: (1) accuracy, (2) relevance, (3) completeness, (4) timeliness, (5) cost-effectiveness, (6) auditability, and (7) reliability. *Accuracy* refers to whether information is accurate (true) or inaccurate (false). *Relevance* refers to whether information is needed and useful in a particular situation. *Completeness* refers to how thorough or inclusive a set of information is. *Timeliness* refers to two conditions: Is the information available when it is needed, and is it outdated when it is received or when it is to be used? *Cost-effectiveness* refers to the relationship between the benefit to be derived from using information and the cost of producing it. *Auditability,* also known as verifiability, refers to the ability to check the accuracy and completeness of information. *Reliability* summarizes how closely information fits the other six attributes. Information is not always perfect. It may not be totally accurate, or it may not be 100 percent verifiable. Reliability takes into consideration the expected averages of the other six attributes. If they are near what was expected, then the information is considered reliable. If it deviates significantly from what was expected, then it is considered unreliable.

It is important to look closely at the information to determine if it is correct and in a form that meets your needs. You can't assume correctness merely because it was generated by a computer.

You must use the information wisely and ethically. *Computer ethics* refers to a standard of behavior that conforms to societal and professional principles for the use of computers and the information they generate. Chapter 2 takes a closer look at this important topic.

OBJECTIVE 1.3
Define the terms computer and information system.

WHAT ARE COMPUTERS AND INFORMATION SYSTEMS?

Two tools that are used to convert data into information and communicate it to the people who need it are computers and information systems. A **computer** is an electronic device that can accept input, process it in a prescribed manner, output the results, and store the results for later use. It is a tool used to process data into information. There is not a single type of computer, rather, a wide assortment with varying capabilities, as we will examine later in this chapter. Figure 1-7 shows a computer that you might recognize, a microcomputer.

A *system* is any set of components that work together to perform a task. An **information system** is a set of components that work together to manage the acquisition, storage, manipulation, and distribution of information. The components of an information system are hardware, software, people, data, and procedures. **Hardware** includes all the physical equipment that make up an information system such as computers and communication equipment. **Software** is the instructions that cause the hardware to do the work. People, like you, make products, deliver services, solve problems, and make decisions. A person who uses computer hardware and software to perform a task is often referred to as an **end-user** or simply **user.** As an end-user of an information system you will need to understand what it can do for you and how to use it effectively to accomplish your information needs. Data also play an important role in an information system; as you saw earlier, they provide the basis for information. The final component in an information system is **procedures,** the instructions that tell a user how to operate and use an information system.

Information systems that are designed for use by an individual user, are called **personal information systems.** You might set up a personal information system on your home computer to manage your financial portfolio. Information systems designed to be used by many users are called **multiuser information systems.** These are found in most businesses and organizations and are vital to their successful operation. Many of today's products could not be produced without the effective use of information systems on the factory floor. Aerospace, automotive, and industrial

Information system components

- Hardware
- Software
- People
- Data
- Procedures

FIGURE 1-7
Most of you have seen or used a microcomputer, such as the ones pictured here.
(Courtesy of Digital Corp. [left] and Apple Computer, Inc. [right]).

manufacturers use information systems to automate production and streamline engineering, speed development time, reduce cost, and keep up with the competition.

OBJECTIVE 1.4
Recognize the importance of possessing a basic level of knowledge, understanding, and skill in using computers and information systems.

WHY LEARN ABOUT COMPUTERS AND INFORMATION SYSTEMS?

You can see that many potential career choices require, or soon will require, an understanding of computers and information systems and the ability to use them; this is called **computer literacy.** This is only part of the story; you'll also be expected to judge the value of, and use the information generated wisely; this is called **information literacy.** You will need both to compete for many jobs. This doesn't mean, however, that you'll have to be a technical wizard, because there are many levels of ability. These range from users who only need to know how to turn the computer on and off and use the software required by their job to generate or gain access to needed information; to those who must decide what data should be gathered and how those data should be processed; to those who repair, install, or design computers and information systems.

Because of the move to an economy based on information, your ability to perform on a job may depend on how well you acquire and use the skills needed to use computers and information systems. Imagine that the marketing department manager plops down a 2-inch-thick pile of statistics and asks you to summarize it and prepare a report to the marketing director at 8 A.M. tomorrow! If you know how to use it, the computer can help.

Computer literacy
- Basic knowledge and understanding of computers
- Ability to use computers effectively

Information literacy
- Effectively judge the value of information
- Wisely use the information generated

Even on a personal level you can see why it is important to learn about these tools. If you have used a computer, then you have had an introduction to this remarkable tool. You already realize its impact on your efficiency and productivity. However, if you have never used a computer, just ask a friend who uses a word processor about the differences in preparing a term paper. Ask him/her to go back to typing rough and final drafts on a typewriter. The answer will be a resounding "No way!"

OBJECTIVE 1.5
Describe the three basic functions that computers perform, and explain the advantage of using a computer to accomplish them.

WHY USE A COMPUTER?

A computer processes data into information through three basic functions: (1) performing arithmetic operations on numeric data, (2) testing relationships between data items by logically comparing values, and (3) storing and retrieving data. These functions allow the computer to calculate numeric data, create documents, and manage data.

If you can perform these functions already, why use a computer? Computers work faster, more accurately, and more reliably than people. Consider the formidable task the Internal Revenue Service faces each year processing millions of tax returns. It would be possible to process them manually; however, this would be extremely difficult, time consuming, and prone to human error. None of us would be too happy to wait years for a refund check or to have payment amounts miscalculated.

OBJECTIVE 1.6
Identify the components that make up a computer.

WHAT HARDWARE MAKES UP A COMPUTER?

Computer hardware includes the system unit, input devices, output devices, and secondary storage devices (see Figure 1-8). The **system unit,** or housing, contains the major components and controls of the computer, that is, the central processing unit and main memory. Hardware that is externally attached to the system unit is sometimes referred to as **peripheral devices.** An **input device** allows instructions and data to be entered into the computer for processing, for example, keyboard and mouse. An **output device** receives information from the computer, for example, monitor and printer. A **secondary storage device** provides permanent or relatively permanent storage of data and instructions. Instructions and data can be reentered without retyping them. Common secondary storage devices are hard disk drives and floppy disk drives.

Basic tasks performed by computers

- Arithmetic operations on numeric data
- Logical comparisons of values
- Storage and retrieval of data

Advantages of computers over humans

- Faster
- More accurate
- More reliable

Types of hardware and examples

- System unit
  - Contains major components and controls, for example, central processing unit and main memory
- Input devices
  - Keyboard
  - Mouse
- Output devices
  - Monitors
  - Printers
- Storage devices
  - Disk drives
  - Tape drives

FIGURE 1-8
The components of a computer system are shown in this photo.
(Photo by Sylvia Dill)

WHAT IS SOFTWARE?

Computer hardware by itself is no more than an extremely expensive paperweight or doorstop without a key to unlock the computer's enormous potential. The key is software. Software, or **computer programs,** are the instructions that cause the hardware to do the work. A computer program consists of numerous instructions, often tens of thousands. There are two main types of software: system software and application software.

System software directly controls and monitors the operation of the computer hardware. The computer is a general-purpose tool designed to perform a wide variety of tasks. **Application software** allows you to perform a specific task or set of tasks such as preparing documents, managing data, performing numeric calculations, creating graphic images, and transferring data between computers electronically. The types of application software that perform these tasks are word processors, database management systems, electronic spreadsheets, graphics programs, and communication programs. Application software includes specialized tasks related to such fields as business, engineering, science, education, and entertainment. Business-oriented applications include accounting programs such as payroll, accounts receivable, accounts payable, general ledger, budgeting, and financial planning which are used in almost every kind of business. Engineering and scientific applications include programs such as computer-aided design (CAD), which automates mechanical drawings; chemical engineering; scientific calculations; and structural analysis. Educational applications include computer-assisted instruction (CAI) that guides a student through a course of study, typing tutors, and grade book programs to assist instructors in the process of recording student scores. Entertainment applications include games, flight simulators, and music programs.

You interact with the application software by entering commands and data. The application software interacts with the system software requesting specific computer hardware resources. You can also interact directly with system software to control the computer hardware (see Figure 1-9). You do not need to personally create computer programs for the computer to be useful. In fact, most people purchase the software they need rather than create it themselves.

HOW DO COMPUTERS TRANSFORM DATA INTO INFORMATION?

Information processing, or more traditionally **data processing,** refers to all the steps associated with converting data into information. These steps include input, processing, output, and storage (see Figure 1-10).

Information processing steps
• Input
• Processing
• Output
• Storage

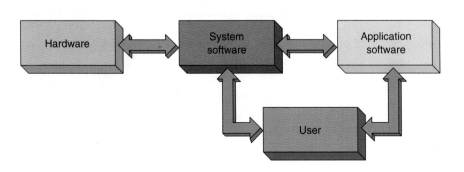

FIGURE 1-9
The relationship among system software, application software, hardware, and the user.

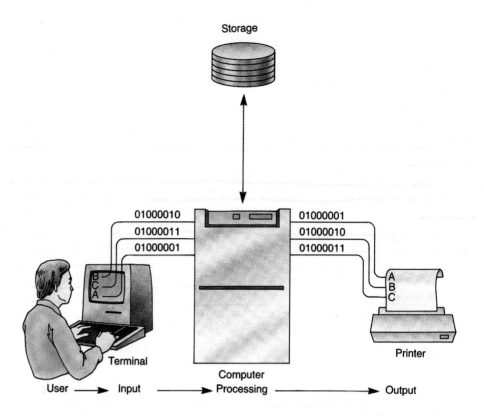

Input refers to the data and instructions entered into a computer for processing and also describes the act of entering data and instructions. It is important that correct data be input because the information generated is based on the manipulation of those data. If the input is incorrect the output will also be incorrect creating a situation referred to as **garbage in, garbage out (GIGO).**

Processing involves performing calculations and logical operations on data to achieve a desired outcome. Be sure that the programs you design or buy will process the data in the manner required.

Output refers to the results of processing and also describes the act of generating results. Once the computer generates the information, it must be output so you can use it. Output takes numerous forms, including informal drafts, formal reports, and graphics. One advantage in using a computer is that a single set of data entered can be manipulated in a variety of ways to produce many different outputs. For example, a company's corporate sales data could be manipulated to produce reports on sales of each product by region, total sales of each product, performance of each individual salesperson, and charts that graphically display these results.

Storage refers to the computer's ability to maintain data or information for use at a later time. A computer has two primary means of storage: internal storage called **main memory,** or **primary storage,** and external storage called **secondary storage.** The instructions in a computer program and the data they work on must be stored in main memory to be executed. Secondary storage preserves programs and data permanently or relatively permanently.

Let's see how this process works. Imagine you work for a newspaper and you've just received 3,000 completed surveys on what readers want in a national health care program. Your editor wants a breakdown of the data by age, income, and political affiliation. She wants the results displayed in both tabular and graphic forms for the paper's editorial page.

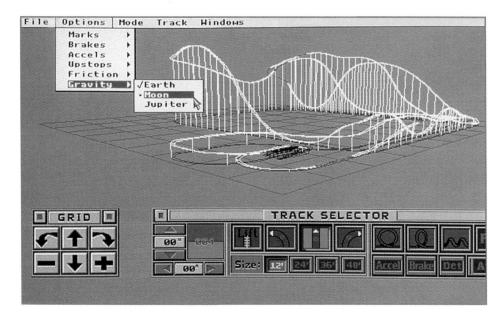

FIGURE 1-11
Computers are used to design
and test rollercoasters before
they are constructed.
(Courtesy of Walt Disney Computer Software)

The first step is to carefully input the data from each survey into the computer. You could use a keyboard to enter the data into an application program called a database management system. This program easily manipulates data to meet your information needs. You enter each individual's age, income, political affiliation, and preferences into the computer.

Next comes processing of the data into the information you need. By selecting the appropriate data manipulation and graphics features of the program, you can extract the information you require and arrange it in both tabular and graphic form.

Once you've generated the information and selected the presentation format, you output the results. They are displayed on the computer's monitor, sent to a printer, or transferred electronically to another computer, or stored for later use. For example, the editor may want to review and approve a printed copy. Later you could retrieve it for modification, if required, and then send it electronically to the computer that controls the typesetting process.

OBJECTIVE 1.9
Identify four basic ways in which computers are used.

WHAT ARE THE BASIC WAYS COMPUTERS ARE USED?

Typically, computers are used for general information processing tasks where output is required in forms that can be read, understood, and used by people (end-users), for example, reports or graphs.

Design and development of products is another way the power of the computer can be used. Products are designed and tested on the computer before resources are spent on actual manufacturing. This saves time and money and is important for expensive products or products that are dangerous for people to test (see Figure 1-11).

Computers can also be used to monitor and control other computers, equipment, or processes (see Figure 1-12), for example, your home environment (heating, cooling, lights, security), robots on assembly lines, or the flight of an airplane.

Another way in which computers are used is to electronically send data from one point to another—a process called **data communication. A computer network**

> **Ways computers are commonly used**
> - General information processing
> - Design and development
> - Monitor and control
> - Data communication

links one computer to another thus making it possible for data to be shared and updated at different locations.

OBJECTIVE 1.10
Understand the limitations of computers.

WHAT ARE THE LIMITATIONS OF COMPUTER USE?

Computers are merely tools, useless without humans. A computer cannot identify a problem to be solved, decide the output needed to solve a problem, identify and collect the data needed to produce output, design the software necessary to transform data into a desired output, or interpret and use the accumulated information to solve a problem. These tasks must be completed by people like you. If a computer is conceived and designed properly, then it becomes a valuable tool allowing you to accomplish your task faster, more accurately, and more reliably.

In some cases, it may seem that a computer is doing its work without the benefit of human involvement, for example, when a computer automatically generates software instructions or initiates a process. However, the *software* that automatically generates other instructions is conceived and designed by humans. The decision criteria that lead to a particular process initiated by a computer are defined and programmed by humans. You play an important part in ensuring the successful use of a computer. In the end the information generated by a computer is only as good as the data that you entered, the quality of the software designed to process the data, and your ability to wisely use the information produced to make decisions and solve problems.

OBJECTIVE 1.11
Define special-purpose computer, general-purpose computer, and embedded processor; specify the criteria used to categorize general-purpose computers and describe the major categories.

HOW ARE COMPUTERS CATEGORIZED?

The two main classes of computers are special-purpose computers and general-purpose computers. A **special-purpose computer** is designed to work on a limited scope of problems, for example, a computer that is modified to control only the environmental factors in a high-rise building, such as heat and humidity. A special-purpose computer that is part of a larger system whose primary purpose is not computational is called an **embedded processor.** These are found in a wide variety of consumer products such as microwave ovens, wristwatches, and video game machines, as well as in automobiles, and robots used in manufacturing. The programs that operate special-purpose computers are generally etched into silicon chips and are not changeable. The silicon chips that contain the instructions etched into them are called **firmware.**

A **general-purpose computer** is designed to work on a wide variety of problems. Simply by using a general-purpose computer and different software, diverse tasks can be accomplished. The focus of this text is on general-purpose computers. There is a wide variety of general-purpose computers. The criteria used to sort them into classifications include architecture (design), processing speed, amount of main memory, capacity of external storage devices, speed of the output devices, the number of users, and the cost.

The architecture of a computer refers to the design of the internal circuitry. It includes the number and type of the components that perform the actual computing tasks.

Processing speed is measured by the number of instructions that a computer processes per second, usually in millions of instructions per second (MIPS). Generally, the larger the classification, the faster a computer can process data.

Main memory includes the internal storage that a computer accesses and uses. Larger computers have more main memory than do smaller computers. Generally, the larger the classification of computer, the larger the number of secondary storage devices that a computer is capable of supporting.

The speed of an output device is how fast it can print or otherwise produce output. Output from dot-matrix and ink-jet printers is measured in characters per second, line printers in lines per minute, and laser printers in pages per minute.

Typically, small computers are single-user computers accessed by only one user at one time. Large computers easily support hundreds of users at one time and are called multiuser systems.

The price of a computer is usually a reflection of the power of the system. Therefore, the larger the classification, the higher the price. The price of a computer also depends on the options purchased. Thus, a complete computer system classified in a lower category may actually cost more than one in a higher category. Small computers range from hundreds to thousands of dollars, and the largest computers cost millions of dollars.

According to these criteria, computers are grouped into four size classifications: (1) microcomputers, (2) minicomputers, (3) mainframes, and (4) supercomputers. You should understand what is meant by each.

Distinctions in computing power are becoming blurred because of technological innovations that increase the processing speed and store greater amounts of data in smaller areas. Therefore, many of the small newer machines have characteristics and capabilities of the large older ones of a few years ago. Figure 1-13 illustrates how the various computer systems overlap in computing power.

Microcomputers

The computer that you will likely come in contact with is the microcomputer. A **microcomputer** is a computer that is built around a single-chip processor called the microprocessor. These computers are relatively small in size, but some of today's models pack as much processing power and speed as larger systems of only a few years ago and at significantly less cost. Microcomputers are designed to be used primarily

Criteria for classifying computers

- Architecture
- Processing speed
- Amount of main memory
- Capacity of external storage devices
- Speed of the output devices
- Number of users
- Cost

Categories of general-purpose computers

- Microcomputers
  - desktop
  - portable
  - laptop models
  - notebook models
  - palmtop models
  - pen-based models
- Minicomputers
- Mainframes
- Supercomputers

FIGURE 1-13
Because technological advances
have increased computing
power and decreased prices,
categorical distinctions among
computer systems are becoming increasingly blurred.

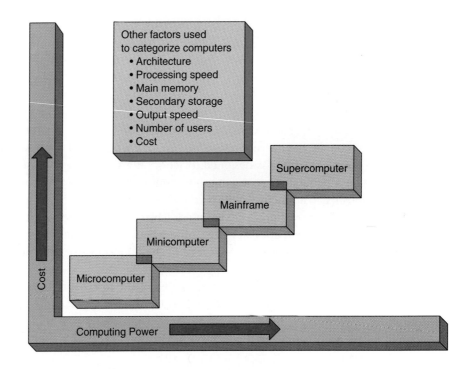

by a single individual, which explains why they are called **personal computers** or PCs for short. However, most microcomputers can share resources if the appropriate software is used and hardware connections are made. Microcomputers are the least expensive computers ranging from a few hundred dollars to several thousands of dollars. PCs are categorized as desktop or portable. A **desktop computer** fits conveniently on a standard business desk.

A term you will often hear is "workstation." A **workstation** is a category of powerful stand-alone desk-top computer whose base price includes a high-end processor, very large main memory, considerable calculating and graphics capability, and all the hardware and software needed to connect it to a network (see Chapter 9). Workstations range in cost from $10,000 to $100,000. Typical users are engineers and architects. The workstation provides the power needed for sophisticated design programs without the expense of larger computers.

Portables are divided into laptop, notebook, palmtop, and pen-based computers. Weight, readability of the screen, layout and ease of use of the keyboard, and durability are some of the most important features to look for in a portable. The advent of truly portable microcomputers has allowed users to take computers where they are needed (see Figure 1-14).

Portable computers have gone through an evolution too in the past few years. The first portables were called transportables, required AC power, and weighed around 30 pounds. Next came the **laptop computer,** which ran on both AC and batteries and weighed around 10 to 15 pounds (see Figure 1-15). Further shrinking in size but increasing power and flexibility resulted in a **notebook computer** (see Figure 1-16). About the size of an $8\frac{1}{2}$- × 11-inch notebook, it is very popular and has both AC and battery power options. Notebook computers weigh around 6 to 8 pounds, have display screens from 7 to 10 inches, and feature keyboards that are smaller than those for desktop microcomputers. However, many challenge desktop models in power and speed. Some notebooks can be inserted into a docking station

FIGURE 1-14

Portable computers have allowed individuals to use computers in a wide variety of circumstances (a) in the library, (b) in the field at a construction site, and (c) on the go.

(Figure 1-14b courtesy of Compaq, Inc.)

a

c

b

to take full advantage of the desktop's peripheral devices, including the full-sized keyboard and large monitor. The docking station uses the notebook's microprocessor and storage units and eliminates the need to transfer data from the notebook to a separate desktop computer to use the desktop's features. A **palmtop computer** weighs less than 1 pound and is as easy to carry around as your wallet or checkbook (see Figure 1-17). It fits easily into your pocket and can provide you with quick access to the data wherever you need it. Palmtops can be connected to your PC to transfer and share information between them. Most operate for up to 60 hours on standard alkaline AA or AAA batteries, which can be easily replaced. Palmtop computers can be used with peripherals such as printers, fax/modems, and integrated circuit cards that supply additional memory and software applications. Drawbacks with palmtops include their small keyboard and display screen. A **pen-based computer** uses a pen-like device to input data rather than a keyboard or a mouse (see Figure 1-18). It is ideal for mobile workers and those who regularly fill out forms, such as law enforcement personnel, insurance claim adjusters, delivery personnel, and doctors.

FIGURE 1-15
These two men are using a laptop computer at a construction site.

FIGURE 1-16
A notebook computer fits easily into a standard briefcase for convenient transport to where you need it.

(Courtesy of International Business Machines Corp.)

FIGURE 1-18
(Above) An insurance claims adjuster uses a pen-based computer to complete a claims form electronically. The information can later be transferred to a computer in the main office and the claim processed.

Minicomputers

Minicomputers are the next step up in processing power, speed, and cost (see Figure 1-19). Minis are designed to accept input from and produce output to a large number of users, supporting from 10 to 100 terminals. Typically the minicomputers perform complex computations such as those involved in the use of CAD programs that create engineering and architectural drawings, transaction processing applications such as order-entry systems, and as interfaces between mainframe computers linked into a computer network. The top-of-the-line minicomputers are designated superminis. Minicomputers range in price from tens of thousands of dollars to several hundred thousand dollars.

FIGURE 1-19
Minicomputers generally have less power than do mainframes. They are used in many small and medium-sized organizations.
(Courtesy of International Business Machines Corp.)

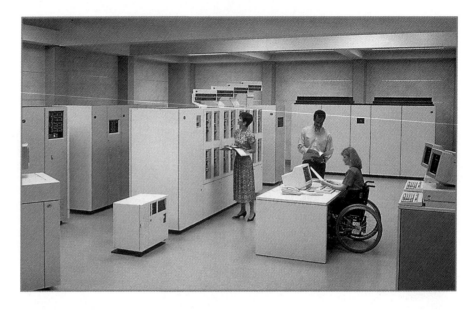

FIGURE 1-21
(a) The Cray YMP supercomputer. (b) Terminals and other hardware needed to support the Cray YMP.

(Photo by Jo Hall [right])

a   b

Mainframes

Mainframes provide an increase in processing power, speed, and cost over minicomputers (see Figure 1-20). They typically handle greater volumes of input, output, and storage activities and can support hundreds of users. The mainframe is for more intensive computational tasks than minicomputers and is associated with the manipulation of large volumes of data by businesses and the government. Because mainframe computers are sensitive to temperature and humidity changes and dust, they are usually found in environmentally controlled computer rooms. Mainframes are priced from several hundred thousand dollars to several million dollars.

Supercomputers

Supercomputers are the most powerful, fastest, and most expensive computers, supporting hundreds of users (see Figure 1-21). A supercomputer is used for complex or sophisticated applications such as weather forecasting (see Figure 1-22), genetic decoding, aerodynamics, and processing of geological data. Supercomputers can process up to several billions of instructions per second (BIPS), but they require environmentally controlled computer rooms and cost millions of dollars.

FIGURE 1-22

A Cray supercomputer produced this three-dimensional schematic simulation of a thunderstorm. The position of the arrows indicates that the low-level rotation is intensifying. This type of simulation helps meteorologists to predict the paths and intensities of severe storms.

(Courtesy of Gene Moore, Phototake, NYC; inset courtesy of Joseph Klemp and Richard Rotunno, National Center for Atmospheric Research.)

HIGHLIGHT 1-2 **Give Me a Break!**

You have probably heard or said these words sometime. They have real meaning for users of computers. Ergonomics experts say that you really do need a break from working long hours at a computer. You can suffer repetitive stress injuries, in the fingers, wrists, neck, shoulders, and back. They may cause chronic pain or permanent damage to muscles, tendons, and nerves. You may be 1 of 10 million computer-related eye cases seen by optometrists annually. Or you may merely suffer occasional eyestrain from long hours of watching the screen with little or no relief.

There are computer programs that educate computer users on do's and don't's. Exercise*Break* shows illustrations of 50 tension-relieving exercises, tells you how to sit at the computer, and lets you set a schedule so the computer reminds you to do the appropriate exercises. "Eyercise" is concerned with your visual needs in mind. It offers relaxation techniques and suggestions for relieving tension and eye strain. "Take Five" suggests minivacations through listening to music, stretching activities, imagining a visual vacation, or practicing guided-imagery exercises to relax tired bodies.

To reduce stress injuries, use furniture that is properly designed and adjusted to your height. Good posture is extremely important. You should be aware of the symptoms of repetitive stress injuries and make changes in your office environment as soon as possible. It is wiser to avoid injury in the first place.

Remember to move around, stretch your arms, legs, back, and eyes—you know, take a break!

SUMMARY

Data are raw facts that convey little meaning by themselves. Information is processed data that is seen in context and conveys meaning to people. The value of information refers to its meaningfulness and usefulness in a particular situation and is judged based on the attributes of information. The attributes of information include accuracy, relevance, completeness, timeliness, cost-effectiveness, auditability, and reliability.

A computer is an electronic device that can accept input, process it in a prescribed way, present the results as output, and store the results for use in later processing. A system is any set of components that work together to perform a task. An information system is a set of hardware, software, people, data, and procedures that work together to manage the acquisition, storage, processing, and distribution of information. A personal information system is designed to be used by an individual user. A multiuser information system is designed to be used by many users.

One purpose of a computer is to transform data into information. Computers accomplish this by performing three basic functions. They perform arithmetic operations on numeric data, they test relationships between data items by logically comparing values and store and retrieve data. The advantage of using computers for these functions is that they perform them faster, more accurately, and with more reliability than humans.

Computer hardware includes the system unit, input devices, output devices, and secondary storage devices. Peripheral devices are hardware that are externally attached to the system unit.

Software, or computer programs, are the instructions that cause the hardware to do the work that you desire. There are two main types of software: system software and application software.

Data are transformed into information through a series of steps referred to as information processing, or data processing. These steps include input, processing, output, and storage.

Computers are used in several basic ways: for general information processing tasks; to design, develop, and test products; to monitor and control other computers, equipment, and processes; and to send data from point to point electronically.

Computers cannot operate alone. They require humans to identify a problem, decide how to solve it, identify and collect the data, design the software, and interpret the information obtained.

A special-purpose computer is designed to work on a limited scope of problems. A computer that is part of a larger system whose primary purpose is not computational is called an embedded processor. A general-purpose computer is designed to work on a wide variety of problems. Simply by using a general-purpose computer and different software, diverse tasks can be accomplished.

General-purpose computers are classified by architecture, processing speed, main memory, external storage capacity, speed of output devices, number of users that can access a system at one time, and the cost of the computer. The classifications include microcomputers, minicomputers, mainframe computers, and supercomputers.

Microcomputers are often called personal computers since they are primarily designed to be used by a single individual. Microcomputers are divided into desktop computers and portable computers. Portables are divided into laptop, notebook, handheld, palmtop, and pen-based computers. Minicomputers are the next step in power followed by the mainframe computer. The most powerful computers are dubbed supercomputers.

VOCABULARY SELF-TEST

Can you define the following?

application software (p. 15)
computer (p. 12)
computer literacy (p. 13)
computer network (p. 17)
computer programs (p. 15)
data (p. 11)
data communication (p. 17)
data processing (p. 15)
desktop computer (p. 20)
embedded processor (p. 19)
end-user (p. 12)
firmware (p. 19)
garbage in, garbage out, (GIGO) (p. 16)
general-purpose computer (p. 19)
hardware (p. 12)
information (p. 11)
information literacy (p. 13)
information processing (p. 15)
information system (p. 12)
input (p. 16)
input device (p. 14)
laptop computer (p. 20)
mainframes (p. 24)
main memory (p. 16)
microcomputer (p. 19)

minicomputers (p. 23)
multiuser information systems (p. 12)
notebook computer (p. 20)
output (p. 16)
output device (p. 14)
palmtop computer (p. 21)
pen-based computer (p. 21)
peripheral devices (p. 14)
personal computers (PCs) (p. 20)
personal information systems (p. 12)
primary storage (p. 16)
procedures (p. 12)
processing (p. 16)
secondary storage (p. 16)
secondary storage device (p. 14)
software (p. 12)
special-purpose computer (p. 18)
storage (p. 16)
supercomputers (p. 24)
system software (p. 15)
system unit (p. 14)
transaction (p. 11)
user (p. 12)
value of information (p. 11)
workstation (p. 20)

REVIEW QUESTIONS

Multiple Choice

1. Which of the following is true about data?
   a. conveys little or no meaning to people
   b. are seen in context and convey meaning to people
   c. are the primary product of processing
   d. are not necessary for processing

2. Which of the following is not a function of an information system?
   a. accepts input
   b. produces output
   c. communicates output in a timely fashion
   d. makes decisions for users

3. Computer literacy means _____.
   a. being knowledgeable in advanced mathematics and electronics
   b. having a complete understanding of how computers work internally
   c. being able to use the most advanced and complex features of a computer
   d. having a general knowledge and understanding of computers

4. Which of the following is not an advantage of computers over humans?
   a. faster
   b. more reliable
   c. more accurate
   d. smarter

5. Which of the following is not a function of a computer?
    a. stores and retrieves data
    b. interprets output
    c. tests relationships logically
    d. performs arithmetic operations

6. A(n) _____ allows information to be retrieved from the computer.
    a. output device
    b. input device
    c. storage device
    d. system unit

7. _____ refers to computer programs that help users perform a specific tasks.
    a. System software
    b. User software
    c. Application software
    d. Hardware

8. _____ involves performing calculations and logical operations on data to produce a desired result.
    a. Storage
    b. Processing
    c. Input
    d. Output

9. Which of the following is false?
    a. Computers process data into information.
    b. Computers are more accurate than people.
    c. Computers can interpret and use information to solve a problem.
    d. Computers are faster than people.

10. Which of the following is the fastest and most powerful category of computers?
    a. personal computer
    b. minicomputer
    c. mainframe computer
    d. supercomputer

Fill In

1. _____ are raw facts that convey little meaning by themselves.

2. Data that have been processed into a form that can be seen in context and convey information to people are called _____.

3. A(n) _____ is an electronic device that can accept input, process it in a prescribed way, present the results as output, and store the results for use in later processing.

4. A(n) _____ is a set of hardware, software, people, data, and procedures that work together to manage the acquisition, storage, manipulation, and distribution of information.

5. _____ refers to being able to judge the value of information and use the generated information wisely.

6. _____ is the components, or physical equipment, that make up a computer.

7. The instructions that cause the hardware to do work are called _____.

8. _____ refers to the input, processing, output, and storage stages involved in converting data into information.

9. _____ refers to the data entered into a computer for processing.

10. A(n) _____ is a computer small enough and light enough to carry around with you.

Short Answer

1. Differentiate between data and information and give several examples of each.

2. To use computers effectively it is necessary to have detailed knowledge of electronics and mathematics. Defend or refute this statement.

3. Describe the three basic tasks that a computer can perform.

4. Describe the advantages that computers have over humans in processing data into information.

5. Identify the components that make up a computer.

6. List the steps involved in transforming data into information and give an example.

7. Tell what is meant by the value of information.

8. Describe four ways in which computers are commonly used.

9. Discuss some of the limitations of computer use.

10. Discuss several ways in which computers and information systems have affected either your personal, educational, or professional life.

Issues for Thought

1. Some airplanes are controlled by computers that do not let the pilot override the computer's control. Do you think this is a good idea? Why or why not?

2. When you make a transaction, many companies use computers and information systems to gather data about you such as your name, address, telephone number, buying habits, and credit history. They then sell this information to other companies without your permission and without giving you the chance to verify the information. What potential problems can you see in this? Explain your answer.

CHAPTER

2

COMPUTER ETHICS, CRIME, AND PRIVACY

OBJECTIVES

2.1 Briefly describe how computer technology can cause ethical and legal issues to arise.

2.2 Define computer ethics.

2.3 Describe a code of ethics for computer professionals.

2.4 Describe some ethical guidelines for computer users.

2.5 Describe how ethics pertain to governments and computing.

2.6 Describe how ethical behavior relates to computing on a network.

2.7 Define how ethical behavior affects global issues.

2.8 Understand how ethics affects information.

2.9 Understand the conflict in determining ethical resolutions to computing issues.

2.10 Define computer crime and describe several types.

2.11 Describe how detection, prevention, and legislation can help reduce computer crime.

2.12 Understand the potential for invasion of your privacy through the unethical or criminal use of computers.

PROFILE

Augusta Ada, Countess of Lovelace

The Countess of Lovelace, as Augusta Ada, daughter of the famous poet Lord Byron was later to be known, seemed destined for greatness from the start. You see, early on Augusta displayed a penchant for the study of mathematics, which her mother, Annabella Milbanke, encouraged and supported.

She was an accomplished linguist. And this expertise with languages found her in the employ of Count Luigi Frederico Menabrea who had written an article on the analytical engine, a predecessor to the computing device designed by Charles Babbage. The fact that she undertook the assignment of translating, from Italian into English, is not remarkable, but what she did with those papers is.

Augusta became great friends with Charles Babbage. Not only did she translate the papers, but she also had the ability to really understand his designs. She actually worked out most of the theoretical principles and the programming behind Babbage's analytical engine and added her own notes and observations. She suggested that for storage, the binary system would be more suitable than the decimal system. She also included looping as part of the design of the analytical engine.

The countess died in 1852, and although it took a while, she has finally been recognized for her accomplishments. Her immortality emerged from her love of mathematics. The other title (besides countess) bestowed on Augusta Ada is "first programmer." She has also been recognized by the U.S. Department of Defense, which named its most complex and far-reaching computer language "Ada."

Computers are neither good nor bad. They simply take data that are entered by people, process it according to instructions developed by people, and present it as output designed to be interpreted by people. Therein lies a potential dilemma—people.

Have you ever made an airline reservation, stayed in a hotel, rented a car, filed your income tax, acquired a social security number? Data about you are in all those files. Imagine what they know about you! Is it an invasion of privacy for someone to accumulate data? Not necessarily, but it could be.

In the forward to a book called *The Rise of the Computer State*, Walter Cronkite mused:

"If—or is it when?—these computers are permitted to talk to one another, when they are interlinked, they can spew out a roomful of data on each of us that will leave us naked before whoever gains access to the information.

"But we must be vigilant against their misuse, either accidentally or intentionally. . . . there is also a danger of losing it all in the green glow from a little phosphor screen."

In this chapter we will look at the issues surrounding computer ethics, crime, and privacy.

OBJECTIVE 2.1
Briefly describe how computer technology can cause ethical and legal issues to arise.

HOW CAN COMPUTER TECHNOLOGY CREATE ETHICAL AND LEGAL QUESTIONS?

Computer technology has affected society. Day-to-day tasks are accomplished faster and more accurately. We use computers to go into space and to write a term paper. Computers allow huge volumes of data and information to be amassed. That, in itself, is not a problem. However, it's what is done with that data and information that leads to legal and moral dilemmas.

In the past, access to data was limited; however, now more users have access to many different kinds of data. How, and to what degree, do you limit or regulate this access?

Ten to 15 years ago copying personal computer software was not the problem that it is today, because in the early 1980s the desktop computer was just a "newborn." Is new software a *product,* or does it provide a *service?* Can it be thought of as an expression of an idea, or is it just a means to change the function of the computer? Various laws and standards may or may not apply depending how you define it.

Laws are not the only thing that new computing technology is affecting. Software developers have moved toward graphical representations of commands and instructions on the computer screen. To the sighted person, this represents an easy method of understanding computers; however, to a blind or visually impaired person, this severely limits their access. Software is not at the stage where it interprets pictures and turns them into sound reliably and conveniently. With text-oriented software, commands and instructions could be synthesized and spoken by the computer. This method brings computing to the world of the blind, but new technologies such as multimedia that combine audio and video are only partially useful to users who are hearing impaired. Closed captions for computers may be one answer. As computer technology advances, developers must take care that in the search to help one group of people, another group is not left out of the loop.

Additionally, standards and codes concerning legal and moral issues must change and adapt as new dimensions are added, for example, networking, virtual reality, and artificial intelligence. These standards, codes, and behaviors fall under the general heading of ethics.

I t sits on your desk, offers legal advice, and doesn't charge. Is it a lawyer? Not really, but it can help prepare your small business or at home legal paperwork. "It" is application software that makes filling out routine, legal documents simpler.

Much of the legal work a small business requires tends to be fill-in-the-blank type. The costs involved while the lawyer asks you questions, you give the answers, and the lawyer prepares the documents are fees that most small businesses would prefer to do without. One product, LegalPoint, from Teneron Corporation, contains over 50 "templates" such as

employment contracts and bills of sale. To fill out the form, the user highlights the question to be answered and the program offers suggestions. The completed document can be loaded into a word processor where it can be edited or a company logo added. The program also offers summaries of many topics that affect a business such as the Fair Labor Standards Act and the Americans with Disabilities Act.

The need for a real, live lawyer still exists. You should always have one review legal forms; but for routine entry of data, computer software may be your lawyer on a disk on top of your desk!

OBJECTIVE 2.2
Define computer ethics.

WHAT IS COMPUTER ETHICS?

Webster's New World Dictionary defines "ethics" as "the study of standards of conduct and moral judgment; the system of morals of a particular person, religion, group, etc." **Computer ethics,** then, could be described as a set of rules that govern the standards or conduct of computer users; principles used with computers and the information they produce. The terms "property" and "stealing" are difficult to define as they relate to software, information, access, and privacy. Although there may be disagreement on what is "right" and what is "wrong" in given instances, there are areas of agreement. Those common areas serve as a beginning and controversies can be handled on a case-by-case basis. To help raise awareness and to develop meaningful discussions on ethics, the Computer Ethics Institute generated the "Ten Commandments of Computer Ethics" (see Figure 2-1). Ethical dilemmas arise among professionals, individuals, governments, on networks, and globally. Many times ethicist are capable of making a case for either side of an example.

OBJECTIVE 2.3
Describe a code of ethics for computer professionals.

WHAT DOES PROFESSIONAL ETHICS EMBODY?

The concept of professional ethical standards is not new. For thousands of years people have recognized the need for regulations or codes of ethics. In Babylon from 1792 to 1750 B.C. one of the greatest kings developed the famous *Code of Hammurabi,* the credo of which was that "the strong shall not injure the weak." The Hippocratic Oath, the code of ethics to which physicians subscribe, dates back to 2000 B.C. Most professional organizations acknowledge the need for principles; a code of ethics offers a framework for accountability. In 1992 the Association for Computing Machinery (ACM) adopted a revised Code of Ethics, as have other professional organizations. The ACM Code asks members to abide by the following eight principles:

Make a contribution to society.
Avoid injury to others; consider long-range impacts.
Be honest.
Be tolerant of others.

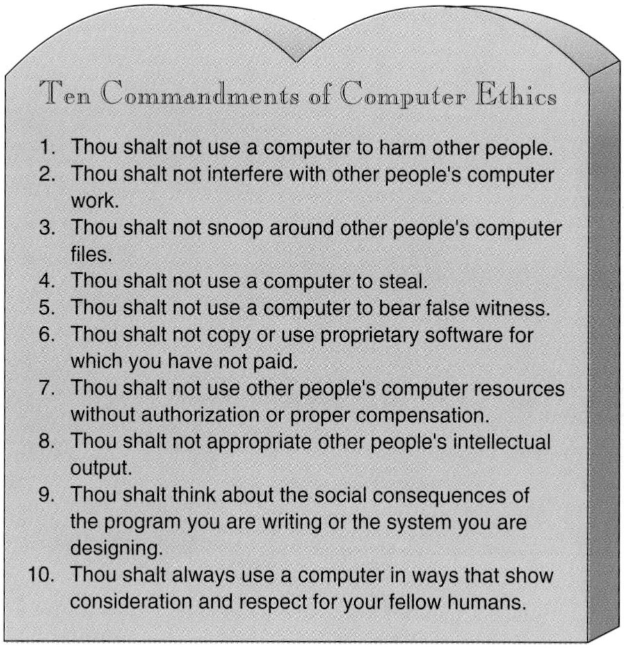

FIGURE 2-1
The "Ten Commandments of
Computer Ethics," as developed
by the Computer Ethics
Institute.

Ten Commandments of Computer Ethics

1. Thou shalt not use a computer to harm other people.
2. Thou shalt not interfere with other people's computer work.
3. Thou shalt not snoop around other people's computer files.
4. Thou shalt not use a computer to steal.
5. Thou shalt not use a computer to bear false witness.
6. Thou shalt not copy or use proprietary software for which you have not paid.
7. Thou shalt not use other people's computer resources without authorization or proper compensation.
8. Thou shalt not appropriate other people's intellectual output.
9. Thou shalt think about the social consequences of the program you are writing or the system you are designing.
10. Thou shalt always use a computer in ways that show consideration and respect for your fellow humans.

Do not condone copyright or patent infringement.

Respect intellectual property.

Maintain privacy.

Revere confidentiality.

You will notice that computers, per se, are not mentioned. In fact this general code could be adapted for other professions. However, a study described in the *Computer Professionals for Social Responsibility Newsletter* indicates that fewer than half of the businesses surveyed had a written code of ethics.

More and more business computers are being linked together to facilitate sharing information. Being connected also allows electronic mail to be sent between computers. This has given rise to new software programs that employers use to monitor their employees. **Electronic work monitoring** lets the employer count an employee's keystrokes, track data entry errors, record the length and frequency of breaks, determine what files have been accessed and for how long, and read their electronic mail (see Figure 2-2). Some of these software monitoring products even have the ability to view the employee's computer screen at the same time as they are working, without the employee knowing it.

The legality of this practice is under constant debate. Even if it is legal, is it ethical? Do employers have the right to ensure that workers are not using company time for personal reasons? Is this a version of spying, or does it have legitimate uses? Borland International found that an employee was passing company secrets to a rival company. Does company security justify monitoring? A recent study by the Communications Workers of America, along with the University of Wisconsin, found that monitored employees have sufficiently greater levels of stress, anxiety, and depression. Certainly this will affect their job performance. Should monitoring practices be announced, or should they take place without employee awareness? The ethics of both could be debated.

Ethics finds its way into big and small businesses. Take, for example, a computer repair business. They make money by performing the service of repair. If a repair is going to cost as much as a new piece of equipment, do they have the "legal" obligation to inform you? the "ethical" obligation to inform? Does a salesperson, who knows a simple repair could be your solution, have the same obligation to inform you of your choices?

FIGURE 2-2
Electronic work monitoring is a controversial workplace practice. According to studies, 10 to 15 million employees are under surveillance annually.

(Courtesy of Honeywell, Inc.)

Ethical situations change as the evolution of ideas change. For example, the trend in software is toward interoperability, that is, add-on programs from one company that will work with software designed by another company. To accomplish this, some aspects of the original must be duplicated. By strictly adhering to copyright laws, this could be seen as infringement. Without some overlap of programs, could new software be written? Where is the line drawn, or is it a fuzzy line?

OBJECTIVE 2.4
Describe some ethical guidelines for computer users.

WHAT DOES INDIVIDUAL ETHICS EMBODY?

Ethical behavior on the part of an individual is basically the choice of the individual. Although there are laws that govern us all, some people will inevitably seek to circumvent those laws. Unfortunately, it is the same with computer use standards. It is up to each of us to behave "ethically" and to persuade other users to behave in "ethical" ways. Some ethical behaviors for individuals include

Refusing to borrow or share illegally obtained programs
Protecting your password and not using another's password
Copying software for backup purposes only
Using appropriate language and behavior on a computer network
Encouraging others to behave ethically

OBJECTIVE 2.5
Describe how ethics pertain to governments and computing.

WHAT DOES GOVERNMENT ETHICS EMBODY?

Although there is no specific code of ethics for all government entities, the U.S. Constitution does set certain standards. For example, the First Amendment of the U.S. Constitution grants us freedom of association and "abridging the freedom of speech or of the press." And the Fourth Amendment guarantees "the right of the people to be secure in their persons, houses, papers, and effects, against unreasonable searches and seizures, shall not be violated and no warrants shall issue but upon probable cause. . . ." The framers of the Constitution had no way of knowing or preparing for the future. So laws are still being written to cover the technological advances. Of course, wiretapping and eavesdropping are limited by state and federal statutes, but what's to prevent another individual from doing it? Of course, it's the personal code of ethics of the individuals that dominates in those situations.

The Currency & Banking Retrieval System is a database where banks and other sources who file with it report transactions of $10,000 or more, as well as smaller, suspicious bank deposits. Is this electronic "snooping" ethical or lawful? The following two examples show how basically the same action by the same government agency results in different ethical conclusions.

An Internal Revenue Service agent used a computer to search the database for questionable cash bank deposits. The records did not look right. Receipts for admissions from a booking agency were not reported. The records were subpoenaed, and the parties in question wound up paying $12 million in taxes, penalties, and interest, along with serving a 21-month jail term. Is this an invasion of private records or merely pursuit of justice? Many people agree that this was the correct procedure by the IRS.

An internal audit of the Southeast region released in 1993 showed that over 300 agents were suspected of using IRS computers to snoop into financial files of celebrities, friends, and relatives. Most would agree that this is not ethical behavior. There are over 50,000 people in the IRS who have computer access to taxpayer data. Even in a large organization, one person's ethical behavior reflects on the whole.

Because the government makes the laws, it is responsible to protect its citizenry from unlawful behavior or unethical action. This brings about interesting conflicts. Should the government give the IRS more power to legally inspect electronic personal files in an effort to gain lawful revenue, or should it protect your right to privacy?

The Federal Bureau of Investigation is implementing an Automated Fingerprint Identification System (AFIS). Their fingerprint files will be digitized, thus allowing electronic cataloging, which makes for increased matching of prints. The system will eventually give the ability to scan a person's fingerprints, much like a scanner in a grocery store. The proposed Interstate Identification Index, along with AFIS, will pull together all criminal information from any state connected with each set of fingerprints. To fight crime, this gathering of data seems to be an acceptable use of modern technology. But could we see the day when this type of computer technology is used when you apply for a driver's license, for example. Could we see a data bank on everyone? When is the line crossed between those who see it as a "right to know" issue, with those who see it as a "right to privacy" issue? As with many ethical questions, just because it's legal doesn't mean it's right.

OBJECTIVE 2.6
Describe how ethical behavior relates to computing on a network.

HOW ARE NETWORKS AFFECTED BY ETHICS?

Electronic networking of computers provides users with a convenient method for accessing a variety of data and information. But publishers and creators of such material are concerned over the recent increase of unethical, but not yet criminal, copying of that material. Copyright laws are unclear in this area so the U.S. Department of Commerce plans to review and release new recommendations for strengthening them. These recommendations were to be put to public hearings. Congress will not take up the issue until after the hearings. The vagueness of network copyright laws leads some people to unethically acquire material not intended for distribution.

Network Rules and Behavior

There are many types of networks: those that connect the office computers, bulletin board services (BBSs) that you access by dialing a telephone number, on-line subscription services (America Online, CompuServe, Delphi, GEnie, and Prodigy are the most common), and worldwide networks such as the Internet (millions of users on over 30,000 connected networks in over 100 countries). Each has rules or expected behaviors that are not always the same since they may have different target audiences. Some BBSs are strictly adult oriented, but most on-line services have rules prohibiting explicit language or obscene material. Parents should monitor access by young children and use the parental control features provided by some networks.

Forums, which are groups of people on a network talking about a certain topic, have unofficial codes of etiquette. Typing in all capitals denotes shouting, and although asking questions that have already been asked a hundred times won't get you thrown in jail, you might not be accepted into the group. A company in San Diego thought they would increase sales by advertising on the Internet. What they got instead was a bunch of angry letters from longtime users who do not see the Internet as a vehicle for this type of commercial endeavor. There is usually a system operator or monitor who informs new members about the general rules and etiquette for the forum.

On a network people are connected by the written word. Because of this anonymity, ethical and criminal abuses can occur. College campuses have been the target of unethical behavior because of the accessibility of network services. At the University of Wisconsin at Stevens Point, the library was forced to shut down for a day because of a bomb threat sent on the campus network. Racist jokes were sent via the Internet from a computer account at the University of Michigan which reached bulletin boards in many countries. At the University of Illinois at Urbana-Champaign and Stephen F. Austin University, two students were charged with threatening the life of the president of the United States using electronic mail. Many students at Dartmouth College missed an exam because someone put a message on the school's network that implied the professor had canceled a scheduled test. Some of the network abuses are fairly harmless, while others are downright criminal.

Network Security

The Computer Emergency Response Team (CERT) was founded in 1989 by the Defense Department to investigate crimes on the Internet. In 1993 they investigated over 1,500 complaints. In 1994, CERT issued an advisory to Internet users because of the high number of break-ins. Software programs designed to look useful were actually stealing passwords. Could unscrupulous behavior mean less information or limited access on the information highway?

In 1986 the Federal Electronic Communications Privacy Act offered protection for a person's electronic mail sent over public networks, but the act does not apply to electronic mail sent via corporate networks. Monitoring of employee E-mail is being addressed by the Privacy for Consumers and Workers Act. It requires that employers notify workers if they are monitoring any electronic mail, communications, telephone calls, or data entry activities. Some believe that an employer has the right to protect its business, while others, like the American Civil Liberties Union, see it as a privacy issue and at the very least want the employer to notify employees who are being monitored.

Censorship Versus Free Speech

Two of the largest on-line services—Prodigy (an IBM and Sears joint venture) and CompuServe (an H&R Block subsidiary)—have different philosophies about their services. CompuServe holds that users publish their own subject matter without approval from them. Prodigy, on the other hand, stirred up great controversy in its attempt to control the contents of its on-line bulletin boards, giving rise to many questions about censorship. CompuServe goes by a user self-policing policy, while Prodigy and some others prohibit profanity outright.

In 1993 a USENET user implemented a program that prevented what he considered irrelevant or abusive messages from being posted on a public network. Preventing someone from posting notices is unacceptable, but should networks post everything? The ethical dilemma that this creates is similar to debates about sexually explicit material in art, movies, and magazines. There is no pat answer, but networks may choose to limit their liability by warning users that material on-line may be inappropriate for children.

Instilling Ethical Network Behavior

Schools are aware of the fact that as more students and others use networks, they need to be informed of the ethical behavior expected with their use. At the University of Delaware all incoming freshmen who want access to the school's computers take a test. The Electronic Community Citizenship Examination tests the student's understanding of ethics and regulations concerning misuse of computer access and copyright restrictions among other topics. Massachusetts Institute of Technology encourages students to report misuses through a program called "Stop It." These initiatives confront abusers and describe how their actions are detrimental to others. Many colleges offer courses where the emphasis is not particularly on what is legally correct but, rather, on what is ethically the right thing to do.

In mid-1994 the National Computer Ethics and Responsibilities Campaign was established with a goal to reduce computer crime over electronic airways. They developed a set of teaching tools to promote ethical behavior on the Internet and other computer networks.

OBJECTIVE 2.7
Define how ethical behavior affects global issues.

HOW DOES ETHICS AFFECT GLOBAL ISSUES?

The Business Software Alliance (BSA) reported that in 1993, 61% of the software used by businesses in Europe were illegally copied. They found over 80% in countries such as the former Soviet Union, Poland, and Spain. Software companies lost over $5 billion in earnings and sales tax revenue. Since 1988 the BSA has filed hundreds of international lawsuits to protect software manufacturers. The Software Publisher's Association estimated that in North America almost one of every two copies of software programs are illegal, which costs software developers billions in lost revenue (see Figure 2-3). Manuals, diskettes, and software were discovered in a major investigation in the Far East that could result in sanctions if those countries do not act to control piracy. Even local legitimate businesses are pressuring government officials to develop stronger copyright laws. Unethical behavior occurring in one country can have wide ranging effects on other countries.

Global ethics deal with the flow, impact, production, dispersal, and utilization of information among nations. Because they have the ability to easily transmit data electronically across borders, governments and big business also have the ability to control that information. Control of the data and information can affect global society by

Widening the gap between those countries that can and cannot afford it—
    creating an information elite
Creating technological, political, and social differences

FIGURE 2-3
It is estimated by the Software Publishers Association that in 1993 more money was
lost to software pirates than McDonald's made.

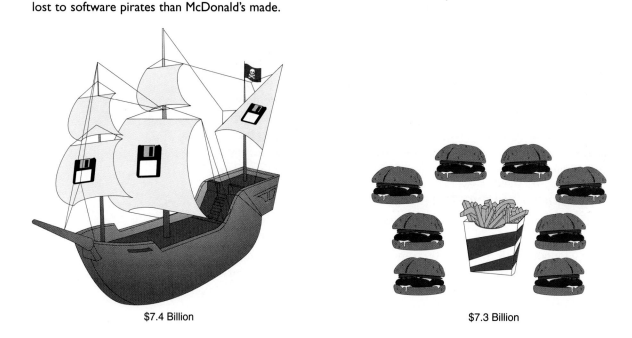

$7.4 Billion $7.3 Billion

Centralizing control of information—those who have it can prescribe how
and who else gets it

Reducing access to information

Creating dependency of Third World countries on developed nations for
economic and information supplies

Incurring economic loss because of computer crime

The focus in the preceding discussions is not on professional, governmental, or
global ethics, but on each of us having an individual stake in the ethical use of computers, data, and information.

OBJECTIVE 2.8
Understand how ethics affects information.

WHAT IMPACT DOES ETHICS HAVE ON INFORMATION USE?

There is a definite need for ethical conduct as it relates to personal information in
computer files. Personal information about each of us is readily available through the
technology of computers. It is not difficult for that information to find its way into
unauthorized hands. The Freedom of Information Act of 1970 allows an individual to
secure the records that federal agencies have collected about them. Table 2-1 gives a
synopsis of legislation dealing with information and computer privacy matters.

Misuse of Information

Is it a misuse of information when your name and buying habits find their way into a
database available for other merchants? Merely buying something from a mail-order
catalog can cause that information to appear in a database that is sold to others. For
example, if you buy a set of gourmet cooking utensils from an all-purpose catalog,
they can put your name on a list to be sold to other chef supply dealers. The chef supply catalog will soon be in your mail box, and after you order a recipe book from

Table 2.1 Computer and Privacy Legislation

- **Freedom of Information Act of 1970** Permits individuals to get copies of the data that federal agencies have gathered.
- **Fair Credit Reporting Act of 1970** Gives people the right to review their credit records.
- **Crime Control Act of 1973** Ensures the security and privacy of data in state criminal records that were produced using federal funds.
- **Privacy Act of 1974** Prevents abuse of a person's privacy, prohibits data collected for one reason to be used for another without prior consent, grants right to see the government information collected, provides copies of that information, allows correction of wrong data, requires the information be current and correct, and keeps them from misuse, to name a few.
- **Tax Reform Act of 1976** Limits IRS access to personal data and restricts sharing of that data with other federal agencies.
- **Copyright Act of 1976** Prohibits books and other written works, including computer programs, from being copied illegally.
- **Privacy Protection Act of 1980** Prevents unwarranted searches of offices and files by government agents.
- **Debt Collection Act of 1982** Specifies prerequisites for releasing bad debt information.
- **Cable Communications Policy Act of 1984** Provides that subscribers are advised if personal information is being accumulated or broadcast.
- **Semiconductor Chip Protection Act of 1984** Gives the chip developer an exclusive ten-year period for rights and prevents others from reproducing chip patterns.
- **Electronic Communications Privacy Act of 1986** Makes interception of computer communications illegal.
- **Computer Fraud and Abuse Act of 1986** Grants jurisdiction to the federal government in matters of computer crimes; pertains to federal government and federally insured financial institution computers.
- **Privacy for Consumers and Workers Act of 1993** Requires employer notification of intent to monitor worker electronic communication; limits the kind and type of monitoring allowed.
- **Copyright Reform Act of 1993** Removes the requirement that copyrightholders register their copyright before they can sue for copyright infringements.

them, your name will be on yet another mailing list to be sold perhaps to a bookstore. In the meantime a profile of your buying habits is being accumulated and added to with each purchase. Many people feel this is a misuse of the information and an invasion of privacy.

Liability for Incorrect Information

Some computer errors are comical; for example, a computer-generated letter announcing that you, "Ms. Philadelphia, PA" are a million-dollar sweepstakes winner, would indicate that your city and state were inserted where your name should have been. Other errors, however, can be devastating if lives are lost through faulty data. What if a patient's medical records became confused with another's because of a data entry error? Just who's liable for incorrect information? The question is ambiguous at best since placing blame is usually quite an involved process, and generally disputes are settled in court. Two ways that software providers are using to protect themselves are (1) verifying and testing their data to make sure their product or service is reputable and (2) entering into contracts in advance with disclaimers that limit their liability.

Software Workability

What happens and who pays when software doesn't do what it's supposed to? Sellers expect the consumers to beware. Consumers, on the other hand, expect the sellers to deliver a software package that "works." Software usually carries no guarantee by the seller. In fact, when there are accidents or losses, blame can be placed on the hardware, software, database, or the user. Any combination of them could be "at fault." Regulations and laws concerning software workability are not yet well defined. This brings us to a series of ethical issues.

OBJECTIVE 2.9
Understand the conflict in determining ethical resolutions to computing issues.

WHY ARE ETHICAL ISSUES DIFFICULT TO RESOLVE?

There are no hard and fast rules and methods that apply in *all* instances as new technology appears; the values also are still emerging. In "virtual reality" where the computer simulates imagery and the user "enters into the picture" a new series of problems are created along with the potential for good. Physicians envision using virtual reality to develop a body suit that may enable a quadriplegic patient to experience movement that is unavailable to them in their "real" world. What if the patient chose to spend time in the computer-generated world instead of living with the challenges of daily life? Professionals must anticipate both positive and negative aspects. Myriad possibilities need to be considered in preparing that code of ethics.

You can see from the following list that computer users are wrestling with issues such as

> Is it a threat to the employee's privacy to use a computer to monitor their work?
>
> Is the employer obligated to compensate an employee displaced by a computer?
>
> Should all data that are input be considered confidential by the individual at the keyboard?
>
> Is it ethical to read someone's electronic mail? view their files? share their password? use their employer's computer for personal tasks?
>
> Is it ethical for a student to use the facilities in the campus computer lab to play games while other students wait for a computer to complete assignments or do research?
>
> Is it ethical for someone to censor messages on computer bulletin boards? post pornographic messages?

The issues are not easily resolved. You will no doubt think of many other issues that should be considered by companies and individuals in formulating codes of ethics.

OBJECTIVE 2.10
Define computer crime and describe several types.

HOW DOES COMPUTER CRIME AFFECT SOCIETY?

A **computer crime** may be described as one where computers and software are used with illegal intentions. Computers allow crimes such as embezzlement, theft, sabotage, and vandalism to be carried out faster and with a lower chance of discovery. Just how costly are computer crimes? Even conservative estimates start in the billions of dollars.

Piracy and Copyright Infringement

Software piracy is the unauthorized duplication of copyrighted computer programs. **Copyright infringement** occurs when the appropriate royalty payment is not made for use of the protected work. Software developers incur the expenses of research and development to produce their programs; thus, each time a "pirated" (i.e., no fee is paid and no royalty is collected by the owner of the work) version is shared, but not paid for, they lose the profit. Federal copyright laws cover most computer software prohibiting unauthorized distribution. Some experts estimate that worldwide piracy costs range from $20 to $60 billion each year. This is obviously a serious concern for software developers. Some methods that developers use to deter piracy are

- Licensing, or allowing the manufacturers to produce the programs upon payment of appropriate royalties to the developer.
- Sealing the packages and using a statement on the outside of the package that only the buyer will use the software.
- "Locking" the programs to prevent the buyer from making unauthorized copies.
- Providing the instructions about using the programs in extensive documentation. Pirates who copy the program will also have to copy the instructions. This can be a real deterrent when the documentation is hundreds of pages in length.
- Educating users. The Software Publishers Association, Washington, D.C., has an interesting approach. It produced a rap video called "Don't Copy That Floppy" aimed at educating preteens about the illegality of copying software. Articles alerting young people about computer crimes are even found in magazines such as *Boys' Life*.

Software pirates have to face the possibility of higher fines and longer jail sentences since President George Bush signed a bill that makes pirating software a felony instead of a misdemeanor. Those who make piracy a business will be looking at five years in prison and as much as $250,000 in fines.

Types of Computer Crime

Computers can be used to commit crimes, such as theft or fraud, but they could be the object of a crime (someone may want to steal the hardware) and computers can also be used in the commission of crimes that are intrinsic to computers, that is, spreading viruses, worms, bombs, and Trojan horses; manipulating data; and stealing data. Employees are being taught how to spot the fraud and forgeries that computer criminals try to pass. Undercover officers conducted sting operations where 30 people were arrested for stealing computer chips that had been sold at three times their value.

VIRUSES, WORMS, BOMBS, AND TROJAN HORSES. A computer **virus** is a program that can get into a computer to destroy or alter data and spread itself to other computers. They are spread through sharing software, downloading files from a bulletin board, or logging on to a computer network (see Chapter 9). John von Neumann (see the profile in Chapter 8) proposed a theory that programs could be designed to automatically multiply, not a problem in itself. But, during the 1970s when criminal users created programs that were destructive and they could multiply quickly, the concept became a real threat. During the 1980s viruses "caught on" and became even worse. They are often set to attack at a specific time or date. For example, the Michelangelo virus wreaks havoc when the computer system is turned on on March 6, the birthday of the famous artist. Now there are hundreds of viruses worldwide. Viruses have been estimated at causing $2 billion in losses a year.

Types of computer crime
• Viruses
• Worms
• Bombs
• Trojan horses
• Data manipulation
• Data stealing

A computer **worm** is a surreptitious program that issues false or misleading commands. It occupies computer memory and spreads quickly as does a virus—they both stop normal computer operation. Because they are not readily apparent it is hard to detect viruses and worms until they have done their damage. In 1988 a graduate student introduced a worm into the Internet, the worldwide network used by universities and government agencies.

A **time bomb** is a program that is set to destroy itself either at a certain time or after a specified number of times the program is run. Time bombs have been used by disgruntled employees who feel they have an ax to grind with the employer. However, the concept has also been used by developers to prevent nonpayment for services. After the software development bill has been paid, the developer tells the purchaser how the bomb can be defused. If payment is not received, the program destroys itself.

The **Trojan horse** disguises itself as a legitimate program, but once it is installed, the rogue program does its damage—garbling data, destroying indexes, or erasing all the data in the computer. Now mail bombs can even be "delivered" via electronic mail services.

DATA MANIPULATION AND DATA STEALING. Data manipulation occurs when a user alters data in the computer. This kind of manipulation ranges from someone changing a grade to accessing and changing medical records or credit records. When a user steals information that has been gathered for a legitimate purpose, it is called **data stealing.** For example, if an address list that has been legally obtained was then sold to someone else for another use, it would be considered data stealing.

There are many reasons for the proliferation of computer crimes. Some of them are

- There are more computers in use.
- More people are familiar with computers and what they can do.
- More computers are linked together and communicating with each other.
- More databases can be accessed by microcomputer users.

Computers are used in the apprehension of criminals too. Automated fingerprint identification systems are set up around the country. Fingerprint records that have been obtained by pressing the inked finger onto a card can be scanned by computers and the information about the patterns and distinguishing features stored in computer files. Later, they can be retrieved and matched to prints found at the scene of a crime. This system was instrumental in convicting the infamous "Night Stalker" in California. So beware. If you commit crimes using a computer, you might be convicted by the computer as well.

The Criminal

Most of the computer crime headlines are given over to the knowledgeable computer user who enjoys the challenge of breaking into large computer systems, usually for the fun of it, without criminal intent, but this is still considered a crime. Not all computer mischief, sometimes called "hacking," is done for fun. One so-called hacker known as "Storm Shadow" was convicted of stealing credit records. Even without criminal intent, hackers cause many millions of dollars of losses. Often you do not hear about these instances because the companies involved are too embarrassed to acknowledge any breach of security. However, the greatest number of computer crimes are committed by insiders—employees of the company. It's very hard to guard against them.

Incarcerating prisoners is expensive, and there is not enough jail space to accommodate new prisoners. Computers are instrumental in the confinement of certain nonviolent criminals. An electronic monitoring device containing a transmitter is attached to the person's ankle. It sends digital signals to the receiver, a microcomputer (seen on the table in Figure 2-4). The microcomputer sends the signals over

FIGURE 2-4
Electronic monitoring can be a viable alternative to incarceration.

Did you ever play the children's game where you are "it" and must give hints to other players about what you're looking at? Now, it's not just a game. Between 10 and 15 million workers are being "spied on" in the United States—by their employers.

Networked computers make their "game" easier. Your desktop computer can be monitored without your knowledge. As of early 1995, Congress had not yet passed an act to require employers to advise when employees are under surveillance. Among the companies who post their surveillance policy are Pacific Bell, Federal Express, and General Motors.

Software programs that are legitimately used for supervising employees can also be used for viewing your electronic mail messages, counting your keystrokes as you work, and timing the number of coffee breaks you take as well as how long you are gone. Although monitored workers suffer stress, job anxiety, and physical ailments according to studies conducted by the Communications Workers of America, E-mail surveillance has uncovered acts of employees passing trade secrets.

If you do not give your employer a full day's work, or you steal programs, or you use company equipment illegally, does the employer have the right to know and act on that knowledge?

Should Big Brother decide?

FIGURE 2-5
Many computer facilities are protected by closed-circuit television.

telephone lines to a host computer located at the correctional institution. By verifying that the offender stays within range of the receiver (approximately 150 feet), or checks in at preset times, it is possible to maintain accurate records of the prisoner's whereabouts. Wouldn't this be an ironic punishment for someone convicted of committing a computer crime?

OBJECTIVE 2.11
Describe how detection, prevention, and legislation can help reduce computer crime.

HOW CAN COMPUTER CRIME BE PREVENTED?

The "best offense is a good defense" is a phrase generally associated with football. In other words you don't have to attack if you can prevent. The best defenses against computer crime are prevention and detection before you have to result to prosecution (see Figure 2-5).

Detection

FIGURE 2-6
A tiny, yet powerful, video camera and lens have been miniaturized so they fit on a single microchip. This allows inconspicuous placement of a video camera in almost any situation such as in a convenience store, warehouse, ATM machine, and elevator.

(Courtesy of TVX, Inc.)

Because computer crime is often committed by a company's own employees, detection is often difficult. If a file is not accessed regularly, the crime may not be discovered for months or years. Once the crime is detected, placing and proving blame may be next to impossible. The criminal usually does not leave evidence such as fingerprints or a paper trail. Investigations require expertise and money. Although there are other employees around, no one can tell who may be committing a crime. One method of detection is through a software feature called an **audit trail** that shows deletions, changes, or additions to a file. The audit trail tells when the action was taken and by whom. Many victims fail to report violations of their computer system; it could be seen as a sign of weakness to a bank, credit company, or investment company's customers. Often managers can't identify signs of criminal computer activity, and law enforcement personnel lack expertise as well. Having a computer crime unit in police divisions is very helpful. Computer law specializations provide the legal profession with ammunition to fight computer criminals.

Closed-circuit television monitoring systems deter hardware theft. Motion, optical, or infrared sensors also detect intrusions. The camera-on-a-chip (see Figure 2-6) acts as a great security guard.

Prevention

There are many techniques to use in the prevention of computer crimes. You can limit access to both the computer area and the computer itself.

CONTROLLING ACCESS TO THE COMPUTER AREA. Businesses protect themselves against criminal loss of computers and data by securing the computers from physical crime, such as theft or vandalism. There are many types of entry systems available from simple lock and key to vision systems. There are basically three types of sophisticated entry systems; knowledge based, possession based, and biometric based.

A knowledge-based system uses a type of keypad into which the user punches a code to gain access similar to those found on some automobiles. With possession-based systems, a person has a magnetically coded card that is inserted into a card reader. The access code on the card is read and matched to valid codes before entry to a building or room is granted (see Figure 2-7). A biometric system takes a unique feature of a person to use as an entry code, for example, recognizing signatures, fingerprints, voices, retinal vein patterns, and physical hand dimensions (see Figure 2-8).

Preventing access to the computer room does not necessarily mean your files are safe. Your computers are accessible through telephone lines via modems. You can disconnect the modem when you are not using it or program the modem communication software to accept calls only from known numbers or automatically disconnect when someone without proper clearance repeatedly tries to log in to your computer.

CONTROLLING ACCESS TO THE COMPUTER. Some computers are equipped with a physical lock and key device to prevent any entries being made. Some software also comes with hardware locks. These devices are connected to the back of networked computers. The software recognizes certain keystrokes that are entered by the user as well as detects that the hardware lock is securely in place before access to the software is permitted.

Controlling computer access

- Lock and key
- Passwords
- Antivirus software
- Encryption

FIGURE 2-8
Hand recognition systems are used to verify physical characteristics of a hand, such as size and shape, so as to control access to restricted areas. Here the device allows only authorized personnel onto the tarmac area at the airport.
(Courtesy of Recognition Systems, Inc.)

But the simplest type of access control is the password. A **password** is a unique combination of characters that a user enters as an identification code. The typed code is compared to a list of acceptable entry codes for that software. Passwords can protect entire programs or selected parts (see Figure 2-9). Users might be able to view certain data, but they may not have the ability to make changes to that data. You should change your password periodically. Programs or data can be compromised by terminated employees, so their passwords or access codes should be withdrawn immediately.

Passwords cannot prevent data from being corrupted by viruses. To prevent viruses from infecting your computer, do not copy software from a questionable origin, and don't let other people use your program disks or your computer. Remember that bulletin boards may contain contaminated software. There are many antivirus software programs available to specifically combat viruses. The three services that this type of software renders are prevention, diagnosis, and recovery. They prevent a virus by running monitoring routines, and if you already have a virus, the program recognizes the identifying codes and then helps eliminate it by erasing the infected files. Unfortunately, piracy and infringement cannot be cured by antivirus software.

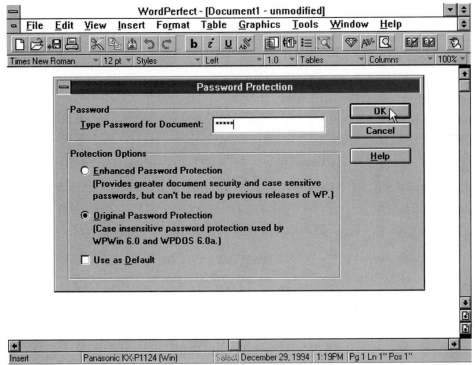

FIGURE 2-9
The WordPerfect password option protects your documents from unauthorized access.

Passwords are effective to a certain extent. However, sophisticated criminals or hackers can learn your code if it is too simple. A higher level of limiting access to your data is through encryption. **Encryption** is a process that makes data indecipherable unless you have the correct "key." PC Tools, from Central Point Software, can produce more than 70 quadrillion encryption combinations. However, if you forget the "key," your data are encrypted forever. So it is wise to keep a backup copy of important files in a secure place.

Government agencies are interested in implementing use of the Clipper chip that encrypts digital communications in phones, modems, and fax machines; it would allow law enforcement officials to access correspondence through these media by suspected criminals. The Clipper chip does not have widespread support. Civil libertarians fear that government control over the encryption codes could lead to abuses in privacy. However, some manufacturers argue that without fully encrypted products, foreign demand will decline.

Disaster Recovery

Even with the best security measures in place, the unthinkable can occur. What happens if someone, either accidentally or with criminal intent, erases or alters your computer files? Software such as Norton Utilities or Rescue can often restore your lost data. This software is used when the hard drive (where all your files are stored within the computer) is faulty or has been reformatted.

Those software programs do not work when physical damage occurs. There are teams of experts called **disaster recovery** teams whose job it is to help recover data that may have been destroyed by criminal damage, fire, flood, electrical surges, or virus attack. They have the ability to recover many files from damaged computers that to you or I would seem impossible. Large businesses that are particularly dependent on their computer system are at risk, but even small businesses can suffer when their normal functions are interrupted. As always, backup copies can avert disasters.

Legislation

With the laws found in Table 2-1 and the constitutional protection afforded us, there should be plenty of legislation to guard our rights. Some scholars feel that the Constitution as it is written covers all possible areas of computer applications; others, however, argue that a new amendment should be added granting our rights and privileges regardless of the technology involved. Legislators are faced with decisions about what actions constitute computer crimes. In 1991 the Computer Crime Unit was organized by the Department of Justice and charged with prosecuting computer criminals. It supports imposing stiffer punishments and expanding the area covered by federal computer crime statutes.

Continued vigilance on the government for new laws and standards will help legitimate computer users stay ahead of the criminals. A government panel representing many federal agencies, called the Working Group on Intellectual Property Rights, is working on amendments to the Copyright Act to better prevent copying on computer networks. The Department of Justice proposed criminal punishments to cover a broader range of activities not previously covered by the Computer Fraud and Abuse Act.

Our laws may not be adequate to deal with the burgeoning problems created by new technologies; therefore, lawmakers must become more knowledgeable about the computers and their operation to assure freedoms for all. Companies or individuals who run afoul of the laws need to be prosecuted, and the sentences should be carried out as imposed. Unless the laws are enforced they will not act as a deterrent.

OBJECTIVE 2.12
Understand the potential for invasion of your privacy with the unethical or criminal use of computers.

HOW CAN PRIVACY ISSUES AFFECT YOU?

The U.S. government is the largest user of computers; it holds more than 4 billion personal files on its citizens. It also funds a majority of computer research. The IRS processes over 100 million tax returns a year. Legislation exists that prevents federal agencies from misusing information they have obtained; however, through a system called matching, they are able to compare data that each agency has on a specific person. For example, deadbeat parents who are not paying child support can be tracked through welfare, social security, and income tax records too. The fact that all these files are accumulated into a centralized database eliminates privacy for any individuals.

Computers are not capable of invading our privacy, but they do make it possible for people to get access more quickly and efficiently to more confidential data in one place than ever before. Privacy invasion by way of computers occurs in two ways: (1) data can be accumulated and organized by almost any agency or company, and (2) data can be shared with other agencies or companies.

Banks, credit card companies, libraries, and even video stores accumulate data on our financial stability, buying habits, reading, and even preferences for leisure-time activities. With all this information about us being readily available to virtually anyone who asks, our desire for privacy takes a back seat to someone else's need to know. Of course, there are legitimate uses for the collection of personal data: the physician who treats us needs to have test results, medical history, and records of prescription drugs. The bank that lends money for our mortgage needs to know how much we make, our credit history, and if we've ever declared bankruptcy. The issues of privacy really revolve around the ethical use of personal data.

Care must be taken when data are accumulated to avoid (1) reporting data inaccurately, (2) accessing or using data illegally, (3) accumulating more data than are required, and (4) combining and exchanging data among various collection agencies.

Just because these records exist may cause no harm, but if they are not current, relevant, or accurate, any decisions based on the data could be harmful.

A hot topic under discussion is the privacy that someone can expect from E-mail, that is, electronic mail delivered to a computer "mailbox." Can you expect that messages delivered in this way are protected from prying eyes as are the letters received in sealed envelopes? The federal government's Electronic Communications Privacy Act does not protect mail sent over private networks. Unless your company has a written policy, the recipient should expect that the employer is accessing those messages, even if just to monitor and maintain its network.

Perhaps if everyone acted in an "ethical" manner, there would be fewer instances of computer crimes and no chance of invasions of privacy.

SUMMARY

As computer users and as recipients of the results of computer use, we must be aware of the potential for unethical behavior by certain people. Computers are not the culprits, but the people associated with the illegal acts are to blame.

A standard of conduct is called ethics. Computer ethics are the standards that govern the use of computers and the information they produce.

The Association for Computing Machinery set forth a code of ethics to which all professional computer users should strive. This code serves as a good model for any business.

The government, because of the nature of its business, has the ability to collect vast amounts of data on its citizenry. It also has the obligation to see that it serves its intended purpose.

The increased use of computer networks has given rise to more opportunities for software piracy. Debates continue over the rights of free speech or the censorship of materials.

Those same electronic networks have made worldwide communication and the sharing of information much easier. Those who have control of the information decide who receives it and how. Unethical use of data and information has widespread effects throughout the world.

Information can be misused. Incorrect information produced by software or software that doesn't work the way it is supposed to affects the usefulness of the information.

Ethical issues are not covered by a well-defined law. For that reason it is difficult to arrive at a consensus of right or wrong for many questionable situations of computer use and abuse.

Computer crime can take the form of piracy and copyright infringement. Types of computer crime include viruses, worms, bombs, and Trojan horses. Criminals are sometimes mischievous computer hackers, but more often than not crimes are committed by an employee or ex-employee.

Computer crime can be reduced if steps were taken to identify and prevent it before it takes place. When computer crime is committed, laws dealing with computers and crime in general should be used to prosecute the criminal.

audit trail (p. 46)

computer crime (p. 42)

computer ethics (p. 34)

copyright infringement (p. 43)

data manipulation (p. 44)

data stealing (p. 44)

disaster recovery team (p. 49)

electronic work monitoring (p. 35)

encryption (p. 49)

global ethics (p. 39)

password (p. 48)

software piracy (p. 43)

time bomb (p. 44)

Trojan horse (p. 44)

virus (p. 43)

worm (p. 44)

REVIEW QUESTIONS

Multiple Choice

1. Which of the following is not an example of ethical behavior as defined by the Association for Computing Machinery?
   a. Be honest.
   b. Maintain privacy.
   c. Make only two copies of software.
   d. Respect intellectual property.

2. Codes of ethics have been traced to _____.
   a. 2000 B.C.
   b. 200 B.C.
   c. 200 A.D.
   d. the Magna Carta

3. The Computer Emergency Response Team was founded to investigate crimes on _____.
   a. federal computers
   b. the Internet
   c. retrieval systems
   d. Prodigy

4. _____ ethics deal with the flow, impact, production, dispersal, and utilization of information between nations.
   a. Professional
   b. Network
   c. Government
   d. Global

5. President Bush signed a bill that made software piracy a(n) _____.
   a. ethical violation
   b. misdemeanor
   c. felony
   d. hacking violation

6. _____ occurs when someone copies a software program illegally.
   a. Program infringement
   b. Software piracy
   c. Data manipulation
   d. Data stealing

7. A computer program that is made to destroy other programs is known as a _____.
   a. computer infection
   b. worm
   c. data manipulation
   d. virus

8. Most computer crimes are committed by _____.
   a. computer professionals
   b. teenagers
   c. employees
   d. persons with a previous criminal record

9. Antivirus software cannot protect your computer from _____.
   a. copyright infringement
   b. time bombs
   c. Trojan horses
   d. worms

10. An encryption device supported by government agencies is called the _____.
    a. Clipper chip
    b. Detector chip
    c. Encrypt chip
    d. Recovery chip

Fill In

1. The study of standards of conduct and moral judgment is called _____.

2. The _____ is a database where cash deposits of over $10,000 can be reported.

3. Two of the largest on-line computer services are _____ and _____.

4. Controlling the contents of an on-line bulletin board is called _____.

5. When software does not work the way it is supposed to, it is a(n) _____ issue.

6. The _____ is the legislation enacted that allows an individual to have access to his or her file accumulated by the federal government.

7. If your computer or data suffer damage in a flood or fire, you would contact a(n) _____.

8. When someone changes data in an existing file, it is called _____.

9. The program that disguises itself as a legitimate program is known as a(n) _____

10. _____ is a process used by federal agencies to compare data on individuals.

Short Answer

1. Briefly describe how problems in terms of legal or moral issues could arise concerning software.

2. Define computer ethics.

3. Should networks be subject to limits on pornography?

4. Describe how control of information can impact the global society.

5. List five reasons why ethical issues are hard to resolve.

6. Why might a company *not* report a computer crime?

7. Recount ways that a computer could be involved in a crime.

8. Describe three ways that developers can protect themselves from piracy.

9. Illustrate how an individual's personal privacy could be invaded by computers.

10. What is matching and give an example.

Issues for Thought

1. There must be a balance between the right to one's privacy and the "need to know." Discuss whether a set of medical records should be allowed to be accessed if the data in them would help others.

2. If you, as the employer, suspected an employee of copying software, what would your course of action be? How would your reaction differ if it were company software that the employee sold or general software, such as a screen saver, that he or she would use at home?

INFOMODULE I
A HISTORY OF COMPUTERS

As soon as humans domesticated animals and started to carry on trade with others, they needed to keep track of numbers. First, people used their fingers. Then, they used notches on sticks, counting stones, and even knots tied in ropes. The abacus, a rudimentary computing device, evolved in different cultures at about the same time. This simple device, which uses beads to represent digits and wires to hold places, is still used today.

PEOPLE AND THEIR CONTRIBUTIONS

As early as the seventeenth century, mathematicians and other scholars were eager to create a machine that could add, subtract, multiply, and divide numbers. Initially, the evolution of computing devices proceeded slowly. Yet, an interesting thing happened with numbers. John Napier, a Scotsman, discovered a way to manipulate numbers that would reduce multiplications and divisions to additions and subtractions—logarithms. Then, Robert Bissaker invented the slide rule, which helped solve complex problems relatively quickly.

Blaise Pascal, a French mathematician and philosopher, invented the first mechanical digital calculator, which could perform addition and subtraction on whole numbers. The Pascaline (see Figure IM1-1), developed around 1640, was a financial failure. It was cheaper to have human labor perform the calculations, workers feared losing their jobs, and only Pascal could repair the machine. However, Pascal's concept of a decimal counting wheel using gears with ten teeth and one carrying tooth wasn't made obsolete until the development of the electronic calculator. A programming language, Pascal, was later named to honor his contributions.

Nineteenth-Century Technology

In 1804, Joseph Marie Jacquard, also a Frenchman, built an automated punched-card machine (see Figure IM1-2) that was used to operate weaving looms. Jacquard's inven-

FIGURE IM1-1
The Pascaline.
(Courtesy of International Business Machines Corp.)

tion used data coded on cards joined to create a series of instructions to automate weaving. This use of programmed instructions was a concept of great importance to modern computers. However, workers in the mills feared this kind of automation would cost them their jobs.

In the 1800s, a British inventor and mathematician, Charles P. Babbage, designed an all-purpose problem-solving machine, the difference engine (see Figure IM1-3), which had a mechanical memory to store results. He also designed, but never built, an analytical engine that would have required half a dozen steam engines and would have taken up the space of a football field. Babbage's concepts led to the modern computer and earned him the title "father of the computer."

Babbage's confidante and partner, Augusta Ada, the daughter of poet Lord Byron, and later Countess of Lovelace, understood Babbage's ideas, recognized their great value, and in the 1840s translated and wrote scientific papers defining them for others. She suggested using a binary system rather than the decimal system for storage. Lady Lovelace is sometimes called the first programmer because she also refined the design of the analytical engine to include the automatic repetition of a series of calculations— the loop. This looping procedure is extremely valuable to today's programmers.

George Boole, a self-taught English mathematician of the 1850s, realized that complex mathematical problems could be solved by reducing them to a series of questions answered either affirmatively or negatively. The binary system of 1's for positive answers and 0's for negative answers is thus implemented. This theory of Boolean logic became fundamental to the design of computer circuitry.

Later, in the 1880s, Dr. Herman Hollerith built the first electromechanical punched-card data processing machine (see Figure IM1-4), which tabulated and sorted the data from the 1890 census. His Tabulating Machine Company was one of the companies that later became IBM.

FIGURE IM1-2
Jacquard's loom.
(Courtesy of International Business Machines Corp.)

FIGURE IM1-3
Babbage's difference engine.
(Courtesy of International Business Machines Corp.)

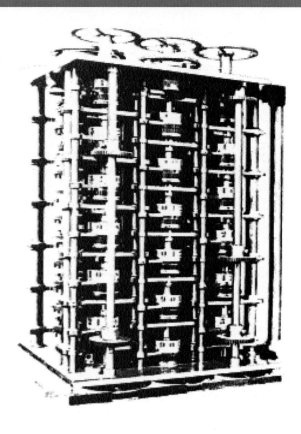

FIGURE IM1-4
Hollerith's punched-card machine.
(Courtesy of International Business Machines Corp.)

Early-Twentieth-Century Technology

There is a time gap in the computer's history after Hollerith. Progress was being made, but nothing spectacular was reported. Then, by 1931 at the Massachusetts Institute of Technology (MIT), Vannevar Bush and his colleagues created, modified, and perfected a differential analyzer, which was an electronic machine that solved simple differential

equations. Although the mechanism resembled a giant dishpan with projecting steel rods, it was a mechanical analog computing device. It performed calculations by the rotation of various shafts.

George Stibitz, a research mathematician at Bell Telephone Laboratory, tinkered with the idea that Boolean logic provided a natural language for electromechanical circuits. His device, created in 1937 from batteries, flashlight bulbs, wire, and tobacco can strips of metal, controlled the flow of electricity. The Complex Number Calculator machine was a binary adder—a basic requirement for all future digital computers. In 1940, Stibitz and his colleague Samuel Williams successfully demonstrated that this device could send calculations over a distance of 250 miles using teletype machines.

In Iowa in 1939, John Atanasoff and Clifford Berry collaborated to build the Atanasoff-Berry Computer (ABC). The ABC (see Figure IM1-5), the world's first general-purpose electronic digital computer, did not generate a lot of interest in the scientific community even though its purpose was to solve simultaneous linear algebraic equations. In fact, when Dr. Atanasoff contacted IBM about his machine, the company said that it would never be interested in an electronic computing machine.

Vacuum Tube Technology

In 1941, during World War II, Konrad Zuse built the first operational general-purpose computer for Germany. His machine used binary logic even though Zuse had not heard of George Boole. Zuse proposed an updated model that used vacuum tubes instead of electromechanical relays to increase the speed 1,000-fold and suggested that the machine be used by the military to compare and evaluate aircraft designs and to break wartime codes. But Adolph Hitler refused funding, saying that the war would be over before the two years Zuse needed to finish the machine.

Fortunately, for the Allies, the Polish secret service smuggled a replica of the German message-scrambling device, Enigma, to the British. Alan Turing, an eccentric English genius, unraveled the mysteries of the Enigma. In 1943, Turing and his colleagues capitalized on the vacuum tube technology that Zuse had wanted to pursue. The British machine could process 25,000 characters per second. In 1950, Turing also constructed the Automatic Computer Engine (ACE), which was touted as the first (arguably) programmable digital computer.

Most of the industries in the United States rallied to support the war effort. Thomas J. Watson, president of IBM, offered to supply thousands of punched-card sorting machines. Watson also knew about and offered IBM's support to Howard Aiken, a Harvard mathematician who wanted to build a general-purpose programmable computer that could calculate cannon shell trajectories. This device was similar to that which Babbage had proposed.

In 1944, Aiken completed the first automatic sequence-controlled calculator, Mark I. It calculated with electromechanical relays and used electricity rather than muscles, effectively replacing Hollerith's gear mechanism. The Mark I was 51 feet long and 8 feet high (see Figure IM1-6) and contained over 750,000 parts strung with 500 miles of wires. It used paper-tape input and punched-card output. Calculations of 23-digit numbers took only 3 seconds. With the Mark I, 6 months of manual calculations could be completed in 1 day.

Technology advanced rapidly, and many people worked on similar ideas simultaneously. As a result, some dates, discoveries, and claims overlap in the history of the computer.

In 1941, John Mauchly, a physicist on the staff at the University of Pennsylvania's Moore School of Engineering, visited Atanasoff in Iowa, where the ABC computer was still in the early stages of construction. Mauchly was impressed with the possibilities of the machine. In 1942, Mauchly and another Moore School colleague, J. Presper Eckert, proposed to build a machine that would compute artillery firing tables for the government. This device was called the Electronic Numerical Integrator and Computer (ENIAC).

At 80 feet long and 18 feet high (see Figure IM1-7), the ENIAC was twice as big as the Mark I. Instead of gears or mechanical relays, the 30-ton device contained over 100,000 electronic components, including 17,468 vacuum tubes. Although the vacuum tubes took up a great deal of space, their use increased the speed of calculations by 1,000-fold. The ENIAC operated on the decimal system, which allowed the punched-card output to be read easily by humans. However, changing programs or operations was extremely difficult because the instructions had to be wired into the circuitry manually. Since it could take the operators as long as two days to manually replug the hundreds of wires involved when changing from one operation to another, the ENIAC was not a particularly efficient general-purpose computer. (Mauchly and Eckert claimed the ENIAC was the first general-purpose electronic digital computer, but on October 19, 1973, a court settlement declared that the Atanasoff-Berry Computer was entitled to that honor.)

The ENIAC was obsolete almost before it was completed, and Mauchly and Eckert planned a successor machine called the EDVAC (Electronic Discrete Variable Automatic Computer). Completed in 1949, EDVAC stored its instructions electronically, using the

FIGURE IM1-6
The Mark I.
(Courtesy of International Business Machines Corp.)

binary system for instruction coding and input. The EDVAC was one of the first two stored-program computers. It consisted of five units: (1) arithmetical, (2) central control, (3) memory, (4) input, and (5) output. Improvements over the ENIAC included reduction of the number of tubes, increased memory, and increased ease of use, including an easier, faster way to set up new problems.

The stored-program concept has been claimed by many. However, the definitive paper outlining this and other differences in design features has been credited to John von Neumann, the special consultant hired by the Moore School for the EDVAC project. Presented in the mid-1940s, John von Neumann's paper "First Draft of a Report on the EDVAC" served as a blueprint for future stored-program computers.

At the same time, an Englishman, Maurice V. Wilkes of Cambridge, incorporated von Neumann's stored-program concept into the EDSAC (Electronic Delay Storage Automatic Computer). The EDSAC was available just before the EDVAC.

Around 1949 at Harvard, An Wang, founder of Wang Laboratories, developed magnetic core memories. When current flows through wires inside a magnetic core, the electricity magnetizes the core in different directions. The direction of magnetization indicates certain data representation to the central processing unit. Subsequently, Jay Forrester at MIT discovered a way to organize magnetic core memories into a grid, providing a more practical application than the previous serial connections. Computers became faster and more reliable, as well as capable of containing larger memories. Magnetic core memory has given way to newer technologies, including semiconductor memories.

In 1951, Mauchly and Eckert formed their own company to create a commercially usable general-purpose computer, the UNIVAC I (see Figure IM1-8). Remington Rand bought the company when Mauchly and Eckert fell upon hard times. The UNIVAC I was the first general-purpose computer designed specifically for business data processing applications. Previously, computers had been used solely for scientific or military applications. The U.S. Census Bureau immediately installed UNIVAC I, using it for over 12 years. In 1954, the General Electric Company in Louisville, Kentucky, used UNIVAC I to process the first computerized payroll. Before long, other companies, including Burroughs (now called UNISYS), Honeywell, and IBM, realized the commercial value of computers and began offering their own machines.

FIGURE IM1-7
The ENIAC.
(Courtesy of International Business Machines Corp.)

FIGURE IM1-8
The UNIVAC I correctly predicted that Dwight Eisenhower would defeat Adlai Stevenson in the 1952 presidential election. A young Walter Cronkite confers with J. Presper Eckert, Jr., and the computer operator.

(Courtesy of UNISYS Corp.)

FIGURE IM1-9
Comparison of size between vacuum tube and an integrated circuit.

(Courtesy of National Semiconductor Corp.)

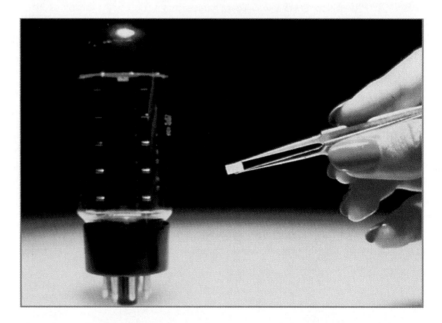

From 1950 to 1952, the U.S. Navy and the Digital Computer Lab at MIT developed the Whirlwind computer, another early vacuum tube stored-program computer. One of the students involved in the Whirlwind's development was Ken Olsen, later the founder of Digital Equipment Corporation. The Whirlwind simulated high-performance trainer aircraft, contained self-diagnostics, and performed 50,000 operations per second, but it was only about 85 percent accurate.

Chip and Computer Technology

Other innovators appeared on the scene in the late 1950s. Both Jack Kilby, at Texas Instruments, and Robert Noyce, at Fairchild Semiconductor, discovered that resistors, capacitors, and transistors could be made from a semiconductor material at the same time and that any number of transistors could be etched on silicon. Thus, the integrated circuit was born and refined (see Figure IM1-9). During this time, the integrated circuit was christened a chip. These 1959 discoveries were finally mass produced in 1962 and were included in the computers of the mid-1960s.

Gene Amdahl's revolutionary IBM System/360 series of mainframe computers was also introduced in the 1960s. They were the first general-purpose digital computers using integrated circuit technology. The IBM System/360 was a "family" of computers. This meant that small but growing companies could start with a relatively inexpensive, small computer system and then, as the company grew, add larger, more powerful computers from the same family. Because the software was compatible, a company could share programs among all the computers in the family. Later, in his own company, Amdahl built a competitive computer that was less expensive, smaller in size, and faster.

Miniaturization, which had come about through various technological innovations, coupled with the commercial success of computers led Ken Olsen and his Digital Equipment Corporation (DEC) to produce the first minicomputer, the PDP-1, in 1963. Its successor, the PDP-8, was the first commercial minicomputer. It was considerably less expensive than a mainframe, and small companies could afford it to computerize their operations.

However, miniaturization was not the only direction for computers. Computers were also becoming more powerful. In fact, the ILLIAC IV was a supercomputer first used at the Ames Research Center in 1972 for solving aerodynamic problems that were too large and complicated for other systems.

Meanwhile, in the mid-1950s, advances were being made in the field of high-level English-like programming languages. FORTRAN (FORmula TRANslator) was developed by John Backus and a group of IBM engineers as the first problem-oriented algebraic programming language. Therefore, its orientation was more toward mathematicians and scientists than computer specialists.

Rear Admiral (Ret.) Grace Murray Hopper was instrumental in developing COBOL (COmmon Business Oriented Language) as the first programming language designed for business data processing. Hopper also helped develop the UNIVAC I's compiler, a program that could translate other programs into machine language, the 1's and 0's that computers understand.

During the mid-1960s, Dr. John Kemeny (a mathematics professor and president of Dartmouth) and his colleague Dr. Thomas Kurtz developed the computer language BASIC (Beginner's All-purpose Symbolic Instruction Code). They later developed a version called True BASIC, which uses structured programming tools to make programs easier to read, debug, and update. Today, numerous other high-level languages, including Pascal, C, and Logo, are in use.

Douglas Engelbart introduced a hand-held device that could roll across a flat surface on wheels and cause a corresponding movement on the computer screen. This device was called a "mouse" because its electric cord looked like a tail. This mouse "roared" and revolutionized the input process.

The term "bit" as an abbreviation for binary digit was coined by John Tukey in 1946. By 1970, Intel had created a memory chip that could store a kilobit of information. A kilobit translates into roughly 25 five-letter words. Another innovation at Intel came from Ted Hoff, who further improved the integrated circuit by compressing 12 chips into 4. Thus, the arithmetic and logic functions of several chips could be contained on one chip, called a microprocessor. This microprocessor, called the Intel 4004 (forty-oh-four), made the development of the small computer, or microcomputer, a possibility. The first chips could handle only four bits of data at a time. However, eight-bit microprocessor chips were developed and used in early microcomputers.

The earliest microcomputer, the Altair 8800, was developed in 1975 by Ed Roberts. Roberts, who has been called the "father of the microcomputer," founded a company called Micro Instrumentation Telemetry Systems (MITS). He developed the Altair to be sold in kit form to consumers (mainly hobbyists) for $395. This computer used an early Intel microprocessor and had less than 1 kilobyte of memory. In 1977, competition for the Altair appeared in the form of Tandy's TRS-80 Model 1, which was available for purchase from Radio Shack stores, and the Personal Electronic Transactor (or PET) from Commodore Business Machines.

The focus was not on microcomputers only. Supercomputers were being updated, too. In 1976, Seymour Cray's Cray-1 supercomputer was delivered to the Los Alamos Scientific Laboratory in New Mexico, and a Control Data Corporation CYBER-205 was used by the Meteorological Service in the United Kingdom for weather predictions.

The first commercial computer store appeared in 1975 in Santa Monica, California. ComputerShack, a retail franchise group selling computer equipment opened for business in 1977 in Morristown, New Jersey. It was to become the leading hardware and software outlet known today as ComputerLand.

The market for software was also growing. In 1974, Bill Gates and Paul Allen developed Microsoft BASIC, a high-level language for microcomputers. The language was used by the MITS Altair in 1975. IBM adopted Microsoft BASIC for its personal computers in 1981, a move that turned Microsoft into a thriving company. Most popular microcomputers—including the Apple II, Commodore 64, and Commodore PET—use Microsoft BASIC. Other successful Microsoft products include PC-DOS and MS-DOS, the operating system software that runs millions of personal computers.

The application software industry got its initial boost because Dan Bricklin, a Harvard Business School student, was not fond of the tedious mathematical calculations involved in the preparation of financial planning sheets—part of the assigned work. Preparing the worksheets was repetitive, requiring numerous hand calculations and recalculations to obtain meaningful results. At times, erroneous calculations in the middle of the worksheet affected other numbers, which had to be recalculated. This method was time consuming and frustrating.

Bricklin thought that an electronic spreadsheet would be practical for businesspeople and other microcomputer owners. He teamed up with friend Bob Frankston, and together, they developed and marketed an electronic spreadsheet. The product, called VisiCalc, was the first of its kind in 1979 and stayed a best-selling package until 1983. At that time, lawsuits prevented timely upgrades from being issued to include 16-bit technology. Eventually, Bricklin sold the company and the rights to VisiCalc to Lotus, Inc., a name recognizable for its spreadsheet package, Lotus 1-2-3. It would become the best-selling program for the personal computer.

Many microcomputer companies have come and gone, but one of the great rags-to-riches stories is Apple Computer, Inc. It was founded by Steven Jobs and Stephen Wozniak on April Fool's Day 1976. The partners' first headquarters was located in Jobs's garage. Wozniak, the technical expert, made a microcomputer affordable for both the individual and the small businessperson. Because Jobs knew very little about circuitry or coding, he provided the marketing impetus for the small company. The first Apple Computers came on the market in 1977. The Apple II was the first PC capable of generating color graphics.

The microcomputer's microprocessor history evolved through a series of competitions between Intel and Motorola primarily. Of course, there are other microprocessing companies, but these two companies have been battling since Intel's 8088 came out in 1979. In 1981, the Intel 8088 was selected as the central processing unit for IBM's personal computer—a microprocessor coup. Then, Motorola's 68000 microprocessors were chosen by not only Apple but also companies that were building workstations. Microprocessors have changed drastically, moving from the 80286 in 1982, to an 80386 in 1985, and subsequently to the 80486 of 1989. With the 80386, a 32-bit microprocessor, Motorola and Intel ended up tied for sales in 1988. With the introduction in 1993 of the Pentium chip, it appears that the 486 is now history in some people's books. It's almost as if even before the chip hits the market, it's successor is in production.

Printers have evolved rapidly over time. The first Epson dot-matrix printer, the TX-80 appeared in 1978, followed by the Hewlett-Packard Laser-Jet in 1984. The following year, the Apple LaserWriter incorporated page description languages so the parameters for the printed page could be specified.

D. C. Hayes and Associates introduced the Hayes microcomputer modem 100 in 1978. Since then Hayes has set the standard for modems and most today are said to be Hayes compatible. The modem was a necessary device for accessing the popular on-line information service, CompuServe, that was founded in 1979.

Another benchmark in the microcomputer revolution was the introduction of the Apple Macintosh in 1984. The Macintosh was visually oriented, and its mouse made it remarkably easy to use. It was praised for its ability to produce graphics and to print text of near typeset quality using Apple's LaserWriter. Logitech obtained mouse technology rights and began producing the popular input devices in 1983.

In 1979, WordStar, a word processing program produced by MicroPro International, became available. The popular microcomputer word processing software package WordPerfect was introduced in 1980. By 1993, a 6.0 release was on the market. Word was introduced as the Microsoft entry into the word processing arena in 1983. Release 5.1 appeared in 1993 too.

Even though business was booming, total sales of microcomputers were still fewer than 1 million units until IBM came along. IBM had been in the business of manufacturing and marketing office equipment and larger computer systems for years. In 1981, IBM presented the IBM personal computer (IBM PC), which used a 16-bit microprocessor. That year, other computer giants, Xerox and Digital Equipment Corporation, also entered versions of microcomputers. Sony, Hewlett-Packard, NEC, North Star, Zenith, and others now have microcomputers on the market.

Adam Osborne introduced a truly portable microcomputer in 1981, the Osborne 1. It weighed only 24 pounds, had memory capacity of 64 kilobytes, and cost approximately $1,795. It could be manufactured in just over 1 hour's time, using only 40 screws to put together the easy-to-find parts.

Time magazine annually honors someone who during the year has made a difference in the world. In 1982, *Time* chose the computer as its "Man of the Year." That same year, Peter Norton produced the popular file recovery program called Norton Utilities for the IBM PC.

By 1984, the IBM PC had become the de facto industry standard (that is, the most popular and widely used computer), with hundreds of companies designing software for it. IBM did not stay at the top of the heap for long, however. Because the IBM PC was the most popular microcomputer, almost every microcomputer manufacturer presented a version of the IBM PC design. These are called IBM PC compatibles, or clones—machines that run the IBM PC software and work with other IBM PC equipment. Some IBM PC compatibles are made by Leading Edge, Tandy, Epson, Kaypro, Compaq, and Dell.

In 1986, the Compaq DeskPro 386 computer, the first to use the powerful 32-bit Intel 80386 microprocessor, was introduced. Compaq became the biggest competition for the corporate market of IBM. The even more powerful 80486 microprocessor first appeared in 1988. In 1987, IBM announced the OS/2 operating system. It had multitasking and multiuser features that made headlines in networking. New network applications, however, were developed more slowly than initially hoped for.

The year 1987 also saw the introduction of PageMaker from Aldus Corp. The program incorporates both type and graphic images on a page. Multimedia application that integrate video, animation, sound, and text began appearing in 1989.

Table I Major contributors to computer development

Date	Person	Contribution
1642	Pascal	The first mechanical digital calculator, the Pascaline.
1804	Jacquard	Used punched cards with weaving loom.
1822	Babbage	"Father of the computer." Invented the difference engine with mechanical memory to store results.
1840s	Augusta Ada	"The first programmer." Suggested binary system rather than decimal for data storage.
1850s	Boole	Developed Boolean logic, which later was used in the design of computer circuitry.
1880s	Hollerith	Built first electromechanical, punched-card data-processing machine, used to compile information for 1890 U.S. census.
1939	Atanasoff and Berry	Built the ABC, the world's first general-purpose, electronic digital computer to solve large equations.
1943	Turing	Used vacuum-tube technology to build British Colossus, to counteract the German code scrambling device, Enigma.
1944	Aiken	Built the Mark I, the first automatic sequence-controlled calculator; used by military to compute ballistics data.
1940s	von Neumann	Presented a paper outlining the stored-program concept.
1947	Mauchly and Eckert	Built the ENIAC, the second general-purpose electronic digital computer; used to compute artillery firing tables.
1949	Wilkes	Built the EDSAC, the first stored-program computer.
1949	Mauchly, Eckert, and von Neumann	Built the EDVAC, the second stored-program computer.
1949	Wang	Developed magnetic-core memory.
1949	Forrester	Organized magnetic-core memory to be more efficient.

(Continued on next page)

The NeXT computer was introduced in 1988 as a computer system for educators. Deliveries began in 1989. That year also saw NEC Technologies, Inc.'s UltraLite laptop computer weigh in at just over 4 pounds. IBM produced a laptop computer in the mid-1980s that was less than a hit. The following year the first pen-based PC, the GRIDPAD, was completed.

The late 1980s also saw Lotus bring suit against other spreadsheet software developers, claiming that their packages infringed on the Lotus copyright, that the competitors' packages looked like Lotus, and that they operated like Lotus. These actions earned the nickname "look and feel" lawsuits.

A nondestructive worm was introduced into the Internet network in 1988 bringing thousands of computers to a halt.

Windows 3.0, a graphical user interface product, released by Microsoft in 1990 sold over 3 million copies. It offered pull-down menus and icons to identify its functions.

Today's history can, of course, be found in computer and noncomputer magazines, newspaper headlines, nightly news, and probably your own classroom.

Table I lists many of the major contributors to the development of computers.

Date	Person	Contribution
Table I Continued		
Date	Person	Contribution
1950	Turing	Built the ACE, which some consider to be the first programmable digital computer.
1951	Mauchly and Eckert	Built the UNIVAC I, the first computer designed and sold commercially, specifically for business data-processing applications.
1950s	Hopper	Developed the UNIVAC I compiler.
1957	Backus	One of a group of IBM engineers to develop FORTRAN.
1959	Kilby and Noyce	Developed and perfected the integrated circuit to be used in later computers.
1960s	Amdahl	Designed the IBM System/360 series of main-frame computers, the first general-purpose digital computers to use integrated circuits.
1961	Hopper	Instrumental in developing the COBOL programming language.
1963	Olsen	With DEC produced the PDP-1, the first minicomputer.
1965	Kemeny and Kurtz	Developed BASIC programming language; True BASIC followed later.
1970	Hoff	Developed the famous Intel 4004 microprocessor chip.
1975	Roberts	"Father of the microcomputer." Designed the first microcomputer, the Altair 8800 in kit form.
1976	Cray	Developed the Cray-1 supercomputer.
1977	Jobs and Wozniak	Designed and built the first Apple micro-computer.
1978	Bricklin and Frankston	Designed VisiCalc, an electronic spreadsheet.
1981	IBM	Introduced the IBM PC with a 16-bit micro-processor.
1986	Compaq	Released the DeskPro 386 computer, the first to use the 80036 microprocessor.
1987	IBM	Announced the OS/2 operating-system technology.
1988	Compaq	Introduced the 80486 microcomputer.
1988	Steven Jobs	Introduced NeXT computer.

TECHNOLOGICAL EVOLUTION OF COMPUTERS

Over time, computers improved in speed, power, and efficiency. The changes are recognized as a progression of generations, each characterized by specific developments.

First Generation (1951–1959)

First-generation computers were powered by thousands of vacuum tubes. The UNIVAC I and others like it were large because of the massive number of tubes that were required. The **vacuum tubes** themselves were large (the size of today's light bulbs). They required great amounts of energy, and they generated much heat. The computer's memory was stored on magnetic storage devices, primarily magnetic tapes and magnetic drums. Most of the data were entered into the computers on punched cards similar to those used in Jacquard's process. Output consisted of punched cards or paper. Binary (machine) language and assembly languages were used to program the computers. Operation was under human control; that is, a human operator had to physically reset relay switches and wiring before a program could be run.

Second Generation (1959–1965)

The device that characterized the **second-generation computers** was the transistor. **Transistors** were made of a semiconducting material and controlled the flow of electricity through the circuits. Transistors were a breakthrough technology that allowed computers to become physically smaller but more powerful, more reliable, and even faster than before. The transistor was developed at Bell Labs in 1947 by William Shockley, J. Bardeen, and W. H. Brattain. It was displayed for the public in 1948, and it won a Nobel Prize in 1956; however, it was not used in conjunction with computers until 1959.

Transistors were less expensive and smaller, required less electricity, and emitted less heat than vacuum tubes. Also, fewer transistors than tubes were required to operate a computer. Transistors were not so fragile as vacuum tubes, and they lasted longer. Because the components were substantially smaller, computers became considerably smaller.

Although magnetic tape was still the most commonly used external storage medium, magnetic disk storage was used so that data could be located more rapidly. MIT developed magnetic core storage in which each core stored one bit of information.

Table 2

Generations of Computers and Their Characteristics

First Generation (1951–1959)
- Vacuum tubes
- Magnetic tape for external storage—some magnetic drum
- Punched cards for input
- Punched cards and paper for output
- Machine and assembly languages
- Human operators to set switches
- UNIVAC I typical example

Second Generation (1959–1965)
- Transistors
- Magnetic-core storage
- Magnetic tape most common external storage, but magnetic disk introduced
- Punched cards and magnetic tape for input
- Punched cards and paper for output
- High-level languages—FORTRAN, COBOL, BASIC, PL/I and others
- Human operator to handle punched cards
- Honeywell 200 typical example

Third Generation (1965–1971)
- Integrated circuits
- Improved disk storage
- Monitors and keyboards for input and output
- More high-level languages, including RPG and Pascal
- First complete operating systems meant less involvement for human operators.
- Family of computers introduced allowing compatibility
- Minicomputers used commercially
- IBM System/360 typical example

Fourth Generation (1971–Present)
- LSI and VLSI
- Magnetic disk most common external storage
- Introduction of microcomputer
- Fourth-generation languages emerged and application software for microcomputers became popular
- Microcomputers used—Compaq DeskPro 386 typical example
- Burroughs B7700 and HP 3000 (minicomputer) typical examples

Fifth Generation (Future)
- True artificial intelligence

Contrasted with tape and drum storage, in which the location of data had to be found first, magnetic core storage made data instantaneously available. Punched cards and magnetic tape were the primary means for input, and punched cards and paper constituted the output.

Programming languages also became more sophisticated. High-level languages resembling English were developed, including FORTRAN, COBOL, BASIC, and PL/I. Like the first-generation computers, second-generation computers were primarily under the manual control of human operators.

Third Generation (1965–1971)

Integrated circuits signified the beginning of **third-generation computers.** Again, computers were smaller, more efficient, and more reliable than their predecessors. Unlike transistors and circuit boards that were assembled manually, **integrated circuits (ICs)** were single, complete electronic semiconductor circuits contained on a piece of silicon, sometimes called chips. ICs could be manufactured by machinery, which ultimately resulted in a lower cost.

Memory technology improved. By 1969, as many as 1,000 transistors could be built on a chip of silicon. Magnetic disks were improved and were used more for storage. Monitors and keyboards were introduced for data input and output. Punched cards lost their preeminence as input and output devices.

A new program controlled the computer and its resources and used them more effectively. This new program was the operating system. It meant that human operators were no longer required, and processing could be done at computer speeds rather than human speeds. High-level programming languages continued to be developed, including RPG and Pascal.

Another phenomenon of this third generation was the concept of families of computers. Businesses that bought computers and programs found that almost before a system was fully adapted, it was outdated or unable to grow with their needs. IBM recognized this problem and created an entire product line, the IBM/360 series, which allowed necessary upgrading or expansion. Programs written for one computer were compatible with any of the machines in the line. Businesses could upgrade or expand their data processing operations as necessary.

Digital Equipment Corporation introduced the first minicomputer in November 1963. Its PDP-1 was substantially cheaper than a mainframe, thus making smaller computers available to yet another business market.

Fourth Generation (1971–Present)

The significant distinction for **fourth-generation computers** lies in the techniques of implementation of integrated circuits by using **large scale integration (LSI)** of chips with several thousand transistors. In the mid-1970s the development of **very large scale integration (VLSI)** produced a chip containing a microprocessor. The development of VLSI made the development of the microcomputer possible. The Intel 80386 microprocessor followed. The Intel 80386 is faster and more powerful than its predecessors.

Magnetic disks became the primary means of internal storage. The proliferation of application programs for microcomputers allowed home and business users to adapt their computers for word processing, spreadsheet manipulating, file handling, graphics, and much more.

Fifth Generation (Future)

Although many people disagree on the start of the **fifth-generation computer** technology, some say that it will begin with the creation and use of a computer with

artificial intelligence (AI). AI indicates the ability to perform humanlike thinking and reasoning. The unofficial original goal was a thinking machine by 1990. Although expert systems are already being used for specialized applications, true artificial intelligence, or computers that can think, are still merely concepts. (Table 2 lists the generations of computers and their respective characteristics.) The future remains to be seen, of course, but since you will be part of the future, you may have some ideas or innovations of your own.

VOCABULARY SELF-TEST

Can you define the following?

artificial intelligence (AI) (p. 68)
first-generation computer (p. 65)
fifth-generation computer (p. 67)
fourth-generation computer (p. 67)
integrated circuits (IC) (p. 67)

large scale integration (p. 67)
second-generation computer (p. 66)
third-generation computer (p. 67)
transistor (p. 66)
vacuum tube (p. 65)
very large scale integration (VLSI) (p. 67)

REVIEW QUESTIONS

Multiple Choice

1. The _____ generation of computers was characterized by vacuum tubes.
   a. first
   b. second
   c. third
   d. fourth

2. The second generation of computers was characterized by _____.
   a. magnetic cards
   b. artificial intelligence
   c. transistors
   d. transformers

3. Integrated circuits signified the beginning of the _____ generation.
   a. first
   b. second
   c. third
   d. fourth

4. The advancement that allowed several thousand transistors to be placed on a single chip is known as _____.
   a. artificial intelligence
   b. large scale integration
   c. first-generation efficiency
   d. vacuum tube technology

5. Some experts say that artificial intelligence represents the entry of the _____ generation of computers.
   a. second
   b. third
   c. fourth
   d. fifth

Fill in

1. First-generation computers are characterized by _____ technology.

2. _____ are made of a semiconducting material and are primarily characteristic of the second generation of computers.

3. Integrated circuits signified the beginning of the _____ generation of computers.

4. The advancement that allowed the incorporation of several hundred thousand transistors onto a single chip is called _____.

5. _____ is the ability of fifth-generation computers to think and reason.

Short Answer

1. What characteristics delineate the first and second generations of computers.

2. Distinguish between third- and fourth-generation computers.

3. What characteristics will appear in the fifth generation of computers?

4. Write a thumbnail sketch of someone you found interesting in this InfoModule.

5. What invention or innovation do you think is most responsible for making the computer a successful product? Defend your choice.

COMPUTER HARDWARE: THE TOOLS OF THE TRADE

OBJECTIVES

3.1 Understand why it is important to learn about computer terminology.

3.2 Explain how data are represented in a computer.

3.3 Describe the central processing unit and state its purpose, define microprocessor, and briefly state why the issues of compatibility and CPU speed are important.

3.4 Describe the components of main memory and their functions.

3.5 Understand the term "input" and the purpose of an input device and define some common devices and applications for which they are used.

3.6 Identify and describe three special-purpose input devices.

3.7 Define optical recognition and describe three methods and devices used to accomplish it.

3.8 Understand the term "output" and the purpose of an output device, differentiate between hard copy and soft copy output, and identify common output devices for each.

3.9 Understand the purposes of ports and device drivers.

3.10 State the purpose of secondary storage and describe the two main types of magnetic secondary storage.

3.11 Identify several different forms of optical secondary storage.

3.12 Recognize common secondary storage problems and possible solutions.

PRO FILE

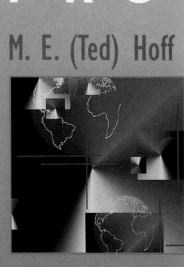

M. E. (Ted) Hoff

It's hard to imagine the world today if it weren't for people with vision like Ted Hoff. Even he probably didn't realize what would become of the work he started on that fateful day in 1969.

After working at Stanford University as a research assistant, Ted Hoff joined Intel Corporation in 1969. At Intel, Hoff led a team that helped a Japanese firm, Busicom, design a custom circuit for its calculator. The Busicom design called for 12 integrated circuit chips, each with 3,000–5,000 transistors. The chips that made up the processor were matched to the specific tasks of the calculator. After reviewing the design, however, Hoff decided it was too complex and would be too expensive to produce. Consequently, he used a totally different approach. He decided to design the calculator around a general-purpose processor, relying more on software than on electronics. Although more memory space was needed to store the software, this approach enabled Hoff to put the entire processor on a single integrated circuit chip, called a microprocessor.

What a chip it was! The Intel 4004 could handle 4 bits of information at a time, and its computational powers came close to those of the ENIAC, one of the early electronic digital computers that required an entire room to house it. This single microprocessor performed as well as some of the early (1960s) IBM machines that cost around $30,000 and had processing units the size of a large desk. Hoff's microprocessor was about ⅛-inch by ⅛-inch and cost about $200. The reductions in size and cost made it possible to design small, relatively inexpensive computers. This discovery heralded the beginning of the microcomputer revolution. Thanks to Ted Hoff's creativeness, microprocessors are everywhere—in our computers, homes, cars, factories, and, yes, still in our calculators.

For most of us, it's not necessary to understand the details of how a computer system works to use it. Just as it is not necessary to understand the details of how an automobile works to operate it. However, in both cases it is helpful to have a general knowledge of the parts, or hardware. This chapter introduces you to the hardware that makes up a computer system. This hardware includes the processor, or central processing unit (CPU), which is the engine that interprets and executes instructions that turn raw data into usable information. It also includes input devices used to enter data into the computer for processing, output devices used to communicate the results of processing to the user, and secondary storage devices used for nonvolatile storage of instructions and information needed or generated by the computer. We'll talk more about these instructions, or software, in the next chapter.

OBJECTIVE 3.1
Understand why it is important to learn about computer terminology.

WHY DO YOU NEED TO KNOW ABOUT COMPUTER TERMINOLOGY?

There is specialized terminology associated with any new subject. The value of understanding computer terms can be seen in the following:

- You load your software and try to run an application but . . . OUT OF MEMORY. You have only 640 *kilobytes* of *RAM* and the software requires at least 1 *megabyte* of RAM.
- You bought the latest release of the drafting software AUTOCAD. You try to install and run it on your computer, but it doesn't work. By reading the instruction manual, you find that it requires a *coprocessor*.
- You buy a computer game and look forward to playing it and enjoying the amazing realistic sounds that it advertises. However, your computer produces only very poor quality sound. Reading the box, you discover you need a *16-bit sound card* to produce the advertised sounds.

You can avoid or solve these problems if you have a general knowledge of the terminology and capabilities of the available hardware. We'll begin our look at computer hardware by talking a bit about the byte.

OBJECTIVE 3.2
Explain how data are represented in a computer.

HOW DOES THE COMPUTER UNDERSTAND WHAT YOU INPUT?

One way humans communicate is by depicting ideas through characters. This representation takes the form of alphabetic (letters), numeric (digits), and other special characters, collectively called alphanumerics.

Computers only recognize two distinct electrical states—ON or OFF. The ON and OFF states are commonly represented with the numbers 1 and 0, respectively. The **binary system** is the number system using only 1's and 0's. Various combinations of 1's and 0's can represent all the numbers, letters, and symbols. For example, the uppercase letter *D* is represented by the binary sequence 1000100. Because the language of the computer, machine language, is based on the binary system, data and instructions must be interpreted into binary code before they can be used by the computer. Fortunately, you do not have to convert data and instructions into binary code since there are computer programs that automatically take care of this.

Data representation

- Bit—smallest unit of data
- Byte—number of bits needed to represent a character
- Word—number of adjacent bits that can be manipulated as a unit

Bits and Bytes

Each individual 1 or 0 is called a bit, a *b*inary dig*it*. A **bit** is the smallest piece of data that a computer can process. To represent an alphanumeric character requires multiple bits. A grouping of bits that represents a character is called a **byte.** A byte typically consists of 8 bits. The byte is the basic unit used to measure the size of memory. However, with today's memory sizes, it is more common to hear the terms *kilobyte* (representing approximately 1,000 bytes, abbreviated as K or KB), *megabyte* (representing approximately 1 million bytes, abbreviated as MB), or *gigabyte* (representing approximately 1 billion bytes, abbreviated as GB) (see Figure 3-1).

Computer Words

Although individual characters are represented by a byte, the computer handles them in units of words. A **computer word** is the number of adjacent bits that can be manipulated as a unit. Depending on the design of its circuitry, computers handle different sizes of words. Common sizes are 16-, 32- and 64-bit words. If the bit string is larger than the maximum word size, the computer breaks it down into smaller strings. This adds additional steps and time to the operation being performed.

You might compare word size and its relationship to computer power and speed as you would the size of a truck to move your belongings. For example, if you have a 16-foot truck, but enough furniture to fill a 32-foot truck; you fill the truck, drive to the new location, empty the truck, and drive back to load the remainder of the furniture. But if you had a 32-foot truck, everything could have been loaded at once and you would have made only one trip thus speeding up the process.

Encoding Systems

How does the computer know how to represent each individual character with all the bits and bytes? An **encoding system** defines how characters are coded in terms of bits using 1's and 0's. The two most widely used encoding systems are ASCII (*A*merican *S*tandard *C*ode for *I*nformation *I*nterchange), developed by several computer manufacturers, and EBCDIC (*E*xtended *B*inary *C*oded *D*ecimal *I*nterchange *C*ode), developed by IBM.

OBJECTIVE 3.3
Describe the central processing unit and state its purpose, define microprocessor, and briefly state why the issues of compatibility and CPU speed are important.

WHAT IS THE CENTRAL PROCESSING UNIT?

The **central processing unit (CPU),** or processor, interprets and executes instructions and controls and communicates with the other parts of the computer. Every

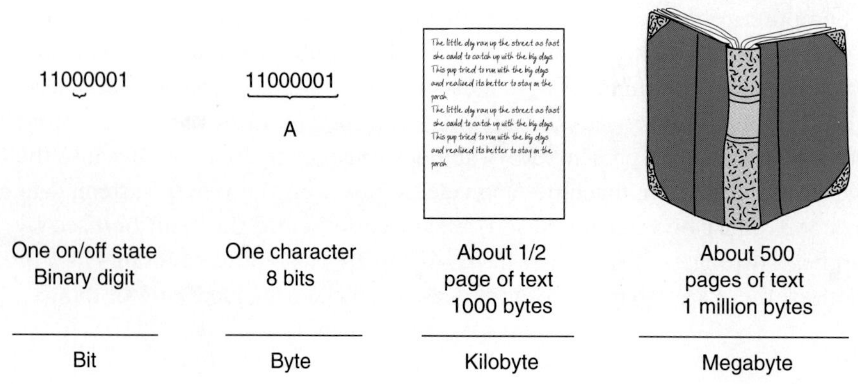

11000001
11000001
A
One on/off state
Binary digit
Bit
One character
8 bits
Byte
About 1/2
page of text
1000 bytes
Kilobyte
About 500
pages of text
1 million bytes
Megabyte

FIGURE 3-1
Comparison of sizes of bits and bytes.

computer has a CPU comprised of the arithmetic-logic unit and the control unit. The **arithmetic-logic unit (ALU)** is the part of the processor that performs arithmetic operations, logic operations, and related operations. The **control unit** retrieves and interprets instructions and directs the ALU and other parts of the computer in response to these interpretations.

Main components of a CPU

- Arithmetic-logic unit (ALU)
- Control unit

The Microprocessor

Microcomputers as we know them would not be possible without technological developments such as semiconductor technology. A complete electronic semiconductor circuit contained on a piece of silicon is called an **integrated circuit (IC).** An integrated circuit, also called a **microchip** or just **chip,** is used for logic and memory circuitry. For example, an IC can be designed to function as part of the ALU or as a memory chip. A CPU is a very complex series of circuits. Until the developmental work by Ted Hoff and others, the parts of the CPU were on separate chips. Hoff combined them onto a single chip. When those circuits are contained on a single chip, it is referred to as a **microprocessor** (see Figure 3-2). The CPU of a microcomputer is a microprocessor. Often, you will hear a microcomputer described by its microprocessor rather than its brand name. For microcomputers there are two main series of microprocessors: Intel (e.g., 80486 and Pentium), used by IBM and compatibles; and Motorola (e.g., 68030 and 68040), used by the Apple Macintosh line of computers.

A microprocessor usually does not carry all the burden of a computer system. Many other chips control other functions, such as sound, video, and peripheral devices. For example, many computers contain a **coprocessor,** which is a chip used along with the main microprocessor dedicated to speed large number-crunching activities. This adds more speed and power to the computer system. The microprocessor and other support chips and circuitry of a microcomputer are contained on the main circuit board, often called the motherboard or system board (see Figure 3-3). Some of these support chips are contained on adapters, that is, circuit boards that can be plugged into receptacles on the motherboard called **expansion slots.**

CPU and Software Compatibility

The circuitry of the different types of microprocessors is very different. This is important to know because software is designed for a specific type of processor. You need to know the type of processor your computer has to ensure that the software will be

FIGURE 3-2
The central processing unit consists of the control unit and the arithmetic-logic unit. In a microcomputer the CPU is combined on a single chip called a microprocessor.
(Courtesy of Intel Corp.)

FIGURE 3-3
The motherboard, or main cir-
cuit board, of a computer.
(Courtesy of Digital Corp.)

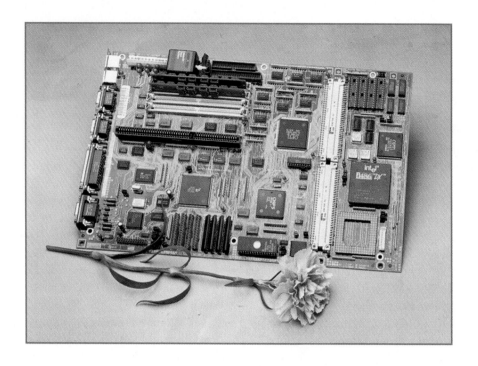

HIGHLIGHT 3-1 **Picture This**

Partners in the *Daily Planet*—yes it is a real newspaper in Telluride, Colorado—realize that a picture is worth a thousand words. They capture
photographs for the paper using an Eastman-Kodak
DCS 2000 digital camera. It is similar to a single-lens
reflex camera, but rather than film and chemicals, it
records images on an internal hard disk. It takes both
color and black-and-white pictures. After the picture is
"taken," it is downloaded into a graphics program
where editing occurs. A desktop publishing program
allows for setting up the text and photograph before
laser printing a page ready for the presses. All this
occurs faster than the 60 minutes required for processing film and converting it to halftones necessary for
printing.

This model, lists for approximately $10,000, so it is
not a household item yet and the digital image quality
is not as high as conventional camera and film, but digital photos contain enough detail for black-and-white
newspaper photographs. Some of the paper's digital
images are stored on a disk drive rather than in a file
drawer of negatives for use in future stories.

Do you suppose a glitch in this computer is called a
shutter "bug"?

compatible. Both Apple and IBM solved many of the compatibility issues by developing computers called Power PCs, each with the ability to run the other's software.

The Impact of CPU Speed

Another important factor concerning CPUs is its speed of operation. A program, such
as a word processor, may run on either a slow or fast processor, but it works much
more efficiently on the faster processor. Other programs, such as multimedia applications that are graphic intensive, use animation and video or produce high-quality
sounds require a high-speed processor.

One factor that affects the speed of a processor is the system clock. The **system
clock** generates electrical timing signals that regulate the operations of the processor and other parts of the computer. Clock speed is measured in megahertz (MHz).
Many microcomputer advertisements tout a particular computer as being "a XX-MHz
computer." Use the clock speed as a general guide for comparison only because there
are many other considerations; switching from a 33-MHz to a 66-MHz computer does
not necessarily mean a twofold increase in computing speed.

Another factor that influences speed is the architecture of the computer—how the circuitry is designed. The links among and within the various units are called buses. A **bus** is an electrical path for signals to flow from point to point in a circuit. A bus that carries a 32-bit word results in faster operations than a bus that carries only a 16-bit word.

Computer speeds are also increased by designing computers that use more than one CPU. A microcomputer that has a single CPU performs only **serial processing;** that is, it must finish one instruction before starting the next. Some microcomputers are designed with additional specialized processors that work in conjunction with the main processor. They relieve the main processor of some tasks such as number crunching and graphic manipulations, thus increasing the speed at which the computer can operate. Many computers, such as supercomputers, are designed with multiple, full-featured CPUs that permit parallel processing. **Parallel processing** allows several processes to be performed simultaneously. Tasks can be performed at speeds much faster than on serial processing computers. Thus, more complex tasks, such as simulations, can be performed.

OBJECTIVE 3.4
Describe the components of main memory and their functions.

WHAT IS MAIN MEMORY?

A CPU holds only one instruction and a small amount of data at one time. However, the tasks we typically ask a computer to perform require numerous, sometimes tens of thousands of, instructions and large amounts of data. The computer stores instructions and data that are waiting to be processed in the internal storage component of a computer called **main memory,** or primary storage. The two most common types of main memory are random-access memory (RAM) and read-only memory (ROM).

Random-access memory (RAM) is the part of main memory in which you enter (write) data and instructions and then retrieve them (read) in a random (nonsequential) manner. The computer automatically manages which portion of RAM the data and instructions are written to and retrieved from. Most of main memory consists of RAM. It is where program instructions and data are temporarily held while waiting to be processed. Many applications require a specific amount of RAM, or they may run slowly, or they may not work at all. However, most computers have provisions for adding more memory. RAM is volatile; it requires electrical current to maintain its contents. Thus, when the power to a computer is shut off, everything stored in RAM is lost.

Read-only memory (ROM) is the part of main memory from which data and instructions can only be retrieved (read). The contents of ROM are generally unchangeable and permanent. ROM is nonvolatile because the contents are not lost when the electric current is turned off. ROM is available as either chips or cartridges. ROM chips are typically located inside the computer on the main circuit board. Their contents are usually set by the computer manufacturer. A very important function is the permanent storage of instructions that tell a computer what to do when it is turned on. ROM cartridges are removable and often used to store games and other programs used by personal computers or game machines. Figure 3-4 illustrates an example of RAM and ROM use in a microcomputer.

In many of today's microcomputer advertisements you will see a reference to cache memory. **Cache memory** is a special type of buffer memory that holds a copy of data or instructions in main memory if they are likely to be needed next by the processor. Cache memory generally increases the speed at which data and instructions can be accessed and thus at which a task is completed. Special software is required to automatically access and manage a cache memory.

Main memory
• Random-access memory (RAM)
• Read/write
• Volatile
• Read-only memory (ROM)
• Read only
• Nonvolatile

FIGURE 3-4
An example of RAM and ROM
use in a microcomputer.

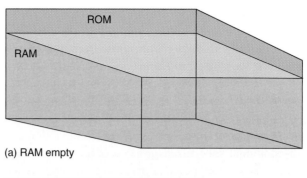

(a) RAM empty

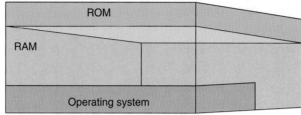

(b) Operating system loaded into RAM

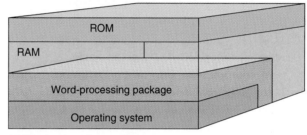

(c) Word-processing package
loaded into RAM

OBJECTIVE 3.5
Understand the term "input" and the purpose of an input device and define some common devices
and applications for which they are used.

WHAT IS INPUT AND WHAT IS AN INPUT DEVICE?

You'll see the term **input** commonly used in two ways. As a noun or adjective it refers to the data and instructions entered into a computer for processing. For example, "What input was used to produce this information?" As a verb it describes the act of entering data and instructions into a computer. This process is often referred to as **data entry.** For example, "Input these journal entries by two o'clock."

An **input device** is the hardware that transfers data and instructions into the computer for processing. The input is converted into a digital form for processing. There are a wide variety of input devices, many with specialized uses. A number of them are described in this section.

Keyboard

The **keyboard** is an input device that resembles a typewriter keyboard (see Figure 3-5). You press individual keys or combinations of keys to send data to the computer for processing. The keyboard will probably be your primary input device with either larger computers or microcomputers. The IBM enhanced keyboard (see Figure 3-6) and the Apple extended keyboard (see Figure 3-7) are two commonly used key-

FIGURE 3-5
New keyboard designs, such as the Apple adjustable keyboard, were developed to help prevent repetitive stress injuries such as carpal tunnel syndrome.

(Photo by John Greenleigh; courtesy of Apple Computer Inc.)

FIGURE 3-6
IBM-PC enhanced keyboard.

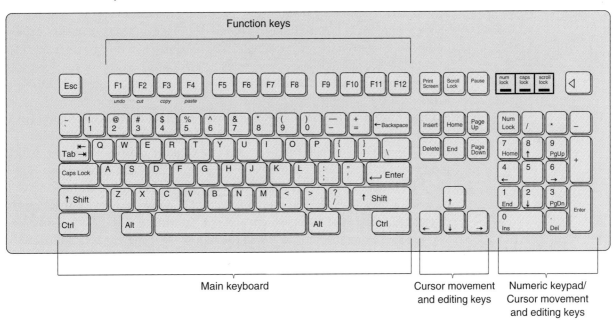

boards. These keyboards are made up of several parts: the main keyboard, the numeric keypad/cursor movement and editing keys, and the function keys. The main keyboard, or central portion, contains the standard set of printable characters. The calculatorlike numeric keypad at one side assists in data entry. On IBM enhanced keyboards some of the keys on the numeric keypad also perform cursor movement and editing functions. Each keyboard also contains a group of keys called function keys (numbered F1 through F12 on the IBM enhanced keyboard and F1 through F15 on the Apple extended keyboard) that are programmable keys. Typically, the function key uses are defined by the operating system or an application program.

FIGURE 3-7
Apple extended keyboard.

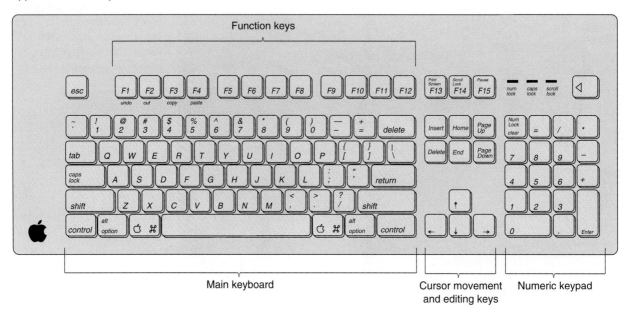

Main keyboard   Cursor movement and editing keys   Numeric keypad

Pointing Devices

A **pointing device** controls an on-screen pointer. A pointing device is often used for actions such as choosing menu items, "pressing" on-screen "buttons" in dialog boxes, and selecting text or other values. A pointer can take a variety of shapes depending upon the circumstances, for example, a rectangular block or arrowhead. Popular pointing devices include the mouse, trackball, stylus or pen, and puck. Head position and eye trackers are pointing devices that give physically challenged individuals access to a computer.

MOUSE. A **mouse,** the most commonly used pointing device (see Figure 3-8), is an inexpensive and easy-to-use complement to the keyboard. A mouse is designed to be easily gripped in your hand and contains one or more buttons on the top which are used to select items and choose commands. Most mice are connected to the computer by a cable; however, a cordless mouse that uses infrared or radio wave technologies is also available. On the underside of a mouse is a device that detects the direction and speed of its movement across a flat surface. This device is usually a ball that is rolled along the surface. When the mouse is moved, the rotation of the ball is translated into a digital signal that controls the movement of the on-screen pointer.

TRACKBALL. A **trackball** is a pointing device with a sphere located on top that is rotated by hand to control pointer movement (see Figure 3-9). In essence, a trackball can be thought of as an upside-down mouse. Whereas the entire mouse is moved, a trackball is stationary and the ball is rotated by hand. A trackball may also contain one or more buttons to initiate other actions (see Figure 3-10).

STYLUS/PUCK. A pen-based computer uses a **stylus** (also called a pen), a pointing device that is pressed against the computer screen as the primary input device. Pen-based systems are designed to read handwriting and make the input process easier and more intuitive to the user. Currently they are being used by people such as inspectors, inventory takers, poll takers, police officers, and rail workers. Users check boxes or fill in blanks on computer displayed forms that are nearly identical to the paper forms they traditionally used. The data can be stored and later transferred to other computers for processing.

FIGURE 3-8
(a) A mouse is a pointing device that is typically used to control an on-screen pointer.
(b) A mouse especially designed for children.
(Courtesy of Logitech, Inc.)

(a)

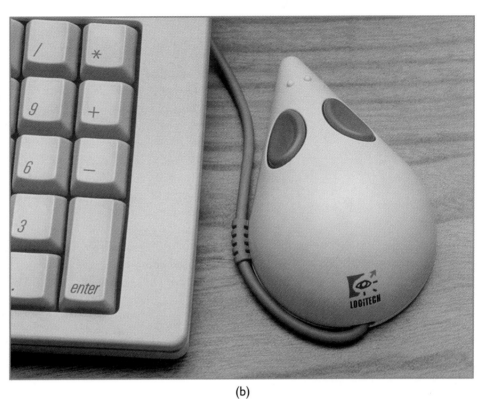

(b)

FIGURE 3-9
(Above) A trackball.

FIGURE 3-10
(Left) A minitrackball can be attached to many notebook computers to control the on-screen pointer.
(Courtesy of Logitech Inc.)

A **graphics tablet** (also called a digitizing tablet) consists of a flat plastic rectangle that contains electronic circuitry below its surface to detect when an object makes contact with the tablet. The graphics tablet is used in conjunction with pointing devices such as the stylus and the puck.

The stylus is pressed against a graphics tablet to draw, point, or select commands or items. Using a stylus offers a great deal of manual control and closely resembles freehand drawing. For this reason it is often preferred by artists for illustrations.

A **puck** is a pointing device that is often used with a graphics tablet (see Figure 3-11). It has a mouselike shape with buttons for selecting items or choosing commands. In addition, a clear plastic piece with crosshairs printed on it extends out from the body. The place where these crosshairs intersect points to a specific location on the tablet. That location is mapped to a specific location on the screen. Because the crosshairs lie on a clear plastic piece, drawings can be placed on the tablet and traced to easily enter them into the computer.

HEAD POSITION AND EYE TRACKERS. Although not common devices to the average user, head position and eye trackers can open up the world of computers to those who cannot use other handheld input devices.

Head position trackers use a headset that emulates a mouse. A control unit that sits on top of the computer measures the change in the headset's angular position and translates this change into cursor movements. The headset also contains an attached mouth tube into which the user lightly puffs to select an item, such as a letter to be entered into a word processing document, from a keyboard that is displayed on the screen.

Eye trackers use video cameras to track the position of the eye's pupils. These data are then translated into screen coordinates. Thus, the eye points to and selects items on the screen.

Touch Screens

A **touch screen** recognizes the location of a contact on the screen (see Figure 3-12) through a built-in grid of sensing lines or a grid of infrared beams and sensors.

Many applications, such as automatic teller machines (ATMs) and information kiosks, use touch screens because they offer an easy and intuitive way for users to

FIGURE 3-11
This engineer is using a puck to help design a new textile plant.

(Courtesy of Burlington Industries, Inc.)

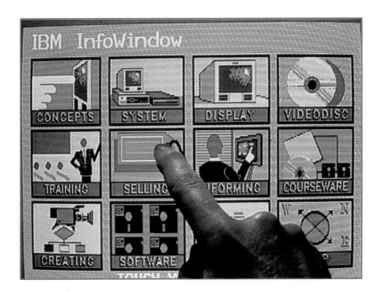

FIGURE 3-12
Touch screens allow users to make selections by simply touching the screen.
(Courtesy of International Business Machines Corp.)

interact with the computer. Also since there are no moving parts, they are durable and stand up to use by numerous individuals.

Speech Recognition

Probably the easiest way to input commands and data into a computer is to speak them. The ability of a computer to accept input by recognizing the speech of a user is called **speech recognition** or **voice recognition.** Currently, systems recognize limited vocabularies spoken by specific individuals. However, developing a system that can recognize the variety of speech patterns and accents that exist still poses significant problems for designers.

Tasks that require intensive use of the hands or eyes benefit from speech recognition. For example, physicians performing surgery could receive information from the computer by simply asking for it. Speech recognition input is also valuable for individuals who have lost some or all of their eyesight or functional use of their hands (see Figure 3-13).

FIGURE 3-13
The IBM Voicetype voice recognition system allows commands and text to be entered by speaking.
(Courtesy of International Business Machines Corp.)

Identify and describe three special-purpose input devices.

WHAT ARE SPECIAL-PURPOSE INPUT DEVICES?

Although many input devices are designed to be general-purpose input devices allowing for their use in a wide variety of applications, some accomplish specific tasks, such as magnetic ink character recognition (MICR), magnetic strips, and hand-tracking devices.

Magnetic ink character recognition (MICR) is the method by which a computer recognizes characters written in a special magnetic ink. The computer determines the shape of the character by sensing the magnetic charge in the ink. Magnetic ink is found on documents such as bank checks and credit card slips because the MICR reader reads the magnetic characters even if the user has written over them (see Figure 3-14).

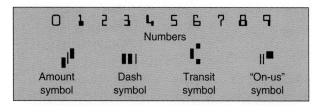

(a) Magnetic-ink character set

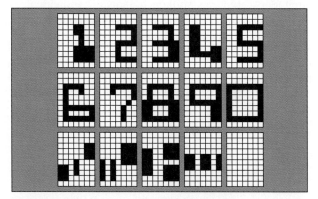

(b) Matrix patterns for magnetic-ink characters

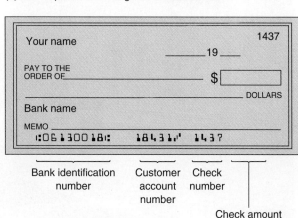

FIGURE 3-14
These magnetic ink characters are bank processing symbols. They represent the check number, customer account number, and bank identification number. Banks use magnetic ink characters on checks to ensure fast and efficient processing.

(c) Sample check

Magnetic strips are thin bands of magnetically encoded data found on the backs of many credit cards and automated teller cards. The data stored on a card vary from one application to another, but they often include account numbers or special access codes.

A **hand-tracking device** is a special-purpose input device that converts the movements of a hand into digital signals (see Figure 3-15). These signals are sent to the computer and can be used to control various functions such as the movement of a graphically produced hand displayed on the screen.

OBJECTIVE 3.7
Define optical recognition and describe three methods and devices used to accomplish it.

WHAT IS OPTICAL RECOGNITION?

Optical recognition is the process of using light-sensing equipment to scan paper or other sources and translate the pattern of light and dark or, in some cases, color into a digital signal that can be used by the computer. Optical recognition does not rely on the magnetic quality of the image, as MICR does. The three types of optical recognition described here are (1) optical mark recognition, (2) optical bar recognition, and (3) optical scanners.

Optical Mark Recognition

Optical mark recognition (OMR) employs mark sensing, one of the simplest forms of optical recognition, to scan and translate the locations of a series of pen or pencil

FIGURE 3-15
(a) Original DataGlove showing fiber optic sensors.
(Courtesy of VPL Research)
(b) Mattel Power Glove, a hand tracker with programmable keyboard used with Nintendo game.
(Courtesy of Mattel Toys)

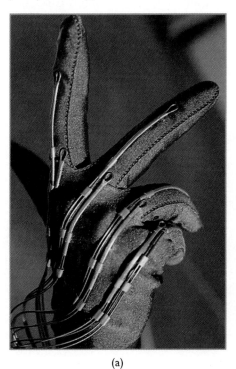

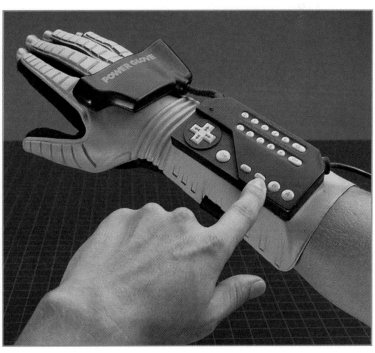

(a)   (b)

FIGURE 3-16
Flatbed scanners resemble a photocopier.
(Courtesy of Hewlett-Packard Co.)

marks into computer-readable form. A common use of OMR is to score test results, for example, answers to multiple-choice questions. An input device called an optical mark reader scans the form and identifies the *positions* of the marks, rather than the shapes, to score the test.

Optical Bar Recognition

Optical bar recognition (OBR) involves scanning and translating a bar code into digital signals to be used by a computer. A bar code is composed of a set of vertical lines of varying widths; it may also include numbers and letters. An input device called an optical bar reader scans and interprets the pattern of lines printed on products. The use of bar codes on products has given businesses faster and more accurate checkout procedures and better inventory control.

Optical Scanners

An **optical scanner,** often simply called a scanner, is an input device that uses light to sense the patterns of black and white (or color) on paper or other medium and convert them into a digital signal. The scanner converts an image into digital form that is stored on disk. Graphical software allows the display and manipulation of the image (light and dark, or color, patterns) sensed by the optical scanner. These graphical images can be saved, manipulated, and incorporated into other programs.

Suppose you wanted to edit scanned text. The optical scanner determines the character's shape and produces a graphic image. However, because it is only an image and not real text, it cannot be edited. **Optical character recognition (OCR)** software translates these images into text files that can be used by programs capable of manipulating text.

Scanners are available in two basic types: **flatbed scanners** and **handheld scanners.** Flatbed scanners resemble photocopy machines (see Figure 3-16) and are the best choice if you need to scan full-page documents. Flatbed scanners take up more desk space and are more expensive than handheld scanners. As its name implies, a handheld scanner is small enough to be held in your hand and must be physically moved across the page by the user. One disadvantage is that it relies on the user's arm movements, thus moving the scanner too fast or in a crooked manner across an image results in distortion of the scanned image (see Figure 3-17).

FIGURE 3-17
Handheld scanners are very popular. They are held in the user's hand and passed over the document.
(Courtesy of Logitech Inc.)

OBJECTIVE 3.8

Understand the term "output" and the purpose of an output device, differentiate between hard copy and soft copy output, and identify common output devices for each.

WHAT IS OUTPUT AND WHAT IS AN OUTPUT DEVICE?

Output is the process of translating data that are in machine-readable form into a form understandable to humans or readable by other machines. The information that is the result of processing is also referred to as output. An **output device** is hardware that enables a computer to communicate information to humans or other machines so that it may be used. Output is divided into two general categories: (1) output that is read and used by people and (2) data that are sent to secondary-storage devices to be used later as input for further processing by a computer or for use by another machine.

Output that is readable by users is categorized as either hard copy or soft copy. **Hard copy** is output that can be read immediately or stored and read later, such as paper. It is a relatively stable and permanent form of output. **Soft copy** is a transient form of output, for example, text on a screen display. It is lost when the computer is turned off. However, if the data used to create that soft copy remain in the computer's main memory or have been saved on disk or tapes, the soft copy can be reproduced repeatedly. In the next sections you will examine hard and soft copy output devices.

Output concepts
● Human-readable output
● Hard copy
● Soft copy
● Machine-readable form

Common Hard Copy Output Devices

Hard copy output devices produce graphics and text on paper, or other media, that are read by people. Printers and plotters are the most common hard copy output devices.

PRINTERS. A **printer** is an output device that produces output, on paper or other media, in the form of text or graphics. There is a wide variety of printers each with differing capabilities and features.

Print quality is a major consideration in choosing a printer for a particular job. Quality is said to be compressed print, standard-quality, near-letter-quality, letter-quality, near-typeset quality, and typeset quality print. The quality of type that a printer produces is determined mainly by its printing mechanism. Figure 3-18 compares print qualities.

This is an example of typeset-quality print.

This is an example of near-typeset quality print.

This is an example of letter-quality print.

This is an example of near-letter quality print.

This is an example of standard-quality print.

This is an example of draft-quality (compressed) print.

FIGURE 3-18
A comparison of the different qualities of print.

FIGURE 3-19
A desktop laser printer.
(Courtesy of Hewlett-Packard Co.)

In general, printers can be categorized by describing how they produce characters on a page. A printer uses one of two basic types of printing mechanisms: impact or nonimpact.

An **impact printer** produces characters when a hammer or pin strikes an ink ribbon, which in turn presses against a sheet of paper and leaves an impression of the character on the paper. This is how an ordinary typewriter works. Large system computers often use impact printers called line printers that print a line of characters at a time and generate thousands of lines per minute. The impact printer most often used with microcomputers is the dot-matrix printer.

The **dot-matrix printer** uses print heads containing 9 or 24 pins. These pins produce patterns of dots to form the individual characters. The 24-pin dot-matrix printer produces much crisper, clearer characters. Dot-matrix printers can typically produce a wide variety of print qualities. Some even offer color printing capabilities. They have a reputation for being very loud; however, some models substantially reduce the noise. Dot-matrix printers are popular with home computer users because they are relatively inexpensive to purchase (approximately $100 and up) and have low operating costs of less than 1 cent per page.

A **nonimpact printer** does not use a striking device to produce characters on paper. Rather, it uses a variety of other technologies. Because nonimpact printers do not hammer against paper, they are much quieter. Nonimpact printers include the ink-jet and laser printers.

An **ink-jet printer** is a nonimpact printer that forms characters on paper by spraying ink from tiny nozzles in the print head. The ink is absorbed into the paper and when dried is permanently bonded to the paper. Ink-jet printers produce high-quality output, comparable to laser printers.

The **laser printer** is a nonimpact printer that is capable of printing typeset quality images on paper using a technology similar to a photocopier. Desktop laser printers typically print a few pages (4–12) per minute (see Figure 3-19). Large system laser printers print thousands of pages per minute.

PLOTTERS. A **plotter** is an output device that reproduces graphic images on paper using a pen that is attached to a movable arm (see Figure 3-20). Plotter applications

FIGURE 3-20

(a) Desktop plotters are used in offices to generate graphics that enhance business presentations. (b) Large plotters allow images such as this circuit diagram to be drawn to a size that users can view in detail.

(Courtesy of Houston Instrument)

(a)

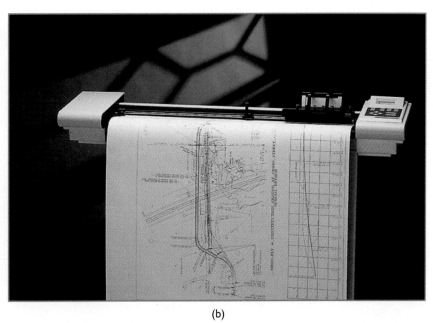

(b)

include creating high-quality graphical images in multiple colors for computer-aided design and drafting and bar graphs and pie charts to enhance business presentations.

Common Soft Copy Output Devices

Ordinarily, users prefer to see output before making a permanent copy. Viewing work before printing permits users to make corrections or to rearrange material. Although most soft copy output appears on a visual display device or screen, a voice output device lets users hear it as well.

MONITORS. The most popular soft copy output device is the monitor (see Figure 3-21). A **monitor** is a televisionlike apparatus that displays data or information.

Monitor quality is often discussed in terms of **resolution,** a measure of the number of picture elements, or pixels, for short, that the display screen of a monitor contains. A **pixel** is the smallest increment of a display screen that can be controlled individually. The more pixels, the clearer and sharper the on-screen image. Resolution is measured in dots per inch (dpi), the number of pixels that a device can display or print in one linear inch.

Let's look at two popular kinds of viewing screens for monitors: cathode ray tube and flat-panel display.

To produce an image on a **cathode ray tube (CRT)** display, an electron beam moves across a phosphor-coated screen. Intensifying the strength of the beam causes the phosphor coating to glow, forming the characters. The most common type of CRT has a display screen of 24 lines of 80 characters each. The standard CRT monitor size for desktop computers has been 14 inches. Other sizes are available, including those used in desktop publishing applications to display two full 8 ½-inch × 11-inch pages at their normal size. CRT monitors are large primarily because of the size of the picture tube.

FIGURE 3-21

Shown here are several monitors used to view output. Note the difference between the color display of the monitor on the left and the monochrome (single-color) display of the monitor on the bottom right.

(Courtesy of TRW, Inc.)

A CRT is too cumbersome to use on portable computers because it is so large and heavy and demands a lot of power. Monitors for portable computers need to be lighter weight and more energy efficient. A **flat-panel display** does not have a picture tube and is manufactured to fit on a battery-powered portable computer. Flat-panel screens do not use an electron gun and therefore do not flicker. The flickering may cause eyestrain and fatigue during prolonged sessions at the computer. Common types of flat-panel displays include the liquid-crystal display (LCD) and gas plasma display (see Figure 3-22).

For your computer to communicate with the monitor it needs a graphics adapter card. A **graphics adapter card** is a circuit board inside the computer that converts the electronic signals sent by your computer into a form usable by the monitor. In some computers this circuitry is built in; in others a separate card must be installed. The graphics adapter card determines the monitor display type. Two common types of graphics adapter cards found in IBM and compatible computers are VGA and SuperVGA. The video graphics array (VGA) offers a resolution of 640 dpi $\times$ 480 dpi. The SuperVGA card has a resolution of 800 dpi $\times$ 600 dpi.

VOICE OUTPUT. Another type of soft copy output is **voice output,** the technology in which a computer uses a voice. Voice output systems are used where a display screen would not work or be appropriate, for example, in automobile warning systems, toys and games, or systems designed for the blind and visually impaired.

Common output devices

- Hard copy
  - Printers
  - Plotters
- Soft copy
  - Monitors
  - Voice output

FIGURE 3-22
(a) Gas plasma display screen. (b) LCD display screen.

(a)

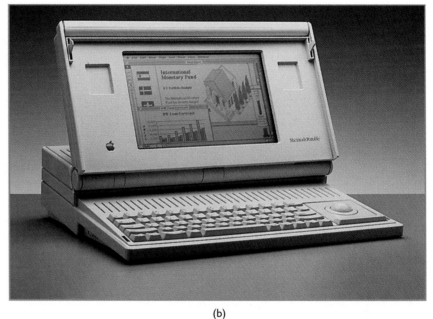

(b)

Speech coding, one type of voice output, is the storage of a bank of human sounds. The sounds are coded and selected to build the words and phrases. You may have heard the supermarket checkout computer give the total of your purchases. **Voice synthesis** is the process of electronically reproducing the human voice in recognizable patterns. Producing these patterns is not easy. The English language and its rules of syntax are enough to confuse many humans. Imagine the difficulty in programming a computer to decipher how to say, "I have read the book and Eric will read the book next."

Understand the purposes of ports and device drivers.

WHAT ARE PORTS AND DEVICE DRIVERS?

You will see a number of pluglike connectors either at the back or on the side of your computer. These are called **expansion ports,** or input/output (I/O) ports. Their purpose is to allow your computer to physically connect to and communicate with peripheral devices. Communication can take place from the computer to the peripheral device, from the peripheral device to the computer, or both ways. The cable that connects a peripheral device to the computer is called an **interface cable.**

A **device driver** is software that allows peripheral devices to communicate with your computer and other peripheral devices. Common examples of peripherals that require device drivers include monitors, printers, and mice. For example, a printer driver tells the computer what kind of printer it will be working with and what type of printing capabilities the printer has (such as font choices and page layout). Device drivers may be part of the operating system and require little or no setup by the user, or they may require installation before a peripheral device is used.

OBJECTIVE 3.10
State the purpose of secondary storage and describe the two main types of magnetic secondary storage.

WHAT IS SECONDARY STORAGE?

Because the contents of RAM are erased every time the power to the computer is turned off, another more permanent means of storage is needed to avoid reentering program instructions and data every time. **Secondary storage** is external to main memory and provides a nonvolatile means for keeping data and instructions for permanent or long-term storage. The contents of secondary storage can be loaded into main memory for use by the CPU.

The two most common types of secondary storage for all sizes of computers are magnetic tapes and magnetic disks. As a rule of thumb, the larger the computer system, the greater the secondary-storage capacity and the faster the computer accesses the data stored there.

Magnetic Tape

Typically, **magnetic tape** is a one-half inch or one–quarter inch ribbon of mylar (a plastic material) coated with a thin layer of iron-oxide material on which data are recorded. The **tape drive** is an input/output device that reads, writes, and erases data on tape.

Magnetic tapes are erasable, reusable, and durable. Tapes store large quantities of data inexpensively; therefore, they are often used as backup storage media. However, magnetic tape is not well suited for data files that are revised or updated often. This is because magnetic tape stores data sequentially; that is, a computer must read every preceding record to get to the data you need.

One-fourth-inch-wide **cassette tape** (see Figure 3-23) that resembles the cassette tape used for audio recording and one-half inch **cartridge tape** (see Figure 3-24) are often used with microcomputers for backing up (making copies of) the contents of a hard disk.

Cartridge tapes and reel-to-reel tape systems are popular as secondary storage media for large computer systems. A **reel-to-reel tape** is magnetic tape placed on open reels typically about 10 ½ inches in diameter (see Figure 3-25), about 2,400 feet long and one-half inch wide. Reel-to-reel tapes are relatively inexpensive and durable and hold many megabytes of data.

FIGURE 3-23
Cassette tapes for data storage are similar to audio cassettes.

FIGURE 3-24
This tape cartridge is approximately one-half the size of a videocassette and holds about 20,000 pages of information.
(Courtesy of BASF Corporation Information Systems.)

Magnetic Disk

A **magnetic disk** is a mylar or metallic platter on which electronic data are stored. The main advantages of a magnetic disk over magnetic tape include the ability to (1) directly access the data stored on it, (2) hold more data in a smaller space, and (3) attain faster data access speeds.

Magnetic disks are used with all sizes of computers. The difference is in the number of disks and the data storage capacity of each disk. Magnetic disks are manufactured in both floppy diskette and hard disk styles.

FLOPPY DISKETTE. A **floppy diskette** is a small flexible mylar disk on which data are stored. They provide an inexpensive, portable means of secondary storage. Two common sizes of floppy diskettes are 5 ¼-inch and 3 ½-inch sizes (see Figure 3-26). Typical formatted capacities are 360 K and 1.2 megabytes for 5 ¼-inch diskettes and 720 K, 1.44 megabytes, and 2.88 megabytes for 3 ½-inch diskettes.

Because floppy diskettes have a limited storage capability, other disks are used, including flopticals and hard disks. *Flopticals* are a high-capacity media that combine the features of magnetic and optical storage. They look like ordinary 3 ½-inch disks but have capacities of approximately 21 MB. The drives for this media are called super floppy drives.

FIGURE 3-25
(a) Magnetic reel-to-reel tape with raw iron oxide.
(Courtesy of BASF Corporation Information Systems.)
(b) Magnetic reel-to-reel tape mounted on tape drives.
(Courtesy of U.S. Department of the Navy.)

(a)

(b)

HARD DISK. A **hard disk** is made from materials such as aluminum instead of mylar and is hard and inflexible. The input/output device that transfers data to and from a hard disk is a **hard disk drive.**

A hard disk has several advantages over a floppy diskette. The rigid construction of a hard disk allows it to be rotated very fast compared to a floppy diskette. Thus, data can be transferred much faster to or from a hard disk because it takes less time to find the storage location. More data can be placed in a smaller area, giving the hard disk more storage capacity than a floppy disk of the same size. The larger capacity of hard disks is often required to accommodate many of today's large programs.

Hard disk drives are available in two different styles, nonremovable and removable. In a nonremovable hard disk drive, the hard disk(s) are enclosed permanently in the drive in a sealed case, which is attached permanently in the computer. In a removable hard disk drive, the hard disk(s) are contained in a removable cartridge that offers the advantages of a hard disk, but is also portable. Several advantages of removable cartridges are that a user can have separate cartridges for each application or user, store them in locations separate from the computer, and transport data easily. Removable media give a measure of security, because when the user leaves, data on the disk do not need to remain in the computer.

Figure 3-27 shows a typical nonremovable hard disk for a desktop microcomputer. Hard disks for portable computers are smaller, ranging from 1.3 inches to 2.5 inches. Removable cartridges for microcomputers have the same speed and capacity as a system with nonremovable hard disks.

Large system computers use a form of magnetic disk called a **disk pack** (see Figure 3-28), a removable device in which several hard disks (a common number is 11) are packed into a single plastic case. Disk packs can be interchanged, giving a virtually unlimited amount of secondary storage.

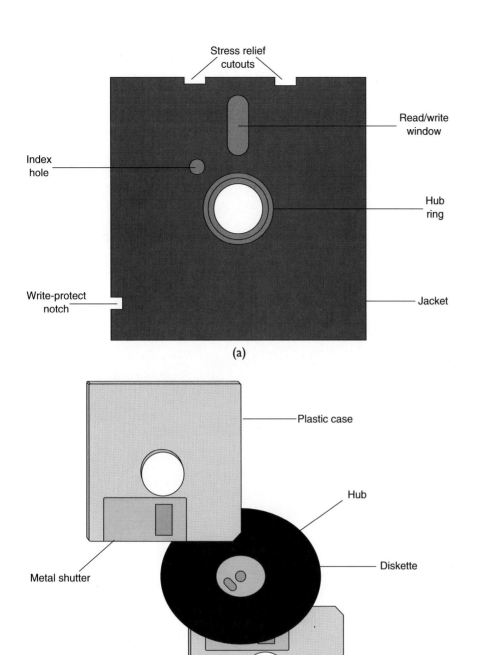

Stress relief
cutouts

Read/write
window

Index
hole

Hub
ring

Write-protect
notch

Jacket

(a)

Plastic case

Hub

Diskette

Metal shutter

Write-protect tab

A protective liner covers
both sides of the diskette.

(b)

FIGURE 3-26
Desktop microcomputers use
5 ¼- and 3 ½-inch floppy
diskettes. (a) The 5 ¼-inch disks
are covered by stiff, protective
jackets that have various holes
and cutouts. The disk drive uses
the hub ring to hold the disk to
rotate it. The elongated
read/write window allows the
read/write head of the drive to
write data on or read data from
the floppy disk. The small hole
next to the hub ring is the
index hole. Through the index
hole, a computer determines
the relative position of the disk
for locating data. The cutout on
the side of the floppy disk is the
write-protect notch. Covering
this opening with a piece of tape
protects data on the disk from
being erased or written over.
(b) The 3 ½-inch disks have hard
plastic jackets and protective
metal pieces that cover the
read/write window when the
disk is not in use. The additional
protection makes the disk less
prone to damage from handling,
dust, or other contaminants.

FIGURE 3-27
The case has been removed from this hard disk drive to show the hard disk and a read/write head.
(Photo courtesy of Seagate.)

FIGURE 3-28
An operator installs a disk pack for mainframe computer storage.
(Courtesy of BASF Corporation Information Systems.)

OBJECTIVE 3.11
Identify several different forms of optical secondary storage.

WHAT TYPES OF OPTICAL STORAGE ARE USED?

Optical technology involves the use of lasers—highly concentrated beams of light. Laser beams read to and write data from the optical storage medium. The laser beam is either reflected back to a sensor or scattered by microscopic pits whose presence or absence in the disk represents a binary 1 or 0. As costs continue to decrease, optical storage may replace magnetic storage as the preferred method of storing data and instructions because it has much larger capacity and greater reliability. However, optical technology is generally read only. Optical storage formats include disks, cards and tape.

Optical Laser Disk

Optical laser disks are metal disks ranging in size from 3 ½-inches to 14 inches. A typical 14-inch disk stores as much as 20 reel-to-reel tapes. Optical disks come in three formats: (1) CD-ROM, (2) WORM, and (3) erasable.

FIGURE 3-29
A CD-ROM has storage capacities of 500 megabytes and more.

(Photo by John Greenleigh/Apple Computer Corp.)

CD-ROM. A common version of the optical disk is the CD-ROM (compact disk, read-only memory). A CD-ROM is convenient for storing data that remain the same (see Figure 3-29). In the past, Price Waterhouse sent over 15,000 auditing professionals a 40-volume printed packet of information. Not only was this costly, but searching for data was difficult. Now the auditors access all this information on one CD-ROM. Other applications well suited to CD-ROM include reference books, annual reports, all types of government statistics, and stock market reports (see Figure 3-30). Today most desktop computers come equipped with CD-ROM.

WORM. Another type of optical disk is the **write-once, read-many (WORM)** optical disk that is written to once and read many times. Data on WORM disks cannot be erased and are thus suitable for long-term storage. They are available in 5 ¼-inch disks with capacities up to 800 megabytes and in 12-inch disks that store up to 3 gigabytes for large computer systems.

ERASABLE DISKS. Erasable optical disks can be erased and written to many times. They are removable and hold up to 1 gigabyte or more of data. They are relatively expensive compared with magnetic hard drives and will probably not see widespread use until the price declines.

Optical Card

An **optical card,** or laser card, is the size of a credit card and has an optical laser-encoded strip that stores approximately 4 megabytes of data. Such cards have many potential uses, most notably as credit records or medical histories.

Secondary storage devices

- Magnetic Tape
  - Cassette
  - Cartridge
  - Reel to reel
- Magnetic disk
  - Floppy diskette
  - Hard disk
- Optical storage media
  - Optical laser disk
    - CD-ROM
    - WORM
    - Erasable
  - Optical card
  - Optical tape

FIGURE 3-30
CD-ROM opens up whole new vistas of education for children. Colorful graphics, sound, and animation capture a child's attention and imagination as they learn about the world around them. Here, a program called Mayo Clinic—The Total Heart teaches them about the heart, heart disease, and how to maintain a healthy heart.

(Courtesy of AST Research)

Optical Tape

Optical tape is similar to magnetic tape in that it is read sequentially, but, data are stored by optical laser techniques. Optical tapes, which are in cassette form, store over 8 gigabytes each. A 15-inch reel of optical tape is capable of storing 1 terabyte (1 trillion bytes) of data, or about a half-billion pages.

OBJECTIVE 3.12
Recognize common secondary storage problems and possible solutions.

WHAT ARE SOME COMMON SECONDARY STORAGE PROBLEMS AND SOLUTIONS?

Each medium has its own niche in the realm of secondary storage. However, problems do arise, such as lost data, slow access to data, and not having enough storage.

Lost Data

So you think your data are safe because you used a command to save your file! Think about these scenarios—operator error, system failure, software defects, viruses, theft, vandalism, site destruction, and Mother Nature. Thankfully, there are ways to protect your data and computer.

BACKUP. Backing up data on a mainframe computer is standard procedure, whether it is convenient or not. Many microcomputer users do not back up their data. If you have ever lost an important file, *backup* is a word you won't soon forget. Whether to guard against hard disk failure, operator error, or natural disasters like fire or flood, backing up your work is worth the effort. In fact, many insurance companies require their customers to perform regular backup procedures to insure their coverage. Tape backup is one of the most common, convenient, reliable, and least expensive methods (see Figure 3-31).

DATA RECOVERY. Even if you did not make a backup, there are software programs that, under certain circumstances, can recover data and programs after they have been "lost." Your operating system or applications like Norton Utilities provide routines for such recovery. There are also companies that specialize in recovering data from damaged disks.

ELECTRONIC PROTECTION. Lightning strikes can easily render your computer's electronic components useless. Lesser known, but potentially as damaging, are variations in electrical power levels. These spikes, surges, sags, and brownouts can have devastating effects on both data and components.

Storage problems and solutions

- Lost data
  - Backup
  - Data recovery software and services
  - Electronic protection
- Slow data access
  - Defragmentation software
  - Head alignment software
- Not enough storage
  - Additional media
  - Data compression

The best protection against lightning is to unplug your computer. Minor electrical spikes can be eliminated with a *surge protector*, a relatively inexpensive device that all computer users should consider purchasing. For complete protection, although expensive, an *Uninterruptable Power Supply (UPS)* delivers a constant level of voltage regardless of any variations in line voltage. Be sure that there aren't too many devices running from the same circuit.

Slow Data Access

This is a problem that you may not realize is happening. Through use, data and program storage become fragmented (i.e., stored in parts rather than as one unit), and read/write heads become misaligned. Both these problems severely reduce the speed at which data are accessed, and in fact, if the heads are misaligned enough the secondary storage device will be unable to access the media at all. One solution is found in programs such as Spinrite, which pieces together fragmented files and helps restore your hard disk to its original performance. There are other software products that test your drives for proper head alignment, rotational speed, and other drive problems.

Not Enough Storage

When secondary storage space runs out, there are both hardware and software solutions to this problem. It's easy to exceed the capacity of available storage. One solution is to purchase a hard disk with larger capacity or add additional disks to your computer system. Further, technologies like digital audio tape (DAT) are available. It uses 8mm tape and stores up to 2.2 gigabytes in a single cartridge. High-capacity optical devices will play a larger role as prices decrease.

Another way to achieve more space on existing secondary storage is through data compression software. *Data compression* works by reducing the size of the file to be stored on disk. Depending on the data compression software you use, up to 50 percent of the available disk space can be made available for storing additional files.

SUMMARY

Letters, digits, and other special characters are collectively called alphanumerics. The binary system that uses only 1's and 0's represents data in a computer.

The smallest piece of data that a computer processes is a bit. A grouping of bits that represent a character is called a byte. A computer word is the number of adjacent bits that can be manipulated as a unit. An encoding system defines how characters are coded in terms of bits (1's and 0's). ASCII and EBCDIC are the two most widely used encoding systems.

A central processing unit (CPU), or processor, is that part of the computer that interprets and executes instructions and controls and communicates with the other parts of the computer. It is comprised of the arithmetic-logic unit (ALU) and control unit.

When all the parts of a CPU are contained on a single chip, it is called a microprocessor. Other chips, such as a coprocessor, often are used to remove some of the processing burden from the microprocessor. The microprocessor and other support chips and circuitry of a microcomputer are contained on the main circuit board, often called the motherboard or system board. Some support chips are contained on adapters, or circuit boards, that can be plugged into receptacles on the motherboard called expansion slots.

Software is designed to run on a specific type of processor. You need to know the type of processor your computer has to ensure compatibility. Knowing the CPU speed is important because some programs require a high-speed processor. The speed of a processor is affected by the system clock, the system architecture, and the number of processors in the computer. A computer with a single CPU must finish executing one instruction before it begins the next, a process called serial processing. A computer with multiple CPUs executes more than one instruction at a time, a process called parallel processing.

The computer's main memory is the internal storage unit of a computer. The two most common types of main memory are random-access memory (RAM) and read-only memory (ROM).

Input refers to the data and instructions entered into a computer for processing or to the act of entering data, which is often called data entry. Input devices transfer data and instructions to the computer for processing. The most commonly used input device is the keyboard.

Pointing input devices control an on-screen pointer. They include the mouse, trackball, stylus, and puck used with a graphics tablet; stylus used with pen-based computers; and head position and eye trackers.

A touch screen is an input device that detects where a computer screen is touched and uses this information to initiate an action.

Speech recognition, or voice recognition, is the ability of a computer to recognize the speech of a user as input.

Some input devices are designed for special purposes. These include the MICR reader used for magnetic ink character recognition, magnetic strips that contain encoded data on cards, and hand tracking devices that digitize the movements of a hand to control computer operations.

Optical recognition is the process of using light-sensing equipment to scan paper, and other media, and translate the patterns of light and dark (or color) into a digital signal that is used by the computer. Optical recognition devices include the optical mark reader for optical mark recognition (OMR), the optical bar reader for optical bar recognition (OBR), and optical scanners used in combination with graphical software or optical character recognition (OCR) software. Optical scanners are available in two basic types: flatbed scanners or handheld scanners.

Output refers to the process of translating machine-readable data into a form that is understood by humans or a form that is read by other machines. The information that is the result of processing is also referred to as output. An output device is the hardware that enables a computer to communicate information to humans or other machines.

Output that people read is categorized as either hard copy or soft copy. Hard copy output devices include printers and plotters. Printers are categorized as either impact or nonimpact printers, based on how the mechanism prints the characters. Common impact printers are line printers and dot-matrix printers. Common nonimpact printers are ink-jet printers and laser printers. A plotter is an output device that uses a pen attached to a movable arm to draw graphic images on paper.

Common soft copy output devices include monitors and voice output systems. A monitor is a televisionlike device that displays data or information. Two popular types of monitor screen displays are the cathode ray tube (CRT) and the flat-panel display. Common types of flat-panel displays include liquid crystal display (LCD) and gas plasma display.

The use of a voice by the computer for output is called voice output. It is used where a display screen would not work or would be inappropriate. Speech coding and voice synthesis are two types of voice output.

Expansion ports, or input/output (I/O) ports, are the pluglike connectors at the back or on the side of the computer whose purpose is to allow the computer to Two types of magnetic disks are floppy diskettes and hard disks. Hard disks are available in two styles, nonremovable and removable. Large computer systems use magnetic disk packs.

Optical technology uses a laser to store data on various media. Optical media include optical laser disks which are available as CD-ROM, WORM, and erasable as well as optical cards, and optical tapes.

Common areas that may cause problems when dealing with secondary storage are lost data, slower data access time, and running out of storage room on the media. Lost data can be combatted by backing up your data, using data recovery software or consulting data recovery specialists, and by using hardware devices that protect against electronic disturbances that damage data. Slow data access times are improved by using software to defragment your disk and align the read/write heads of the drive. Purchasing additional storage capacity or using data compression on your current storage media adds additional storage space. Data compression is a method of reducing the size of a file to create more space on the storage media.

VOCABULARY SELF-TEST

Can you define the following?

arithmetic-logic unit (ALU) (p. 75)

binary system (p. 73)

bit (p. 74)

bus (p. 77)

byte (p. 74)

cache memory (p. 77)

cartridge tape (p. 92)

cassette tape (p. 92)

cathode ray tube (CRT) (p. 89)

central processing unit (CPU) (p. 74)

chip (p. 75)

computer word (p. 74)

control unit (p. 75)

coprocessor (p. 75)

data entry (p. 78)

device driver (p. 92)

disk pack (p. 94)

dot-matrix printer (p. 88)

encoding system (p. 74)

expansion ports (p. 92)

expansion slots (p. 75)

eye trackers (p. 82)

flatbed scanners (p. 86)

flat-panel display (p. 90)

floppy diskette (p. 93)

graphics adapter card (p. 90)

graphics tablet (p. 82)

handheld scanners (p. 86)

hand-tracking device (p. 85)

hard copy (p. 87)

hard disk (p. 94)

hard disk drive (p. 94)

head position trackers (p. 82)

impact printer (p. 88)

ink-jet printer (p. 88)

REVIEW QUESTIONS

Multiple Choice

1. The number of adjacent bits that can be stored and manipulated as a unit is called a _____.
   a. byte
   b. nibble
   c. word
   d. MIP

2. A microprocessor contains both the _____.
   a. ALU and main memory
   b. control unit and RAM
   c. RAM and ROM
   d. ALU and control unit

3. When application software, such as a word processor, is loaded into a computer, it resides in _____.
   a. RAM
   b. the operating system
   c. ROM
   d. the instruction set

4. Which of the following input devices is the most common?
   a. Keyboard
   b. Stylus
   c. Trackball
   d. Mouse

5. A _____ is a pointing device that fits in your hand and controls an on screen pointer as it is rolled along a flat surface.
   a. trackball
   b. keyboard
   c. stylus
   d. mouse

6. One of the most complex input techniques, in which a user speaks into a microphone, is called _____.
   a. speech recognition
   b. voice output
   c. voice coding
   d. voice synthesis

7. The output that can be read immediately or stored and read later is called _____.
   a. hard copy
   b. soft copy
   c. optical recognition copy
   d. machine-readable copy

8. Printers produce characters on a page using two basic types of printing mechanisms; they are _____.
   a. electrical and mechanical
   b. impact and nonimpact
   c. hard and soft
   d. dot matrix and ink jet

9. CD-ROM is a type of_____.
   a. optical laser disk
   b. main memory chip
   c. magnetic disk
   d. operating system

10. A WORM drive uses a(n) _____ as its storage medium.
    a. magnetic disk
    b. magnetic tape
    c. optical disk
    d. punched tape

Fill In

1. _____ is a type of internal memory that can only be read from and not written to.

2. ASCII and EBCDIC are two types of _____ systems.

3. The smallest unit of data that a computer recognizes is called a(n) _____.

4. A _____ is a pointing device with a sphere located on top that is rotated by hand to control pointer movement.

5. _____ and _____ are pointing devices that enable individuals with motor disabilities to use a computer.

6. A(n) _____ is an input device that recognizes the location of a touch on the screen.

7. A screen display is an example of _____ copy output.

8. A(n) _____ is an output device that uses a pen attached to a movable arm to draw graphic images on paper.

9. A _____ is a type of storage media made from materials such as aluminum instead of mylar and is hard and inflexible.

10. Optical technology uses_____to write and read data.

Short Answer

1. What two major units comprise the CPU? Briefly describe the function of each unit.

2. What does the term *volatile* mean as it pertains to computer memory?

3. Describe the roles that RAM and ROM play within a computer, the main purpose of each, and the factors that distinguish the two types of memory.

4. Define pointing device and describe several devices that fit this category.

5. Give examples of situations where speech recognition would be a valuable input method.

6. What is meant by optical recognition? Describe three types of optical recognition.

7. Describe the two basic types of printing mechanisms used in printers and give examples of printers that use them.

8. Compare the two kinds of screens for monitors.

9. What are the advantages of magnetic tape over magnetic disks?

10. Describe several secondary storage problems that computer users might encounter. Give suggestions for avoiding these problems.

1. Bring in several computer advertisements to discuss. Are you able to decipher them yourself? Can you determine the speed, amount of memory, peripheral equipment? Discuss how you would choose one for a specific task.

2. Optical scanners have made it relatively easy for individuals to digitize and incorporate text and graphics from nearly any source into their documents. From an ethical standpoint, what limits do you think should be placed on scanning and using preexisting text and graphics in your own materials without permission? Defend your position.

COMPUTER SOFTWARE: THE BRAINS BEHIND THE BRAWN

4.1   Understand the two basic types of software.

4.2   Define operating system, describe its major
      functions, and discuss several ways it is typically
      used in day-to-day computer operation.

4.3   Describe several capabilities of operating sys-
      tems.

4.4   Contrast three types of user interfaces.

4.5   Understand the purpose of a disk operating
      system and an operating environment and
      identify four major microcomputer operating
      systems and their associated environments.

4.6   Describe the purpose of a utility program.

4.7   Define application software and describe the
      two broad categories into which they are
      grouped.

4.8   Define integrated software.

4.9   Identify concerns of those getting started on a
      new application software package.

4.10 Define the terms computer programming,
      computer program, programmer, programming
      language, and language translator program and
      describe the five categories of programming
      languages.

PROFILE

Peter Norton

Oops! That sound started the rest of Peter Norton's life. Norton, a Southern Californian, appears to be an average all-American kind of guy. He's in his forties, and rather than "dressing for success," his work attire consists of rolled-up shirt sleeves and a tie loosened casually.

Norton lost his job in the late 1970s when the aerospace industry suffered huge cutbacks. He took computer programming jobs to tide him over. Then came the celebrated "Oops" when he deleted an important file accidentally. Now, it's clear that was a fortunate accident. As a programmer, Norton was sure there must be a better, more efficient, way to recover the lost file. He didn't want to have to reenter everything. So he applied those programming skills and successfully created a computer program to recover the data from that lost file.

Peter Norton Computing, Inc. (PNCI), was formed in 1982, based on that new program, dubbed Norton Utilities. With the Norton name boldly proclaimed, he felt obliged to deliver the best quality. And since he was the programmer, owner, and sole public relations expert, it wasn't long before he had to hit the road in an effort to market the product. Norton visited computer stores and user groups trying to generate sales. To do this, he prepared technical notes and left them for potential buyers. A publisher from Brady Books came across these pamphlets and recognized that Norton had a talent for writing about technical topics in a highly readable form. Shortly thereafter, Norton's first computer book, *Inside the IBM PC,* was published and became an immediate best-seller. It has now become an industry standard. In fact, since 1983 Norton's books have been translated into 14 languages and over 1 million copies have been sold.

The original PNCI offices were in the Norton home. Business hours depended on the family's schedule. A programmer was finally hired to help, and he was forced to share work space with Mrs. Norton. At day's end the programmer had to move his files and papers out of the way so the table could be set for dinner.

In 1988 Norton was named "Entrepreneur of the Year" by Arthur Young and *Venture.* Norton's philosophy was to work as long as it was fun; he didn't set out to make lots of money. But PNCI was one of the fastest-growing private companies in America, and in 1990 Symantec Corp., a publicly held software company, worked out a merger deal. Norton's share is estimated at a $100 million. The office isn't at the kitchen table anymore, and Norton is much too busy enjoying his family, doing philanthropic work, and collecting contemporary art.

Oops! Is that tomorrow's Picasso?

hapter 3 introduced you to the hardware components of a computer. However, software is required to direct it to perform the desired task(s). This chapter introduces two types of software: system software and application software. You'll learn what they are and what they can do for you, and you'll take a brief look at the tools used to create software: programming languages and language translators.

OBJECTIVE 4.1
Understand the two basic types of software.

WHAT TYPES OF SOFTWARE MAKE A COMPUTER USEFUL?

Computer hardware cannot perform alone. To accomplish any task, it must be given a series of instructions, called **software,** or **computer programs,** telling it what to do. Software is an intellectual creation that is independent of the medium (e.g., disk or tape) that it is stored on. There are two basic types: system software and application software.

Types of software

- System software
  - Controls hardware
- Application software
  - Performs specific tasks

    System software refers to programs designed to perform tasks associated with directly controlling and utilizing computer hardware and to determine how application programs will run. System software does not accomplish specific tasks for a user, such as creating documents or analyzing data.

    Application software refers to programs that allow the user to accomplish specific tasks, such as creating a letter, organizing data, or drawing graphs. Together, system and application software direct the hardware to perform the tasks you wish to accomplish with a computer.

    Software acts as a connection, or interface, between you and the hardware. **Interface** describes how two parts are joined so that they can work together. System software and application software provide an interface to the hardware. Figure 4-1 shows the functional relationship among system software, application software, hardware, and a user. Next we'll look at two types of system software: operating systems and utility programs.

OBJECTIVE 4.2
Define operating system, describe its major functions, and discuss several ways it is typically used in day-to-day computer operations.

WHAT IS AN OPERATING SYSTEM?

An **operating system (OS)** is a core set of programs that gives the computer the instructions it needs to operate, telling it how to interact with hardware, other software, and the user. Hardware resources include peripheral devices (monitors, printers, etc.), memory, and the central processing unit. The OS establishes a standard interface between the user and the computer system.

    Before an OS can be used, however, it must be loaded into the computer's memory. This happens during the booting process. To **boot** a computer means to load the OS, which prepares the computer for operation.

    The portion of the OS that is in use resides in main memory, so the computer receives and executes the details of an operation at computer speeds. An OS dramatically increases the efficiency of a CPU, because it takes the burden of detailed programming off a programmer or computer user. Today, all computers use an operating system.

FIGURE 4-1
The relationships among system
software, application software,
hardware, and a user.

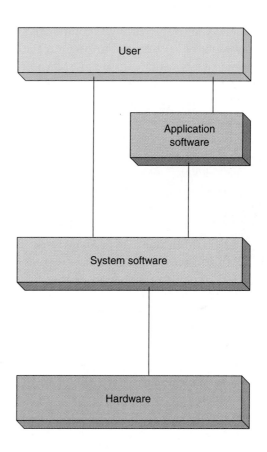

Major Functions of Operating Systems

The major functions of an OS are to provide resource management, data management, job (task) management, and a standard means of communication between the
user and the computer. The resource management function allocates CPU time, main
memory, secondary storage, and input and output devices for use.

The data management functions govern the input and output of data and their location, storage, and retrieval. For example, it supervises the transfer of characters between
the CPU and the keyboard, monitor, printer, and other input or output devices. It also
stores, organizes, and retrieves information on disk. The job management function prepares, schedules, controls, and monitors jobs submitted for execution to ensure the
most efficient processing. A job is a collection of one or more related programs and
their data. The OS also establishes a standard means of communication between the
user and the computer system providing a user interface and a standard set of commands that control the hardware.

Typical Day-to-Day Uses of an Operating System

Operating systems manage resources and route information inside the computer. The
most common use is for executing application programs. This is typically done by typing in the application program's filename at a prompt, selecting the filename from a
menu, or selecting an icon representing the application program from the computer
screen. The OS continues to work behind the scene while the application software is
running. It responds to requests for computer resources and carries them out. For example, to store data, you select a "SAVE" option. The OS directs and stores the data on the
disk, but the action is not seen by the user. When software works without additional user
direction, it is said to be transparent. Much of what the OS does is transparent to the user.

You will also use the OS to format floppy diskettes. Formatting prepares a disk to store files and data by organizing it so your computer can locate and read data from it. All diskettes must be formatted before the computer can use them.

Another common use of the OS is for creating directories to organize files. A directory is a catalog of filenames and other subdirectories stored on a disk. Its purpose is to organize and group files and directories so that you can locate them easily. You could easily become overwhelmed by a long list of files if directories were not used to organize them. It is a good plan to keep all the files that belong to a particular project together in the same directory.

You will use the OS to display a list of the files stored on a particular disk. In addition, it is useful to verify that there is enough room available on a disk to save a file.

A very important function of an OS is protecting and backing up your files by copying them to other disks for safekeeping. This procedure ensures that you won't lose valuable programs or data because of damage to a disk or accidental erasure.

You will also use the OS for computer housekeeping operations, for example, erasing files that are no longer needed, moving files from one directory to another for better organization, and renaming files to make their content more evident.

OBJECTIVE 4.3
Describe several capabilities of operating systems.

HOW DO OPERATING SYSTEMS DIFFER?

Capabilities vary from one OS to another. For example, large computer OSs must service and address the needs of numerous (possibly hundreds) of users, application programs, and hardware devices. They also typically provide a host of security and administrative tasks, such as keeping track of and reporting on computer usage to management. Most microcomputer operating systems accommodate only a single user and only a handful of peripheral devices. Therefore, they tend to be smaller and less sophisticated than large computer operating systems.

OS capabilities can be described in terms of the number of users, the number of simultaneous tasks they perform, and the type of processing they allow. A particular OS may incorporate one or more of the capabilities discussed in the paragraphs that follow.

Operating system capabilities

- Number of users
  - Single user
  - Multiuser
    - Time sharing
- Number of tasks
  - Single tasking
  - Multitasking
- Type of processing
  - Multiprocessing
  - Interprocessing
  - Real-time processing

Number of Users

A **single-user operating system** allows only one user at a time to access the computer. Most microcomputer operating systems, such as DOS, are single-user access systems. A **multiuser operating system** allows two or more users to access a computer at the same time. This OS was developed because many computers have greater computing capacity than can be exhausted by one user. The actual number of users depends on the hardware and the OS design. Although this capability is usually associated with larger computers, it is sometimes found in microcomputers.

To facilitate a multiuser system, time sharing is sometimes employed. A **time-sharing operating system** allows many users to access a single computer. This capability is typically found on large computers where many users need access at the same time. The attention of the CPU is shifted among the users on a timed basis controlled by the OS. As long as the computer does not have more users than the OS can handle, it appears that each user has uninterrupted access to the CPU. TSO is a time-sharing operating system used on many mainframes.

Number of Tasks

A **single tasking** operating system allows only one program to execute at a time, and that program must finish executing completely before the next program begins. Many microcomputer operating systems work like this. The goal of this OS is maximum ease of use and minimum professional support. A **multitasking** operating system allows a single CPU to execute what appears to be more than one program at a time.

Type of Processing

There are numerous processing methods used by computers. Three that you may have heard of include (1) multiprocessing, (2) interprocessing, and (3) real-time processing.

A **multiprocessing** OS allows the simultaneous execution of programs by a computer that has two or more CPUs. Each CPU is either dedicated to one program or dedicated to specific functions and then used by all programs. Many computers, such as mainframes and supercomputers, have more than one CPU and use multi-processing operating systems.

Interprocessing, also called dynamic linking, is a type of processing that allows any change made in one application to be automatically reflected in any related, linked application. Let's say you wanted to incorporate a spreadsheet graph into a word processing document. Without interprocessing capabilities, if you made a change in the spreadsheet data that affected the graph, you would have to generate the new graph, delete the old graph from the word processing document, and then insert the new graph. In Microsoft Windows this capability is called object linking and embedding (OLE).

In some situations, getting a response in time to correct or modify an event is critical to ensure safe and efficient operations. For example, it would be important to be notified of faulty or defective parts in a space shuttle engine, or of a nuclear reactor that has exceeded a specific temperature, in time to correct the situation. An OS with **real-time processing** capabilities allows a computer to control or monitor the task performance of other machines and people by responding to input data in a specified amount of time. Most real-time operating systems are written for a specific application such as monitoring the vital signs of an intensive-care patient in a hospital.

Other processing methods include virtual machine processing, where a number of different operating systems are used concurrently, and virtual memory, also called virtual storage, where secondary storage devices are used as an extension of main memory.

OBJECTIVE 4.4
Contrast three types of user interfaces.

HOW WILL I INTERACT WITH AN OPERATING SYSTEM?

User interface types

- Command line
- Menu driven
- Graphical

Each OS has a **user interface,** the portion of a program that users interact with—entering commands to direct the operating system and viewing the results. User interfaces take three forms: (1) command line, (2) menu driven, or (3) graphics based (see Figure 4-2). A **command-line interface** requires a user to type the desired response at a prompt using a special command language. This interface is usually considered more difficult to learn and use because commands must be looked up or memorized. However, once you learn the commands this can be a fast and efficient entry method. A **menu-driven interface** allows the user to select commands from a list (menu) using the keyboard or a pointing device such as a mouse. A **graphical user interface (GUI)** typically includes some or all of the following parts:

- icons, which are graphical images that represent items, such as files and directories

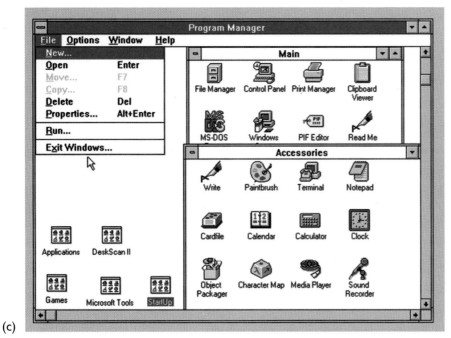

```
C:\WP60\BOOK1>dir

Volume in drive C is MS-DOS_5
Volume Serial Number is 1ADD-AA42
Directory of C:\WP60\BOOK1

         <DIR>       08-28-93   11:38p
    ..   <DIR>       08-28-93   11:38p
SSP    1    103600   07-25-93    9:54p
SSP    2     68491   06-22-93   11:00p
SSP    3    120981   08-13-93    5:26p
SSP    4    105739   08-13-93    5:28p
SSP    6    117460   08-28-93    3:06p
SSP    7     94761   08-28-93    3:17p
SSP    5     58891   07-29-93   10:52a
       9 file(s)      669923 bytes
                    50098176 bytes free

C:\WP60\BOOK1>
```

(a)

MS-DOS Shell

File   Options   View   Tree   Help

| Open |
| **Run**... |
| Print |
| Associate... |
| **Search**... |
| View File Contents   F9 |

| Move...   F7 |
| Copy...   F8 |
| **Delete**...   Del |
| Re**n**ame... |
| Change Attributes... |

| Cr**e**ate Directory... |

| Select All |
| Deselect All |

| E**x**it   Alt+F4 |

C:\WP60\BOOK1*.*

	SSP	.1	103,600	07-25-93
	SSP	.2	68,491	06-22-93
	SSP	.3	120,981	08-13-93
	SSP	.4	105,739	08-13-93
	SSP	.5	58,891	07-29-93
	SSP	.6	117,460	08-28-93
	SSP	.7	94,761	08-28-93

Disk Utilities

F10=Actions   Shift+F9=Command Prompt   11:59p

(b)

Program Manager

File   Options   Window   Help

| New... |
| **Open**   Enter |
| Move...   F7 |
| Copy...   F8 |
| **Delete**   Del |
| **Properties**...   Alt+Enter |
| **Run**... |
| E**x**it Windows... |

Main

File Manager   Control Panel   Print Manager   Clipboard Viewer

MS-DOS   Windows   PIF Editor   Read Me

Accessories

Write   Paintbrush   Terminal   Notepad

Cardfile   Calendar   Calculator   Clock

Object Packager   Character Map   Media Player   Sound Recorder

Applications   DeskScan II

Games   Microsoft Tools   StartUp

(c)

- a graphical pointer, that is controlled by a pointing device, typically a mouse, to select icons and commands and move onscreen items
- on-screen pull-down menus that appear or disappear controlled by the pointing device
- windows that enclose applications or objects on the screen
- other graphic devices that let you tell the computer what to do and how to do it, for example, option boxes, check boxes, dialog boxes and buttons.

OBJECTIVE 4.5
Understand the purpose of a disk operating system and an operating environment and identify four major microcomputer operating systems and their associated environments.

WHAT TYPES OF OPERATING SYSTEMS AND ENVIRONMENTS ARE USED ON MICROCOMPUTERS?

A variety of operating systems are available for microcomputers. Many of the basic functions performed are similar, but there are some differences. These include the fact that each is designed to run on a specific processor or set of processors; each has a unique user interface; each has its own set of capabilities defining the number of users, the number of tasks, and the type of processing allowed; and each supports a specific set of application software.

An **operating environment** is software that enhances the functions of an operating system and improves its user interface. Common added functions include support for larger amounts of main memory, multitasking, and an enhanced user interface that is either menu driven or graphics based. Operating environments need an OS as a foundation, because they can't function on their own. They logically sit on top of the OS (see Figure 4-3).

Some common operating systems for microcomputers include DOS, Windows95, OS/2, the Apple Macintosh operating system, and various versions of Unix. We'll look at these and their associated operating environments next.

DOS

Currently, DOS (Disk Operating System) is the most common OS in use on IBM and compatible microcomputers. While not officially declared a standard, it has become what is known as a de facto standard; that is, DOS is recognized as the most popular and widely used OS. Microsoft Corp. makes MS-DOS and IBM makes PC-DOS; both are usually termed just DOS.

DOS was designed as a single-user, single-tasking OS—the computer accommodates only one user and one application program at a time. DOS uses a text-based, command-line user interface. In other words, to direct the OS to perform a function, the user types a command at the prompt to enter it. To use a menu-driven interface, you run the DOS shell command, which supports a mouse.

Adding an operating environment to DOS improves the user interface and ease of use and increases its functionality. Microsoft Windows is the most popular operating environment used with DOS. It adds a GUI to DOS that allows access to programs and commands using icons, menus, and a mouse. Another popular operating environment for DOS is GEOS from GeoWorks, Inc.

Windows95

Microsoft's Windows95 is a 32-bit operating system for IBM and compatible computers. It does not require DOS and offers a more intuitive and easy-to-use GUI than

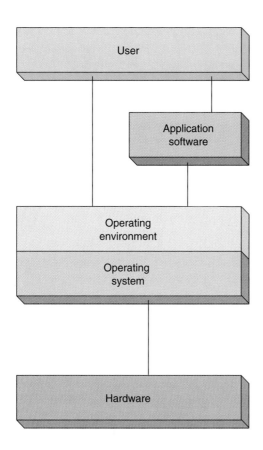

FIGURE 4-3
The operating environment is an interface between the user and the operating system.

previous versions of Windows. It is a single-user, multitasking OS. In addition to running new 32-bit software applications, it also runs existing DOS and Windows programs.

OS/2

OS/2 (Operating System 2) is an OS created by IBM and made available in 1988. OS/2 is a single-user, multitasking OS that runs applications made for other operating systems including DOS. However, software designed specifically for OS/2 cannot be run on DOS-based computers. OS/2 comes bundled with a GUI operating environment called Presentation Manager.

Macintosh Operating System

The Apple Macintosh OS, called the System, made its debut in 1984. It runs on the Motorola 68000 series of microprocessors. The System has little in common with DOS or OS/2. However, the newest version of Windows incorporates many Macintosh-like features. Early versions of the System were single-user and single-tasking; however, current versions include support for multitasking. The operating environment of the System called, the Finder, provides a GUI. MultiFinder is a version that allows multitasking. The System and Finder always come bundled together when purchasing a Macintosh. The intuitiveness and the ease of use that it brought to the OS helped make the Macintosh a popular microcomputer.

Unix

Unix is a multiuser, multitasking OS that uses a command-line user interface. It is often used on high-end microcomputers called workstations by professionals such as engineers and architects. Some users find Unix difficult to work with because of its structure, including the large volume of commands. Several operating environments are available to give Unix a GUI and make it easier to use. Popular operating environments for Unix are OSF/Motif and SUN/OpenLook.

OBJECTIVE 4.6
Describe the purpose of a utility program.

WHAT ARE UTILITY PROGRAMS?

Another type of system software that you are likely to use is called a utility program. **Utility programs** perform a wide range of functions in support of the OS. Some utility programs are bundled with the OS when you purchase it and are invoked through it; they appear to be part of the OS. Others are purchased as separate products. Utility programs perform functions such as copying data from one storage device to another, converting data from one format to another, restoring damaged or accidentally erased data, and diagnosing (detecting, locating, and describing) problems with hardware and software, to name a few.

OBJECTIVE 4.7
Define application software and describe the two broad categories into which they are grouped.

WHAT IS APPLICATION SOFTWARE?

If you head for the computer to write a letter or assemble data for a report, the OS alone is no help. Application software refers to programs that help a user perform a specific task faster, more efficiently, and thus more productively than could be accomplished manually. Application software tells system software how to direct the hardware to perform desired functions.

Application software is written for a specific OS. So when you buy application software, make sure the version is compatible. Some application software is available in several versions for different operating systems; others have specific hardware requirements, such as a particular microprocessor or a minimum amount of main memory.

Application software can be grouped into two broad categories: (1) generalized and (2) specialized. **Generalized application software** is software that can be applied to a wide variety of tasks. The generalized application software programs that are most used on microcomputers by businesses and at home include word processors, electronic spreadsheets, database management system, graphics, and communications. For example, using a generalized spreadsheet program, you can create one spreadsheet to calculate your household budget and another to calculate your taxes. Chapters 5 through 9 focus on generalized application software.

Specialized application software performs a specific task and cannot be changed or programmed for a different task. For example, a payroll application program is designed exclusively for payroll functions. It cannot do other tasks, such as word processing. Popular specialized application software includes business-oriented programs, vertical market programs, engineering and scientific programs, educational programs, and entertainment programs.

Business-oriented applications include accounting software (e.g., payroll, accounts receivable, accounts payable, general ledger, budgeting, and financial planning, which are used in almost every kind of business), banking software, financial software, and investment software. Vertical market software handles the unique needs of specific markets (businesses), such as medicine and health services, legal services, the automotive industry, and property management. Engineering and scientific applications (see Figure 4-4) include programs such as computer-aided design (CAD), which automates mechanical drawings; chemical engineering; scientific calculation; and structural analysis. Educational applications include computer-assisted instruction (CAI) that guides a student through a course of study, library services, student services, typing tutors, and grade book programs to assist instructors in the process of recording student scores. Entertainment applications include games, flight simulators, and music programs.

FIGURE 4-4
The U.S. Coast Guard Ice Patrol maintains records of potentially dangerous icebergs adrift in the North Atlantic by obtaining information using specialized application software that gathers and analyzes data from the computerized side-looking airborne radar. Here, a technician monitors a computer display, watching for and tracking the coordinates of icebergs such as the one pictured. ·
(Wolfgang Kaehler. Inset: Courtesy of International Ice Patrol U.S. Coast Guard.)

OBJECTIVE 4.8
Define integrated software.

WHAT IS INTEGRATED APPLICATION SOFTWARE?

Integrated software is a category of application software that combines a number of applications, such as word processing, database management, spreadsheet, graphics, and communications, into a single package. The applications are generally integrated in two major ways. First, data are easily transferred from one to another. This helps users coordinate tasks and allows them to easily merge data created by the different applications. Second, a consistent interface is provided so that once a user learns a task, such as printing a file, in one application, they perform the task in the same way for all the applications.

Cost is another reason to use integrated software. It is generally less expensive to buy one integrated software package than to buy each application separately. However, integrated software generally doesn't offer the full range of features that stand-alone applications do. Integrated software packages vary in both the applications they contain and the functionality of those applications.

Common integrated software packages include Microsoft Corp.'s Works for Windows; Spinnaker Software Corp.'s PFS:WindowWorks; GeoWorks, Inc.'s GeoWorks Pro; and Lotus Development Corp.'s LotusWorks.

OBJECTIVE 4.9
Identify concerns of those getting started on a new application software package.

HOW DO I GET STARTED WITH A NEW APPLICATION PROGRAM?

Getting started on a new application software package

- Determine system requirements before buying
- Read documentation on installing and getting started
- Make backup copies of master disks
- Run installation program
- Load application program
- Use manuals, on-line help, and tutorials to learn program

It is important to know the system requirements before you purchase application software. These are the capabilities your computer must have to run the software, including the amount of memory, type of microprocessor, and the operating system in use. These facts are usually found on the outside of the software package, so check them before you buy. You'll also want to buy the latest version of a program. Software manufacturers upgrade their products, removing bugs (errors) and adding new features. Numbers are generally used to distinguish between versions. Usually if you have an older version you can update to the latest version by paying a small fee to the software manufacturer.

When you finally bring an application program home, there are a number of things to do before you start using it. First, look over the documentation and carefully *read* all materials that apply to getting started. The manuals provide you with all the instructions for using and installing the program. You can avoid mistakes by reading them first to become familiar with the entire process.

Another important task is learning how to make backup copies of the program disks. Having a backup copy protects your investment. If anything goes wrong and the disks are damaged or erased during installation or use, the original set is intact.

When you buy a new program it has to be installed on your computer. To **install** a program means to prepare it to work with your computer. Application programs contain an installation program, typically called INSTALL.EXE. The **installation program** is responsible for getting the application up and running. It guides you through the installation process by presenting a screen menu of setup options. The options may include choosing the type of monitor, printer, or other peripheral device with which you work. For example, an installation program typically asks you to identify your printer and then installs the appropriate device driver.

Nearly everyone has seen computer arcade games—they're fast and entertaining and provide a challenge. But what about "real" games—like checkers or chess. How good is a computer when matched against the best humans?

Many stores sell computer chess and checkers games that give the novice or average player a competitive battle. They are not much of a challenge to the top players. But the days of human dominance are slowly coming to an end. Along with increased memory capability and the speed of today's computers, programmers are creating new software that are turning the tide.

The 1994 Harvard Cup Humans Versus Computer Intel Chess Challenge was won for the first time by a computer program called WChess. It won against four grandmasters and drew against two other opponents.

In checkers, humans are still hanging on. Marion Tinsley became world champion in the mid-1950s and held the title until retiring from competition in 1992 as grand master emeritus. In 1992 he played against a program called Chinook and won. He is scheduled to play an improved Chinook that has the ability to store over 250 million moves. That accounts for every move possible with eight or fewer pieces on the board. It analyzes 12 million plays a minute—a formidable challenge. The Boston Computer Museum will host the man versus machine game with the winner to be recognized by the International Checkers Hall of Fame and British Draught Federation as world checker champion. Let the games begin!

If you install the program on a hard disk drive, the installation program also copies the application program files from the floppy diskettes onto your hard drive. Generally, the files on the master diskettes are stored in compressed form and require the installation program to convert them and store them on your hard disk.

Once the program is installed, it can be loaded. To **load** a program means to bring it into main memory. Both system and application software play a role in loading a program. For example, let's say you are using an OS with a command-line interface. If the command to load a word processor is WP, you type in that command at the prompt and press the Enter key. But, before anything happens, the command sequence WP(ENTER) must be interpreted by the computer. This function is the responsibility of the OS which identifies symbols typed from the keyboard as commands and performs the indicated task. In this example, it loads the word processing application program. The command is interpreted and the operating system looks on the disk for the file WP.EXE to bring it into main memory and the application program takes over loading the rest of the files associated with the word processor. The manuals that come with the application software as well as any available on-line help and tutorials will teach you to use and get the most out of the program. You are now ready to be productive.

OBJECTIVE 4.10
Define the terms computer programming, computer program, programmer, programming language, and language translator program and describe the five categories of programming languages.

WHAT IS COMPUTER PROGRAMMING?

The details of creating software are beyond the scope of this text, but we'll briefly examine a few general concepts. As stated earlier, a computer program, or software, is a set of instructions intended to be executed by a computer to perform a useful task. **Computer programming** involves designing, writing, modifying, and testing instructions given to the computer so it can complete a task. A **programmer** is an individual who translates the tasks that you want a computer to accomplish into a computer language that the computer understands. A **programming language** is a set of written symbols that tells the computer hardware how to perform specified operations. Of the hundreds of different programming languages available, all fit into one of five general categories: (1) machine, (2) assembly, (3) high-level, (4) fourth-generation, and (5) fifth-generation languages.

Categories of programming languages

- Machine
- Assembly
- High level
- Fourth generation
- Fifth generation

Machine Language

Machine language is a binary code made up of 1's and 0's, the only language that a computer understands. Machine language is a **low-level language** that requires programmers to have detailed knowledge of how computers work, since every detail of an operation must be specified. Because it uses only 1's and 0's, it is easy to make an error but very difficult to find and debug (correct) it. Easier-to-use programming languages have been developed, but they must ultimately be translated into machine language by a language translator program before a computer can use them. A **language translator program** is a system program that converts programming language code into machine language.

Assembly Language

The next higher level is assembly language, also classified as a low-level language. **Assembly language** uses mnemonics in place of 1's and 0's to represent the instructions (see Figure 4-5) A **mnemonic** is an alphabetical abbreviation used as a memory aid. For example, instead of using a combination of 1's and 0's to represent an addition operation, a programmer might use the mnemonic *AD*. The language translator program used to translate assembly language code into machine language is called an **assembler.**

High-Level Language

A **high-level language** contains instructions that closely resemble human language and mathematical notation and does not require that a programmer have detailed knowledge about the internal operations of a computer. High-level languages are much easier to learn and use than either machine or assembly languages. Typically, less time and effort are required for high-level programming because errors are easier to avoid and correct. Popular high-level languages include FORTRAN, COBOL, BASIC, Pascal, and C (see Table 4-1). Figure 4-6 shows an example of a C language program, a commonly used high-level language for developing software.

A high-level language must also be translated into a machine language before it can be used by a computer. Two different language translator programs are used: (1) compilers and (2) interpreters. A **compiler** translates a whole program written in a human-readable high-level or assembly programming language into machine language all at one time before the program is executed. An **interpreter** translates a program into machine language one line at a time, executing each line after it is translated.

Types of language translator programs

- Assemblers
- Compilers
- Interpreters

FIGURE 4-5
This is a comparison of assembly codes (mnemonics) and machine language instructions
for a program that computes and prints out the result of 2 × 4.

Assembler code (mnemonics)	Machine-language instructions

```
sseg                    segment stack          0100
                        db 256  dup (?)         110010   100000   1111000   100000   110100   100000
                                                111101   100000   100000
sseg          ends                              11110
dseg                    segment                 10111000
data                    db "2 x 4 =  "          1010000
                                                11101000
dseg          ends                              11111100
cseg                    segment                 10111000
assume        cs:cseg,ds:dseg,ss:sseg,es:nothing  10001110   11011000
start         proc far                          10111000
                        push ds                 10001110   11000000
                        mov ax,0                10111010
                        push ax                 10111011
                        call main               10001101   110110
start         endp                              10111111
                                                10110000   00000010
main                    proc near               10110011   00000100
                        cld                     11110110   11100011
                        mov ax, dseg            00001100   110000
                        mov ds, ax              10100000
                        mov ax, 0b000h          10111001
                        mov es, ax              10100100
                        mov dx, 0               1000111
                        mov bx, 0               10110000   10000111
                        lea si, data            10001000   00000101
                        mov di, 32848           11100010   1111000
                        mov al, 02h
                        mov bl, 04h
                        mul bl
                        or al, 30h
                        mov al,  data+9
msgsb:        mov cx,9
lbl:
                        movsb
                        inc di
                        mov al, 135
                        mov [di], al
                        loop 1b1
main                    endp
cseg                    ends
                        endstart
```

Table 4-1

- FORTRAN(FORmula TRANslator) was introduced in 1957 and is the oldest
  high-level programming language. It was designed primarily for use by scientists,
  engineers, and mathematicians for solving mathematical problems. FORTRAN is
  well suited to complex numerical calculations.
- COBOL (COmmon Business-Oriented Language) is a widely used programming
  language for business data processing. It was specifically designed to manipulate
  the large data files typically encountered in business.
- BASIC (Beginner's All-Purpose Symbolic Instruction Code) was developed at
  Dartmouth College in the mid-1960s to provide students with an easy-to-learn,
  interactive language on a time-sharing computer system. Because novices could
  learn and begin programming in a few hours, BASIC has become the most popular
  language for microcomputers. It is available for many microcomputers in use today.
- In the late 1960s, Niklaus Wirth of Zurich developed Pascal, naming it after
  Blaise Pascal, the French mathematician and philosopher who invented the first
  practical mechanical adding machine. Pascal is suited to both scientific and file
  processing applications. It was originally designed to teach the concepts of structured programming and top-down design to students.
- The C programming language, developed at Bell Laboratories in the early 1970s,
  incorporates many advantages of both low-level and high-level languages. Like
  assembly language, C gives programmers extensive control over computer hardware, but because C uses English-like statements, which are easy to read, it is
  often classified as a high-level language. C also incorporates sophisticated control
  and data structures, which make it a powerful, but concise, language.

FIGURE 4-6

An example of a program
writen in the high-level language
C that computes the sum and
average of ten numbers.

```
#include <stdio.h>

main ()
    {
        int i, num;
        float sum;

        printf("Enter numbers \n");
        sum = 0;
        for (i = 0; i < 10; i++)
          {
              scanf("%d",&num);
              sum = sum + num;
          }
        printf("Sum = %3.1f\n",sum);
        printf("Average = %3.1f\n",sum / 10.0);
    }
```

Fourth-Generation Language

The different categories of languages are sometimes labeled by generations—from lowest to highest. Machine languages are considered the first generation; assembly languages, the second generation; and high-level languages, the third generation. A **fourth-generation language** is one of a variety of programming languages that requires much less effort creating programs than high-level languages. The objectives include increasing the speed of developing programs, minimizing end-user effort to obtain information from a computer, decreasing the skill level required of users (they concentrate on an application rather than the coding and solve their problems without a professional programmer), and minimizing maintenance by reducing errors and making programs easy to change. The sophistication of fourth-generation languages varies widely. These languages are usually used in conjunction with a database and include database query languages, report generators, and application generators.

Fifth-Generation Language

Many individuals consider natural languages to be **fifth-generation languages. Natural languages** do not require the user or programmer to learn and use a specific vocabulary, grammar, or syntax. A natural language closely resembles normal human speech. For example, if a user enters the command "Get me sales figures for January 1995," a computer that understands natural language interprets this and supplies the desired information.

Because of the complexity of interpreting a command entered in human speech format, natural languages require very powerful hardware and sophisticated software. Although advances have produced computers with enough power, a deficit exists in the development of programming languages and techniques.

SUMMARY

The instructions that direct the operations of a computer are called software. There are two basic types of software: system software and application software.

The most important type of system software is the operating system. It is software that controls and supervises a computer's hardware and provides services to other system software, application software, programmers, and users of a computer.

The major tasks of an operating system are resource management, data management, job management, and providing a standard means of communication between a user and the computer.

Operating system capabilities can be described in terms of the number of users they accommodate at one time, how many tasks they run at one time, and how they process those tasks.

An operating system can be designed as a single-user OS that allows only one user at a time or as a multiuser OS that allows two or more users to access a computer at one time.

Operating systems can be designed for single tasking, allowing only one program to execute at a time, or for multitasking, allowing a single CPU to execute two or more programs.

There are numerous processing methods used by computers including multiprocessing, interprocessing, and real-time processing.

The user interface of an operating system is the portion of the program with which users interact. It can be command line, menu driven, or graphics based.

Popular microcomputer operating systems include MS-DOS, Windows95, OS/2, the Apple Macintosh operating system, and Unix. An operating environment is software that improves its user interface and enhances the functions of an operating system. Popular operating environments include Microsoft's Windows for DOS, the Presentation Manager for OS/2, Finder and MultiFinder for Apple Macintosh, and OSF/Motif and SUN/OpenLook for Unix.

Utility programs are a type of system software that perform a wide range of functions in support of the operating system.

Application software programs direct a computer to complete a task for the user. There are two broad categories of application software: generalized and specialized. Generalized application software can be applied to a wide variety of tasks and includes programs such as electronic spreadsheets, data managers, word processors, graphics, and communications. Specialized application software performs a specific task and cannot be changed to perform a different task. Such software includes business-oriented, vertical market, engineering, and scientific programs; educational programs, and entertainment programs.

Integrated software allows several programs to share the same user interface and data.

When getting started on a new application software package, determine the system requirements before buying, carefully read the documentation on installing and getting started, make backup copies of the master disks, and run the installation program. After installation, load the application program and use the manuals, on-line help, and tutorials that are available to learn to effectively use the program.

Computer programming involves designing, writing, modifying, and testing instructions given to the computer so it can complete a task. A programmer is an individual who translates the tasks that you want a computer to accomplish into a programming language that the computer understands. A programming language is a set of written symbols that tells the computer hardware how to perform specified operations. Programming languages fit into one of five general categories: (1) machine, (2) assembly, (3) high-level, (4) fourth-generation, and (5) fifth-generation languages. A language translator program is a system program that converts programming language code into machine language. These include an assembler for assembly language and compilers and interpreters for high-level languages.

Can you define the following?

application software (p. 109)
assembler (p. 120)
assembly language (p. 120)
boot (p. 109)
command-line interface (p. 112)
compiler (p. 120)
computer program (p. 109)
computer programming (p. 119)
fifth-generation language (p. 122)
fourth-generation language (p. 122)
graphical user interface (GUI) (p. 112)
generalized application software (p. 116)
high-level language (p. 120)
install (p. 118)
installation program (p.118)
integrated software (p. 118)
interface (p. 109)
interpreter (p. 120)
interprocessing (p. 112)
language translator program (p. 120)

load (p. 119)
low-level language (p. 119)
machine language (p. 120)
menu-driven interface (p. 112)
mnemonic (p. 120)
multiprocessing (p. 112)
multitasking (p. 112)
multiuser operating system (p. 111)
natural languages (p. 122)
operating environment (p. 114)
operating system (OS) (p. 109)
programmer (p. 119)
programming language (p. 119)
real-time processing (p. 112)
single tasking (p. 112)
single-user operating system (p. 111)
software (p. 109)
specialized application software (p. 116)
system software (p. 109)
time-sharing operating system (p. 111)
user interface (p. 112)
utility programs (p. 116)

REVIEW QUESTIONS

Multiple Choice

1. Programs designed to perform tasks associated with directly controlling and utilizing computer hardware rather than accomplishing a specific application for a user are called _____.
   a. communications software
   b. specialized application software
   c. system software
   d. application software

2. A(n) _____ controls and supervises the hardware of a computer.
   a. operating system
   b. specialized application
   c. database management system
   d. interface

3. Which of the following is not a major function of an operating system?
   a. resource management
   b. providing a means of communication between user and computer
   c. solving specific user tasks
   d. data management

4. An operating system with _____ capabilities allows a single CPU to execute what appears to be more than one program at a time.
   a. multitasking
   b. time sharing
   c. multiprocessing
   d. real time

5. An operating system with _____ capabilities allows a computer to control or monitor the tasks of other machines and people by responding to input data in a specified amount of time.
   a. real time
   b. multitasking
   c. multiprogramming
   d. interprocessing

6. A(n) _____ is software that enhances the functions of and changes the user interface of an operating system.

    a. disk operating system

    b. user interface

    c. operating environment

    d. application program

7. A _____ employs icons, pointers, pull-down menus, windows, and devices such as option boxes, check boxes, dialog boxes and buttons.

    a. user interface

    b. graphical user interface

    c. menu-driven interface

    d. command-line interface

8. _____ is the software that tells the computer how to solve a problem or perform a particular task; it helps the user work faster, more efficiently and more productively.

    a. Application software

    b. An integrated program

    c. A device driver

    d. An interface

9. A(n) _____ is a set of written symbols that tells the computer hardware how to perform specified operations.

    a. assembler

    b. interpreter

    c. compiler

    d. programming language

10. _____ is the only programming language that a computer understands.

    a. Fourth-generation language

    b. Machine language

    c. Assembly language

    d. High-level language

Fill In

1. To _____ a computer means to load the OS which prepares the computer for operation.

2. _____ is a capability of an operating system that allows a single CPU to appear to execute more than one program at a time.

3. The operating system capability that allows simultaneous execution of programs by a computer that has two or more CPUs is called _____ .

4. A(n) _____ is software that enhances the functions of an operating system and improves its user interface.

5. Software that can be applied to a wide variety of tasks is called _____.

6. _____ is a category of software that combines a number of applications in one package and allows them to share data and use a common interface.

7. The _____ program is responsible for configuring a new application program to work with your hardware and copying its files to your hard disk.

8. _____ involves designing, writing, modifying, and testing instructions given to a computer so it can complete a task.

9. A _____ is an individual who translates the tasks that you want the computer to accomplish into language that the computer understands.

10. A language translator program that translates an assembly language program into machine language is a(n) _____ .

Short Answer

1. What is an operating system?

2. Discuss three ways that operating systems differ.

3. Describe several ways in which you might use an operating system in day-to-day computer use.

4. Identify and describe three types of user interfaces.

5. Why would you want to add an operating environment to an operating system?

6. List and briefly describe four operating systems commonly used with microcomputers.

7. Identify the two broad categories of application software and give examples of each.

8. Describe several tasks involved in getting started on a new application software program.

9. What are the advantage(s)/disadvantage(s) of using integrated software?

10. What is computer programming?

Issues for Thought

1. Think about your chosen profession. How might computers and software enhance your productivity? Describe several ways in which you see software changing or affecting your profession.

2. What effect do you think the design of a user interface has on a user? Is the graphical user interface best for both beginners and professionals?

INFOMODULE II

LAYING A SOLID FOUNDATION FOR BUSINESS WITH INFORMATION SYSTEMS

Every day, people buy goods and services. Who buys what? Why? How much does it cost to make? How much should we sell it for? How much inventory is left? The answers to these and many other questions provide enormous amounts of data for businesses.

Thanks to computer hardware and software, we are able to collect and store vast amounts of data. To turn raw data into useful information and to manage it, successful businesses develop information systems. In this Infomodule you'll learn the basic types of information systems and how they are used in business and industry.

WHAT IS AN INFORMATION SYSTEM?

Chapter 1 described an **information system** as a set of people, data, procedures, hardware, and software that works together to manage information. They are used to gather data; process data into reliable, accurate, and usable information; and distribute the information in a timely fashion for use in decision making, problem solving, and control. Creating, processing, and distributing information are the predominant tasks of most business workers today. An individual who performs such tasks is called a **knowledge worker**.

Information systems are the foundation of most businesses. The ways in which they are used affect the growth, productivity, and profitability of an organization. Because the success or failure of an information system can make or break a business, it must be carefully designed and developed. The next section examines one method used for developing information systems.

HOW ARE INFORMATION SYSTEMS DEVELOPED?

The **system development life cycle (SDLC)** is the structured sequence of operations required to conceive, develop, and implement a new information system. The term *cycle* indicates that a newly designed information system does not last forever; ultimately, it needs replacement, and the development cycle starts over again. The cycle may begin in response to a problem in a current information system that is not performing well or in response to a new opportunity for which no information system currently exists.

Developing an information system throughout the SDLC involves continual and clear communication among the users and system personnel—the professionals responsible for designing and implementing the information system.

A **user** is a person who will utilize an information system once it has been installed. Users include the operators who run computers and individuals who require information from the system. System personnel include system analysts, system designers, and programmers. A **system analyst** determines the information processing needs of the users. A **system designer** is a specialist who designs a system to fulfill the users' information needs. A **programmer** codes the instructions in a programming language so a computer can solve the problem. In large organizations, these positions are usually separate and distinct; however, in some cases, particularly small companies, one person may do all or several of the tasks. The SDLC can be broken into four major phases: (1) analysis, (2) design, (3) implementation, and (4) maintenance (see Figure IM2-1).

System Analysis

System analysis includes identifying a system problem or new opportunity, analyzing the current system in light of the problem or new opportunity, and justifying the development of a new system or modifying an old system to solve the problem or meet the opportunity.

The system analysis phase is crucial in developing an information system that satisfies the information needs of users. Users work with system personnel to identify the true nature of a problem or opportunity. Then they help develop a system to provide the information to solve that problem or maximize that opportunity. If a problem or new opportunity is not correctly analyzed, the resulting information system may be useless or even detrimental to an organization.

System Design

The **system design** phase includes the logical system design stage and the physical system design stage. **Logical system design** shows the flow of data through an information system, in effect, the information system blueprint. Much like an architect's blueprint, it is a series of charts, graphs, and data layouts. They describe the input documents that the information system will process, the way the documents will look, and the computer records needed to store data generated by the input documents. They also describe the output documents and reports required by users of the information system including how the output will look (format), who receives the output (distribution), and how often the output will be produced (frequency). The logical system identifies the sequence and method by which documents are input and used to update computer records and then to produce user-desired documents and reports.

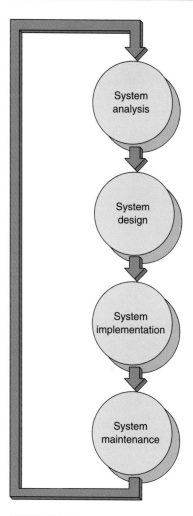

FIGURE IM2-1
System development life cycle.

These tasks must be carefully planned because the remaining stages in the SDLC are dependent on the logical design stage. Even the smallest error can be magnified throughout the cycle so that it becomes a major problem when the new system is implemented. In addition, design errors identified early in this stage can be corrected much more quickly and cheaply than those found later.

The purpose of the **physical system design** stage is to convert the system blueprint into the specific hardware and computer programs transforming the logical design into a working information system. This stage includes hardware acquisition. The programs are created during this stage. A typical business information system contains hundreds of thousands of lines of program code. Each line represents a separate operation for the computer to perform. Often many programmers are needed, and their efforts must be coordinated.

System Implementation

The **system implementation** phase of the SDLC includes testing, installation, and training steps. Then, the system is released to its users. Managers must ensure that the system has been thoroughly tested and is as free from errors as possible. Frequently, managers must also budget the type and amount of training that the users need.

In **testing,** a new information system is checked to ensure that its parts are correct. Development of an information system incurs a huge expenditure of money and is often critical to the success of an organization, so a system should not be delivered to the users without thorough testing.

After the successful testing of an information system, installation is performed. During **installation**, a system is made operational. It may require considerable capital to support both people and equipment.

Training involves one of the most important tasks in the implementation of a new information system. The primary purpose of training is to make users and others familiar with the system so that they can work with it effectively.

System Maintenance

System maintenance is the last phase in the SDLC of an information system. After a system has been tested and installed and the users trained, it enters the maintenance phase. Information systems are maintained by a special group of programmers known as **maintenance programmers**. Maintenance may span several years, during which time minor modifications are made to meet the changing requirements of users. The maintenance costs of an information system are normally considerably higher than the development costs. Eventually, the system reaches a point where routine maintenance is no longer sufficient and the SDLC begins again.

WHAT TYPES OF INFORMATION DO MANAGERS NEED?

Managers make decisions, and each one needs specific types of information to make good decisions. A **manager** is responsible for using available resources—people, materials/equipment, land, information, money—to achieve the goals of an organization.

Management is divided into three basic levels: (1) strategic (top-level) managers, (2) tactical (middle-level) managers, and (3) operational (low-level) managers (see Figure IM2-2).

Strategic (top-level) managers make decisions involving the long-range, or strategic, goals of an organization (see Figure IM2-3). A strategic manager, such as the chief executive officer of Chrysler, might be required to decide whether a new plant should be opened or a new sports car produced.

Tactical (middle-level) managers are concerned with short-term, tactical decisions directed toward accomplishing the organizational goals established by the top-level managers. A tactical manager for Chrysler might decide how long to advertise a new car on television in a particular state.

Operational (low-level) managers are directly involved with the day-to-day operations of business (see Figure IM2-4). They are responsible for seeing that the tactical decisions of middle-level managers are implemented. An operational manager at Chrysler might decide to use a newer, less expensive method for cleaning paint-nozzle jets.

WHAT ARE THE BASIC TYPES OF INFORMATION SYSTEMS?

Several types of information systems exist to accommodate the differences in information needs of individuals in an organization. These include transaction processing systems, management information systems (MISs), decision support systems (DSSs), and executive support systems (ESSs). Each is described in the paragraphs that follow.

Transaction Processing Systems

A **transaction** is a business activity or event. Transactions include buying a product such as a shirt at a department store or a service such as cable television from a local provider. The information system that helps manage these transactions is a **transaction processing system (TPS)**.

FIGURE IM2-2
Levels of management, types of decision making, and information needs.

Strategic manager

1. Long-range, strategic decisions
2. Summarized past and present information
3. Future projections
4. Use of internal and external information sources

Tactical managers

1. Short-term, tactical decisions
2. Fairly detailed past and present information
3. Primarily internal and some external information sources

Operational managers

1. Immediate, operational decisions
2. Detailed, current information focused on specific topic
3. Internal information sources only

FIGURE IM2-3
This manager evaluates internal and external information before making decisions.

FIGURE IM2-4
This manager checks purchase order requests.

Transaction processing systems provide information on current transactions and perform routine record-keeping functions. They also provide information for operational management personnel managing the day-to-day activities of an organization. A TPS performs several functions, including collecting data, validating input, processing data, updating computer records, and generating output.

Some transaction processing systems commonly seen in business organizations include accounts payable, order entry, accounts receivable, inventory control, payroll, and general ledger. These systems are grouped into one broad category—accounting information systems.

Management Information Systems

A **management information system (MIS)** provides information to managers for use in problem solving, control, and decision making. An MIS provides information both in hard-copy reports and in on-line retrieval. They are used for highly structured, recurring situations where information requirements are known in advance.

Often, a TPS feeds information to an MIS. For example, an MIS can use the sales information gathered by an order-entry TPS over several years to evaluate the performance of the sales staff. The TPS provides the actual sales data, but the MIS furnishes the summarized reports on the sales staff. With the report(s), a manager attempts to detect and solve any performance or personnel problems regarding the sales staff.

An MIS is used in all areas, including planning, marketing, finance, manufacturing, human resources, and project management, primarily by tactical management. An MIS makes internal and external operations more efficient.

Decision Support Systems

A **decision support system (DSS)** is an interactive, information system that helps users solve management problems. An **interactive system** allows a user to communicate one-on-one with a computer. A DSS contains a set of related programs and data to help with analysis and decision making in an organization. At a minimum, it includes a database related to the types of decisions being made and modeling software (e.g., a spreadsheet) to test alternative solutions. More powerful modeling software such as Integrated Financial Planning System (IFPS) and graphics software are often included.

Although different levels of management benefit from decision support systems, they are used predominantly by tactical management to create models that assist in analysis and decision making. A DSS can present several tentative solutions for one problem. The user does not have to rely on anyone else for computer support. Information is available almost immediately. A DSS does not make decisions for users, but it does support managers by providing information. The user first evaluates information supplied by a DSS, then using judgment, intuition, and experience he or she reaches a decision.

There are numerous DSS applications in business organizations. Some of the most important and widely used applications are in financial planning, manufacturing, new product development, plant expansions, and employee performance evaluation (see Figure IM2-5). For example, in financial planning, a bank would use a DSS for budgeting and analyzing the impact of changes in money market rates, financial regulations, and interest rates.

Executive Support Systems

Executive is usually synonymous with strategic, or top-level, management. An executive has the responsibility of setting long-range planning goals and a strategic course for an organization. An information system that caters specifically to the information needs of executives, such as managerial planning, monitoring, and analysis is called an **executive support system (ESS)**.

An ESS incorporates a large volume of data and information gathered from the external environment of an organization. External information is used in conjunction with information generated by a TPS in the functional areas (e.g., marketing, accounting, and production) of the organization to accommodate the executive's specialized information needs. An ESS plays a vital role in summarizing and controlling the volume of information an executive must read. The executive assigns values to each source of information to place emphasis on sources deemed most important. Thus, ESSs can be tailored to meet the specific needs of each executive in an organization.

HOW ARE INFORMATION SYSTEMS USED IN BUSINESS?

This section looks briefly at ways that information systems are used in several areas of business. These are typical descriptions but by no means the only ways that information systems are organized and named. Figure IM2-6 shows an organizational chart of the functional areas to be examined—accounting, finance, marketing, production/operations, and human resources. Each area may be supported by its own information system, although there can also be sharing of information among them.

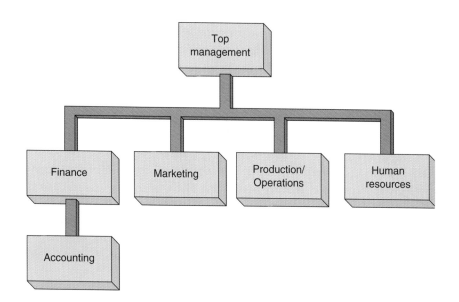

FIGURE IM2-6
Several functional areas of business.

Accounting Information System

An **accounting information system** uses transaction processing systems to record data that affect the financial status of the organization. Referred to as operational accounting systems, they maintain a historical record of the transactions. They also produce reports such as balance sheets and income statements that give a financial picture of the organization.

Accounting was one of the first business areas to incorporate computer-based information systems. It readily lends itself to computerization for several reasons. Accounting transactions generate large amounts of data that need to be processed regularly and stored, accurately and quickly. Processing is relatively simple and easy to implement on the computer. Management can establish appropriate controls and error-checking procedures to ensure the security and accuracy of the data. In addition, accounting systems are designed to maintain an audit trail so data stored in the system can be traced back to the original transaction. Accounting information systems are made up of a number of subsystems. The more common ones include accounts receivable, accounts payable, payroll, and general ledger systems.

Financial Information System

A **financial information system** provides data on the acquisition of funds and the allocation and control of those financial resources. While an accounting information system focuses on recording data generated by daily operations, financial information systems focus on planning and control. In doing so, they rely heavily on a DSS, which in turn draws data from the transaction processing systems of the accounting information system.

Financial calculations are complex, with many variables and numerous possible interactions. The calculations are often repeated many times with minor changes to answer "what-if" questions. Financial information systems are less concerned with absolute accuracy than accounting information systems are because many of the financial variables are future oriented and difficult to predict precisely.

Financial information systems are made up of numerous subsystems. Among the common ones are requirements analysis, planning, cash management, credit management, and capital expenditure systems.

Marketing Information Systems

A **marketing information system** involves gathering details about day-to-day sales transactions, managing and controlling marketing operations, and planning sales and strategies for the future. A marketing information system deals with existing products and markets and plans for future products and markets. It relies equally on transaction processing systems, management information systems, and decision support systems.

A marketing information system can be broken into two subsystems: a sales system and a marketing system. The sales system records data about transactions, for example, customer names, item numbers, quantities ordered, and billing and shipping addresses. This information is recorded using a transaction processing system.

The marketing system focuses on planning and control and relies on both the MIS and DSS. The MIS uses data generated by the sales system to provide information on how well products and sales staff are performing. Management may use this information to adjust activities to meet organizational goals. A DSS helps plan for the future by forecasting sales, planning pricing, and designing promotional strategies. A marketing system is broken down further into numerous subsystems. Some of them are order-entry, customer profile, product management, sales management, sales forecasting, advertising, and market research systems.

Production/Operations Information System

The **production/operations information system** gathers and processes data about all the activities involved in producing goods and services. Those data, when turned into information, are used to plan, monitor, and control the production/operations process. Such a system helps an organization work more efficiently. Production scheduling is planned better and the work load is balanced with the available production capacity. Production/operations information systems enable continuous monitoring, feedback, and control of production/operations. This results in stricter quality control and leads to better products and greater productivity. Production/operations information systems can reduce inventory costs by enabling better control of raw materials and finished goods with fewer occurrences of depleted inventories.

The production/operations information system is also composed of a number of subsystems. Several of the more common are the master production schedule, materials requirement planning, capacity planning, engineering, production control, plant maintenance, process and numerical control, and physical distribution systems.

Human Resources Information System

The **human resources information system** in most organizations involves recruitment, placement, evaluation, compensation, and development of employees. Its goal is the effective and efficient use of an organization's human resources by management. The information should allow management to meet the personnel needs of a business and create effective personnel policies and programs.

HOW ARE INFORMATION SYSTEMS AFFECTING INDUSTRIES?

Applications for computers and information systems proliferate in industries as people recognize their advantages. The following paragraphs discuss some of the ways they are used in industries, such as manufacturing, banking, investment, retail, and health care.

Manufacturing

A manufacturing firm transforms raw materials into finished goods. It relies on engineering activities, such as planning and designing new products. It depends heavily on information from both the MIS and DSS. A manufacturer is also concerned with procurement of raw materials, which may be finished goods from another manufacturer. This area of manufacturing relies on a TPS to monitor inventories and generate purchase orders as needed. The MIS and DSS are instrumental in inventory planning and control and scheduling efficient use of facilities to maximize productivity. Finally, a manufacturing firm fabricates finished goods, which requires making or acquiring components and assembling them into finished products. A TPS gathers data about the fabrication process, while an MIS supplies management with information to control the fabrication process.

Most manufacturing companies realize that to be competitive they must computerize their factories—either partially or fully. The use of computers to control machines in the manufacturing process is called **computer-aided manufacturing (CAM)**. To be fully automated and integrated, a company must link the different parts of the manufacturing process with all other aspects of the company. Automation and integration of operational activities and managerial functions throughout the entire manufacturing enterprise is called **computer-integrated manufacturing (CIM)** (see Figure IM2-7).

Technicians and assemblers at
the Convair Division of General
Dynamics Corporation in San
Diego are using a"paperless"factory system that replaces up to
90 percent of manufacturing
paperwork in the final assembly
area of the Tomahawk cruise
missile. Accessing the system
through bar codes, assemblers
receive instructions at their
workstation computers. The
system maintains configuration
control and is being adapted to
other factory areas to maintain
high quality and reduce the cost
of manufacturing. Convair produces the Tomahawk cruise missile for the U.S. Navy and the
U.S. Air Force.

(Courtesy of General Dynamics Corp.)

Banking

Banking is the most computer-intensive industry in the United States because accuracy
is demanded, and a great volume of repetitive transactions occur daily. Transaction processing systems are particularly important. In addition, computers and information systems help banks plan and control their accounting and reporting operations and enable
them to provide new and improved services.

The most widely used computer application in banking is demand-deposit, or check
account banking. This TPS generates monthly customer statements and supplies information to management on account activities.

Computers and information systems also make on-line banking possible, where customer accounts are immediately updated after a transaction. Each teller station has a terminal and operates online when accessing accounts to cash checks or make deposits (see
Figure IM2-8). Most banks and branch offices also have automated teller machines (ATMs),
where cash is dispensed to customers any time of the day or night (see Figure IM2-9).

FIGURE IM2-8
A bank teller's computer terminal and printer are linked to the
bank's mainframe computer to
process customer transactions.

FIGURE IM2-9
Automated teller machines are linked to a bank's mainframes and offer individuals easy and convenient access to their bank accounts.
(Courtesy of Diebold, Inc.)

Computer-based information systems are important advantages in lending. Consumer, commercial, and mortgage loans are all analyzed by computers. Sometimes an information system is used to evaluate the creditworthiness of a customer. The information system generates customer statements and management reports, such as loan analysis, interest, and tax reports. Many banks also include credit card services and trust management, which are handled by computers.

In addition, computers and information systems provide electronic funds transfer (EFT), a computerized method of transferring funds from one account to another. Huge amounts of money are moved, worldwide, in this way every day.

Investments

The investment industry uses information systems to record transactions, process billing information, and prepare monthly statements. Computers in the stock market keep track of stocks being traded on the floor of the New York Stock Exchange (see Figure IM2-10). On an average, over 140 million shares are traded daily, far beyond the capacity of the old ticker-tape machines. Although some transactions are still completed by specialists, the turn-around time for a market order processed by a computer is approximately 75 seconds.

Investors in the stock market need current facts about the financial condition of their investments. Computers permit the quick and easy retrieval of financial statistics through on-line information services. Services, like The Dow-Jones News Retrieval give traders the instant financial data they need for making decisions on stock trading. Others include Standard & Poor's Compustat and Wharton's Econometric.

Computer analysis of the variables that affect the financial position of a firm result in improved forecasts on market prices of securities. Many brokers use computers to help analyze their decisions to buy, sell, or hold securities for the portfolios of their clients. Interestingly, the computer was blamed for aiding the stock market disaster of October 1987. Critics claim that the automatic trading ability of the computer fueled the fire of the panic in the market.

Retail Sales

The area of retail sales includes many repetitive transactions that lend themselves to computer technology. Although each sale is different, the basic recording process remains the same. Consequently, retail stores use a TPS to record transactions. In addition to basic applications such as accounting and customer billing, computers are useful in merchandising and forecasting and analyzing sales. Retail purchases made with credit

FIGURE IM2-10

The New York Stock Exchange relies on computers to process and manage the large volume of data generated each day. Computers are also important in individual offices, where stockbrokers keep clients informed of late-breaking developments.

(Courtesy of International Business Machines Corp.)

cards also involve computers. The computer notifies the sales clerk when consumers attempt to charge above their approved credit limits.

An important computer application is the point-of-sale (POS) system . A POS system typically consists of cash register–like terminals that are on line to a computer in the store or to a unit that stores and transmits data over communication lines to a computer at a regional center. A POS terminal with a laser scanner reads sales data from items containing a product code (see Figure IM2-11). A POS system allows management to analyze the effects of sales and advertising quickly and accurately.

Health Care

The health care industry uses computer-based information systems for traditional data processing operations such as billing patients, controlling inventory, calculating health care statistics, and maintaining patient histories. They also use systems for more challenging tasks, such as scheduling lab and operating room times, automating nurses' stations, and monitoring intensive-care patients.

FIGURE IM2-11
Optical scanning systems read sales data from a product code and speed the checkout process.

(Courtesy of International Business Machines Corp.)

In addition, the technology enables doctors and other health care technicians to (1) test for and diagnose diseases and illnesses faster and more accurately, (2) design prostheses and reconstruction models, (3) build and use devices to monitor vital signs and other bodily functions, (4) design and test pharmaceuticals, and (5) offer choices in lifestyle and job selection to people who are physically challenged.

Some computerized methods that aid physicians in diagnosing diseases and illnesses include digital subtraction angiography, sonography, and computed tomography. In sonography, beams of high-frequency sound waves penetrate a patient's body, and the computer translates the rebounding echoes into an image that the doctor reads. In digital subtraction angiography (DSA), pictures are first made by a digital X-ray scanner; a contrasting agent is introduced into the body, and a second image is made. The computer subtracts the first image from the second and leaves an image that shows what has changed. Computed tomography (CT) scanners view different sections (or slices) of the body from many angles by moving X-ray tubes around the body. The scanner converts the X-ray pictures into a digital code to create high-resolution images.

Programmers and engineers work closely with physicians to design prostheses and create models for reconstructive surgery. By using diagnostic scanning procedures, technicians can digitize an accurate picture of damaged bone and visually compare it with a prosthesis design for fit and function. Then the actual prosthesis is built, usually with the help of computer-aided manufacturing machinery to ensure that precise measurements are met.

Computer-controlled devices are another important area of medical technology for patients who need constant monitoring, such as those in intensive-care units, post operative recovery rooms, and premature-baby nurseries.

Pharmaceuticals are influenced by computerization. Development of a new drug is time consuming and costly, involving years of research and experimentation and costing millions of dollars. Thousands of compounds have to be made and tested before a new drug can be released for production and human use. Computer graphics techniques save drug researchers time by simulating, in 3-D, the shapes of molecules. Because the shape of a molecule usually determines its behavior, biochemists can accurately predict how various molecules should be combined. In addition, some computers are programmed to simulate various attributes of test animals so that toxicity can be checked or the safety of certain procedures can be verified by computer simulation without endangering human or animal life.

For physically challenged people, devices that stimulate muscles to move (with patterned electrical stimulation) continue to be improved. The computer stores a signal of brain-wave muscle patterns, reads the signal, and gives an electrical stimulation to the appropriate muscle group to cause movement. Tendon injuries are being treated in this way, and improvement has been shown in patients paralyzed by strokes, accidents, or cerebral palsy. Some patients, with damaged spinal nerves causing paralyzed limbs, walk and ride bicycles using attached electrodes and adapted equipment.

Computers and information systems have had, and continue to have, a tremendous and far-reaching effect on nearly all aspects of the business community.

VOCABULARY SELF-TEST

Can you define the following?

accounting information system (p. 132)

computer-aided manufacturing (CAM) (p. 133)

computer-integrated manufacturing (CIM) (p. 133)

decision support system (DSS) (p. 130)

executive support system (ESS) (p. 130)

financial information system (p. 132)

human resources information system (p. 133)

information system (p. 126)

installation (p. 128)

interactive system (p. 130)

knowledge worker (p. 126)

logical system design (p. 127)

maintenance programmers (p. 128)

management information system (MIS) (p. 130)

manager (p. 128)

marketing information system (p. 132)

operational (low-level) managers (p. 128)

physical system design (p. 127)

production/operations information system (p. 133)

programmer (p. 127)

strategic (top-level) managers (p. 128)

system analysis (p. 127)

system analyst (p. 127)

system design (p. 127)

system designer (p. 127)

system development life cycle (SDLC) (p. 126)

system implementation (p. 127)

system maintenance (p. 128)

tactical (middle-level) managers (p. 128)

testing (p. 127)

training (p. 128)

transaction (p. 128)

transaction processing system (TPS) (p. 128)

user (p. 126)

REVIEW QUESTIONS

Multiple Choice

1. The structured sequence of operations required to conceive, develop, and make operational a new information system is called _____.
    a. project management
    b. a system development life cycle
    c. a system analysis
    d. a system blueprint

2. A(n) _____ records and manages transactions.
    a. management information system
    b. transaction processing system
    c. executive support system
    d. decision support system

3. A(n) _____ provides information for situations that recur and are highly structured where the requirements are known in advance.
    a. decision support system
    b. executive support system
    c. transaction processing system
    d. management information system

4. Which of the following information systems caters to the needs of strategic management?
    a. executive support system
    b. transaction processing system
    c. decision support system
    d. management information system

5. An information system that automates and integrates the entire manufacturing enterprise results in _____.
    a. manufacturing automation protocol (MAP)
    b. computer-aided manufacturing (CAM)
    c. computer-aided design (CAD)
    d. computer-integrated manufacturing (CIM)

Fill In

1. A(n) _____ is a set of people, data, procedures, hardware, and software that work together to achieve the common goal of information management.

2. An individual who creates, processes, and distributes information is called a(n) _____.

3. _____ involves making minor changes in an information system in response to changing user requirements.

4. _____ managers are directly involved with the day-to-day operations of business.

5. A(n) _____ provides information to managers for use in problem solving, control, and decision making for highly structured, recurring situations where information requirements are known in advance.

Short Answer

1. Define system development life cycle (SDLC) and list and describe its four major phases.

2. Identify the different levels of management and the types of information each needs.

3. List and define the four basic information systems described in the Infomodule.

4. Recount several ways that information systems are used in the accounting, financial, marketing, production/operations, and human resources areas of a business.

5. Describe several ways in which the manufacturing, banking, investment, retail sales, and health care industries use information systems.

CHAPTER 5

DOCUMENT PREPARATION: WORD PROCESSING AND DESKTOP PUBLISHING

OBJECTIVES

5.1 Define word processing.
5.2 Describe the benefits of using a word processor.
5.3 Summarize the basic functions of a word processor.
5.4 Describe several features that add significant power to a word processor.
5.5 Understand what is meant by the term desktop publishing.
5.6 Describe the benefits of desktop publishing.
5.7 Contrast desktop publishing and word processing.
5.8 Understand the limitations of desktop publishing.
5.9 Identify fundamentals of document design.

PROFILE

Alan C. Ashton and Bruce W. Bastian

"We're perfect!" Well, that's what it might sound like when people at the Orem, Utah–based offices of WordPerfect answer the phone. Today sales are in the hundreds of millions of dollars, and the word processing software for IBM PCs and compatibles is offered in approximately 20 languages found in more than 80 different countries of the world. WordPerfect is one of the more popular word processing programs.

The WordPerfect story began in the late 1970s when Allen C. Ashton, a computer science professor at Brigham Young University (BYU), developed a program so a computer could produce organ music. During this time, the Wang computer was popular; it was a computer specifically dedicated to word processing tasks. After reviewing the manual that described the functions of the word processor, Ashton felt confident that with his musical editing expertise, he could create a more efficient program. So, he did. However, Ashton did not promote his ideas at that time; the specifications lay dormant.

A BYU music student, Bruce Bastian, was trying to computerize marching band formations as part of his graduate project. As the venture became more involved, it was clear that a computer science advisor would be helpful. Enter Ashton, who ultimately encouraged Bastian to forsake music and pursue a computer science degree. They planned to go into business after Bastian's graduation, calling themselves Satellite Software International (SSI). One of the first problems the budding entrepreneurs faced was a scarcity of funds. Thus began a series of exciting coincidences.

During the late 1970s, the Orem city council was looking into the purchase of a computer, specifically the Data General minicomputer. However, they also wanted the ability to accomplish word processing using that equipment. Unfortunately, the software was not available. It was time to resurrect the word processing specifications. Now Bastian's background and creativity in music played an instrumental (pardon the pun) part. He wrote the clear and concise programming code for the program that would be called the SSI word processing program (SSIWP). By March 1980 the software was being sold to other Data General minicomputer users.

The developers wanted to make their program available for other computer users, but there was no standard machine to adapt to. Until 1981, that is, when the IBM PC appeared on the scene. By November 1982 an IBM version of SSIWP was released. Because there was some name confusion with MultiMate (a competitive PC word processor now part of Ashton-Tate Corp.), which also used the acronym SSI for Software Systems, Inc., the new name WordPerfect was coined. It's been part of our vocabulary since early 1986.

Most of you won't be required to know much technical information about computers. However, many will be expected to understand and use application software to accomplish a specific task or solve a problem. Because microcomputers are a productivity tool for both business and personal use, and because people are more likely to use microcomputers than large computer systems, our discussions focus on application software for microcomputers.

This chapter describes two types of application software used to prepare documents: word processors and desktop publishing software.

OBJECTIVE 5.1
Define word processing.

WHAT IS A WORD PROCESSOR?

At some time, almost everyone needs to write something—a personal letter, business letter, memo, term paper, or perhaps a manuscript for the great American novel.

A **word processor** is application software that creates and manipulates text-based documents. It can be thought of as an electronic equivalent of the typewriter. Anything written with a typewriter, or pen and paper, can be done with a word processor. However, as you will discover, the capabilities of a word processor go far beyond those of the typewriter. In fact, you have probably already been introduced to computers through their word processing functions. Popular word processors include WordPerfect, AmiPro, and Microsoft Word. **Word processing** is the term that describes the act of entering, editing, and printing text with a word processor. Most popular word processing software is available in DOS, Windows, and Macintosh versions.

One of the first software packages available for personal computers was the word processor. Today, word processors are probably the most popular generalized application software for microcomputers. Anyone who regularly works with words can benefit from using a word processor (see Figure 5-1). So pervasive is the technology that virtually every current document you read originated on a word processor.

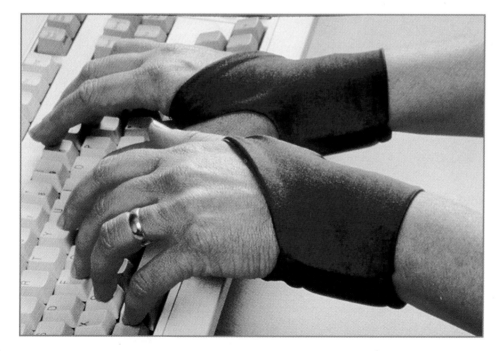

FIGURE 5-1
Even though word processors have simplified data entry they have introduced various hand and wrist injuries. Wrist protectors such as these from MouseMitt help protect against the stress associated with repetitive hand movements.
(Courtesy of MouseMitt International)

FIGURE 5-2
Design engineers work with scale models to determine ergonomic office environment that offers optimal working conditions and comfort for the user. These designs have been incorporated into this office setting.

(Main photo courtesy of TRW, Inc.)

With the increased use of word processors and other application programs, people are spending greater amounts of time at the computer. Therefore, it is important to consider issues of comfort and health, ergonomics, in the design of the workplace (see Figure 5-2).

OBJECTIVE 5.2
Describe the benefits of using a word processor.

WHY USE A WORD PROCESSOR?

People who use word processors find two significant advantages over a typewriter: (1) speed and efficiency in creating the documents, and (2) freedom to concentrate on the subject without concern for the mechanics of writing and typing (see Figure 5-3).

With a word processor it is not necessary to retype pages or use correction fluid to cover words or lines. Typographical errors can be corrected and editing changes can be made on the screen before the text is ever printed. Words and paragraphs can

Benefits of using a word processor

- Speed and efficiency
- Concentration on subject matter rather than mechanics

FIGURE 5-3
Here an instructor uses a word processor to type a lesson plan for her class.

(Photograph by Sylvia Dill)

be moved anywhere in the text, and characters can be changed, inserted, or deleted with a few keystrokes. Even spelling can be automatically checked. The final printed document is clean and neat, with no corrections visible.

Word processors offer an enormous advantage over typewriters because they allow you to type as fast as you are able without worrying about typographical errors. Corrections can be made later. This process is ideal for those whose minds work much faster than they can type. It is easy to lose your creative thought if you are worried about typing properly. Once the thought has been captured, it is easy enough to edit and polish the writing later. With a word processor, the writer concentrates on the subject and getting the point across to the reader rather than the physical aspects of writing or typing.

OBJECTIVE 5.3
Summarize the basic functions of a word processor.

WHAT DOES A WORD PROCESSOR DO?

The three basic functions common to word processors are (1) entering, saving, and editing text; (2) formatting; and (3) printing the document.

Entering, Saving, and Editing Text in a Document

The **edit window** is the work area for entering and editing a document. Depending on the particular word processor, you will either be in an edit window or you will use your mouse to click on pull-down menus or toolbars from which you can select the edit window. An empty edit window is analogous to a clean sheet of paper in the typewriter. Text is entered through the keyboard, stored electronically in the computer, and displayed on screen in the edit window. Most documents contain more text than will fit in the edit window. To see text that is not currently in the edit window, use the cursor movement keys to scroll through the document.

The cursor, which marks the point of present activity on the screen, is found in the edit window. This point indicates where the next character will be entered or where the next operation begins. The cursor is controlled by either cursor movement keys or a mouse, depending on your system. Once you memorize the ways in which the cursor can be moved, you speed up the editing process.

> **Basic functions of a word processor**
>
> - Text entry and editing
> - Formatting
> - Printing

FIGURE 5-4

Many word processors have a windowing capability so that a user can see and edit two or more different parts of the same document or two or more different documents at the same time. This photo shows WordPerfect with multiple windows open.

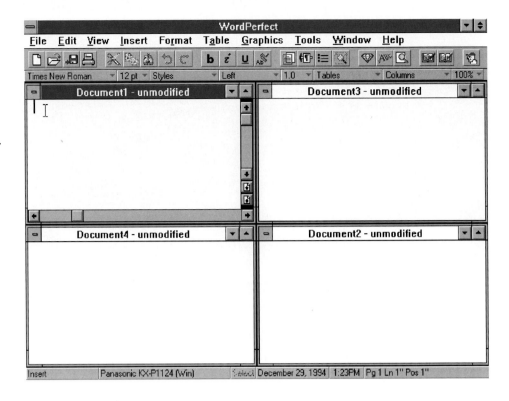

Many word processors allow more than one window at a time to be displayed. This means that a user can view two portions of a document at the same time or see portions of two separate documents (see Figure 5-4). The window in which the cursor currently resides is called the **active window.** A keystroke combination or mouse selection moves the cursor between the windows giving you access to several documents simultaneously.

The **status line** provides information about the current document and the system and is found at the top or bottom of the display screen (depending on which word processor you are using). It may include the disk drive the file being used came from; the name of the document; document number; page, line, and column position on which you are working; the amount of available memory; and current mode of operation (see Figure 5-5). This information is helpful if you are switching back and forth between documents.

ENTERING. Before you begin typing on a typewriter, you insert and align the paper and set margins, tab spacing, and line spacing. Word processors incorporate default settings for parameters like margins, tab settings, line spacing, and page length. **Default settings** are values used by a program unless the user gives other instructions. They allow you to start typing immediately. However, you can choose different parameters.

One headache of typewriter use is remembering to return the carriage at the end of a line of type. If you concentrate on your handwritten notes as you type, you may not be aware that the end of the line is getting closer. With a word processor it is not necessary to keep an eye on the right margin. You just continue typing while the program performs a **wordwrap,** automatically putting the words on the next line and continuing until you press Enter (Return). Then the cursor moves to the next line and begins a new paragraph. If the text is not supposed to go to the end of the line, for example, in a typed column of names, just press the Enter (Return) key after each item in the list is typed. A "hard return" is created when the user strikes the Enter key; however, when the software forces a wordwrap, it is called a "soft return."

FIGURE 5-5
WordPerfect's edit window and status line.

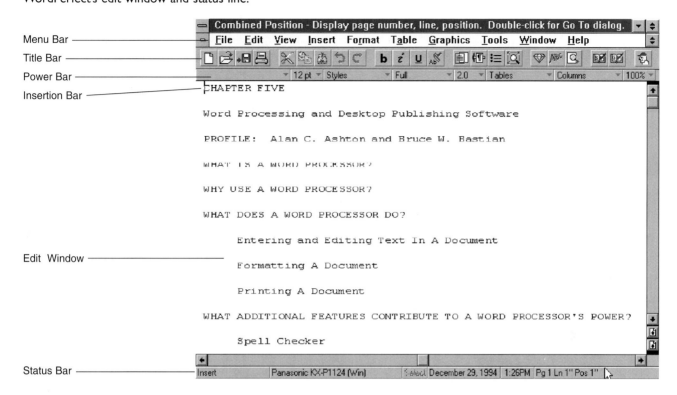

Menu Bar
Title Bar
Power Bar
Insertion Bar

Edit Window

Status Bar

SAVING. As you enter the document you should save it to a disk to avoid accidental erasure by power outage, electrical surge, human error, or other problem. Saving protects your document and allows you to retrieve it from the disk later to edit or reuse it. Use a descriptive name so that it can be easily identified. As a rule, you should save your work often. Whether you do this every 5 minutes or 15 minutes depends on how difficult it would be to recreate any lost work. Some word processors have a timed automatic saving feature. Your work is saved every few minutes, even if you forget to manually do so.

EDITING. Even the best typist makes an occasional mistake, and after reading through a document, you may decide to add or remove some text. Characters, phrases, or blocks of text can be inserted into the existing document. If the program is in the **insert mode,** the existing text automatically shifts to make room for the new text. However, in the **typeover mode,** entries strike over and replace existing text. Most word processors automatically default to the insert mode when loaded.

Characters, phrases, or blocks of text can also be deleted from the document either with the Backspace key or the Delete key. The remaining text shifts left to fill the space of the deleted text.

Your document may present its point more appropriately if you move some of the text or clarify certain portions by deleting text. Editing like this creates a lot of work for a typewriter, but not for a word processor. **Block editing** permits units, or blocks, of text—characters, words, sentences, paragraphs, sections, or even pages— to be moved, copied, deleted, saved, or altered as a unit (e.g., changing print style to boldface, underline, or italic). First, mark the entire text to be changed, and the whole block of text is then manipulated according to further instructions (see Figure 5-6).

FIGURE 5-6
Block of text marked for editing.

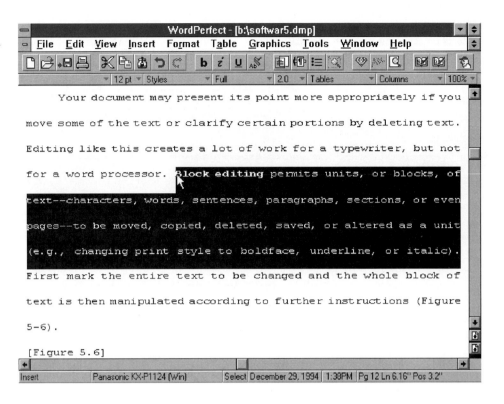

Suppose you have just finished a 20-page report and discover that you misspelled a proper name throughout. It would be tedious and time consuming to search through the entire document to correct the spelling, and there is no guarantee that you would find all the occurrences. Word processors offer a **search and replace** feature that easily finds text and makes corrections throughout an entire document with only a few keystrokes.

In a "simple search," the program looks for a specified string of characters (the misspelled name, in this case), highlights it, and stops. You decide whether to correct it, remove it, or move on. In a "conditional search," the user specifies a replacement string; the program searches for and locates all occurrences of a particular string of characters and inquires at each instance if the existing string should be replaced with the new one. If so, the program replaces the string with the specified change or correction. In a "global" search and replace, the program searches the document so that when each instance of a specified string is found it is automatically replaced.

The following example shows how using the search and replace feature saves time. If your term paper quoted Dr. Emerson Gorfsnorben numerous times, you could type a short version such as "deg." Then later, you search the document for the abbreviated text and the computer replaces it with "Dr. Emerson Gorfsnorben." You type the full name only one time.

Formatting a Document

Format refers to how the elements of a document are arranged on the display screen or how it will appear after it is printed; controlled through the use of various formatting features of a word processor. Some are specified before entering the document (e.g., margins), others during entering and editing (e.g., boldface), and still others after the document is completed but before it is printed (e.g., headers and footers). One attraction of a word processor is that the formatting options can easily be changed.

Not all format characteristics appear on the screen as they will when printed. Some word processors indicate formatting through embedded codes. These codes are communicated from the computer to the printer before printing starts. When they are used most word processors provide a preview feature so you see what the document will look like when it is printed (see Figure 5-7). Adjustments can be made, if they are needed.

Perhaps you have some statistics that you've tried to arrange in a tabulated fashion, but when the page is printed you see they are not aligned under one another. This occurs when a proportional type font is chosen because it allocates space differently, for example, the letter *i* takes up less space than the letter *m*. Using the space bar to align the text is not successful because actual alignment of proportional fonts is not always displayed on the screen. Word processors with a graphical interface have a **WYSIWYG (What You See Is What You Get)** capability, which means that you see how the document will look on the screen before it is printed. Misalignment does not occur with a fixed font because each letter is the same width.

Several formatting features that change the appearance of your document include margin settings, justification, tab settings, line spacing, page breaks, automatic page numbering, centering, headers and footers, and character enhancements (see Figure 5-8).

Often there are specific requirements on how much white space, or margin, is to be left around the text. **Margin settings** are the specifications that allocate space on the left, right, top, and bottom of a printed document. You might choose to have the text justified. **Justification** is the feature that aligns the text flush with the left margin (i.e., left justified), or flush with the right margin (i.e., right justified), or full justified (i.e., spreads the text to fill to the margins) (see Figure 5-9). When you choose full justification, the text on your screen *may* not appear to be justified, but it will print appropriately. Examples of justified print can be seen in magazine articles as well as this text.

Just as a typewriter indents paragraphs (usually five or six spaces from the margin), a word processor also provides **tab settings** to make indentations. Most also have a tab feature that automatically aligns columns around the decimal points.

Traditionally, word processors measured margins, tabs, and other positions on the screen by character positions. Today, many—even those that use a text interface—measure in graphic terms, that is, in inches rather than by character position on the screen. For example, one word processor might set a left margin at 1 inch, and another might set it at 10 or 12 character spaces. Using the measurements in inches allows more precise placement of text and graphics in a document.

You have probably submitted a report typed in double-spaced format. This makes a document easier to read and provides space for written corrections or comments. A word processor gives you choices, for example, half space, single space, double space, or triple space. Spacing can be set for the entire document or be applied to certain text in the document.

A word processor automatically indicates a **soft page break,** that is, the point where the text ends on one page and begins on the next. Unless you indicate otherwise, the program generally expects that you are printing on 8 ½-inch $\times$ 11-inch sheets of paper, so a soft page break might occur at 9 inches, or after 54 text

FIGURE 5-7
(a) Split screen showing embedded codes. (b) Preview screen showing how document will look when printed.

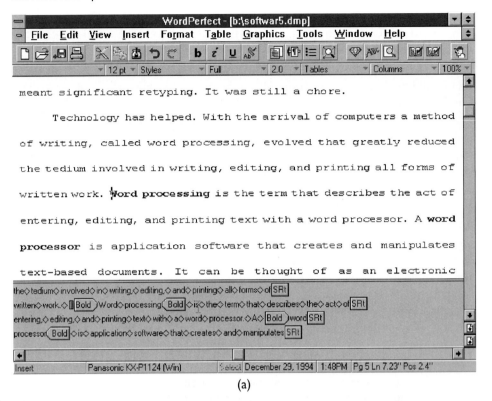

(a)

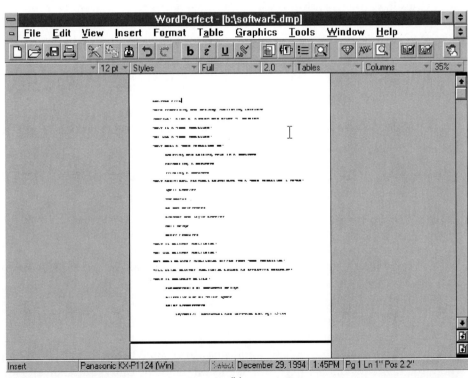

(b)

FIGURE 5-8
Document showing format features.

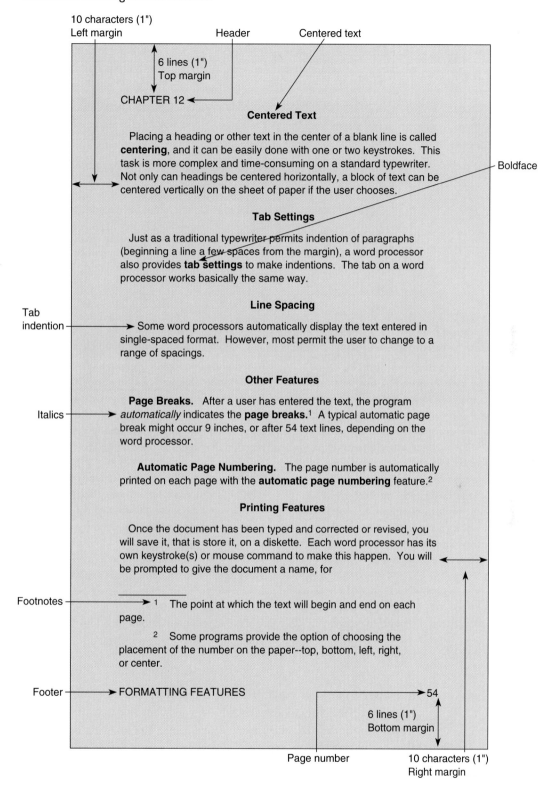

Left Justification. The feature that aligns the text flush with the margin is called justification. It is used to make the right margin evenly aligned, the left margin evenly aligned, or both. The justification of the text may not show on the screen, but will when the document is printed. This style of blocking text can be seen in commercially generated books and magazines.

(a)

Right Justification. The feature that aligns the text flush with the margin is called justification. It is used to make the right margin evenly aligned, the left margin evenly aligned, or both. The justification of the text may not show on the screen, but will when the document is printed. This style of blocking text can be seen in commercially generated books and magazines.

(b)

Full Justification. The feature that aligns the text flush with the margin is called justification. It is used to make the right margin evenly aligned, the left margin evenly aligned, or both. The justification of the text may not show on the screen, but will when the document is printed. This style of blocking text can be seen in commercially generated books and magazines.

(c)

HIGHLIGHT 5-1 Author! Author!

You should know that the book *Just This Once* was written by a computer. No, not by someone sitting at a computer keyboard using word processing software—the computer actually "wrote" the book. First, however, the computer had been programmed to "think" like the late author Jacqueline Susann. In fact, an expert system was created by Scott French who used passages obtained from Susann's previous novels, *Valley of the Dolls* and *The Best of Everything*, to provide the data required for the knowledge base. The best-selling author's use of verb tense, sentence structure, the ratio of dialog to action, even the length of time between passionate love scenes were all analyzed.

Susann's style was matched so well that one reviewer indicated that the book was indistinguishable from her previous works. Watch your local bookstores for more books written by expert systems. Unless, this time "once" happens to be enough.

Or you may want to try your own hand! Did you ever dream about writing the next *Star Wars*? A screen play isn't your style? How about a novel? Even if you haven't the foggiest idea of where to begin, there is software to the rescue.

Using the ability of one of Hollywood's best screenwriter instructors, John Truby, StoryLine takes you through the creative process of writing. A template guides your story and the software keeps it credible with proven building blocks. It helps you keep track of as many as ten characters in a scene at a time. If you stray too far from the plot, StoryLine warns you and offers suggestions through examples from classic films such as *The Godfather*.

Is the great American novel waiting inside you—or your computer?

lines, depending on the defaults of the word processor. You can override the soft page break and specify exactly where you want the text to stop on one page and begin on another by choosing a **hard page break.** This feature forces selected text to be printed on separate pages, for example, title page, table of contents, index, or bibliography.

Automatic page numbering prints the page number on each page. Some programs provide the option of deleting the page number from certain pages or choosing the placement of the number on the paper—top, bottom, left, right, or center.

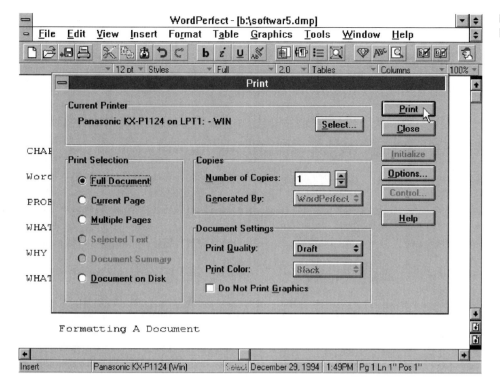

FIGURE 5-10
Example of printing options.

Term papers and other written materials often have a title page where headings are usually centered. Placing a heading or other text in the center of a blank line is called **centering.** You know how tedious and time consuming it can be to center headings using a typewriter. On a word processor, this task is accomplished with one or two keystrokes.

Sometimes specific text is to be included at the top or bottom of each page. For example, a report's title and the author's name could be printed at the top or bottom of every page. A **header** is a line (or lines) of text repeated at the top of each page. A **footer** is text that appears at the bottom of each page. The information in the header or footer is keyed in just one time for the entire document rather than page by page; the program automatically inserts the appropriate text on the specified pages. The header and footer appear on the document when it is printed, but often do not appear on screen.

You may want to place specific emphasis on certain words or phrases in some documents. Most word processors permit **character enhancement** to the text style when it is printed. Typically, they include **boldface** or *italics*, underlining, or a ***combination.***

Printing a Document

The bottom line in using a word processor is to produce a printed document. You will generally be presented with several print options from which to choose (see Figure 5-10). For example, you might tell the program to print only the first page, several specific pages, or all of the pages. You can also specify sections (blocks) or paragraphs to be printed. More than one copy of the same document can be printed. Many word processors permit choosing paper sizes other than the standard 8 ½-inch × 11-inch size, assuming that the printer is capable of handling different sizes.

Popular sizes of paper are 8 ½ × 14 (legal), business envelopes, and various mailing labels. Other options include choosing the printed quality of the type such as draft or near letter quality.

Laser printer developments in the last few years have made near-typeset-quality printing affordable so that many small businesses produce their own newsletters, magazines, and brochures. The results often look as good as those done by a commercial printer. Because the trend is for word processors to include more page layout features, laser printers are becoming more popular. Some laser printers are equipped with a special page description programming language, such as PostScript, that gives you precise control over nearly every detail of a printed page. Modern laser printers offer an almost unlimited variety of type styles, called fonts, in a wide range of sizes. A **font** includes all the letters, numbers, and symbols of one style of type, in one size. A collection of all available sizes of one font is called a **typeface**. Laser printers have several fonts built in. Additional fonts, called soft fonts, can be added to your system by loading them from cartridges or disks. Although in some fonts the characters appear on the computer screen, the printer may not be capable of printing that particular character in that font. In that case, a blank space is printed.

OBJECTIVE 5.4
Describe several features that add significant power to a word processor.

WHAT ADDITIONAL FEATURES CONTRIBUTE TO A WORD PROCESSOR'S POWER?

Developers of word processors make them as versatile as possible for a broad spectrum of users. Some common features that add significant power to a word processor are described in the paragraphs that follow.

Spell Checker

Checking for and correcting spelling errors has always been a tedious aspect of writing. A typist stops in the middle of a sentence to look up the correct spelling in the dictionary. Many word processors have a **spelling checker** to quickly and easily locate misspelled words and typographical errors in a document (see Figure 5-11). Each word in a document is compared to those in the dictionary of the word processor, usually between 20,000 to over 100,000 words. Words that are either misspelled or not in its dictionary are highlighted and options for the correct spelling are presented. The user decides whether to replace the word with one of the recommendations of the spelling checker.

However, *misused* words that are correctly spelled are not detected. For example, in the sentence "I placed the book over their," the spelling checker cannot know that the word "their" is used incorrectly; it merely verifies that the word is *spelled* correctly.

Thesaurus

Sometimes writers get stuck using the same word over and over. Many word processors contain a **thesaurus** that suggests alternative words to offer more variety or precision than those used originally. Usually, the thesaurus is accessed by highlighting the word to be replaced. With the correct command or keystrokes, a list of synonyms (and often antonyms) is presented on the screen. Sometimes, the synonyms have sublists of synonyms (see Figure 5-12).

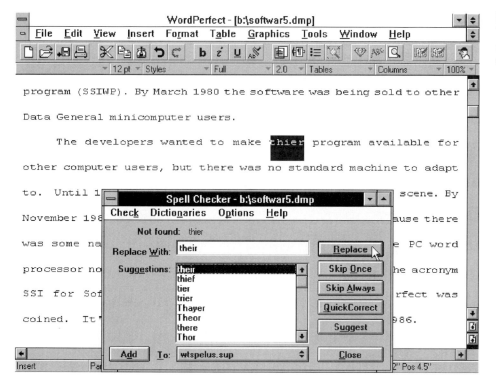

FIGURE 5-11
The spell checker will present options to your misspelled word.

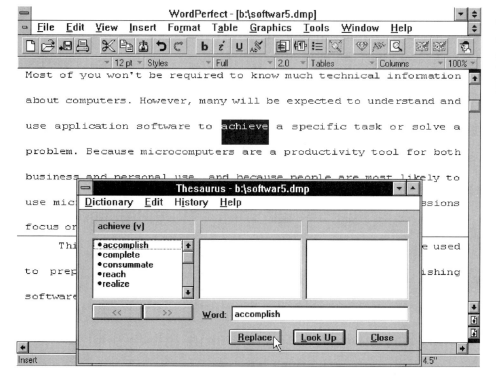

FIGURE 5-12
Thesaurus in use. The word for which you wish to find a more appropriate term is highlighted. The thesaurus presents several possibilities.

FIGURE 5-13
A grammar checker can detect
incorrect sentence structure.

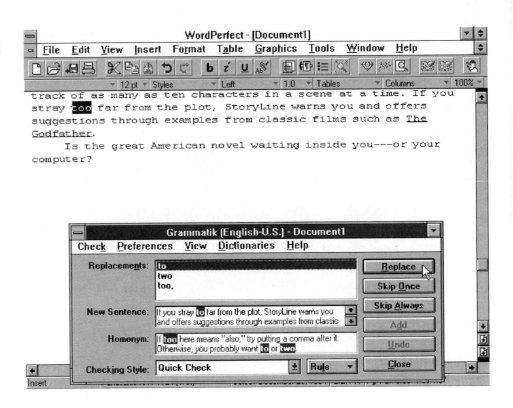

CD-ROM References

CD-ROM disks, while read only, offer the advantage of a large amount of storage.
Thus, many reference materials are available in CD-ROM format, including books of
quotations, almanacs, encyclopedias, atlases, and dictionaries. Access to these materials allows the writer to quickly search and retrieve many different types of information that could be included in a document.

Grammar and Style Checker

It's easy to forget to put a period at the end of a sentence when you're trying to finish your work on time. Some word processors have a **grammar and style checker** that points out potential problems with punctuation, grammar, sentence structure, and writing style. They find mistakes such as using the wrong verb tense (see
Figure 5-13).

Mail Merge

A particularly helpful option for business users is the **mail merge** feature, which
permits a form letter to be addressed and personalized automatically to any number
of addressees. With mail merge, a form letter is created containing specially coded
characters that tell the word processor where to insert variables such as names and
addresses. Once the process is complete, the computer merges the form letter with
the variables to produce multiple "original" letters. With mail merge, each recipient's name appears in the body of the text. And, even though hundreds or thousands of these letters may have been sent, each looks and sounds like a personal letter. Such mass customizing would have been impossible without refinements in
word processing.

Other Features

A math function that performs simple calculations is useful to those who create documents that are mainly text but that include some columns and rows of numbers.

With this feature, calculations can be done automatically while writing a financial report or an accounting statement.

As our language has developed, it has created certain conventions about the ways written information should be presented for maximum effectiveness. Readers expect visible signals that alert them to a change of topic or to a particularly important passage. Thus, document preparation involves more than merely putting together a series of sentences.

Although writers still need to know when to apply these conventions, word processors make them easy to include, either as the document is being written or after the first draft has been completed. Most word processors include features for creating footnotes, endnotes, and subscript/superscript notations. In addition, writers mark segments of text to be used for other purposes—for example, to indicate words and phrases in the text to automatically generate an outline, a table of contents, or an index. These are slow, tedious, and error-prone tasks when performed manually, but with a word processor, these functions are automated and are completed faster and easier.

Page layout features are included in many word processors so that businesses or personal users can type, design, and publish professional-looking newsletters, brochures, flyers, or pamphlets on their own. One feature creates newspaper-style columns. When the first column is full, the type flows to the top of the next column and begins to fill that column. Several options of type faces, styles, and sizes are usually available with a program, assuming that your printer can accommodate them. Many word processors also allow graphic images to be combined with text. Separate page layout software discussed in more detail shortly is available for more complex publishing efforts.

OBJECTIVE 5.5
Understand what is meant by the term desktop publishing.

WHAT IS DESKTOP PUBLISHING?

Desktop publishing (DTP) is a concept that combines the use of microcomputers with word processing, page composition software, and high-quality laser printers. Page composition software, typically called desktop publishing software, permits placement of graphic elements in the document where desired and then "flows" the text around the photo, chart, or illustration. Popular DTP software programs are PageMaker and Ventura Publisher.

Large corporations that want to publish in house, managers of small businesses, and writers who decide to self-publish use this software to produce annual reports, booklets, brochures, manuscripts, and newsletters. Figure 5-14 shows a document produced using DTP.

Graphic elements to be included in the document are produced in one of three ways: (1) generated at a computer, using DTP software or paint and draw programs and a mouse; (2) digitized, using a scanner; or (3) copied from proprietary clip art or photos on a disk or CD-ROM.

Creating graphic elements for desktop publishing
- Computer generation
  - Page composition software
  - Paint and draw programs
- Digitizing (scanners)
- Clip art

DTP software enhances the document by incorporating lines in a variety of widths and lengths. Paint and draw programs, such as MacPaint, PC Paintbrush, Adobe Illustrator, and others, allow you to create original artwork directly on the monitor with a drawing device such as a mouse (see Figure 5-15). These programs have enhanced the eye appeal and readability of documents through company logos or letterheads, cartoons, or other graphic illustrations.

A scanner "reads" a photograph or other graphic representation and converts the image into a pattern of electronic digits. The data are stored in a file and can be imported into the document.

FIGURE 5-14
This publication was designed, created, and printed with a desktop publishing system. Notice the graphics and variety in type styles.

(Photo by Larry Hammil.)

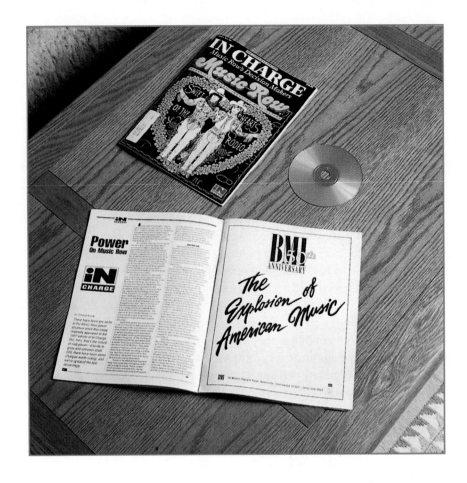

FIGURE 5-15
Specialized text, headings, logos, or art can be created using a paint program such as NeoPaint and incorporated into the desktop publishing document.

(Courtesy of NeoSoft Corp.)

Young children take to computers like "ducks to water." Computers are becoming an integral part of primary and secondary education. Workers in all types of occupations use or are being trained to use computer technology on the job. But what about those who are well into their retirement years? Is it a case of "You can't teach an old dog new tricks"? Certainly not!

Take Californians Sam and Frieda Block. Technophobia (fear of computers) was not a problem. They bought their first computer when they were in their seventies. A programming course enabled Frieda to write and solve math problems, which she would do "just for fun . . . ." She also learned to keep records of her sister's medical records and bills.

Sam, who was deaf since childhood, used a typewriter or a telecommunication device for the deaf (TDD) to communicate with friends and family. The TDD required special equipment and using a typewriter was frustrating because he couldn't hear the bell ding at the end of each line. At age 83, Sam learned to write letters on the computer, but he also plays games and helps people with their taxes too.

The Blocks have gone on line with Prodigy, and Sam easily communicates with friends all over. The pressure is now on the rest of the family to go on line and be as "computer literate" as mom and dad.

A common and cost-effective method of adding visual information to DTP documents is through clip art or photos. **Clip art** consists of images on floppy disk or CD-ROM available from a variety of publishers. Clip art is also included with some DTP software. Photo CDs contain digitized photos that can be incorporated into documents. The user selects appropriate illustrations or photos from these files, imports them into the DTP software, and positions them on the screen.

OBJECTIVE 5.6
Describe the benefits of desktop publishing.

WHY USE DESKTOP PUBLISHING?

To appreciate fully the benefits of DTP, it is necessary to understand the traditional process of preparing professional-looking documents using typography and a print shop. The first step is creating the basic text, using a typewriter or microcomputer. Second, decisions must be made about type styles and sizes, headlines, borders, and other elements that make the document more attractive or readable. A professional typesetter then rekeys the document and produces "galley proofs," which are returned for proofreading by the author. After checking for errors, the text is corrected and cut and pasted according to the design layout. In addition to "pasting up" the text in columns, space must be left to accommodate photographs and other illustrations. Finally, this document is ready for the printer's camera to make printing negatives. It is said to be "camera ready" and is sent to a commercial printer who prepares a photographic plate and prints the finished document on a press. The cost for a commercially printed document runs between $50 and $250 per page.

By contrast, DTP allows the computer user to create high-quality documents in less time and at a significantly lower cost. The unique qualities of a DTP system lie in the **page composition software.** It is basically visually oriented or graphics oriented and involves positioning and aligning text, graphics, and other elements of the document page entirely on the screen.

Besides the time and cost savings, DTP helps the originator control the creative process from start to finish, thus preventing errors and misunderstandings due to poor communication among originator, typesetter, and printer. It assures

Benefits of using desktop publishing

- Reduced cost
- Less time
- More control

consistency of appearance and quality in the case of documents that need to conform to a specific layout, such as newsletters and reports, which are produced on a regular basis.

OBJECTIVE 5.7
Contrast desktop publishing and word processing.

HOW DOES DESKTOP PUBLISHING DIFFER FROM WORD PROCESSING?

Desktop publishing versus word processing

- Desktop publishing
  - Better graphic handling
  - Typographical control
  - Column control
- Word processing
  - Text based
  - Less expensive

As word processing programs have become more sophisticated, some blurring has occurred between the capabilities of word processors and DTP. Word processors such as WordPerfect, Word and AmiPro now incorporate many DTP features. However, many mid- and low-end word processors remain substantially different as outlined next.

DTP differs from basic word processing in its ability to handle graphics, typographical control, and column control. It is far superior in permitting text and graphics to flow around each other in a document. You can easily curve text around irregular shaped objects.

Second, DTP provides greater control over layout of the document through changing or mixing type styles (incorporating several on the same page); increasing or decreasing the size of letters; kerning (stretching or squeezing text); creating headlines; adding, removing, or substituting one illustration for another; creating decorative special effects like headlines and borders; and merging all these elements quickly and with a minimum of effort. In short, DTP software is used to design the "look" of the document page.

Third, DTP gives the user much better control over the text in columns. This is important since many of the applications for DTP involve documents such as newsletters that may incorporate many columns.

Although most DTP programs have provisions for creating and editing text, this step is often performed using word processing software because of its specialized and sophisticated text creation features. The text document is then imported into the DTP document and manipulated to include the graphic elements.

A DTP system requires more advanced hardware than most word processors. The computer must have greater amounts of main memory and disk storage to work efficiently with graphics and text. A high-resolution monitor is recommended. Most require a mouse to direct operations and to manipulate elements on the screen quickly. Scanning devices allow DTP programs to import photographs, drawings, and other visual elements into a document. Professional-quality documents would be impossible without laser printers, which produce high-resolution copy. On the other hand, system requirements for word processing are considerably less expensive.

OBJECTIVE 5.8
Understand the limitations of desktop publishing.

WILL USING DESKTOP PUBLISHING ENSURE AN EFFECTIVE DOCUMENT?

No. New users of DTP software should realize that even the most sophisticated program is at best a very limited substitute for typographic experience and design ability. These skills come from training and practice. More than one purchaser of a DTP system has been disappointed to discover that the first document was not as attractive or professional looking as those seen in advertising promotional material. DTP maximizes the creative abilities of users who are responsible for producing professional-looking documents and who are willing to learn. If in doubt, seek the advice of an experienced graphics artist before distributing your document to the public.

OBJECTIVE 5.9
Identify fundamentals of document design.

WHAT IS DOCUMENT DESIGN?

Document design is the methodology that combines text and artwork or graphics into a final product. Many businesses use DTP to create their own publicity brochures, flyers, manuals, newsletters, and even technical journals with tables, charts, and graphs, rather than have an external source prepare them.

Fundamentals of Document Design

It's essential to have a plan in mind and take into consideration the tools you have available. Plan a general idea of the layout by sketching your proposed design. Decide what message, what look, what market you want to reach, and what facts, data, or graphic devices you need.

Then a style sheet should be assembled. The **style sheet** for a document is like a blue print or master plan; it sets out specifications, such as what typeface and point size will be used; what spacing will be inserted between letters, lines, and paragraphs; what margins and paragraph indentation to set. For longer documents or reports, you must look at page numbering and the possibility of using headers or footers. A style sheet maintains continuity for your document(s).

You may be adding lines, shapes, and possibly colors. So some elementary design principles are important factors to consider:
- Repetition
- Harmony
- Contrast
- Rhythm
- Unity

Repeating a line, shape, or color generates a feeling of harmony. However, too much repetition produces boredom. You must strike a balance. Balance can be either symmetrical, where identical shapes in a design are placed equidistant from the center of the page, or asymmetrical, where shapes are neither identical nor are they placed equidistant from the center. Or you could choose a visual balance where color and shape creates a harmonious design. Contrast in color, shape, or size also adds appeal to a design. A sense of rhythm or movement is achieved by using wavy lines or patterns in contrast to fixed lines or patterns. A good design has unity which suggests that all the elements function collectively.

Now that you've planned the basics and you know what you need to execute that design, let's examine some of the components of typography—white space, type, and graphics.

Effective Use of White Space

White space, also called blank space, offers the reader's eye a resting place. It contrasts with the print or graphics found on the remainder of the page. The mar-

- Margins
- Paragraph indentation
- Between column space
- Around headlines
- Between letters and words

gins found at the top, bottom, and sides of the page are considered blank spaces. But the area at the indentation for paragraphs, between columns, around a headline, as well as spaces and lines between words and letters are also considered white space, even if your medium is colored paper. Readability specialists and psychologists advise that uniform spacing between words creates a document that is easiest and fastest to read. There are two ways to assure this uniform spacing: leading and kerning.

Leading (rhymes with wedding) refers to the amount of space between lines. **Kerning** is a method for adjusting the space between characters. A font that is not proportional allocates the same space to each letter. However, when a proportional font is used, letters, especially capitals, are not the same size (larger letters take up more space) so they appear to be spaced too far apart. For example, the letters *W* and *M* take up more space than do the *I* and *J.* Kerning decreases the space between those combinations that are not equal.

Hyphenating words at the ends of lines also adds white space. A higher reading rate is achieved if words are hyphenated properly. Whenever a word is hyphenated, there should be at least two letters on each line, and there should be no more than three lines in a row ending with hyphens.

Color Enhancement

White space is important, but color also conveys a message. It highlights or emphasizes a point. There are two color separation processes: spot color and four-color printing.

Spot color adds color for borders, headlines, or other areas where a page full of print needs a high interest break. Usually there are only two colors involved—one for print (often black) and then another color. Of course, the printer has to have the capacity for color printing.

Four-color printing offers thousands of colors by combining cyan, magenta, yellow, and black. Additional programs must be purchased to use the four-color separation process. Some DTP programs offer add-on packages capable of two- and four-color separation where color distortions can be corrected.

Even if you do not choose to add color to your document, another method of adding interest is through different typefaces and font sizes.

Typefaces and Fonts

- Serif
- Sans serif
- Pitch
  - Fixed
  - Proportional
- Weight
- Orientation

A typeface refers to the design of a set of characters; it is a representation of the type. Some examples of common typefaces include Helvetica, Courier, and Times Roman (see Figure 5-16). Typefaces have various qualities such as serif or sans serif, pitch, weight, type, and orientation. The characters in a serif typeface have finishing decorations, called feet and hats. The typefaces are appropriate for the main text of a document, for example, Times Roman, Garamond, and Baskerville. The characters in a sans serif typeface have no decorative feet or hats. They are often found in headings rather than the main body of text and include, for example, Helvetica. Pitch refers to the horizontal spacing between characters. In a fixed-pitch typeface each character takes up the same amount of space. In a proportional typeface, as noted earlier, spacing depends on the width of each particular character. The **weight** of a typeface refers to the width of the characters and can be light, medium, or bold. **Orientation** refers to the direction the letters print on the paper. In portrait orientation, the characters print across the width of the paper. In landscape orientation, the characters print lengthwise down the paper. A typeface can set the mood for your document: some are suitable for personal use, others present a more professional look.

FIGURE 5-16
Examples of typefaces.

This is an example of Times Roman. (10 pt. type)
This is an example of Times Roman. (12 pt. type)

This is an example of Helvetica. (10 pt. type)
This is an example of Helvetica. (12 pt. type)

This is an example of Courier. (10 pt. type)
This is an example of Courier. (12 pt. type)

This is an example of Century Schoolbook. (10 pt. type)
This is an example of Century Schoolbook. (12 pt. type)

This is an example of Arial. (10 pt. type)
This is an example of Arial. (12 pt. type)

A font is a set of alphanumeric characters that all share the same characteristics. As we noted earlier, Times Roman is an example of a typeface and 12-point Times Roman is an example of a font as are 12-point bold Times Roman or 10-point italic Times Roman. A **point** is a measurement of a font's size. The American Point System measures the height of type or the length of lines of type. Common point sizes are from 6 to 72 points. In a 72-point font, each character would be 1 inch tall. Most fonts include standard letters and numbers as well as symbols for language, mathematical, monetary, and legal use. However, some fonts consist entirely of symbols for scientific or mathematical uses.

Graphics Enhancement

Graphics can add high interest to a document. A graphic as simple as a bullet (●) enhances entries in a list of items. And borders around the paper's edge or lines drawn around text to form boxes offer easy, high-interest graphics. There are other graphics elements that you can use in document designing. Word processing programs have many of their own graphics that can be used. But there are drawing and painting programs that allow you to create your own graphics and then import them into a DTP program. Scanners can "read" a graphical image directly into your computer where you can adapt it to your design. Another source of graphical images is contained in clip art. Found in other software packages, clip art depicts graphics for special occasions, holidays, even borders. But a problem exists if there are too many distractions from the text or message that you are trying to relay. Moderation is a good rule of thumb.

When you start putting the white space, text, and graphics together to finalize your document, the following guidelines should be considered: balance, unity, and sequence. Good balance is achieved if the placement of each element gives a sense of stability. You may place the elements on the page so they appear to be unbalanced, but the design can still give a sense of stability in placement. Unity is achieved if a single theme carries the message. Your design should encourage the reader along a definite reading path to make your point. You want the reader to comprehend the message you are sending through your design.

Page Design and Readability

Professionals have devised tests to determine the readability of documents. **Readability** is measured on various indexes; the end result being that the person reading understands and can use what has been written. In fact most textbooks have been evaluated by readability experts. Some of the factors that affect readability are the level of language used, the length of sentences, the style of writing, and the way the type appears on the page. For easiest readability, type should be consistent, well laid out, and proportioned on the page.

Choose one typeface and point size throughout the main part of the document. Introduction of too many typefaces creates a lack of harmony. Titles or headlines should be varied in weight and style so that they stand out from the remainder of the text. For the highest readability levels, avoid long blocks of text using italics, script, bold, or all capital letters.

When laying out your document, refer to the draft design plan. Remember also that vertically rather than horizontally set type is extraordinarily hard to read. Widow and orphan lines also defeat readability. A so-called **orphan line** occurs when one line of a paragraph begins at the bottom of a page. The **widow line** results when a paragraph ends with only one line at the top of the next page.

You may have to experiment with various strategies before obtaining the "look" you're after. But the fundamentals of design to remember are: be subtle and keep your concepts simple.

SUMMARY

Word processing involves using a word processor to enter, edit, and print text. A word processor is application software that manipulates text-based documents. Word processors are used extensively in business, schools, and homes.

Word processors improve the speed and efficiency of creating a document and allow the user to concentrate on the subject rather than the mechanics of writing and typing.

A word processor has three basic functions: entering, saving, and editing text; formatting; and printing.

The edit window is the work area for entering and editing text. Most word processors allow access to multiple windows. The window containing the cursor is the active window. A status line provides information about the current document and system. Unless otherwise instructed, a word processor uses default settings for parameters such as margins, tabs, and line spacing so you are able to begin typing immediately.

Wordwrap is the feature that automatically moves text that runs past the right margin down to the next line. Save your document often to avoid accidentally erasing or losing the text.

Text can be entered in one of two ways: through the insert mode where existing text automatically shifts to the right to make room for the new entry or through the typeover mode where entries strike over and replace existing text.

The search and replace feature allows you to find text and make corrections throughout a document. Block editing permits units of text to be acted on as a single component.

The format of a document refers to how it looks on screen or after it is printed. Formatting features may appear on the screen only as embedded characters or be displayed as they will print in a WYSIWYG environment.

Several frequently used formatting features include margins, justification, tabs, line spacing, page breaks, automatic page numbering, centering, headers and footers, and character enhancements. Word processors provide a variety of printing options including specification of how many copies, which pages to print, and what quality of print.

Word processors also include a number of additional features that add to their power. These include a spelling checker, thesaurus, CD-ROM reference materials, grammar and style checker, mail merge, math functions, endnotes, footnotes, subscripts-superscripts, outline, table of contents and index generators, and page layout features.

DTP is a concept that combines the use of microcomputers with word processors, page composition software, and high-quality laser printers. Page composition software, usually called DTP software, permits placement of graphic elements in a document where desired and allows text to be flowed around photos, charts, or illustrations. Benefits of DTP include reduced time and cost of preparing a document and the ability to maintain control over the process. Graphic elements used in DTP are created in one of three ways: computer generated, digitized, or pulled from a clip art disk.

VOCABULARY SELF-TEST

Can you define the following?

active window (p. 146)

automatic page numbering (p. 152)

block editing (p. 147)

centering (p. 153)

character enhancements (p. 153)

clip art (p. 159)

default settings (p. 146)

desktop publishing (p. 157)

document design (p. 161)

edit window (p. 145)

font (p. 154)

footer (p. 153)

format (p. 148)

grammar and style checker (p. 156)

hard page break (p. 152)

header (p. 153)

insert mode (p. 147)

justification (p. 149)

kerning (p. 162)

leading (p. 162)

mail merge (p. 156)

margin settings (p. 149)

orientation (p. 162)

orphan line (p. 164)

page composition software (p. 159)

point (p. 163)

readability (p. 164)

search and replace (p. 148)

soft page break (p. 149)

spelling checker (p. 154)

status line (p. 146)

style sheet (p. 161)

thesaurus (p. 154)

tab settings (p. 149)

typeface (p. 154)

typeover mode (p. 147)

weight (p. 162)

white space (p. 161)

widow line (p. 164)

WYSIWYG (What You See Is What You Get) (p. 149)

word processing (p. 143)

word processor (p. 143)

wordwrap (p. 146)

Multiple Choice

1. Which application software is best suited for manipulating text-based documents?
    a. desktop publishing
    b. word processor
    c. graphics software
    d. database management system

2. For writing a business letter a user could best be helped by which software?
    a. database management system
    b. desktop publishing program
    c. communications program
    d. word processor

3. Which of the following is not a benefit of using a word processor?
    a. documents can be created quicker
    b. writer concentrates on subject rather than mechanics of writing and typing
    c. allows faster and more creative data analysis
    d. documents can be created more efficiently

4. A(n) _____ is a line (or lines) of text repeated at the top of each page. It usually doesn't appear until you print the document.
    a. header
    b. footer
    c. wordwrap
    d. index

5. _____ features are used to control how a document will look when it is printed.
    a. Editing
    b. Text entry
    c. Formatting
    d. Printing

6. A(n) _____ gives the user a list of synonyms that might replace a word in a document.
    a. spell checker
    b. editor
    c. thesaurus
    d. footer

7. Complex documents that combine numerous graphic elements and text can best be produced using which of the following?
    a. word processor
    b. desktop publishing software
    c. graphics software
    d. paint and draw software

8. Photographic images can be incorporated into a desktop publishing document through the use of _____.
    a. a scanner
    b. clip art
    c. painting program
    d. drawing program

9. Kerning is a capability of desktop publishing software that _____.
    a. colors text
    b. squeezes and elongates text
    c. draws graphic images
    d. imports drawings

10. Predrawn art on floppy disk or CD-ROM available from a variety of publishers is called _____.
    a. text
    b. scanner art
    c. clip art
    d. desktop art

Fill In

1. The act of entering and editing text with a word processor is called _____.

2. A(n) _____ is used to manipulate text-based documents.

3. The _____ feature allows text that extends past the right margin to be placed on the next line.

4. The _____ is located at the top or bottom of the display screen and provides information about the current document and the system.

5. The _____ allows existing text to automatically shift to make room for new text.

6. The word processor automatically indicates the page break known as a _____ page break, while a _____ page break occurs when the user overrides the computer.

7. To make all the text align against the left or right margins is called _____.

8. The way a document looks on screen or after it is printed is called its _____.

9. A(n) _____ locates misspelled words and typographical errors in a document.

10. The concept of combining microcomputers with word processing software, page composition software, and laser printers is called _____.

Short Answer

1. Contrast the terms word processing and word processor.

2. Discuss the benefits of using a word processor.

3. Describe the difference between the insert mode and the typeover mode.

4. Describe the three options of the search and replace feature.

5. What is block editing?

6. Compare the functions of a spell checker to a thesaurus.

7. Briefly describe how the word processing function of mail merge works.

8. Describe the benefits of desktop publishing.

9. Describe three ways in which graphic elements are created for use in desktop publishing.

10. In what basic ways does desktop publishing differ from word processing?

Issues for Thought

1. Desktop publishing software and many word processors incorporate graphics into a document. The advent of scanners allows you to easily scan any available graphic. Should you scan artwork created by someone else, modify it, and use it in your own document? Should permission or credit be given for the original artist's inspiration and work that led to the modified version used in your document?

2. Using desktop software does not guarantee that the document produced will convey the message you want. Have the class break into small groups to design a one-page flyer enticing people to buy a product. Discuss each design and comment on the different layouts.

CHAPTER 6

DATA MANAGEMENT: DATABASE MANAGEMENT SYSTEMS

OBJECTIVES

6.1 Understand why data should be stored in an organized manner.

6.2 Describe the basic hierarchy of data organization.

6.3 Describe the advantages of using a database.

6.4 Describe a database management system.

6.5 Explain the functions of a database management system.

6.6 Define the term relational database.

6.7 Understand how you ensure the validity of data in a database.

6.8 Identify ways to maintain privacy in a database.

6.9 Define how an image database differs from a text-based database.

6.10 Describe some special-purpose databases.

PROFILE

E. F. Codd

Experience is one of life's best teachers. Most of us can see how something can be done by doing it. Some, however, can see how something is done and devise a new and better way of doing it. So it was with Edgar F. Codd, the creator of the relational database structure. Codd received his master's degree in mathematics from Oxford University in England in 1949. Later, he incorporated the mathematical concepts he learned at Oxford to develop his strategy for a database management system. This development did not happen overnight, for Codd had 20 years of computer experience before proposing his ideas on a relational database model.

Codd, who was born in England and served as a pilot for the Royal Air Force in World War II, was employed at IBM in 1949. He helped design IBM's first stored-program computer, the IBM 701. Codd also lived briefly in Canada, where he managed the computer center for the Canadian Guided Missile Program. A short time later he returned to and became a citizen of the United States.

Twenty years later, Codd found himself at a seminar on database management systems where he saw something amiss. Finding data was a potentially complex process under this current structure. Codd reasoned that by using sound mathematical principles, called predicate logic, the database could be simplified into tables. In mathematical terms, these tables were called relations. Codd's idea thus became known as a relational database structure.

New ideas are not always welcomed, and Codd struggled for years to persuade IBM to accept his concept. In fact, it took until 1981 before IBM announced its first relational database product. Still, perseverance paid off for Codd, as the relational model became the standard for databases.

The battles were not over, though. Codd had to fight to recover from a serious fall that left him in a coma. Although he eventually retired from IBM in 1985, Codd was not one to rest on his laurels. He and a friend formed a company, Codd and Date Consultants, to continue improving the relational database model. New fronts on the battlefield arise from the proponents of object-oriented databases, who say the relational system is outmoded. But don't count Codd out just yet.

oduct oday's society thrives on information. To meet an increasing demand for information, we require more and more data to be gathered, stored, and manipulated. In fact, many people require so much data that it has become impossible to manually manage and extract the information needed in a timely fashion. To solve this problem, microcomputers have been called upon to help manage and store the data gathered. In this chapter you will read about microcomputer database management systems, a type of application software used to manage data.

OBJECTIVE 6.1
Understand why data should be stored in an organized manner.

WHY SHOULD YOU ORGANIZE DATA?

Organization of ideas or tangible objects is the key to productivity. Finding the right wrench in a toolbox is easy if they are laid out smallest to largest rather than scattered. The same logic applies to data storage.

Imagine for a moment that you are the instructor of a class in which there are 30 students. You assign grades weekly for tests, homework, and computer lab reports. During each week of a 16-week semester, you collect and grade material from all three sources. When you finish grading each piece of work, you mark the student's name and grade on a piece of paper and toss it onto your desk. Each week you accumulate another 90 pieces of paper. At the end of the semester you must find over 1,400 pieces of paper, organize them, and calculate a grade for each student. This method is not very productive, is it?

The same haphazard data entry into a computer would render the data virtually useless. To be effective and achieve the most efficiency, you must systematically organize the data. In the example, by initially setting up a plan, many problems would be prevented. You could keep a grade book with a row for each student's name. You could break down the columns following the names to record grades for each test, homework assignment, and computer lab report. At the end of the semester, you could then locate and average the grades much more easily.

Computer data must be organized, just as any other data, to be used most productively. The next section describes how data are arranged into a hierarchy.

OBJECTIVE 6.2
Describe the basic hierarchy of data organization.

HOW ARE COMPUTER DATA ORGANIZED?

The hierarchy of computer data organization, starting with the most general to the most specific is database, file, record, field, byte, and bit. A **database** is a cross-referenced collection of files designed to minimize repetition of data. It could be compared to listing all the gradebooks from all the instructors together so any of the data contained in them could be accessed from one place.

A **file** is a collection of records (similar groups of data) that fit under one name or heading (see Figure 6.1). An instructor's grade book is an example of a file. All data in the grade book deal with students and their grades.

A file may be further separated into records. A **record** is a collection of related data items. Information about a particular student, such as the name and test scores, is an individual record. The information in the record pertains to that student only, but all of that information is related to class grades.

Hierarchy of data
• Database
• File
• Record
• Field
• Byte
• Bit

In a record, space must be allocated for data. Each individual classification of data stored in the record is called a **field.** Each record may contain one or more fields. Using the instructor example, there are many fields: student's name, one for each test grade, one for each homework grade, and one for each computer lab report grade.

To round out the hierarchy, each character in a field is represented internally to the computer as a byte. Each byte is composed of 8 bits. Remember that a bit is the smallest unit of data the computer can recognize.

OBJECTIVE 6.3
Describe the advantages of using a database.

WHY USE A DATABASE?

Advantages of a database

- Reduced data redundancy
- Improved data integrity
- Data independence
- Improved data security
- Data consistency
- More powerful data manipulation
- Easier data access and use

A database has many advantages in keeping track of data over "paper and pencil" methods. Following are some:

- A database *reduces data duplication*. For example, a customer's name and address may appear only once in a database, while that data may appear in 20 to 30 files. Whenever a customer address changes, updating all the affected files would be both time consuming and prone to error.
- A database *improves data integrity*. Since a particular piece of data appears in only a limited number of locations, future uses of the data are more apt to reflect any change or addition. For example, if a customer notifies the bank of an address change and the address is stored in only one location, then all other files—checking account, savings account, out-

FIGURE 6-1
Organization of data by file, record, field, byte, and bit.

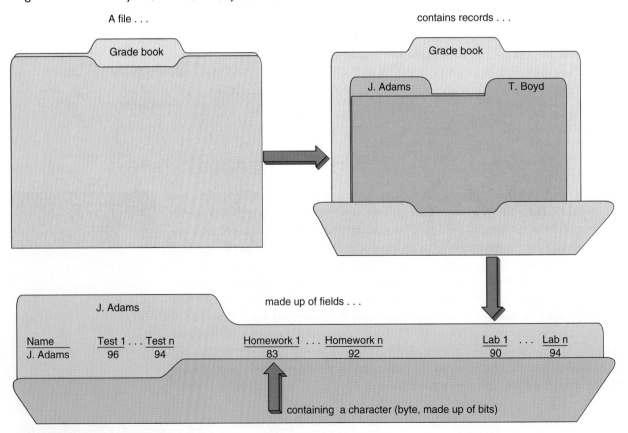

standing loans, bank-issued credit card, tax reporting, and solicitation—will reflect the new address.

- A database *maintains data independence*. The structure of the database requires that data be independent; that is, deleting or changing selected data does not affect other data in the database. If a manager quits his or her job, for example, data concerning his or her office furniture, telephone number, travel expenditures, and other nonsalary items are not destroyed when the manager's name is deleted from the current employee database.

- A database *improves data security*. Most database systems maintain their own security, and since all the data are in one place, security is easier to maintain.

- A database *maintains data consistency*. The kind, type, and size of data are consistent for all applications. For example, the size of a specific field is the same for all applications using the database.

- A database allows more *powerful manipulation of data*. Because the data stored in a database can be cross-referenced and combined, users are able to perform much more sophisticated data manipulations than with an independent unrelated file system.

- A database permits *easier access and use*. Database features include methods that make retrieval of data simple. Data can also be retrieved in multiple groupings. Furthermore, you find data more easily and under a variety of conditions than would be possible without the use of a database. Database management systems are programs specifically designed to provide the user access to the database.

OBJECTIVE 6.4
Describe a database management system.

WHAT IS A DATABASE MANAGEMENT SYSTEM?

A microcomputer **database management system (DBMS)** is the software that allows a user to store, organize, and retrieve data from a database. It is the interface among programs, users, and data in the database. Database management systems for microcomputers include Access, Paradox, dBASE, and FoxBase.

Basically, anyone who needs to organize sizable collections of data finds it helpful to use a database management system to electronically store and retrieve data (see Figure 6-2). Typical users include librarians, stockbrokers, and small-business owners, among others. A librarian might use a DBMS to manage special collections of books, records and CDs, or maps. Stockbrokers might use one to keep track of clients, portfolios, and prospective clients. A small-business owner might use a database management system to control inventory, organize employee records, or gauge the responsiveness of mailing lists.

A popular application that involves integration of several different files is in accounting. These files include the general ledger, accounts receivable, accounts payable, and payroll files. Other applications that require integration of several files include financial management, travel agency management, medical office management, and real estate management.

At home you might use a DBMS to record personal information for tax or insurance purposes. You might also use it to organize names and addresses, your CD collection, your coin collection, and so on (see Figure 6.3).

A DBMS should provide the user a method to easily access data as well as protect the integrity of the data. It provides the user a means of developing other applications

FIGURE 6-2

In 1974, approximately 55 zoos in North America and Europe began pooling data on their animals. By the end of 1986, over 70,000 living specimens from over 200 zoos in 16 countries had been cataloged. From this database, reports covering census, breeding, age and sex distribution, and population trends are routinely generated and distributed to participating zoological facilities. Personnel at the Columbus Zoo record pertinent data about that zoo's tiger population.

(Main photo copyright by Kjell B. Sandved.)

FIGURE 6-3
Database screen showing address records in a file.

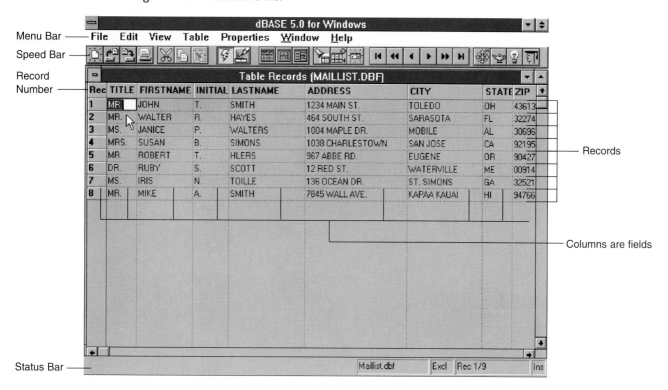

Menu Bar

Speed Bar

Record
Number

Records

Columns are fields

Status Bar

through the database software. Networking is becoming more and more fundamental in business, so the microcomputer DBMS should accommodate multiple users.

OBJECTIVE 6.5
Explain the functions of a database management system.

WHAT DOES A DATABASE MANAGEMENT SYSTEM DO?

The exact features of a microcomputer DBMS vary. Most, however, contain features that allow them to perform basic functions including creating the database, maintaining the database, organizing the database, querying the database, generating reports, and creating customized database applications.

Creating the Database

The first step is to define the problem that you want the database to solve. Suppose you want a list of all regular customers in each region and mailing labels so that you can send promotional and special sales notices to them. First, decide what information the database should provide. In this case, it is the customer's name and address. Each piece of data should be contained in its own field. The individual data items include title, first name, middle initial, last name, street address, city, state, zip code, and telephone number.

Before any data are entered, the organization, or *structure*, of the database must be defined. By defining the data structure, you tell the program how to treat the fields in each record. This includes naming the field, determining the data type (e.g., character, numeric, and date), setting the length of the fields (i.e., the number of characters), and, where necessary, specifying additional information such as the number of decimal places or the format for a date entry.

Functions of a microcomputer database management system

- Entering data
- Maintaing data
- Organizing data
- Querying the database
- Generating reports
- Creating customized applications
- Connectivity

FIGURE 6-4
The data structure for a database file is created using the
database design screen.

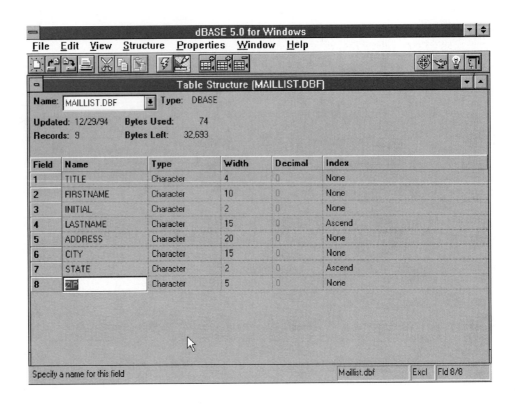

A field name identifies the data stored in that field; for example, CUSTNAME indicates that the field contains the customer's name. The type of data to be stored in the field must also be identified. For example, a field that contains the price of a product to be used as part of a calculation, such as multiplying the price times a number of items, must be designated as numeric. Remember when setting the length of the fields, to account for the longest entry. For example, if you allow ten spaces, cities like Philadelphia, New Brunswick, and San Francisco will overflow the field.

The structure of a database file is created using the **database design screen**. The database design screen is where names, types, width, and other factors for each field in a database file are defined. Figure 6-4 shows an example of a data structure for the mailing list file.

Fields can be designated as key fields when defining the data structure. **Key fields** uniquely identify a record. For example, when extracting information from the database, customer names may be arranged in alphabetical order by the key field LASTNAME. Once the data structure has been defined you can begin entering data.

Database management systems allow users to customize the input screen used for entering data by defining a screen form. A **screen form** describes the layout for entering data into a record. The fields are positioned according to the user's preference and serve as an output screen where field alignment is determined for printing (see Figure 6-5).

Maintaining the Database

The contents of a database rarely stay the same. The change may be to a field in an individual record, or it may involve an entire record within the file. In the mailing list file, for example, you may add a new customer or update the address of another. The maintenance functions most often utilized are updating data in a record and adding or deleting records from your file.

Updating is the process of changing the contents of a record or records in a file. It may involve adding to, deleting from, or changing the contents of an existing

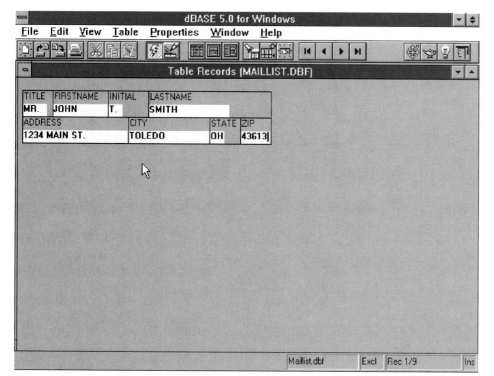

HIGHLIGHT 6-1 Fore!

"I think this shot calls for a five iron." Swoosh! There it goes, but unfortunately there goes your back with it. So where do you turn? The local doctor, the caddy, your uncle? No, try the computer.

That's right, the computer. The Centinela Hospital Fitness Institute has developed a computer application that tracks golf stars like Arnold Palmer, among others, on the PGA and the Senior PGA Tour. Through the use of dBASE, a microcomputer database program, the hospital employs a mobile medical unit to follow the golfers around, gathering statistics about injuries, strength and flexibility, and physiological data.

The database program allows the hospital to store, organize, and update the information gathered in a

timely and efficient manner. The hospital then uses this information and correlates it with their research in the field of biomechanics. These data can then be used to analyze the golfers' techniques and come up with training suggestions that will improve the game or reduce the chance of injury.

Called the "Amateur Golfer Improvement" program, it combines the sciences of computer engineering and medicine. While the medicine part is best left to the doctors, this application is more user-friendly for the hospital employees and less costly than those run on mainframes.

Other clients of the hospital who will require their own specialized programs include the Los Angeles Dodgers and the Harlem Globetrotters.

---

record, for example, entering a new address or telephone number for a person in your mailing list file. You keep the data current by accessing records in a file and changing the field contents.

To change the data, most database management systems provide two methods for accessing and viewing the records. An **edit mode** typically shows you the contents of an individual record and allows you to edit each field (see Figure 6-6a). The **browse mode** typically shows an entire screen full of records and permits you to edit each field (see Figure 6-6b).

Adding to a file means placing an additional record or records into an existing file, for example, entering a new person to a customer file or a new employee in a personnel file. Some programs append the added records at the end of the file; others

FIGURE 6-6

(a) The contents of one record in the Edit mode; (b) records are displayed one screenful at a time in the Browse mode.

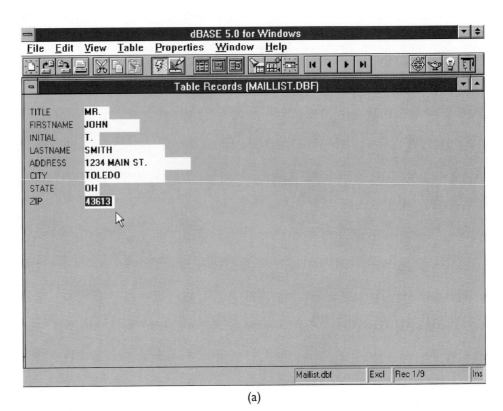

(a)

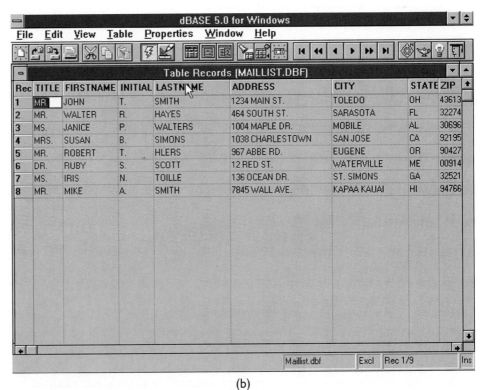

(b)

place them in a spot vacated by previously deleted records; still others make it possible to insert a new record at any point in the file.

Deleting involves removing records from a file. A record may be deleted in direct response to a delete command or it may be a two-step process in which the records are first "marked" for deletion. Once marked, the records can be either "unmarked" to keep them in the database or deleted which permanently removes them from the database. Individual fields within a record can also be deleted.

Extra care should be taken when deleting data to avoid removing a field or record unintentionally because after the data are deleted, they are no longer available. Often, a prompt such as ARE YOU SURE? (Y/N) will appear on the screen before the deletion takes place. It is wise to keep a backup copy of the file in case of accidental deletion.

Organizing the Database

Usually, it is easier to read and make sense of data if they are arranged in a previously designated order. For example, data could be arranged alphabetically by last name or numerically by invoice number. Two methods of organizing the records in a file are sorting and indexing. Both methods are similar in that they order records numerically or alphabetically and in ascending or descending order. However, they differ in the way the sorted records are stored. In the mailing list database, if you request that the address labels be printed in order by zip code, you could receive postal discounts for presorted bulk mailings.

Sorting reorders records in a file according to a desired condition after which the original file is saved in the sorted order. A sort "physically" reorders the records and most programs save them under a new filename. However, if you sort a file in several ways, naming each new file, valuable disk space is quickly consumed (see Figure 6.7).

The process of **indexing** creates a file which contains the user's sorted-data conditions. Indexing allows many different sort orderings without affecting the integrity of the original file and consumes much less disk space since the index file contains only the conditions on which the file was sorted. A simple index may be created in which ordering of data takes place according to the contents of one field. Complex indexing orders the records according to the contents of multiple fields. For example, you might index the records by last name and state. The index lists the records alphabetically by the customer's last name, from A to Z, for Allen, then by state name from A to Z for Alaska, and so on.

Querying the Database

Probably the most important function of a database program is the ability of the user to query the database. A **query** is the process of extracting data from a database and presenting it in a requested format. Queries are accomplished through the use of a database query language. A **database query language** acts as an interface between users and a DBMS. It helps users easily manipulate, analyze, and create reports from the data contained in the database. They make it easy for people, other than programmers, to use a database management system. The quality of the query process determines how fast and efficiently the data are retrieved.

Generating Reports

For the majority of cases, data extracted from the database will be communicated to others through a paper report. These reports may be simple printouts of the screen or custom layouts created in the database program (see Figure 6.8).

Sometimes it is necessary to print only the raw data rather than to arrange the output into a more formal report. Database management systems allow you to print the screen contents at any time. Data in a record can be sent to the printer in the same format as it appears in the screen form.

Many times, however, you require customized output to meet particular needs. This customizing is possible by using a report generator. A **report generator** defines how the output is to appear when printed. In addition to customizing the placement

FIGURE 6-7
(a)Records sorted alphabetically
by last name; (b)records sorted
by state.

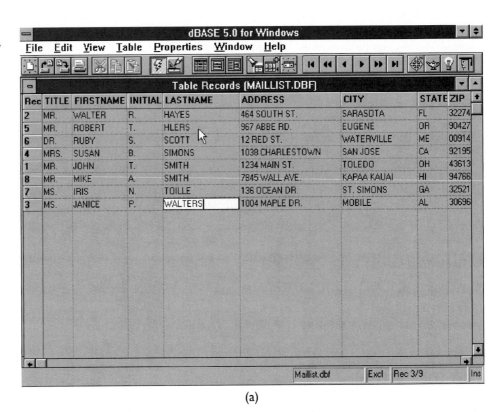

(a)

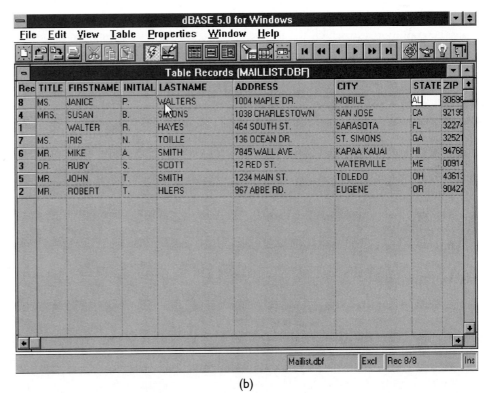

(b)

of fields, most report generators allow you to incorporate headers, footers, formatting, and mathematical and statistical functions.

The header section of a report is found at the top of the report page and contains items such as date, page number, column headings, or perhaps a company logo. The footer, like the header, is a separate section of the report, found at the bottom of the page. The footer may contain page numbers, the user's name, or other relevant infor-

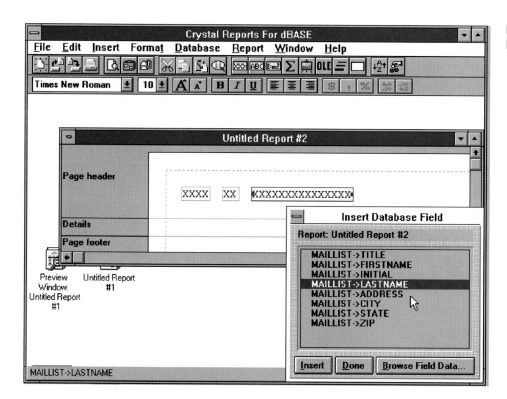

FIGURE 6-8
Database report screen.

mation. Formatting features control the way a report looks by setting margins, justifying text, and indicating page lengths and spacing between lines. Most report generators contain features that perform mathematical and statistical functions such as calculating column subtotals, grand totals, averages, and counts.

Creating Customized Database Applications

Any of the microcomputer database programs will probably fulfill the needs of a typical home user. In business, however, there is a need for custom applications to efficiently manage a task. There are two basic methods that allow development of customized applications in many microcomputer database management systems—a database programming language or an application generator.

A **database programming language** is a language specific to the database that allows you to create applications customized to your needs. The database language commands let you create and control how data are entered, processed, and retrieved from the database. The programmer is responsible for coding all menus, data entry screens, output forms, and the features that tie the database program together.

An **application generator** is a separate program that removes some of the burden of coding an entire custom application. The user gives the program instructions through a series of questions and answers. The application generator simplifies customizing an application by generating much of the program code. An application might display a start-up menu of choices or provide instruction screens to guide a user. You don't need to be a programmer to take advantage of the power of an application generator. Templates for database applications, such as accounting systems, can be purchased.

Connectivity and the Database

Microcomputer database programs are available as both single-user and multiuser products. Single-user programs cannot be used by multiple users in a network environment. Multiuser microcomputer database programs can be purchased in file-server architecture or client-server architecture. Basically, with the file-server arrangement, the database program runs entirely on the user's system, and the network server merely stores the data files that are shared among the different users. This method does not take advantage of the computing power of the server. In a **client-server architecture,** the processing of an application is split between a client and a server. The client portion is the user's microcomputer, which typically controls user interaction with the database management system. The server portion can be another microcomputer, minicomputer, or mainframe that performs tasks such as data management, information sharing between clients, and sophisticated network administration and security features. Using the processing power of both the client and the server computers increases the processing power available and the efficiency with which it is used.

In addition to multiuser support, many microcomputer database programs allow the user to integrate data from other applications. Examples include writing a letter using a word processor and importing (bringing in) it into the database program to perform a mail merge with data in the mail list file or exporting (sending out) data from the database to create a graph in a graphics program. Another desirable feature is for the database program to work with different data file formats from other database programs.

OBJECTIVE 6.6
Define the term relational database.

WHAT IS A RELATIONAL DATABASE?

A **relational database** is composed of many tables (somewhat equivalent to a file) in which data are stored. Tables in a relational database must have unique rows, and the cells (the intersection of a row and column—equivalent to a field) must be single valued (i.e., each cell must contain only one item of data, such as a name, address, or identification number). A **relational database management system (RDBMS)** allows data to be readily created, maintained, manipulated, and retrieved from a relational database. The power of the relational database is in the way it can be queried. Most microcomputer databases are relational in nature.

In a relational database, data relationships do not have to be predefined. Users query it and establish data relationships spontaneously by joining common fields. Two basic query styles used in a relational database are (1) query by example and (2) structured query language. In **query by example,** the database management system displays field information and users enter inquiry conditions in the desired fields. For example, if a user wants to list the employees whose salaries are greater than $25,000 and sort the items in ascending order by department number, the screen might appear as in Figure 6-9.

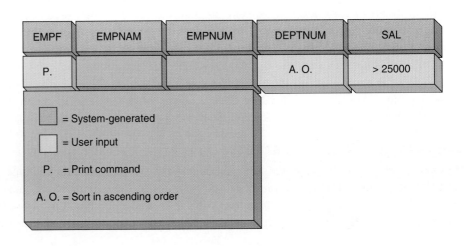

FIGURE 6-9
A database query language that uses the query-by-example approach.

```
SELECT      EMPNAM, EMPNUM, DEPTNUM, SAL
FROM        EMPF
WHERE       SALARY > 25000
ORDER       BY DEPTNUM
```

FIGURE 6-10
A database query language that uses the structured query language approach.

Structured query language (SQL) is the standard database query language used with relational databases. Using SQL the inquiry in Figure 6-9 would appear as it does in Figure 6-10. This tells the DBMS to use the fields EMPNAM, EMPNUM, DEPT-NUM, and SAL from each record in the employee file (EMPF) if the employee's salary is greater than $25,000 and to sort that list by department number.

OBJECTIVE 6.7
Understand how you ensure the validity of data in a database.

HOW CAN DATA VALIDITY BE MAINTAINED?

A business depends on its ability to acquire the right data at the right time. But, even more important, the data must be accurate. This means insuring careful data entry. Since most data errors can be traced to their point of entry, most database management systems provide a method for detecting errors at that point through validity checks. Checking data for appropriateness and accuracy is called **validating.** Data entry checks can be built into the database application to prevent invalid data from being entered. These checks are often set as the data structures are being defined. Validity checks may be accomplished in the microcomputer database program by

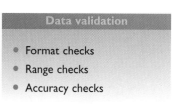

Data validation

- Format checks
- Range checks
- Accuracy checks

- Format checking—determining if data are in the correct format, for example, numeric or text

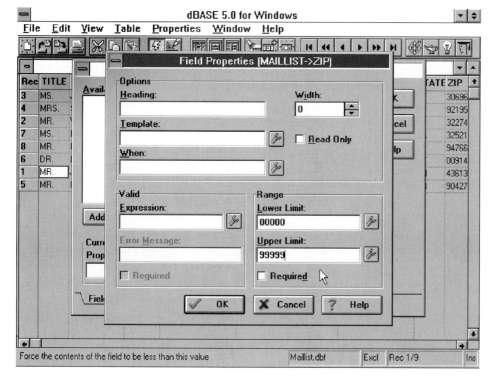

FIGURE 6-11
Screen showing setting of range check.

- Range checking—determining if the data fall within an acceptable chosen range, for example, greater than 100 but less than 500 (see Figure 6-11)
- Accuracy checking—making sure that an entry is possible, for example, cross-checking a product number with the product numbers in an inventory file

Starting out with the correct data helps to ensure that the data the user retrieves will be free of errors.

OBJECTIVE 6.8
Identify ways to maintain privacy in a database.

HOW CAN DATA BE KEPT PRIVATE IN A DATABASE?

Data security

- Data encryption
- Passwords
- File-locking

Data stored in a file are often sensitive or confidential in nature. Therefore, a user may want to restrict data access to only authorized personnel. This is especially true in a multiuser environment. Data **encryption** is a way to code data so they appear as a scrambled display of alphanumeric characters if retrieved by unauthorized persons. Database software provides features that limit or prevent unauthorized access.

A database can be designed so that a password grants access to the entire database or only certain files. A **password** may be a letter, number, or a combination of both designed to prevent data access unless the exact entry code is used. It can be designed so that the user needs one password to view the file and another password to change, add, or delete anything in the file.

Data security is especially critical when the database is run on a network, where more than one person has access to the files at the same time. Sometimes, however, unintended deletions, additions, or changes occur when two people work with the same file. Errors occur because one person does not know what the other is doing—one person's update may be accidentally deleted by the other. Database management software can restrict access or lock the file to prevent accidents like this. **File-locking** and **record locking** are procedures that permit only one user to access a file or record at a time. The file or record cannot be manipulated by a second person until it is released by the first person.

HIGHLIGHT 6-2 Database Coupon Clipping

Many of you fall into that group of consumers who clip coupons. You know the routine: read the Sunday paper, find scissors, cut out the coupons, lose some, file the rest in your coupon organizer; then when you go to the store you forget to bring the coupons! Like any other filing system, only if the data are organized will they be of any use. At some grocery stores databases might make paper coupons obsolete.

Von's, one of the nation's largest supermarket chains, has implemented the database concept to benefit both consumers and marketers of food products. With a program called Target Von's, the consumer uses a magnetic card that, when the appropriate product is scanned, will result in automatic deductions from the bill. Forgot your coupons? No problem!

The suppliers of the products benefit too. By using your card, data are gathered on what items you bought and what marketing group you fit into. This allows the store to tailor their inventory to its consumers' needs. Marketers query the database to pinpoint exactly which customers should receive promotional literature. For example, a 50 cent coupon would be incentive to keep a "regular customer" buying their product, while a $1.00 coupon might encourage consumer's who use a rival's product to switch product loyalty.

Maybe this type of database marketing will give you more time for the crossword puzzle.

OBJECTIVE 6.9
Define how an image database differs from a text-based database.

WHAT IS AN IMAGE DATABASE?

An **image database** is database software that allows storage of both pictures and text (see Figure 6-12). Because images comprise large volumes of data and require large amounts of storage and long transmission times to bring the pictures to the screen, microcomputer databases stored only text until recent years.

However, enhancements in data storage techniques paved the way for color images to be stored in a database much like text. The technique, called compression technology, reduces the file size to a small percentage of the original without significantly reducing the quality of the picture. For example, with compression technology, a color drawing that requires 10 megabytes or more of memory could be reduced to approximately 1 megabyte.

Data compression has created many applications for image databases, including picture inventory files for museums and insurance companies. Seng Jewelers of Louisville, Kentucky, uses an image database to maintain inventory control, provide a record of repairs done for clients (before-and-after pictures), and aid in appraisals. Databases of maps and satellite images use geographic information systems. Picture security systems are another application of image databases. Image databases in the real estate business allow prospective buyers to browse through full-color pictures of homes without leaving the confines of the office (see Figure 6-13).

Image databases require a video camera or graphics scanner, an image capture and compression circuit board that plugs into the computer, and the appropriate image database software.

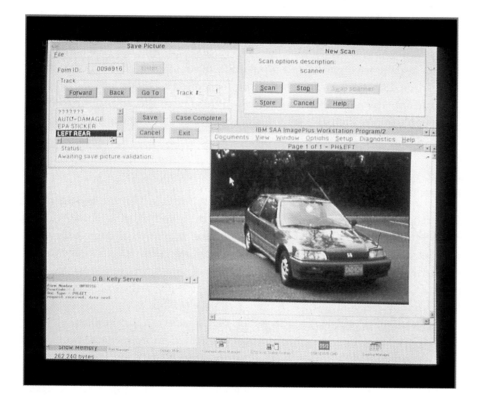

FIGURE 6-12
An image database allows the storage of both text and graphic images.

(Courtesy of International Business Machines Corp.)

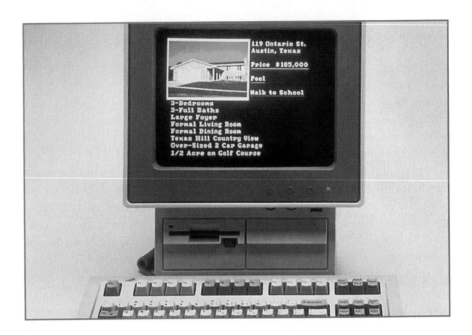

OBJECTIVE 6.10
Describe some special-purpose databases.

WHAT ARE SPECIAL-PURPOSE DATABASES?

The software programs discussed in previous sections are called general-purpose database programs. They are not set up for any particular use. The user defines the screen layouts and the types of data to be input. The format for a report is also designed by the user. Many applications require only some parts of the program.

Specialized database programs are just that—designed to fit a narrow field of use—for example, programs that are set up to use only as class lists for teachers, genealogy programs for cataloging family trees, and various financial databases. These programs usually have predefined input and output screens. The types of data that can be entered are limited. They may allow for limited modification.

Personal information managers (PIMS) are specialized programs that include applications such as your own address and phone number lists, appointment schedules, and to-do lists.

SUMMARY

The hierarchy of computer data organization, starting with the most general to the most specific is database, file, record, field, byte, and bit. A database is a cross-referenced collection of files designed to minimize repetition of data. A file is a collection of records that fit under one name or heading. A record is a collection of related data items. Each individual classification of data stored in the record is called a field. Each character in a field is represented internally to the computer as a byte. Each byte is composed of 8 bits.

The advantages of using a database are that it reduces data duplication, improves data integrity, maintains data independence, improves data security, maintains data consistency, allows powerful manipulation of data, and makes data easier to access and use.

A database management system (DBMS) is software that allows the creation, manipulation, and retrieval of data from a database. It acts as the interface among programs, users, and data in the database. The basic functions of a DBMS include creating the database, maintaining the records, organizing the data, querying a database, generating reports, and creating customized applications.

When creating a database you first need to define the problem, decide what information you want, and determine the data items needed to produce the desired output. The user should carefully defining the data structure, that is, telling the program how to create the fields in each record. The data structure is created using the database design screen. Screen forms can be designed to define the layout for entering data into a record.

A DBMS permits the user to update, add, and delete data in a database. It also allows for placing data in a specified order, through sorting or indexing.

Database management systems allow you to query the database, that is, make a request for information. This is done through the use of a database query language. Report generators let you define how the output appears when printed.

Database programming languages allow creation of customized applications to give control over input, processing, and output of data. Application generators take some of the details of coding the program off the user.

Database programs can be designed to work in single- or multiuser environments. In a file server architecture, the database program runs entirely on the user's system, and the network server merely stores the data files that are shared among the different users. In a client server architecture, the processing of an application is split between a "front-end" client and a "back-end" server. Using both the client and the server computers increases the processing power and improves the efficiency.

A relational database is composed of many tables in which data are stored. Tables in a relational database must have unique rows and cells with single values. The relational database management system (RDBMS) is the software that uses the relational database design. The two basic query styles used by a RDBMS are query by example and structured query language (SQL).

Security and validity are concerns to every user. Many database programs have built-in features that protect the integrity of the data and ensure the confidentiality of the data.

An image database is software that stores both pictures and text. Personal information managers (PIMs) are specialized programs that include applications such as address and phone number lists, appointment schedules, and to-do lists.

VOCABULARY SELF-TEST

Can you define the following?

application generator (p. 181)
browse mode (p. 177)
client server architecture (p. 182)
database (p. 171)
database design screen (p. 176)
database management system (DBMS)
(p. 173)
database programming language (p. 181)
database query language (p. 179)
edit mode (p. 177)
encryption (p. 184)

field (p. 172)
file (p. 171)
file-locking (p. 184)
image database (p. 185)
indexing (p. 179)
key fields (p. 176)
password (p. 184)
personal information manager (PIM)
(p. 186)
query (p. 179)
query by example (p. 182)
record (p. 171)

record-locking (p. 184)
relational database (p. 182)
relational database management system
(RDBMS) (p. 182)
report generator (p. 179)

screen form (p. 176)
sorting (p. 179)
structured query language (SQL) (p. 183)
updating (p. 176)
validating (p. 183)

REVIEW QUESTIONS

Multiple Choice

1. Which of the following is the correct hierarchy of data?
   a. file, database, record, field, byte, bit
   b. database, file, field, record, bit, byte
   c. database, file, record, field, byte, bit
   d. field, file, database, record, byte, bit

2. A librarian who wants to keep track of a special collection of books easily and efficiently would use _____.
   a. desktop publishing software
   b. database management software
   c. a word processor
   d. a scanner

3. TEXT and NUMERIC are different kinds of _____ that the user specifies before data are entered.
   a. design forms
   b. validation methods
   c. data managers
   d. data types

4. Updating, adding, and deleting are all types of _____ functions.
   a. maintenance
   b. retrieval
   c. utility
   d. security

5. Changing the contents of a record in a file is called _____.
   a. browsing
   b. updating
   c. indexing
   d. sorting

6. _____ is a data-organizing method where the reordered records are stored in their reordered sequence.
   a. Sorting
   b. Manipulating
   c. Ordering
   d. Indexing

7. A _____ is used to define how the output of a database management system will appear when printed.
   a. database programming language
   b. database query language
   c. report generator
   d. data structure

8. Which one of the following is a method of querying a database?
   a. DBMS
   b. SQL
   c. asking
   d. indexing

9. Checking to see if data fall within acceptable limits is called _____.
   a. range checking
   b. accuracy checking
   c. file-locking
   d. format checking

10. An image database differs from a text database because of its ability to store and retrieve _____.
    a. words
    b. data
    c. reports
    d. graphics

Fill In

1. A _____ is a cross-referenced collection of files.

2. Before data are entered into the database, the data _____ must be defined.

3. Fields specially designated to be used when retrieving data are called _____ fields.

4. A(n) _____ is created to define the layout for entering data into a record.

5. A(n) _____ is a request for information from a database.

6. In _____ the database management system displays field information and users enter inquiry conditions in the desired fields.

7. _____ is the standard database query language used with relational databases.

8. Format checking, range checking, and accuracy checking are all methods of _____ data entry.

9. _____ is a procedure that permits only one user to access a file at a time.

10. A type of database that incorporates pictures and text is called a(n) _____ database.

Short Answer

1. Briefly describe why it is important to organize computer data.

2. What are the advantages of a microcomputer database management system?

3. Why must care be taken when initially defining the data structure?

4. Describe the difference between the edit mode and the browse mode.

5. Contrast sorting and indexing.

6. Describe the two basic relational database query methods.

7. Describe the difference between file server and client server database architectures.

8. What is a validity check and describe three types of validity checks?

9. What can be done to ensure data confidentiality?

10. What is the importance of using compression technology with image databases?

Issues for Thought

1. Multiple-user databases increase the potential that an unauthorized user may gain access to sensitive or personal data. You've noticed that a coworker left a note out that contains the code and password required to access the payroll compensation data for your organization. Disclosure of compensation data often leads to tension and jealousy among workers and to poor performance by disgruntled employees. Given the possible consequences, how should this incident be treated? Should you talk directly to your coworker? Should you go straight to management? How should management react? How should your coworker react?

2. Databases are maintained by companies of their customers' names and addresses that may be subsequently sold to others. You probably have received unsolicited mail because of this practice. Discuss the benefits, drawbacks, and potential for misuse.

7

WORKING WITH NUMERIC DATA: THE SPREADSHEET AND OTHER USEFUL TOOLS

OBJECTIVES

7.1 Understand what spreadsheet software is.

7.2 Describe several benefits of spreadsheet software.

7.3 Explain several ways in which spreadsheet software is used.

7.4 Identify and summarize the basic functions of spreadsheet software.

7.5 Describe three additional features commonly integrated with spreadsheet programs.

7.6 Briefly describe the layout of a well-designed spreadsheet.

7.7 Describe other programs used for numeric manipulation.

PROFILE

Mitchell Kapor

How does a self-described "nerd" make it big in the world of entrepreneurship and business? Mitchell Kapor did it by combining an interest in personal consciousness, antiwar activism, and interdisciplinary study of linguistics, psychology, and computer science at Yale University.

After college, Kapor entered the working world as a stand-up comic, disk jockey, and teacher of transcendental meditation. Instead of following the usual path toward corporate success by earning an MBA degree, he took his master's in psychology and became a counselor in the psychiatric unit of a small hospital.

Still, Kapor, who grew up in a middle-class Brooklyn family, was on his way to becoming a multimillionaire. Kapor first veered toward computer entrepreneurship when he came across an Apple II. While at Yale, he had found that working with mainframe computers was extremely frustrating. This was not so with microcomputers; they were easy to use and program. Kapor was captivated. He began doing freelance programming in the BASIC language for other new owners of microcomputers. His first programming job was to create a small database of patient information for a doctor.

This simple beginning led Kapor to an alliance with Jonathan Sachs, a former Data General Corporation programmer. The two devised an electronic spreadsheet that was sophisticated enough to appeal to the business world, yet could be run on a microcomputer. The two developers called their program Lotus 1-2-3. Their spreadsheet, designed for the IBM personal computer and compatibles, could make projections, display results, and sort data. The documentation for Lotus was clear and concise, and the program did what it promised. Moreover, it was fast.

Lotus 1-2-3 revolutionized accounting on small computers in much the same way word processors changed writing with typewriters. Spreadsheet programs convinced the business community of the value of the relatively new microcomputer, and were the impetus that sent IBM PC sales soaring. With an alluring product, the powerful thrust of IBM's sales, and Kapor's expertise, all the elements for success were in place. First-year sales projections for Lotus were $3 million, but actual sales were $53 million.

Kapor resigned as chief executive officer of Lotus in 1986 to spend time with his family, to continue his study of linguistics at MIT, and to consult at Lotus. Kapor's "retirement" did not last long, however, because by 1988 he was involved in another enterprise—ON Technology, developing more software for information and communications in both groupware and hypertext applications. Then in 1990, Kapor backed yet another company—GO Corp. GO's primary product is a microcomputer that recognizes handwritten input.

The earliest methods that humans used to count items included tying knots in ropes and marking notches on sticks. Then came the abacus, a wooden frame with wires and beads for calculating. Gradually, as a numbering system developed, the paper and pencil approach started. Each item to be counted was assigned a number, and the numbers could be added, subtracted, multiplied, and divided. As time went on, a sophisticated means of tracking and managing these numbers was devised. For ease in manipulating the numbers and dollar amounts, paper was divided into rows and columns; the paper was called a *spreadsheet*.

Today, users equipped with microcomputers and spreadsheet software manipulate numbers in rows and columns faster, more accurately, and more reliably than ever before. Spreadsheet users—including small-business owners, teachers, students, and especially corporate accounting giants—are asking for, and getting, faster programs with even more capabilities, including a spreadsheet in three dimensions.

OBJECTIVE 7.1
Understand what spreadsheet software is.

WHAT IS SPREADSHEET SOFTWARE?

A spreadsheet is simply a means of tracking and manipulating numbers—organizing them into rows and columns. You may have seen paper spreadsheets similar to the one in Figure 7-1. Your checkbook ledger is also a type of spreadsheet. With the development and advancement of the computer and its capabilities, the paper spreadsheet was computerized. **Spreadsheet software** instructs the computer to manipulate rows and columns of numbers, make calculations, and evaluate algebraic formulas. Figure 7-2 illustrates an electronic version of the paper spreadsheet shown in Figure 7-1. Popular spreadsheet programs include Microsoft Excel and Lotus 1-2-3.

Early spreadsheet programs like VisiCalc were rather crude by today's standards, because they were severely limited in the volume and size of jobs that could be handled. But with more sophisticated hardware and software, programs improved to such an extent that most of today's computer spreadsheets allow at least 256 columns and as many as 32,766 rows, for a possible total of over 8 million spaces for entries. A paper spreadsheet of only 65 columns and 254 rows stretched out would be over 3 ½ feet long and more than 5 feet wide. Now consider that some spreadsheet programs allow as many as 32,000 columns and 32,000 rows—over 1 billion cells!

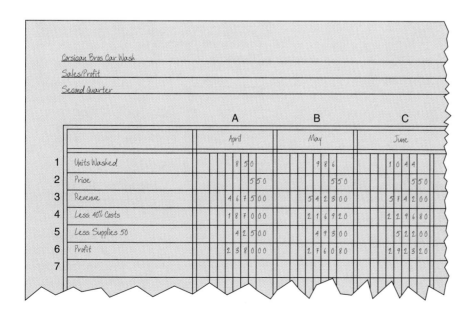

Corsican Bros Car Wash
Sales/Profit
Second Quarter

		A	B	C
		April	May	June
1	Units Washed	850	986	1044
2	Price	550	550	550
3	Revenue	467500	542300	574200
4	Less 40% Costs	187000	216920	229680
5	Less Supplies 50	42500	49300	52200
6	Profit	238000	276080	292320
7				

FIGURE 7-1
A paper spreadsheet.

Describe several benefits of spreadsheet software.

WHAT ARE THE BENEFITS OF A SPREADSHEET?

Spreadsheet processing is one of the most popular computer applications; it brings the shortcuts, speed, and accuracy to numerical functions that word processors bring to writing. Data are moved, copied, and deleted easily, eliminating messy erasures and the need for correction fluid.

One of the most powerful benefits of a spreadsheet is the speed and power with which the computer makes accurate calculations and recalculations. Because data in a spreadsheet are usually dependent on other data, changes made in one value often result in changes in related values. This requires time-consuming and tedious manual recalculation in a paper spreadsheet. Spreadsheet software provides automatic recalculation of all dependent values. You no longer have to worry about which values are dependent or how long or difficult it is to make all the changes manually. Simply enter a new value and the spreadsheet does the rest.

Like other applications, spreadsheet software provides you with reusable data. Recreating even relatively simple paper spreadsheets each month can take many hours to prepare the paper forms and handwrite the entries. Valuable time is wasted in rewriting the same column and row labels from month to month on blank paper forms. With spreadsheet software, a **template,** or blank form, that contains any standard information that doesn't change, can be created for the required report. You simply load the template, make minor modifications, as needed, and then enter your data.

Spreadsheet software often requires repetitive keystrokes or commands where the speed and power of the macro is especially useful. A **macro** is a file that contains a series of previously recorded keystrokes or commands that can be quickly executed with one or two keystrokes. In addition, the data in the spreadsheet can be used

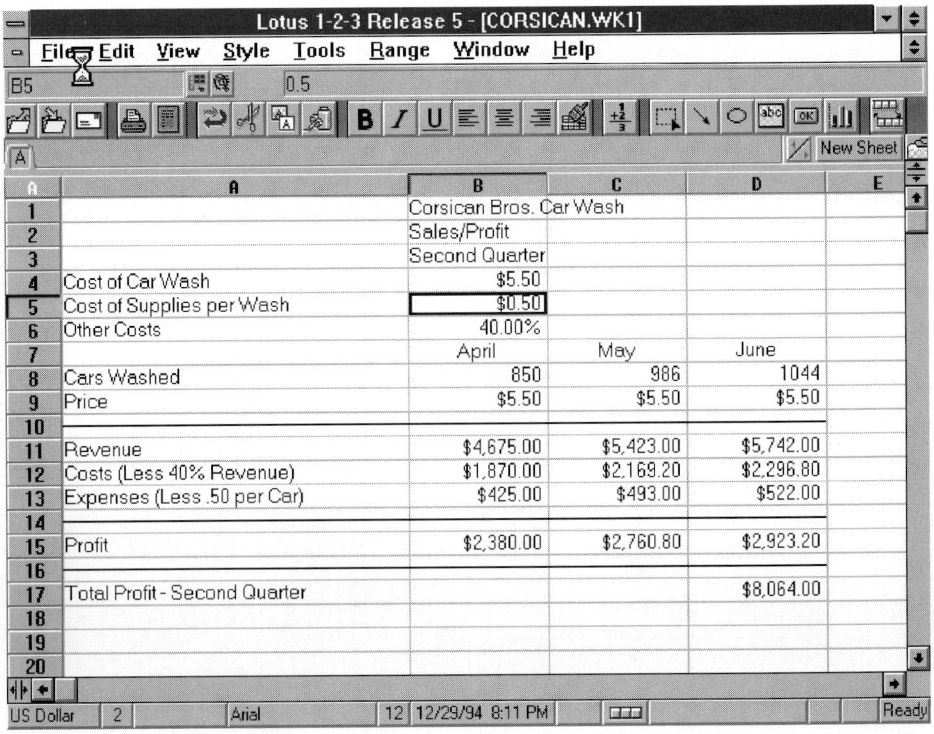

FIGURE 7-2
A screen of the paper spreadsheet as it appears when created electronically.

to create graphs and charts to represent the data visually. (Business and analytical graphics are discussed in Chapter 8.)

OBJECTIVE 7.3
Explain several ways in which spreadsheet software is used.

WHAT ARE SOME COMMON USES OF A SPREADSHEET?

A problem is a candidate for an electronic spreadsheet if it has the following characteristics:

- Can be written in mathematical terms
- Is repeated regularly
- Will be edited or revised
- Is made up of both variable and fixed information
- Must be neat and legible

Examples include periodic business reports, daily ledgers, individual tax information, and class grade sheets.

Businesspeople maintain important information, such as sales, expenses incurred, costs of doing business, inventory control, and projections of profits or losses using spreadsheet programs. They make sales forecasts, analyze competitors' statistics, compare discounts and markup costs, and prepare financial information, such as profit/loss statements and income statements for their banks (see Figure 7-3). For example, bankers use spreadsheets to track day-to-day monetary transactions, create loan amortization schedules, make interest rate computations, and evaluate potential customers' loans, among other tasks. Engineers and scientists store empirical data, perform statistical analyses, build complex graphs, and prepare complex mathematical models using spreadsheet programs. Individuals may use spreadsheets for tracking cash flow, preparing household budgets and personal financial statements, or figuring annual income taxes (Figure 7-4). A spreadsheet created in a table format could help students learn mathematical facts.

OBJECTIVE 7.4
Identify and summarize the basic functions of spreadsheet software.

WHAT ARE THE BASIC FUNCTIONS OF A SPREADSHEET?

Although the actual features of spreadsheets vary from program to program, they all perform basic functions that include creating and saving a worksheet, editing, formatting, manipulating, and printing a worksheet.

Creating and Saving a Worksheet

Figure 7-5 shows a **worksheet,** the name often given to a data file created by a spreadsheet program. Once data are entered, the power of the electronic spreadsheet can be demonstrated. The numbers down the left side of the screen constitute the **row** grid, and the alphabetic characters across the top of the worksheet represent the **column** grid. A combination of these grid labels identifies specific points on a worksheet. The point at which imaginary row and column grid lines intersect is the **coordinate,** or the address of that particular point. In Figure 7-5, coordinate A1 is the point where a line down column A intersects a line across row 1. The box formed by the imaginary lines at each coordinate is a **cell.** The highlighted box in Figure 7-6 is the **cell pointer;** it indicates the **active cell,** or "current" cell. The cell pointer's size changes to reflect the width of the column it is marking. A flashing dash within the cell pointer is the **cursor,** which indicates the beginning of the next entry.

Cells

- Imaginary row and column lines intersect at the coordinate
- Highlighted box formed by imaginary row and column lines is the cell pointer
- Cell pointer indicates the active cell or "current" cell
- Flashing dash inside the cell pointer is the cursor

FIGURE 7-3

The New York Stock Exchange is a busy place where trade decisions must be based on the latest data available. Computers play an important part in furnishing stockbrokers with the latest prices. This broker informs his client of late-breaking developments from data displayed on the screen in his office.

(Main photo: Preston Lyon/Index Stock, Inc.)

Parts of a worksheet

- The window, area where entries are displayed
  - Row grid, the numbers down the left side
  - Column grid, the alphabetic characters at the top
- The control panel and status line areas contain valuable information about activity on the worksheet.

The worksheet has two main parts: the **window,** the visual display area on the screen, and the **control panel** and **status line** areas, which provide valuable worksheet activity information.

The worksheet control panel often found at the top of the screen provides specific information about the worksheet, including the coordinates where the cursor is positioned, the cell width, whether the cell is protected from unauthorized change, and any contents or entry in the cell.

A status line may include other information about the worksheet. For example, in Lotus 1-2-3, the status line at the bottom of the screen in Figure 7-6, gives the current date and time, error messages and other status indicators such as NUM (number lock on), CAPS (all caps selected), or a prompt indicating that the worksheet should be recalculated.

Commands are generally selected from a main command menu. There are submenus listed under most menus because spreadsheets have several hundred or more commands from which to choose (see Figure 7-7). Usually, this is done by moving

FIGURE 7-4
An accounting student uses a laptop computer and a spreadsheet software program to complete classroom assignments at home.

FIGURE 7-5
The typical worksheet screen.

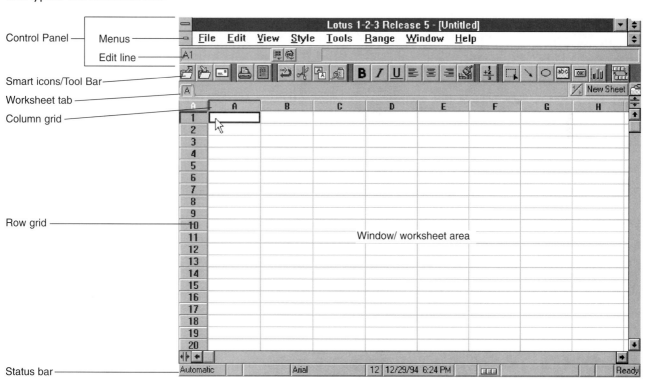

FIGURE 7-6
The cell B5 at column B, row 5 is the active cell.

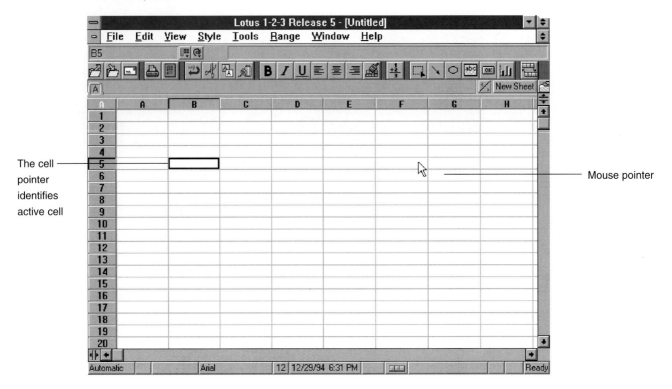

The cell pointer identifies active cell

Mouse pointer

FIGURE 7-7
Submenu selections under the main menu heading.

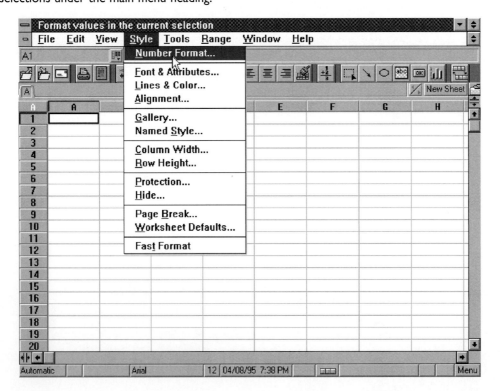

the cursor or mouse pointer to the desired option and selecting it. Sometimes commands are invoked by various keys or key combinations. Frequently used commands are often included in a Tool Bar or Button Bar for easy access. Icons can be used for quickly selecting those features, and the Tool Bars and Button Bars can generally be customized.

MOVING AROUND THE WORKSHEET. Because the window lets you see only a small portion of a worksheet at any time—approximately 80 spaces across and 20 lines down—you must scroll the cell pointer "off the screen" to view the rest of the worksheet. The cell pointer can be scrolled past the right-hand margin and below the bottom of the monitor screen.

The arrow keys move the cell pointer in the direction that the arrow points—for example, the down arrow moves the cell pointer downward one cell at a time. Using various keys and key combinations (such as Home, End, PgUp, PgDn), you can move the cursor over larger distances quickly instead of one cell or row at a time. The mouse lets you choose the appropriate cell by clicking on its coordinate. Another method of moving rapidly involves the "go to" feature, in which you designate the coordinate and, with appropriate keystrokes, move the cursor automatically to that particular cell. For example, to reach coordinate Z100, you could use arrow keys to scroll to the right 25 cells, and downward 99 cells, move the mouse directly to Z100 and click on it, or select a function key such as F5 and type Z100 to go directly to that coordinate.

DEFAULTS. Although default settings vary among spreadsheets, and can be reset by the user, some common ones are as follows:

- The columns are all the same width—they contain the same number of spaces.
- All entries that begin with a letter are left-justified in the cell.
- All entries that begin with a number are right-justified in the cell.
- The worksheet is automatically recalculated whenever a number is changed.
- Numbers appear without commas or beginning and ending zeros.

ENTERING LABELS, VALUES, AND FORMULAS. Different types of data are entered into the cells. You must know the type of data because the computer views entries based on identifying characteristics. The three types of entries are labels, values, and formulas.

A **label** is text that identifies some aspect of the spreadsheet—Figure 7-8(a). A label placed at the top of the worksheet to indicate the contents might appear like this:

Bookcase Company
Profit and Loss Statement
for the period January to March

Other entries that require labels include the column and row headings, and any other words or text required to identify or clarify the spreadsheet information. Some programs automatically recognize any entry that begins with an alphabetic character or certain special characters as a label. Many programs include an **automatic spillover** option; if the cell label is too long to fit the column width, the text continues on, or spills over, into the next cell. If a label begins with numbers or other special characters that normally indicate a value, for example, a street address or a year, specific keystrokes are required to tell the computer that the entry is a label, and not a value.

A **value** is a constant that can be entered by itself into a cell or as part of a formula. In Figure 7-8(b) the upper left of the screen indicates that the value 5.5 is entered in cell B4. **Formulas** are the mathematical equations entered into the spreadsheet program to perform calculations. Formulas may contain constants, cell references that do not contain labels, built-in functions, or range names.

> **Cell entries**
>
> - Labels
> - Values
> - Formulas

A cell reference refers to the contents in another cell. For example, if cell B3 contained the value 200 a formula created in cell D10 could use that value by referencing the cell address as follows: +B3 * .15. This formula commands the spreadsheet to multiply the value found in cell B3 by the constant .15.

In Figure 7-8(c), the formula @SUM (B15..D15) is found in cell D17. The computer understands that the entry in that cell is the total of cells B15, C15, and D15. Therefore, $8064.00 appears in the cell, but the formula (not the total) for the cell entry is shown above the input line. The computer completes the calculation and enters the result where specified.

A special character entry is usually required to identify a cell reference that begins a formula as a value and not a label. The plus sign (+) character is a common example, used to indicate that the entry following it is a value, not a label. The entry in cell D17 begins with the built-in function SUM. To indicate that the entry is a formula, it should be preceded by the appropriate keystrokes—in this case an @ sign. In some programs, you toggle, or switch, between label and value entries just by using certain keys.

BUILT-IN FUNCTIONS. Most spreadsheets have **built-in functions** where formulas for solutions to certain standard problems have already been created and stored in the program. Typical functions include mathematical, statistical, financial, date, string, logical, and tabular. Table 7-1 describes these built-in functions. Most spreadsheets have dozens of built-in functions, and their names vary from program to program. The spreadsheet reference manual and on-line help provided with the software explain the functions offered by a particular spreadsheet. Common built-in functions include SUM, AVG, and MAX, which respectively total, find the average, and determine the maximum value in a list of numbers. They are usually identified to the program as functions, not labels by a symbol, such as the @ sign.

DEFINING AND NAMING A RANGE OF CELLS. Designating a **range of cells** is a method of selecting specific contiguous cells. The range can consist of only one cell or two

FIGURE 7-8

The cell pointer is positioned to show (a) an example of a label entry, (b) an example of a number entry, and (c) an example of a formula entry.

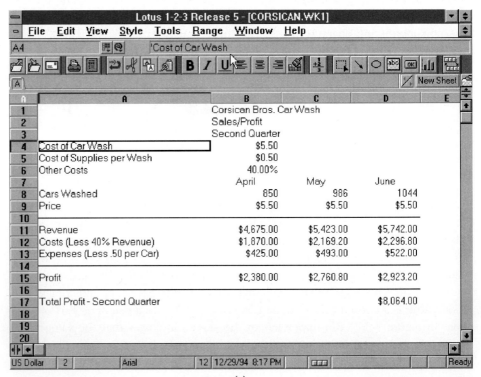

(a)

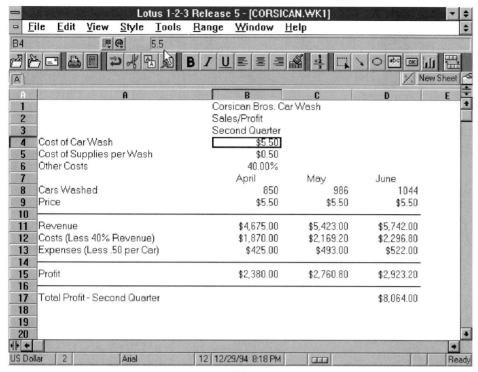

(b)

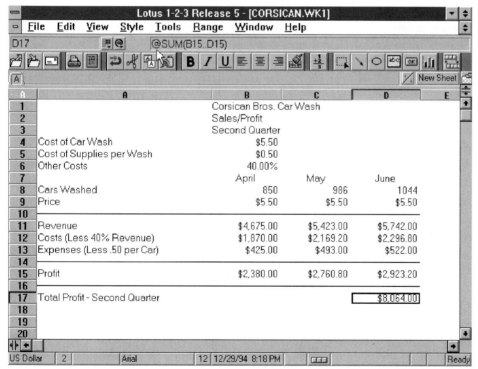

(c)

Table 7-1 Built-in functions

Mathematical function	Performs a mathematical transformation on a single value and returns a single value—for example, a SQRT(x) determines the square root of a value.
Statistical function	Accepts a list of values and provides summary statistics about those values (for example, an average function returns the average value from a list).
Financial function	Calculates the effect of interest rates on sums of money over time (for example, a payment function calculates the payment that will pay off the principal of a loan borrowed at the specified interest rate after the specified number of payments have been made).
Date function	Calculates with dates and times (for example, it can automatically enter the date and time in a report).
String function	Performs operations on text (for example, a length function indicates the number of characters in a string).
Logical function	Tests the condition of cells or performs comparisons to determine what value should be entered in a cell (for example, an IF function enters one value in the cell if the condition is true and another value in the cell if the condition if false).
Table function	Retrieves an entry from a table (for example, a "value look-up" function can search an income tax table that has been entered into the spreadsheet to find a specific number).

or more cells. A designated range can be copied, moved, deleted, saved, printed, or otherwise treated as a unit. This feature is a time-saving device when a large worksheet is in use.

A range of cells can be named for ease in identification. Going back to Figure 7-8(b), the cell containing the cost of the car wash (B4) could be named COST. Then, the formula at cell C11 for finding the revenue could be stated as the number of cars washed times the cost, or +850 * COST.

Named ranges simplify a formula and make it more readable and understandable. The following formula calculates the total royalty payable on sales recorded in cells D4 to D10, applying the royalty rate stored in cell B4.

@SUM(D4:D10)*B4

The range D4 to D10 could be named SALES, and the value in cell B4 could be named ROYALTYRATE (see Figure 7-9). These named ranges could be used in the formula as follows:

@SUM(SALES)*ROYALTYRATE

ORDER OF CALCULATION. Most spreadsheet programs solve the formulas that are entered using the normal order of mathematical operations. That is, they assume that operations enclosed in parentheses are done first, exponentiation next, then multiplication and division before addition and subtraction.

Normally, if operators are of equal precedence, the evaluation is from left to right. For instance, by default the problem 10 + 10/2 will be calculated as 10 divided by 2 = 5; then the addition is completed (10 plus 5 = 15). This problem solved left to right would be 10 + 10 = 20 divided by 2 = 10.

SAVING A WORKSHEET. The Save feature stores a worksheet on secondary storage. You can then recall the file at a later time and continue working or editing that particular worksheet.

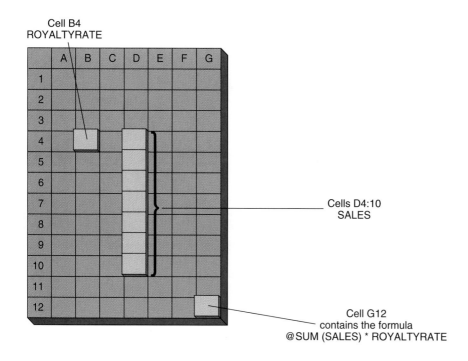

Cell B4
ROYALTYRATE

Cells D4:10
SALES

Cell G12
contains the formula
@SUM (SALES) * ROYALTYRATE

FIGURE 7-9
Named ranges can be used in a formula to make it more readable and easier to understand.

The Exit feature quits a worksheet without saving. An existing worksheet can be loaded and changed and then exited without overriding the original data stored on the worksheet. In some cases you may want to create a duplicate, or second copy, and save it under a different name in order to protect the values in the original. You could do this using the Save As feature.

Retrieve or Open are typical spreadsheet commands that access an existing worksheet that has been saved. You select the Retrieve command or its equivalent from a menu, and enter the name of the desired worksheet or select it from a list.

Editing a Worksheet

From time to time you may need to update or change a worksheet to fix a typographical error, an incorrect value, or an erroneous formula. To avoid inaccurate results, you should always carefully check the entries; never assume they are correct. Labels, values, and formulas can be easily edited or updated by either completely retyping the entry for a cell and reentering it or using the edit mode to correct specific characters in an entry.

However, changing a value or formula often affects numerous other dependent cells in a worksheet. Most spreadsheets have an **automatic recalculation** feature as a default, which automatically recalculates the entire worksheet after a new figure is entered. This ability to quickly edit and recalculate a worksheet is the basis for one of the spreadsheet's most powerful uses—the "what-if" analysis.

What-if analysis involves changing entries on a worksheet, viewing the outcome, and comparing it to the original worksheet to determine the effect. It allows you to see how an increase or decrease in one or more entries affects the end result. Be sure to keep a copy of the original plan for comparison. For example, what if you decided to buy a used car at a certain price: how would that choice affect other areas of the budget, such as car insurance, loan payments, automobile repair expenses, and other living expenses? What if you buy this year's model instead, and the payments are higher? A spreadsheet analyzes the effects on all these areas so that the purchase can be more closely evaluated (see Figure 7-10). In addition to calculating set data values to arrive at a total, the opposite can be done.

FIGURE 7-10
Here spreadsheet software is being used to analyze long-range effects before making important business decisions.

Sometimes called backsolving, the user sets a target value, such as the total sales of a department, and recalculates to show the sales each salesperson must make to reach that target.

Formatting a Worksheet

The **format** process includes various instructions and techniques that change how the contents of the cells are displayed. Format changes are made in one of two ways: (1) globally, which affects the entire worksheet, or (2) individually, which affects a particular cell or range of cells.

ATTRIBUTES. The characteristics or formatting commands available in most spreadsheets are called **attributes.** Attribute commands

- Change column widths
- Set precision of numbers (the number of decimal places)
- Set justification (left, centered, or right)
- Determine number formats, that is, how the number appears (some number format choices are shown in Table 7-2)
- Establish character attributes (boldface, underline, italics)
- Set data types (text or value)
- Change how negative values appear—in parentheses, or preceded by DB (debit) or CR (credit), or in red
- Lock cells (prevent cell entries from being changed)
- Hide cells (the cell contents are not displayed on screen).

TITLES. The **titles** feature freezes rows or columns so they stay in the window when the rest of the worksheet is scrolled regardless of which row or column of the worksheet is being viewed. This feature is especially helpful when there are many rows and columns of numbers to scroll through and review. When the titles scroll off the window, it is difficult to remember what the numbers represent.

INSERT AND DELETE ROWS/COLUMNS. One formatting choice that improves readability is inserting or deleting blank rows and columns. Adding rows increases the space between headings and numbers in the spreadsheet. To add an entire row, for example, the underline or other character can be inserted by first creating a blank

Table 7-2 Common Number Format Choices

Integer	Whole Number
Dollar	Dollar sign ($) and two decimal places
Floating point	Decimal point followed by specified number of places
Expotential	Scientific notation
Commas	Numbers displayed with commas
Leading $	Leading dollar sign ($) placed before any other format
Percent	Displayed using a percent (%) sign
Foreign currency	Displayed using foreign currency symbol, such as DM for Deutsche marks (German money)

row and then filling it with a repeating character. New columns or rows can be created to accommodate entries not originally planned, such as when a company adds a new product line. Figure 7-11 shows a spreadsheet before adding some formatting instructions. Figure 7-12 shows the same spreadsheet after formatting.

Manipulating a Worksheet

Electronic spreadsheets have many features that make them more efficient than paper spreadsheets. For example, portions of a spreadsheet can be moved or copied and mathematical formulas are all recalculated by the computer. Spreadsheet features allow you to present and manipulate values in many ways. We'll look at some features in the paragraphs that follow.

COPYING. The copy feature selects an existing cell (or range of cells) and replicates it in another cell(s) of the worksheet. To copy labels or values, simply identify both the range of cells to be copied and the range of cells into which they are to be copied.

Copying formulas is a bit more involved. Sometimes you will want exactly the same formula using exactly the same cell references in both places. In this case, the computer

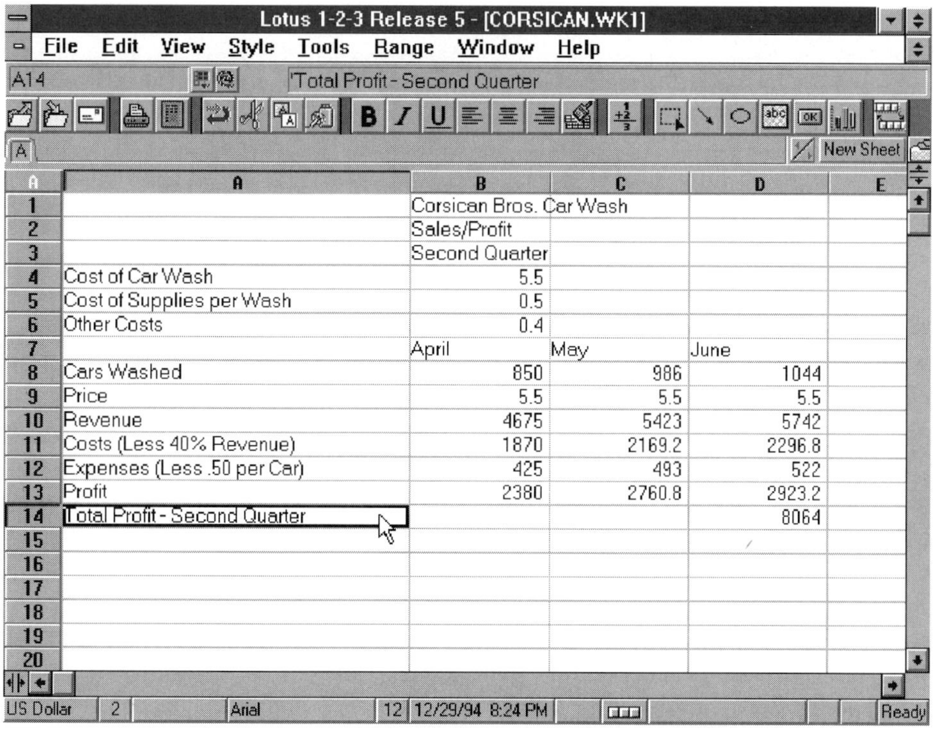

FIGURE 7-11
A spreadsheet before formatting.

FIGURE 7-12
A spreadsheet after formatting.

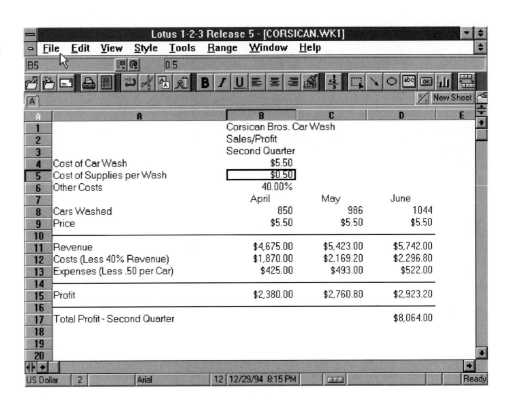

Copying formulas

- Absolute cell reference
- Relative cell reference
- Mixed cell reference

must be instructed to copy the formula using **absolute cell reference.** For example, if the formula in cell D1 in Figure 7-13(a) is copied to cell D2 using absolute cell reference, it appears exactly the same and evaluates in both instances to 10 (i.e., 5 + 5).

Usually, however, you will want a similar calculation but different cell references. Then, you instruct the computer to copy the formula using **relative cell reference.** For example, if the formula in cell D1 of Figure 7-13(b) is copied to cell D2 using relative cell reference, it changes to B2 + C2 and evaluates to 6 (i.e., 3 + 3).

There may also be times when you want some references in the same formula to be relative and others to be absolute. In that case, you instruct the computer to copy the formula, using **mixed cell reference.** Each cell reference is specified as either absolute or relative. For example, if the formula in cell D1 in Figure 7-13(c) is copied to cell D2 using relative cell reference for cell B1 and absolute cell reference for cell C1, the formula in cell D2 will be B2 + C1, which evaluates to 8 (i.e., 3 + 5).

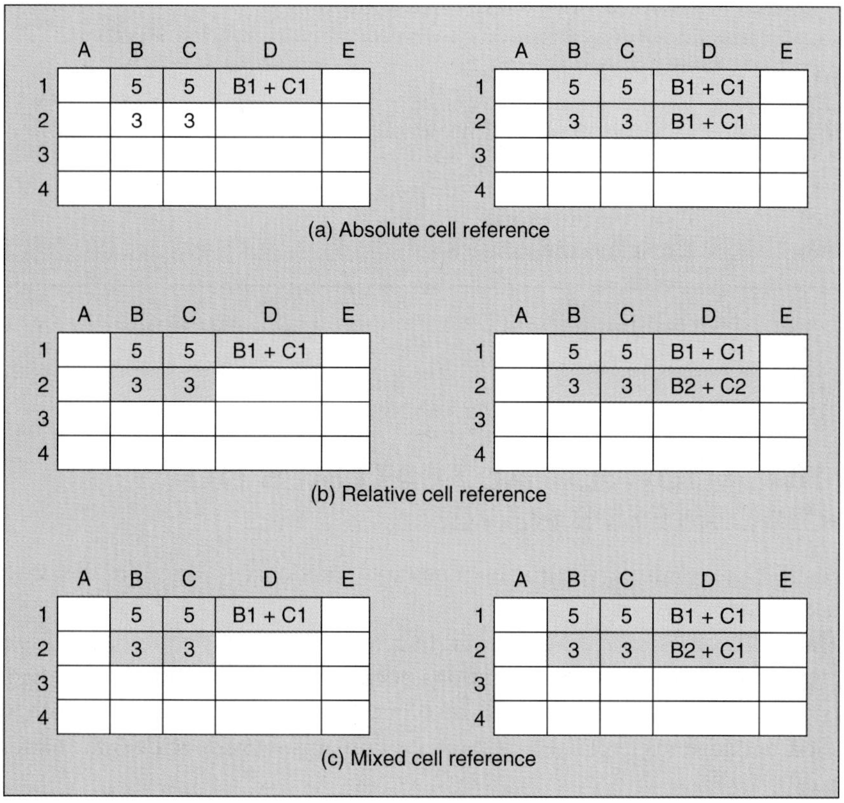

FIGURE 7-13
Cell references: (a) absolute, (b) relative, and (c) mixed.

(a) Absolute cell reference

(b) Relative cell reference

(c) Mixed cell reference

MOVING. The move feature allows repositioning the contents of individual cells or ranges of cells from one location to another. You can redesign the appearance or layout of the spreadsheet. When a range of cells is moved, any formula in the spreadsheet that will be affected by the move must be corrected. If the contents of cell B2 is moved to cell B10, and the formula in cell E2 is 2 * B2, then the formula will have to be edited to 2 * B10. You need to be aware of these potential problems when moving cells.

SORTING. Many spreadsheets sort information by rows or columns, alphabetically or numerically. You can arrange the spreadsheet in date order, organize in ascending or descending dollar amounts, and so on.

LINKING. Changing data in one spreadsheet often necessitates a change in another spreadsheet. Spreadsheets can be linked for use at the same time. This results in a typical 2-D worksheet becoming a 3-D or multidimensional. A **multidimensional spreadsheet** helps you visualize spreadsheet cells as solids having three dimensions, rows, columns, and depth. This 3-D capability helps users divide large applications into more manageable units, consolidate information from many separate spreadsheets, create a centralized database, and summarize results on multiple worksheets that have identical layouts.

Printing a Worksheet

Printing produces a hard (paper) copy. You usually access a special print menu, and then indicate the size of paper, number of copies, and margin parameters. The row-and-column grid designation lines can be deleted at this point to give a more formal appearance.

A printer that accommodates paper wider than the 8 ½-inch standard is often desirable. Some programs print sideways, that is, across the length of the paper, thereby offering more space to print additional columns side by side.

Table 7-3 Database Functions

DAVG	Computes the average
DCOUNT	Counts the nonblank cells
DMAX	Indicates the largest number
DMIN	Indicates the smallest number
DSTD	Computes the standard deviation
DSUM	Computes the total
DVAR	Computes the variance

OBJECTIVE 7.5
Describe three additional features commonly integrated with spreadsheet programs.

WHAT ADDITIONAL FEATURES DO SPREADSHEETS HAVE?

Spreadsheet programs vary, but some common additional features are described in the next sections.

GRAPHING. The data entered and saved in a worksheet can be the basis for generating graphics—pictorial representations such as pie charts, line charts, and bar charts. The data to be graphed must be identified, the type of graph chosen, titles specified, and legends explained. (Chapter 8 contains more specific information on graphics.)

DATABASE. You may want to analyze the data; for example, compute the average, count cells, find the largest and smallest number, determine standard deviation, find the sum, and discover the variance. To accomplish this easily, the worksheet data may be set up as a database. Each row is equivalent to a record and each cell, a field. Typical database functions are listed in Table 7-3. Each item listed is preceded by the letter "D" to indicate that it is a database function.

DESKTOP PUBLISHING. Many spreadsheet programs are integrated with desktop publishing features that allow for the production of high-quality reports. You can print using a wide variety of fonts; add emphasis with lines, boxes, shades, and colors; and incorporate graphs into a report.

OBJECTIVE 7.6
Briefly describe the layout of a well-designed spreadsheet.

WHAT ARE THE CHARACTERISTICS OF A WELL-DESIGNED SPREADSHEET?

Of course, merely loading spreadsheet software into a computer cannot guarantee either the accuracy or effectiveness of any spreadsheet you create. It must be organized logically so that changes in one part will not adversely affect other parts. The most obvious characteristic of a well-designed spreadsheet is that it accomplishes the goal(s) for which it was designed. It must also exhibit the characteristics of accuracy, readability, and consistency. An accurate spreadsheet is free of errors in both the source data and the formulas.

The readability of a spreadsheet is determined by how easily a user ascertains a spreadsheet's purpose, assumptions, and any important information about the values and formulas in the spreadsheet. Factors that affect readability include the visual appearance, the organization of the content, the length of the words and sentences used, the complexity, and how well it takes into account the knowledge and needs of its users. A spreadsheet makes consistent use of design elements such as using standardized terminology in headings, labels, and documentation. Careful planning before entering data into the program ensures that your spreadsheet will exhibit these characteristics.

Spreadsheet design refers to the way the values, labels, and formulas are arranged in the rows and columns of a spreadsheet. The design has much to do with its success, and some time spent planning up front can save headaches later. Two basic methods for spreadsheet design are a free-form approach or a structured-block design approach.

As its name suggests, in a **free-form approach** values, labels, and formulas are entered without any preplanned structure. This approach is often employed by people who are learning how to use a spreadsheet program. The free-form approach can be useful for small spreadsheets where the data are not changed and the developer is the only user.

However, as spreadsheets grow larger and more complex, and as the number of users grows, a **structured-block design approach** improves the design, understandability, and usefulness of the spreadsheet, because the design is planned in advance.

Block design involves defining and positioning a number of blocks of cells, each with a specific purpose. The blocks are positioned to meet the objectives of a particular spreadsheet. Some common blocks used are documentation, input, calculation, output, and macro. When using the block design method or creating large and complex spreadsheets, you will want to first sketch it on paper. Figure 7-14 shows a block design.

DOCUMENTATION BLOCK. The **documentation block** supplies information about a spreadsheet, but it does not contain the actual data. It is typically located at the upper left corner so that it is immediately available when the spreadsheet is loaded. Basic documentation that is helpful includes the title, the filename under which it is saved, the date it was prepared, the date of the last revision, the name of the person who developed it, and the name of the user or users. Documentation is important even if it is only for your own use.

Spreadsheet blocks

- Documentation
- Input
- Calculation
- Output
- Macro

INPUT BLOCK. The **input block** is that portion of the spreadsheet set up to contain variable data used in formulas. For example, the interest rate and loan amounts that change are entered into cells in the input block. Formulas that use these values refer to the cell address where the data are contained. When the data change, you change only one cell in the input block instead of locating and changing every formula that contains those data.

CALCULATION BLOCK. The **calculation block** is the area of the spreadsheet that includes formulas and fixed data. It may consist of one block, or it may be divided into several blocks each serving a particular function. For example, the calculation block for a financial statement spreadsheet may be divided into separate calculation blocks for the balance sheet, income statement, and retained earnings statement. Fixed data are unlikely to change and are therefore included here rather than in the input block. Formulas that perform calculations are also found in this block. The entries here should all be clearly identified with row and column labels to identify the contents of the cells and show the relationships among them.

OUTPUT BLOCK. The **output block** is the portion of a spreadsheet where the results of the calculations are displayed. In a free-form approach, the results of calculations may be displayed in many places. Even when the results are arranged in an orderly

FIGURE 7-14
A block design for a spreadsheet.

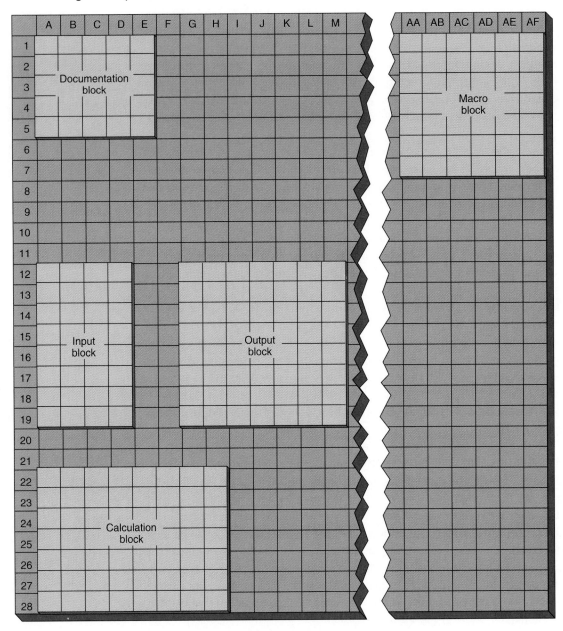

and consistent style under the columns, they may be difficult to find and read. An output block allows you to summarize the output in one place. It is generally near the input block so results from changes can be readily seen. You don't have to look through the entire spreadsheet to find those changes.

MACRO BLOCK. Macros automate various operations such as printing portions of a spreadsheet. The **macro block** is the portion of the spreadsheet where the macros are located. It should be placed in a part of the spreadsheet that will not be affected by changes made elsewhere. Two common locations are in the far right columns as far away from the input and calculation blocks as possible or in the top left immediately following the documentation block. Each line of a macro should be documented with a comment line. You should also include information in the documentation block about the location, purpose, and any cautions about the use of the macro.

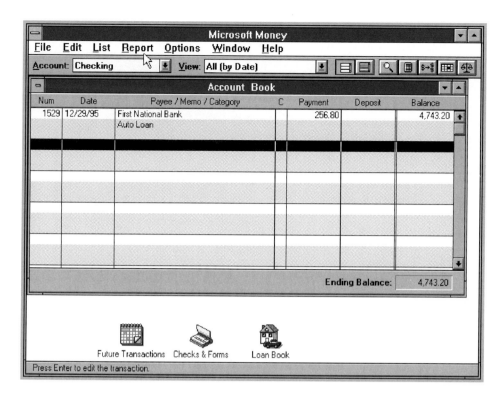

FIGURE 7-15
Microsoft Money checkbook
page.

OBJECTIVE 7.7
Describe other programs used for numeric manipulation.

WHAT ARE OTHER POPULAR NUMERIC MANIPULATION SOFTWARE?

Spreadsheet software does not fit every situation involving numeric manipulation. Other number-crunching software includes accounting, personal finance managers, data analysis, and data modeling.

Accounting

Spreadsheet software is not designed to handle all the complex modern-day accounting needs of many businesses. **Accounting software** is designed specifically to manage more complex financial transactions in greater volume than ordinary spreadsheet software. Accounting software must reflect any change in one account to all other accounts that pertain to that transaction. This could be hundreds or even thousands of accounts. Accounting software is also designed to keep historical records of each transaction, which allows for future auditing.

Personal Finance Managers

Personal financial managers offer users a computerized checkbook, savings account, and loan account in addition to many other specialized programs (see Figure 7-15). According to the 1994 Consumer Technology Index Survey, personal finance software is second in use to entertainment in the home computer market. Microsoft Money and Quicken are popular personal financial managers (see Figure 7-16). With financial managers, you track your investments and determine the amount of money needed to reach a particular goal, such as putting a child through college or preparing for retirement. Many personal finance managers offer on-line bill paying. Tax preparation software is a very popular type of financial management program. The user electronically files tax returns and sends them off to the Internal Revenue Service.

Number-crunching software
• Accounting
• Personal financial managers
• Data analysis
• Data modeling

FIGURE 7-16
Microsoft Money check.

Data Analysis

Like spreadsheet software, data analysis programs are used to perform numeric calculations. However, many of the data analysis programs handle much more math-intensive operations. Engineers and scientists perform analysis by looking at data and how they vary under different situations. Exponentials, differentials, integrals, and complex geometry are mathematical functions common to these programs. The key to math programs such as Mathcad or Mathmatica is the ability to represent a math-

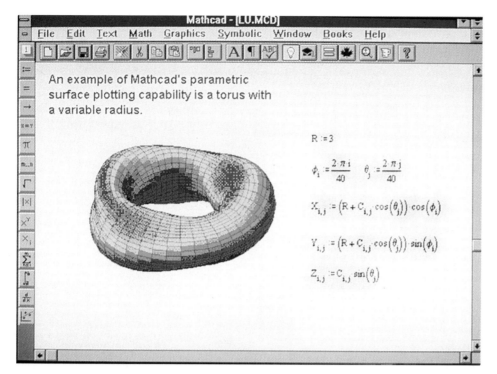

An example of Mathcad's parametric surface plotting capability is a torus with a variable radius.

$$R := 3$$

$$\phi_i := \frac{2 \cdot \pi \cdot i}{40} \qquad \theta_j := \frac{2 \cdot \pi \cdot j}{40}$$

$$X_{i,j} := \left(R + C_{i,j} \cdot \cos\left(\theta_j\right)\right) \cdot \cos\left(\phi_i\right)$$

$$Y_{i,j} := \left(R + C_{i,j} \cdot \cos\left(\theta_j\right)\right) \cdot \sin\left(\phi_i\right)$$

$$Z_{i,j} := C_{i,j} \cdot \sin\left(\theta_j\right)$$

FIGURE 7-17
A Mathcad screen showing a graphic representation of mathematical equations.
(Courtesy of Mathcad ® PLUS 5.0, copyright 1994. Printed with permission from MathSoft, Inc.)

ematical equation graphically. Some mathematical relationships are easier for scientists to interpret when they can be "seen." The results of an analysis can be presented in 2-D or 3-D. With some of these programs, you can integrate the graphs with text and use mathematical notation (see Figure 7-17).

Statistical analysis software tests for relationships among two or more variables (see Figure 7-18). This software is used in various applications from forecasting employment trends to weather analysis. During hurricane season you may see the National Weather Service show probable land strikes for a particular storm. While statistics are not 100 percent accurate, they are often helpful in predicting general trends.

Data Modeling

To **model** means to use mathematics to describe a situation or a physical object. Spreadsheet programs are used to model financial and other business-related data. These models then predict the fiscal health of the company or help determine future development plans.

Physical modeling uses mathematical formulas to manipulate numeric data into shapes. **Simulation** is the ability to imitate an object or process and to make it respond to different situations as if it were real. One common application is training pilots. Flight simulators give a realistic view and feel of takeoff and landing.

Computer simulation software is often used by scientists and engineers to test objects, such as a new bridge design. The bridge can be tested under various load and weather conditions and checked for stress-related problems. This can also be done to existing objects as well. Engineers in San Francisco modeled the Golden Gate Bridge and subjected it to an 8.3 magnitude earthquake. This simulation showed which parts of the bridge needed reinforcements.

Computer simulations allow different models to be tested safely, economically, and repeatedly rather than constructing the actual model. Simulations can be created to represent anything from the size of subatomic particles to entire galaxies.

FIGURE 7-18
Statistical program such as
STATGRAPHICS graphically displays the relationships among
two or more variables.

(Courtesy of Manugistics, Inc.)

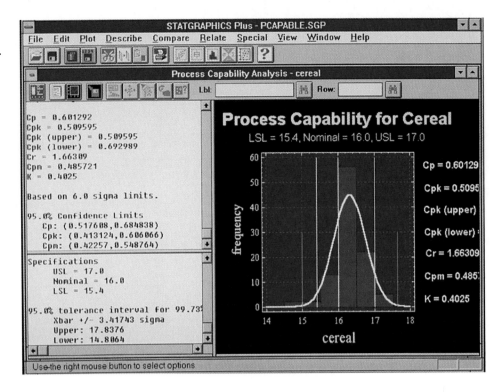

Visualization software allows researchers to "see" what may not be readily visible. At the Scripps Research Institute, the molecular biology department is using visualization software and other programs to visualize and study molecules interacting with proteins. This research will aid the development of new drugs to fight disease. Scientists in the AIDS Vaccine Program use molecular modeling and image technology to study how cells become infected with HIV.

Computer modeling can be fun and games, too. Entertainment software lets you build and manage cities and fight wars on battlefields, some of which are found in deep 3-D outer space.

SUMMARY

A spreadsheet is a tool that is used to track and manipulate rows and columns of numbers. Spreadsheet software uses a computer and special programs to do those same manipulations faster, more accurately, and more reliably than paper spreadsheets.

Spreadsheet software makes editing and recalculating easier. It provides the ability to easily perform "what-if" analyses, develop reusable templates, and create graphs and charts to view data visually.

A spreadsheet is appropriate if the problem can be stated in a mathematical format, and if the problem is to be repeated, edited, revised, made up of both variable and fixed data, and required to be neat and legible.

Worksheet is a name given to a data file created by a spreadsheet program. The numbers down the left side are the row grid and the alphabetic characters across the top are the column grid. At the intersection of an imaginary line drawn from any point on each grid lies the coordinate, or the address of a point on the worksheet. The box thus formed is called a cell. The cell pointer identifies the cell that is available for use called the active cell or current cell, which contains the cursor, the flashing dash.

The worksheet display on a computer monitor includes the window (where entries are displayed) and the control panel and status line areas (where useful information about the worksheet is typically displayed). There are three types of entries: labels, values, and formulas.

Spreadsheets include built-in functions containing solutions to commonly encountered problems. Most spreadsheets have dozens of built-in functions that offer shortcuts; users do not have to write formulas for these built-in functions.

A range of cells can be selected to be edited or acted upon; it may be one cell or a specified portion of the spreadsheet. Naming a cell or a range of cells offers ease in identification when the range is moved from one place on the spreadsheet to another, copied, or specified for use in a calculation.

Mathematical operations are performed following standard rules of operation, that is, values in parentheses, exponentiation, multiplication and division, addition and subtraction.

The Save feature stores a worksheet on a disk while the Exit feature quits a worksheet without saving. Typographical errors and wrong values are corrected by editing the spreadsheet.

Formatting, or changing the look of the worksheet, is accomplished globally or on a range of cells.

Data entered into a worksheet are easily manipulated by copying, moving, sorting, and editing cell entries and recalculating formulas. Formulas that are created can be copied to other cells, but they must be referenced in one of three ways: absolute cell reference, relative cell reference, or mixed cell reference.

A worksheet is printed so that a hard copy of the information can be distributed and used.

Spreadsheet software is often integrated with graphing, database, and desktop publishing functions.

Spreadsheet design refers to the way the values, labels, and formulas are arranged in the rows and columns of a spreadsheet. Block design involves defining and positioning a number of blocks of cells, each with a specific purpose. Some blocks used are: documentation, input, calculation, output, and macro.

Spreadsheet software does not fit every situation involving numeric manipulation. Other number-crunching software includes accounting, personal finance managers, data analysis, and data modeling.

Can you define the following?

absolute cell reference (p. 206)
accounting software (p. 211)
active cell (p. 195)
attributes (p. 204)
automatic recalculation (p. 203)
automatic spillover (p. 199)
block design (p. 209)
built-in functions (p. 200)
calculation block (p. 209)
cell (p. 195)
cell pointer (p. 195)
column (p. 195)
control panel (p. 196)
coordinate (p. 195)
cursor (p. 195)
documentation block (p. 209)
format (p. 204)
formulas (p. 199)
free-form approach (p. 209)
input block (p. 209)

label (p. 199)
macro (p. 194)
macro block (p. 210)
mixed cell reference (p. 206)
model (p. 213)
multidimensional spreadsheet (p. 207)
output block (p. 209)
personal financial managers (p. 211)
range of cells (p. 200)
relative cell reference (p. 206)
row (p. 195)
simulation (p. 213)
spreadsheet design (p. 209)
spreadsheet software (p. 193)
status line (p. 196)
structured-block design approach (p. 209)
template (p. 194)
titles (p. 204)
value (p. 199)
what-if analysis (p. 203)
window (p. 196)
worksheet (p. 195)

REVIEW QUESTIONS

Multiple Choice

1. A _____ is software that manipulates rows and columns of numbers.
   a. database management system
   b. word processor
   c. design program
   d. spreadsheet program

2. The numbers at the left of a worksheet screen are the _____.
   a. control panel
   b. row grid
   c. column grid
   d. cell coordinates

3. A data file created by a spreadsheet program is called a _____.
   a. database
   b. document
   c. template
   d. worksheet

4. A _____ is the text that identifies various aspects of the worksheet.
   a. label
   b. value
   c. cell
   d. formula

5. Which of the following cannot be contained in a formula?
   a. labels
   b. cell coordinate
   c. built-in functions
   d. constants

6. Changing entries on a worksheet, viewing the outcome, and comparing it to the original worksheet to determine the effect is called _____.
   a. "what-if" analysis
   b. exiting
   c. manual recalculation
   d. creating a template

7. _____ features change the look of the worksheet or make it more understandable.
   a. Scrolling
   b. Editing
   c. Formatting
   d. Windowing

8. Selecting specific contiguous cells in a worksheet is known as _____.
   a. setting defaults
   b. entering a label
   c. defining a range
   d. designating titles

9. Which of the following blocks is used to enter variable data into a spreadsheet?
   a. documentation block
   b. calculation block
   c. input block
   d. macro block

10. Formulas and fixed data are included in the _____ block.
   a. macro
   b. input
   c. documentation
   d. calculation

Fill In

1. A worksheet form containing standard information that doesn't change and can be called to the screen where new data are entered is known as a(n) _____.

2. When referring to cell B3, "B" refers to the _____ and "3" refers to the _____.

3. The _____ is the flashing symbol inside the cell pointer; it indicates the position where the next character typed will appear or the next entry will occur in a worksheet.

4. SUM, SIN, and MAX are examples of _____ functions in a spreadsheet program.

5. _____ , _____ , and _____ are the three types of entries made in a worksheet.

6. A(n) _____ format change affects the entire worksheet.

7. Values, labels, and formulas are entered into a spreadsheet without any preplanned structure in the _____ design approach.

8. The _____ block supplies information about a spreadsheet.

9. Software designed specifically to manage financial transactions with more complexity in greater volume than ordinary spreadsheet software is called _____.

10. The ability to imitate an object or process and to make it respond to different situations as if it were a real object or process is called _____.

Short Answer

1. Describe several benefits of spreadsheet software over a paper spreadsheet.

2. List several professional and personal uses of spreadsheets.

3. Give examples of the three types of entries that can be made in spreadsheets.

4. Describe how you derive the coordinate, or address, of the cell of a worksheet.

5. What is the standard order of mathematical operations? Explain why knowing the order of operations of a particular spreadsheet program could be critical.

6. Describe the difference between value, label, and formula.

7. Describe the "what-if" function in a spreadsheet.

8. What is spreadsheet design and describe two approaches.

9. Briefly describe the various spreadsheet blocks.

10. What is the difference between accounting software and general spreadsheet software?

Issues for Thought

1. Your job necessitates using spreadsheets designed and created by other individuals. Before relying on the information generated by these spreadsheets to make decisions, what questions should you ask concerning their design?

2. Many people are not particularly adept at money management. Do you think using a computer personal financial manager would help? What advantages and pitfalls can you see?

DATA PRESENTATION: GRAPHICS SOFTWARE, MULTIMEDIA, AND HYPERTEXT

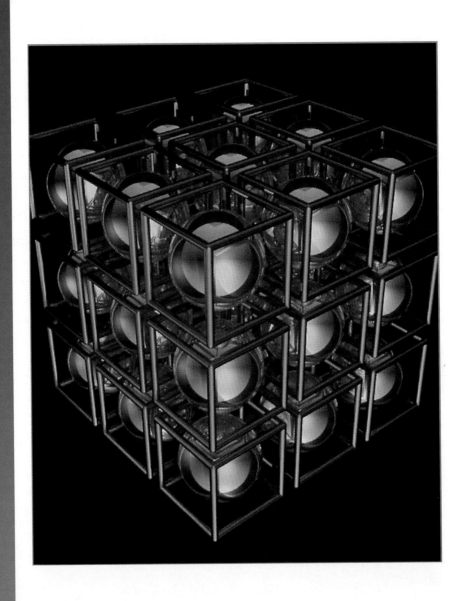

PROFILE

John von Neumann

"You know that he's a Martian disguised as a human being." That's what the neighbors said.

Who was this alleged alien whose findings would have a resounding impact on the future of computers? Well, in a 1945 scientific draft paper that has served as the basis for the logic structure of subsequent computers, he explained how the computer processed information. This man was John von Neumann—a pioneer of the "stored-program concept." Von Neumann proposed a way to encode instructions so they could reside inside the computer. He based his theory on the idea that an internally stored program would save many hours of laborious, manual work needed to reset switches and wiring that were required to reprogram the early computers. This increased the speed at which calculations were performed and led to what many say was the beginning of the computer age.

Von Neumann, who was born in Budapest, Hungary, in 1903, studied in Germany at the Göttingen University, a prestigious center of mathematical research.

Friends and acquaintances were baffled by his ability to calculate complex mathematical problems in his head. He had the power of total recall and could recite entire books from memory many years after he had read them. Von Neumann employed this ability to accumulate a vast array of jokes, anecdotes, stories, and risqué limericks to amuse his friends. On the other hand, the highways were unsafe with the reckless von Neumann behind the wheel because he was known to drive on either side of the road; once he even asserted that a tree jumped in front of his car, causing an accident. Perhaps this combination of awe-inspiring and creative intellect combined with his idiosyncrasies is why neighbors gossiped!

In the 1930s, von Neumann moved to the United States. He went to Princeton and soon immersed himself in studying hydrodynamics—the principles of fluid motion. His knowledge of hydrodynamics, a crucial aspect in designing atomic bombs, enabled von Neumann to produce a mathematical model that showed exactly how bombs would perform. This work apparently appealed to von Neumann as a "problem" to be solved, not a question of lives to be lost.

Was it chance, in 1944, that brought Herbert Goldstine and von Neumann together at a train station? Regardless, it was there that the two mathematicians met and talked about a computing machine that Goldstine was working on—the ENIAC, one of the first operational electronic digital computers. The ENIAC fascinated von Neumann; he now devoted his energies to thinking about something more important than bombs—computers.

While examining von Neumann for a shoulder injury in 1955, doctors discovered he had bone cancer. His life prognosis was six months. Perhaps the radioactivity exposure during the atomic bomb testing was responsible. At any rate, von Neumann's death at 54 was a tremendous loss.

Von Neumann doubted that a computer could duplicate the functions of the brain. Unfortunately, he did not live to see the miniaturization of parts that may someday make artificial intelligence a reality.

I t's been said that "A picture is worth a thousand words." Indeed a picture often clears up the meaning of muddled verbal descriptions. Computer graphics is one of the fastest-growing areas of microcomputer applications. This chapter focuses on how graphics are used to display data.

OBJECTIVE 8.1
Understand what constitutes computer graphics and what graphics software is.

WHAT ARE COMPUTER GRAPHICS AND GRAPHICS SOFTWARE?

Computer graphics are those images that are created or modified through the combination of the computer, software, and the user. The images produced may be text, still pictures, animations, or combinations thereof.

Graphics software is the program that permits the computer and the user to create, manipulate, and output graphic images from simple line drawings to complex 3-D images.

The user provides the creativity to produce the graphic images that communicate the user's ideas to the intended audience. Graphics applications range from modeling complex concepts (see Figure 8-1) to entertaining children (see Figure 8-2).

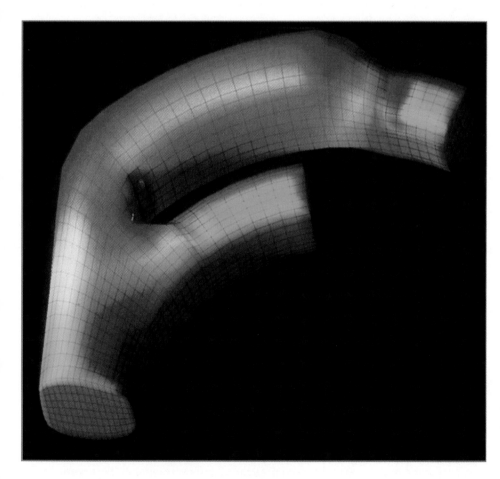

FIGURE 8-1
The degree of pressure inside this manifold is indicated by the color in this graphic image.
(Courtesy of IBM Visualization Systems)

FIGURE 8-2
With Kid Cad, children create graphic screens just for the fun of it or to start their career as an architect.

(Courtesy of Davidson & Associates, Inc.)

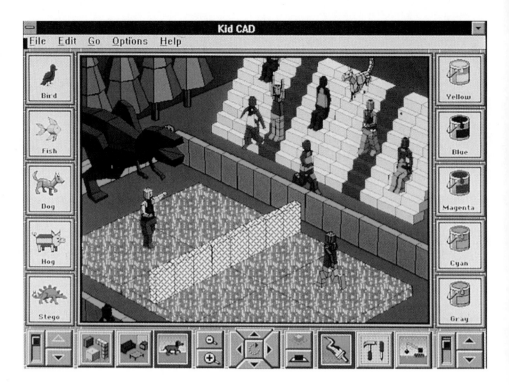

OBJECTIVE 8.2
Contrast vector and raster graphics.

WHAT IS THE DIFFERENCE BETWEEN VECTOR AND RASTER GRAPHICS?

Computers generate graphic images using either vector or raster methods. Images that are created as a set of lines are called **vector graphics.** They are generated through mathematical formulas that determine the length, position, and orientation of an object. A vector graphic, such as a circle, is handled as a single entity. It can be scaled and retains its shape. Vector graphics are also called **object-oriented graphics.**

In contrast, **raster graphics** is a collection of dots arranged to form an image. The image is stored in memory locations that correspond to pixels on the screen. The image may appear to have jagged instead of smooth edges. These graphics are also called **bit-mapped graphics.**

OBJECTIVE 8.3
Describe the main types of graphics software.

WHAT ARE THE MAIN TYPES OF GRAPHICS SOFTWARE?

Types of graphic software

- Paint and draw
- Design
- Chart/graph
- Presentation graphics
- Image editing

Graphics software for microcomputers can be divided into five main types: paint and draw programs, design programs, chart/graph programs, presentation graphics programs, and image-editing programs.

Paint and Draw Programs

For many of us, drawing a straight line or a round circle without the proper tools can be a disaster. Fortunately, there are paint and draw programs. They contain the tools used by artists, illustrators, advertising agencies, and businesses to create original art and illustrations, business forms, logos, and letterheads. Whether you use a

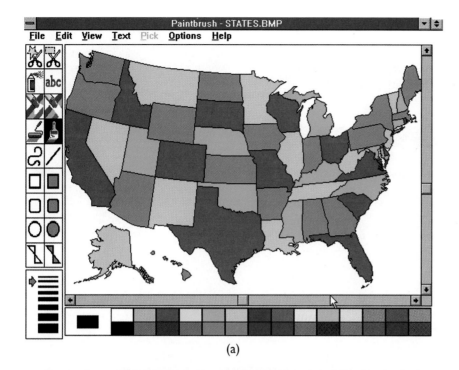

(a)

(b)

FIGURE 8-3
Paint (a) and draw (b) programs
are used to draw illustrations
or create original art.

([b] courtesy of Time Arts)

draw program or a paint program depends on the type of graphic chosen: vector or raster. Some programs combine aspects of both (see Figure 8-3).

Draw programs use vector graphics to create both freehand and line drawings. Instruments with which to draw are selected from menus or chosen by clicking on representative icons. A pencil often represents freehand drawing. Drawing objects consist of lines, squares, circles, and text, among others. They can be shaped, scaled, colored, and otherwise manipulated to create the final picture. CorelDRAW, CA-Cricket Draw, and IntelliDraw are popular drawing programs.

Paint programs use raster graphics and provide better color editing and create detailed graphics. In addition to creating pictures, paint programs contain "artist" tools like a paintbrush, spray can, air brush, and paint roller, all capable of producing

FIGURE 8-4
You can almost "feel" the texture on this computer-generated basketball.

(Courtesy of Image Software)

FIGURE 8-5
Paint programs incorporate such "tools" as brushes, pens, paint cans, and opaque and transparent paint to create images like this.

(Courtesy of Lasergraphics, LFR)

different textures and shades of color (see Figure 8-4). Paint programs, because they work with bit-mapped graphics, allow you to blend, smooth, and sharpen the outlines from one image into another (see Figure 8-5). The colors and types of tools in a program are part of its *palette* (see Figure 8-6). The number of colors available is determined by how many bits represent a pixel. For example, if one bit (0 or 1) is used, there are 2 colors. If two bits (00, 01, 10, or 11) are used, then there are 4 colors possible; four bits mean 16 colors, and so on. To display pictures of near-photographic quality, 24 and 32 bits are required for each pixel. PC Paintbrush, CorelPAINT!, CA-Cricket Paint, and BrushStrokes are examples of paint programs.

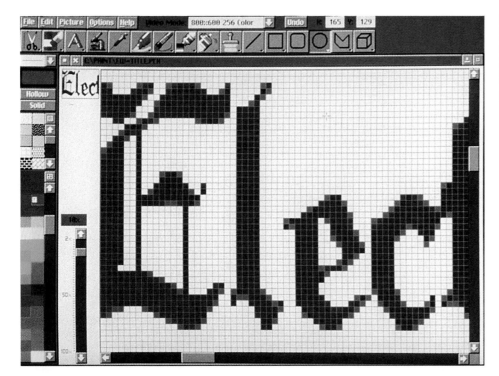

FIGURE 8-6
Here part of a word is zoomed
to permit precise editing.
Notice the color palette at the
left and the tool bar above.

(Courtesy of NeoSoft Corp.)

Design Programs

Design programs aid in applications involving the development of products or structures. These programs are generally vector based and permit the user to complete the designs much faster and with greater flexibility than with traditional pencil and paper. There is no need to erase or redraw manually.

Computer-aided design (CAD) is software for designing and drafting. CAD programs are found primarily in the fields of engineering, industrial design, and architecture. Figure 8-7(a) shows one step in the design process called a wire-frame drawing. Figure 8-7(b) shows a rendered version of the wire-frame drawing. CAD programs can also be used in **simulations,** that is, artificially creating an environment for testing products or processes (see Figure 8-8).

Chart/Graph Programs

A **chart/graph program** is used mainly to display numerical data in a graphical form. These images are usually created by the computer as bit-mapped graphics. The data are represented in a variety of chart or graph types, including bar, line, pie, scatter, stacked-bar, three-dimensional, and surface graphs.

The chart or graph programs may be separate, stand-alone software, or they may be part of another program, often a spreadsheet program. Unlike a paint or draw program, the user does not actually draw the graphs, but rather decides what type of graph format the data should take. Figure 8-9(a) shows a simple bar graph, while Figure 8-9(b) shows an embellished bar graph. Pictorial representation makes it easy to compare data or to spot trends that might otherwise be difficult to see from a page of numbers.

Presentation Graphics Programs

A **presentation graphics** program combines the features of paint programs and chart programs. It produces basic drawings and graphs and contains features to help create, organize, and sequence a slide presentation, generate audience handouts, and

FIGURE 8-7
(a) A wire-frame drawing;
(b) a rendering of the wire-frame drawing.
(Courtesy of Ralph Semrock)

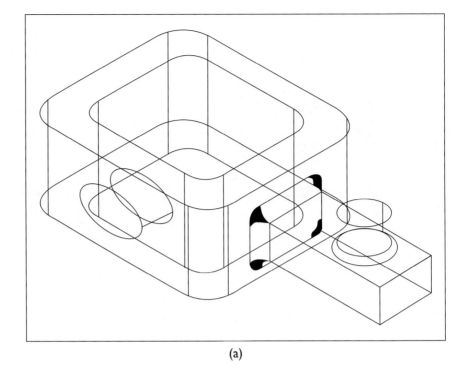

(a)

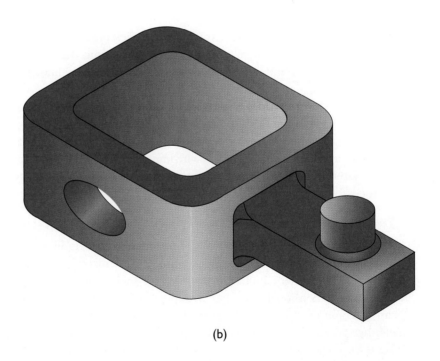

(b)

produce overhead transparencies, speakers' notes, and flip charts. The presentation graphics program can sequence and present a slide show on a large screen monitor (see Figure 8-10), with 35mm slides, or show them on a large screen projector. A **slide show** displays a series of graphics on the monitor in a predetermined order, for a predetermined time period. This feature helps the user produce a script and graphs, as well as specify the sequence, timing of, and slide transitional effects (such as "fade" and "wipe") of a presentation. This produces the same effect as using 35mm photographic slides and a slide projector.

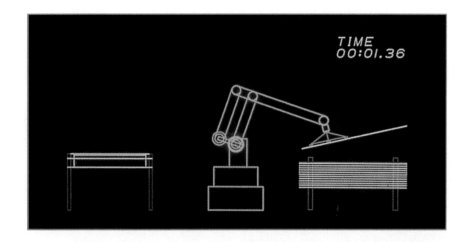

TIME
00:01.36

FIGURE 8-8
CAD software is used here to analyze and simulate how a robot will move in its factory floor environment. The operator can check work cell design elements, such as interference in the motion of the robot or "hand" with other work cell components.

(Reprinted with permission from Calma Co., a wholly owned subsidiary of the General Electric Co., U.S.A.)

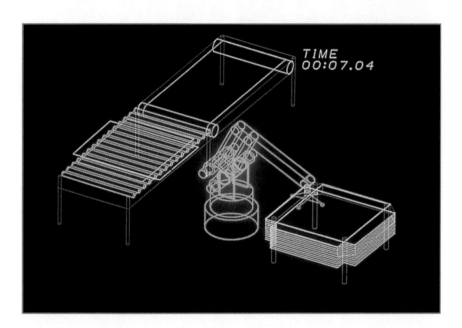

TIME
00:07.04

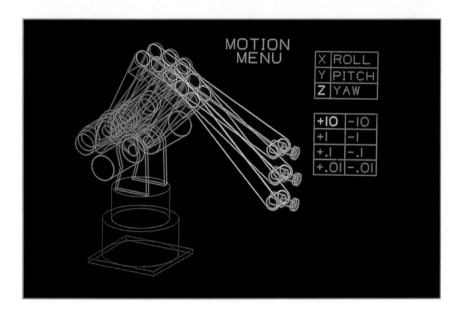

MOTION
MENU

X	ROLL
Y	PITCH
Z	YAW

+10	-10
+1	-1
+.1	-.1
+.01	-.01

FIGURE 8-9
(a) A simple bar graph;
(b) an enhanced bar graph.

(Courtesy of Lasergraphics, LFR)

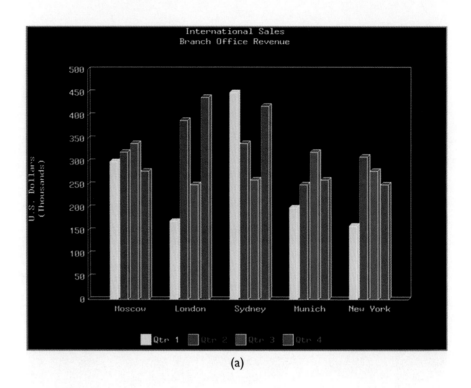

(a)

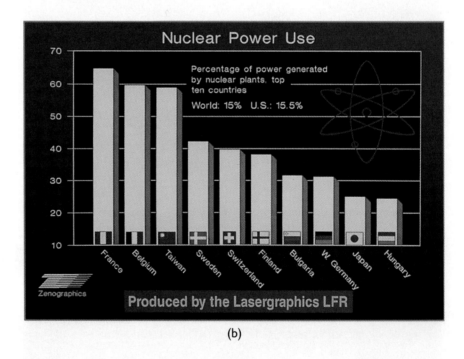

(b)

Animation is the ability to simulate motion. This feature links and sequences a series of individual graphics to create essentially a desktop video. Engineers see how various parts of an object, normally hidden from view, interact. Animation can also serve as a teaching tool for example, showing students how the moving parts of an internal combustion engine operate. Popular presentation graphics programs include Microsoft PowerPoint, Freelance Plus, and Aldus Persuasion.

FIGURE 8-10
The graphically designed system can be presented to a group as part of the presentation on a large screen monitor.

(Courtesy of Mitsubishi Electronics America)

Image-Editing Programs

Image-editing programs allow the user to modify a graphic or photographic image (see Figure 8-11). The image-editing programs may be part of a paint and draw program or stand-alone programs. Photographs, pictures in a magazine, or any other scannable image can be edited. For example, you could scan a photograph, crop it (cut out the background), and place it in a different background. With image editing you improve a bad photograph by enhancing color, altering shading, and changing the brightness and contrast. Image-editing programs include CA-Cricket Image, Image Assistant, and Picture Publisher.

Morphing is the process of progressively transforming one image into another. (see Figure 8-12). Images of people can be changed into other people or objects. Motion pictures, such as the *Terminator* series, *Dr. Jekyl and Ms. Hyde,* and television commercials often implement this technology.

OBJECTIVE 8.4
Discuss how graphics enhance various professions.

WHERE ARE COMPUTER GRAPHICS USED?

Some people may think of graphics as only charts and graphs that represent numerical or statistical data. However, the ability of the computer to display graphical images extends far beyond graphs. This section shows graphics being used in other ways.

FIGURE 8-11
This scanned image of a model is artistically altered as though looking through a glass block window.

(Courtesy of Corel Corp.)

FIGURE 8-12
Morphing software allows you to make a monkey of yourself.

(Courtesy of HSC Software)

Design and Testing

Computer-aided design and computer-aided manufacturing (CAD/CAM) use graphics programs so engineers are able to design new parts or systems much faster than manual drafting. An entire drawing does not have to be scrapped because of changes made to one part of it. Chemical engineers in Alaska use CAD to redesign oil well piping systems. Electronic engineers draw circuit schematics; civil engineers draw bridges and other structures; mechanical engineers draw machine parts; and biochemists design new drugs (Figure 8-13). By experimenting with various computer-aided designs, engineers create different models to test under varying conditions. A graphic design also makes it easier to envision the final look of a product (see Figure 8-14).

FIGURE 8-13
This researcher designs pharma-
ceuticals using a CAD system.
(Courtesy of G.D. Searle & Co.)

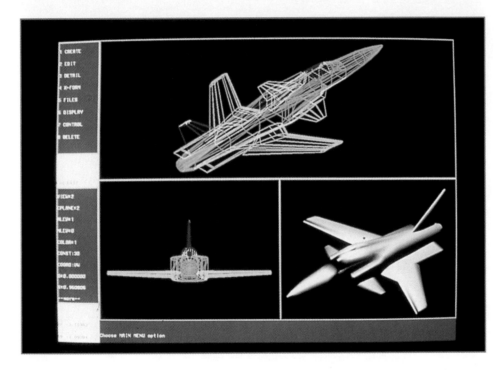

FIGURE 8-14
3-D CAD lets engineers or
designers explore design alternatives and test a product
before manufacturing.
(Courtesy of CADKEY, Inc.)

The yacht hulls of many of the America's Cup entries are designed by computer. These designs can be tested under all kinds of simulated water, wind, and weather conditions before being transformed into models and finally into real vessels with multimillion-dollar construction costs (see Figure 8-15).

Simulation and Training

A computer can simulate a hazardous workplace to allow people to train in a safe environment. The simulations mimic routine operations as well as occasions when things go awry. Graphic simulations allow a trainee to learn from situations that would ordinarily be too costly or too dangerous to recreate.

FIGURE 8-15

Supercomputers analyzed millions of pieces of data before coming up with the optimum design for the hull this 12-meter sailing yacht. Plausible designs were suggested and tested (by simulation) for seaworthiness and speed.

(Leo Mason/Image Bank. Inset: Courtesy of Cray Research, Inc.)

Pilot trainees are put into realistic mockups of plane cockpits. The computer graphics simulate all sorts of takeoffs, flying, combat, and landing conditions. A crash here is not fatal. Errors are reviewed and situations tried again. A commercial airline pilot might fly for dozens of years and hundreds of thousands of miles without experiencing what it is like to be caught in a wind shear or face the terror of losing all engine power. However, a computer simulation that creates these conditions gives the trainee some degree of readiness should the actual situations ever occur.

Real-life training is an important component when it comes to operating lake or oceangoing vessels. Having a mishap with an 800-foot ship would not appear on a list "things to do today." However, personnel need to be trained on a variety of ships that sail to different ports. It is impractical and expensive to train staff in each situation and location.

Computer simulators with sophisticated programs offer this training at the Maritime Training & Research Center in Toledo, Ohio. The simulators make it possible to give training not only in the local harbor, but through the use of geographical databases, training can be done in a variety of harbors, including Los Angeles, Long Beach, Tampa Bay, Jacksonville, Beaumont, Halifax, the St. Lawrence River, and the Strait of Canso.

The marine simulator includes many ship models that can be used by deck officers and engineers who require advanced training to maintain their current licenses or to move up in rank. The integration of the proper computer hardware and software, especially databases and graphics, allow the user to model many situations.

Grounding a ship on a sandbar is a lesson best learned in the classroom.

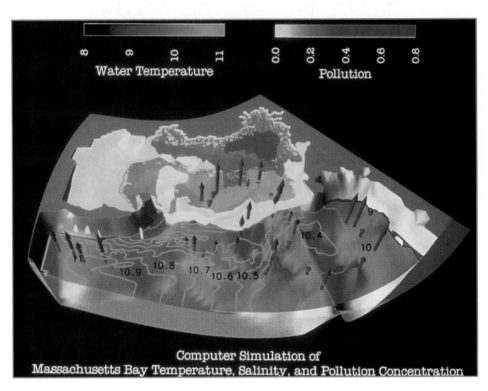

FIGURE 8-16
Scientists can analyze multiple effects on a body of water by graphically representing each variable. Here the arrows indicate differences in salinity.
(Courtesy of IBM Visualization Systems)

Analysis and Modeling

The ability of the computer to store and retrieve graphic images in real time allows different professionals to employ the computer as an analysis tool. Through graphical representations, climatologists "see" temperature variations. When comparisons are made over time, they are able to analyze the data and correlate changes in the environment with changes in temperature (see Figure 8-16). Graphic animation of hurricanes and other violent weather permits meteorologists to study their origins.

Medical personnel diagnose diseases through computer graphics. When linked with a scanner, a computer renders a three-dimensional image of the patient's brain so doctors are able to examine the organ in great detail from every angle, without performing invasive surgery (see Figure 8-17). Black-and-white X rays that are computer enhanced and produced in color reveal more information about the examination

FIGURE 8-17
Multiple views of a patient's
brain are analyzed for radio-
therapy treatment of a tumor.
(Courtesy of IBM Visualization Systems)

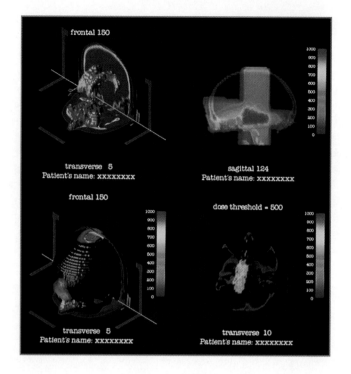

area. In the field of biology, computers create molecular models to demonstrate nature's building blocks in visible form. Veterinary science students dissect computer images rather than actual laboratory animals.

OBJECTIVE 8.5
Identify graphs and charts used to represent data.

WHAT ARE THE COMMON TYPES OF GRAPHS AND CHARTS?

Developers of graph and chart software and presentation graphics software try to create programs that reinforce the rules of good design. They make it easy for the amateur to create good graphs and charts by including suggestions on what type of graph you should use, how to add color effectively, and when to implement various other features. However, users still need to plan their graphics carefully.

Graphs and charts can be developed from spreadsheet data and output through a graphics component of the spreadsheet. They are also developed through data input into a stand-alone graphics program.

Sometimes, a basic graph with no frills will suffice. But, to be most effective in a formal presentation, the user should design a dynamic graph that will impress the point upon an audience. Attention to proper design is important. A poorly designed chart or graph can be very dull, or worse, misleading.

In general, a good presentation graph should
- Be simple
- Be accurate and easy to interpret
- Make a visual impact on the intended audience

Depending on the message you wish to convey, different methods of displaying those data are used. These include bar, line, and scatter graphs and pie, organizational, and flow charts.

Good business graph design

- Simple
- Accurate
- Visual impact

Bar Graphs

Bar graphs show comparisons or relationships among data items and are probably one of the most commonly used graph types. They appear in a variety of forms and are best used to show comparisons of distinct categories. A nontechnical audience is best served by this display. Data are shown using rectangular bars. Figure 8-18 shows several of the many variations of bar graphs.

Bar graphs with vertical bars are sometimes called column graphs, best used to show how data vary over time, while horizontal bar graphs show how values compare at a given time. Clustered-bar graphs, where multiple bars are side by side, allow comparison of several items at once.

Stacked-bar graphs, both horizontal and vertical, combine the features of bar graphs and pie charts. They let you show side-by-side bar comparisons as well as how the parts of a single bar compare.

Line Graphs

Line graphs show trends and emphasize movement and direction of change over time. Points are plotted on the graph and then are connected by straight or curved lines (see Figure 8-19). Multiple trends can be shown, but you need to use different line types or use a legend that clearly identifies each line. Line graphs provide a better method for showing continuous data items.

Area Graphs

Area graphs combine the features of line graphs and stacked-bar graphs (see Figure 8-20). They resemble line graphs with the area shaded below each line. Like stacked-bar graphs, their appearance should follow the same guidelines. In addition to showing

Graph/chart types

- Bar graph
- Line graph
- Area graph
- Scatter graph
- High-low graph
- Pie chart
- Organizational chart
- Flow chart

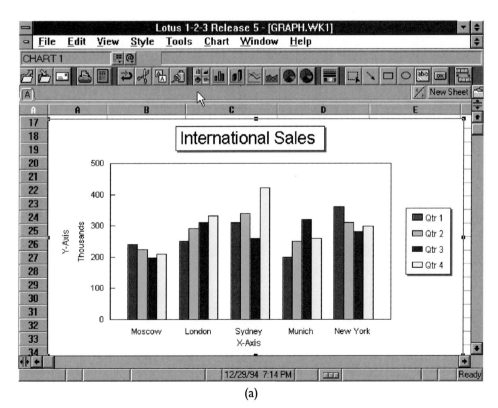

(a)

FIGURE 8-18
(a) Bar graph, (b) horizontal stacked bar graph, and (c) 3-D bar graph.

FIGURE 8-18
continued.

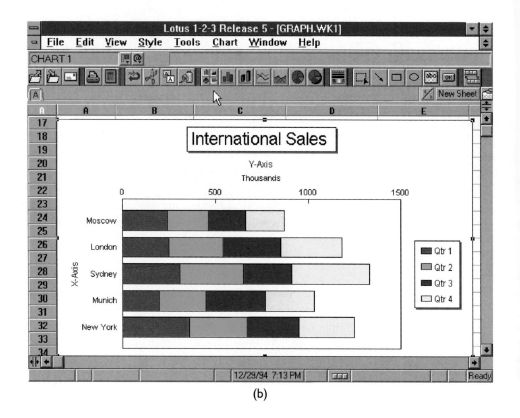

(b)

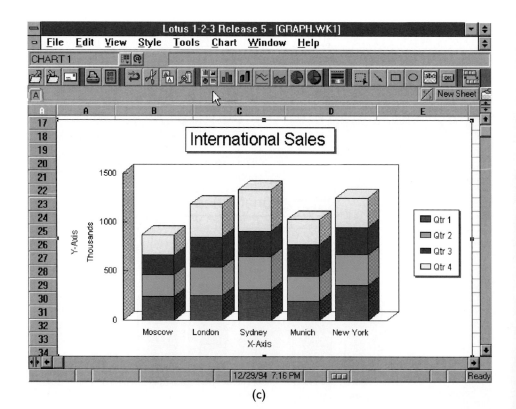

(c)

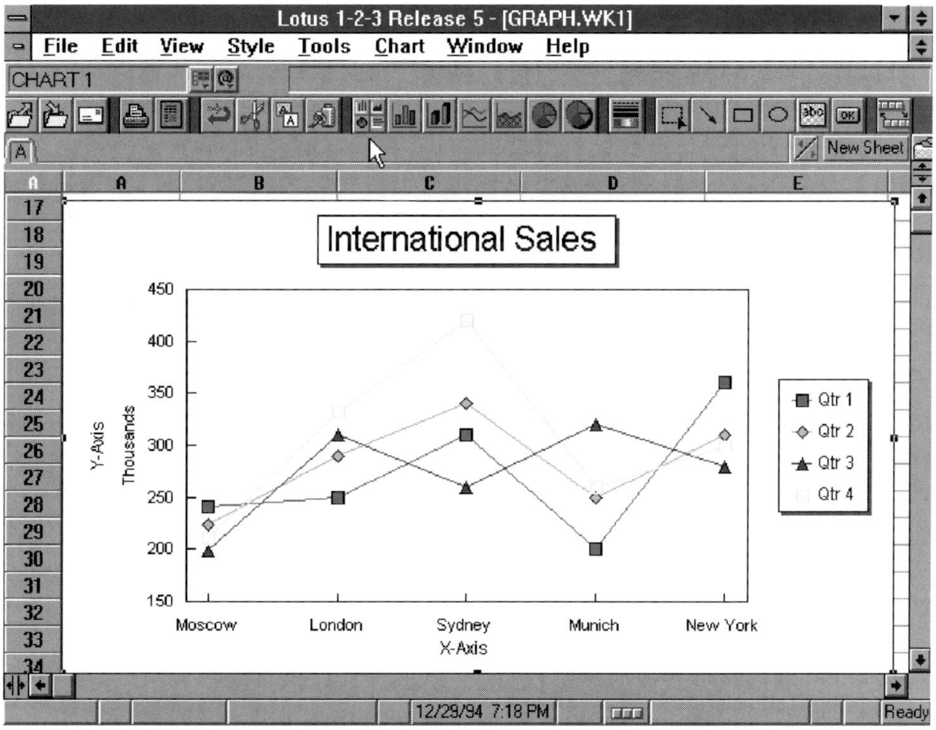

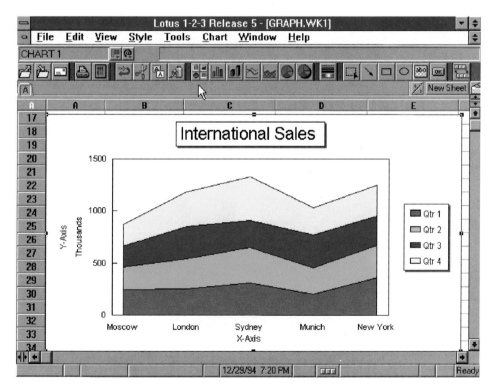

FIGURE 8-19
Line graph.

FIGURE 8-20
Stacked-line graph or area graph.

trends, they can also show the importance of one data item over another at a specific time. The area graph provides an alternative if there are too many data items to plot on a stacked-bar graph.

Scatter Graphs

A **scatter graph** shows the correlation between sets of data. These are also called X-Y graphs. If one set of data increases and the other set decreases relative to the first set, the correlation is negative. If both sets of data increase (or decrease) at the same rate, the correlation is positive (see Figure 8-21). If there is no relationship between the two sets of data, the correlation is zero.

High-Low Graphs

High-low graphs are special types of line graphs that plot minimum and maximum values over time. These are often used to plot stock market prices or temperature variations. The marks for the high and low data points are usually of different types.

Pie Charts

A **pie chart** displays part-to-whole relationships. The entire amount is represented by a circle, or pie, and individual wedges represent parts of the pie. Often these wedges indicate a percentage of the whole (see Figure 8-22). Individual segments may be colored differently or exploded to draw attention to or highlight that particular wedge.

Organizational Charts

Organizational charts display a hierarchy of data. They are often used to display supervisory levels describing how company departments are laid out (see Figure 8-23).

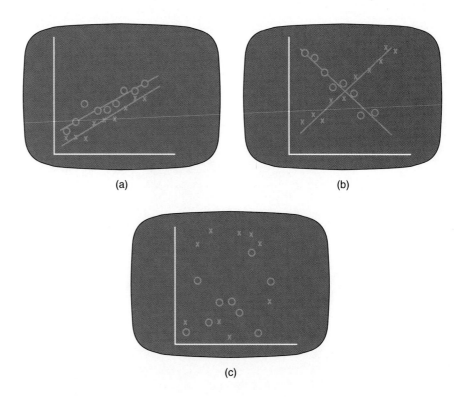

(a)

(b)

(c)

FIGURE 8-21
Scatter graphs: (a) positive correlation; (b) negative correlation; (c) zero correlation.

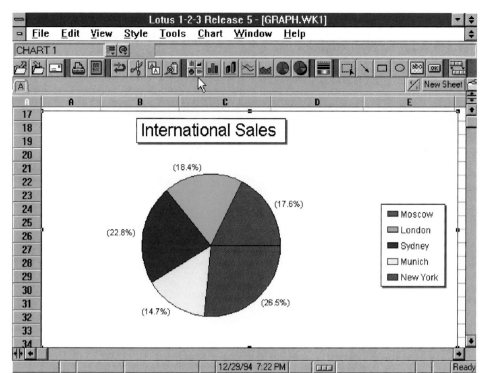

FIGURE 8-22
Pie chart.

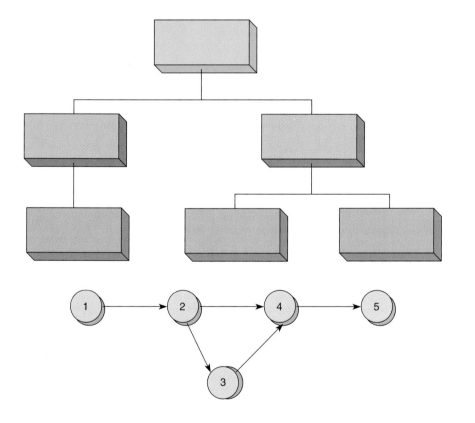

FIGURE 8-23
An organizational chart.

FIGURE 8-24
A flow chart.

Flow Charts

Flow charts display how events are sequenced. They may include how much time is involved to complete each event or merely represent the specific order of events—what must be done first, second, and so on (see Figure 8-24).

FIGURE 8-25
As shown in the expression on these children's faces, multimedia makes learning fun.

(Jeff Haeger, courtesy of Apple Computer Inc.)

OBJECTIVE 8.6
Define multimedia.

WHAT IS MULTIMEDIA?

Multimedia is the integration of high-quality sound, still and motion video, text, animation, and graphics in a complete system. While the foregoing is a detailed description, it may be characterized in one word—communication. It's an exciting way to stimulate the senses, a means to address many levels of comprehension (see Figure 8-25). Multimedia enables the user to read text about a subject and see the topic. Multimedia is a passive medium. Television and motion pictures are multimedia—they combine all the elements just described. However, a multimedia computer lets the user control the presentation, that is, *interactive multimedia*.

Because of the interactive environment of multimedia, educators have found that many students learn and retain information better when provided with multimedia presentations. The biggest drawback to multimedia in the past was its cost. This is no longer the case, and there are many more applications using multimedia today.

OBJECTIVE 8.7
Describe various applications for multimedia.

WHAT ARE SOME MULTIMEDIA APPLICATIONS?

Some popular multimedia applications are found in education, resource materials, training, business, and home and entertainment.

Without a doubt, the majority of interactive multimedia is used in education where it has the potential to help students of all age levels (see Figure 8-26). The California State Board of Education adopted a seventh-grade science multimedia application called "Science 2000." This nontextbook curriculum actively engages stu-

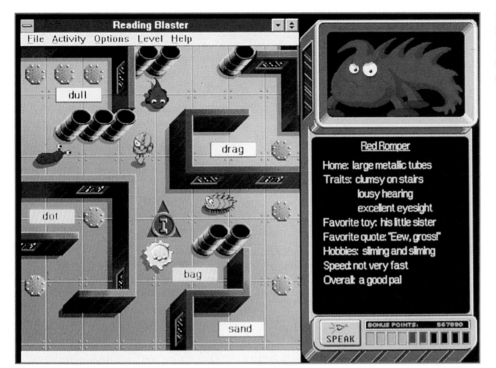

FIGURE 8-26
Students learn to read with the help of animation, graphics, and sound.
(Courtesy of Davidson & Associates)

Multimedia applications

- Education
- Resource materials
- Training
- Business
- Home and entertainment

dents in the learning process. Teachers personalize the software by adding their own knowledge. Other states are incorporating more multimedia applications into their school systems, for example, the Texas Learning Technology Group course in Chemistry I.

The Southeastern Universities and Colleges Coalition for Engineering Education (SUCCEED) is dedicated to changing the way engineering courses are taught by developing multimedia applications. For example, in a course in dynamics, which is the study of objects in motion, students will be able to see the motion, freeze it, and study it in real time.

Gateway Stories, from the Center for Applied Special Technology, Inc., is multimedia software that scans books and adds sound and speech. These stories are then "read" by students who would not ordinarily have access to the mainstream materials.

Reference materials such as encyclopedias, atlases, and dictionaries are a natural for multimedia. An interactive multimedia encyclopedia permits the user to see and hear the topics being researched (see Figure 8-27). The "Presidents" by The National Geographic Society gives information about all the Presidents of the United States and lets the user hear them "speak." "The CD Sourcebook of American History" is a collection of over 600 documents representing approximately 20,000 pages of text including the Declaration of Independence as well as Patrick Henry's famous "Give me liberty or give me death" speech. Multimedia makes it possible to explore worlds that would not otherwise be possible. The human body, outer space, ocean depths, and foreign countries are all destinations to which a student might travel without leaving the classroom.

Many companies offer interactive job training through multimedia applications. United Airlines adopted this type of system to educate flight attendants about aircraft equipment, emergency preparedness, world geography, and cultural awareness. Because there are training locations throughout the world, employees take their disks as they travel and learn at their own pace.

FIGURE 8-27
Neil Armstrong's famous quote,
". . . one small step for man . . ."
can be heard just as it sounded
back in 1969.

(Courtesy of Compton's NewMedia)

In the business world multimedia is finding new uses every day. It is used to sell products by creating dynamic and interesting sales promotions, and to communicate with customers long after the sale. Traditional meetings take on new life when presentations include video, audio, and animation to enhance the usual graphs and charts. Some companies produce and distribute their annual reports on CD-ROM. disks. The reports may contain videos of products or processes, or perhaps even show the company president's address so the stockholders can see and hear it.

Home use is another popular place to find interactive multimedia. Children learn the alphabet and explore the wonders of the zoo. Even cookbooks have changed: the only thing missing is the aroma (see Figure 8-28). If you just want to be better informed about your body, medical books are available. (see Figure 8-29).

Multimedia lets you see and hear about potential vacation spots, view video clips of your favorite sports hero, or preview a scene from a classic movie. And, if entertainment is your main goal, multimedia has its fair share of games to satisfy your need to conquer other worlds. Multimedia gives home games the fast action and graphic ability of arcade-type games. It becomes a necessity as these games employ more full-motion video than ever before.

In April 1993, a multimedia museum of memories opened in Washington, D.C. These memories from 1933 through 1949 are depicted in the world's largest networked multimedia system—the faces, voices, and stories of the Holocaust. Visitors are able to track someone of their age and gender through this time via 24 personal computers that access a network containing the compressed digital information.

OBJECTIVE 8.8
Define the characteristics that make up multimedia.

WHAT MAKES A COMPUTER SYSTEM A MULTIMEDIA SYSTEM?

Integrating text, graphics, audio, and video requires certain hardware and software (see Figure 8-30). In the past you had to "put together" a system to run multimedia

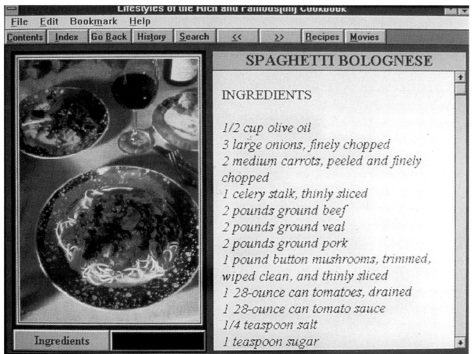

FIGURE 8-28
Lifestyles of the Rich and Famous,
a graphical cookbook.
(Courtesy of Compton's NewMedia)

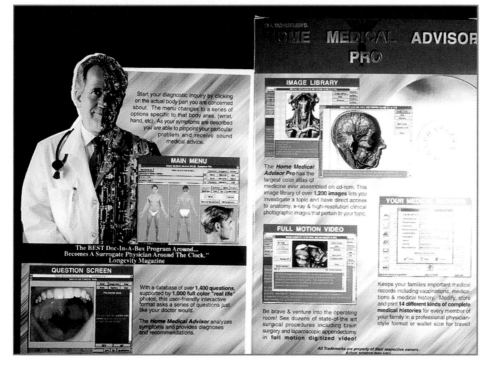

FIGURE 8-29
Medical books assist in locating
the answers to many health-
related questions.
(Courtesy of Pixel Perfect Software)

applications. Video and sound boards, CD-ROM drives, and speakers were purchased separately. However, because of the demand for such machines, manufacturers now supply the necessary hardware and software as standard equipment. In fact, multimedia computers are offered at a relatively low enough cost so this system is becoming standard, even for home use. What sets a multimedia system apart from ordinary computer systems is its ability to handle animation, sounds, and video as part of an integrated package.

FIGURE 8-30
Computer systems capable of
multimedia are becoming the
standard for home use.
(Courtesy of AST Research, Inc.)

Both audio and video take a tremendous amount of storage—full-motion color video requirements are about 40MB per minute. Although much of the data are compressed, even text, in the amounts used by some applications, takes a large amount of storage. CD-ROM technology made multimedia available to the PC user. The typical 3 ½-inch floppy diskette holds approximately 1.44MB, while a CD-ROM disk holds 650MB, or more. Using CD-ROMs, portable computers can become multimedia machines (see Figure 8-31).

Animation

Animation is the simulation of movement by displaying a series of successive images on the screen. To be successful and to appear fluid, the individual images, or frames, must be displayed at a speed that fools the eye into appearing as constant motion. To accomplish this on-screen, the images are displayed at a minimum of 14 frames per second (fps). For example, the classic Disney cartoons, which were all hand drawn, are displayed at about 28 fps. Television runs at 30 fps. Many multimedia programs make use of animation. Distinct programs create graphics in different ways, although the faster the fps, the better the animation will appear. *Tweening* makes the animation process simpler because it fills in the steps from one frame to another. For example, you could instruct a graphics program to take a hand-drawn circle and make it into a square in a prescribed number of steps. Tweening automatically redraws and displays each step so that it looks like a smooth transition from one object to another.

Three-dimensional graphics are almost as common as their two-dimensional counterparts. They are drawn or shown in 2-D media (height and width) such as a computer screen. The third dimension (depth) is added by giving perspective through the use of shading or color gradients. Three-dimensional graphics are found in animation and can be rotated, stretched, or otherwise moved to give the viewer a sense of being in the animation.

FIGURE 8-31
Multimedia goes where you go with this portable system.
(Courtesy of MPC Technologies Inc.)

HIGHLIGHT 8-2 Magic Dragons and 3-D Software

What would you call the person who developed a 3-D imaging system used for applications such as molecular modeling, flight simulations, and computer-aided-design? Would you call him an entrepreneur, inventor, or capitalist? How about dragon master?

In fact, Lenny Lipton, who wrote the lyrics to "Puff, the Magic Dragon," the memorable song by Peter, Paul, and Mary, is the developer behind CrystalEyes. Lipton's company StereoGraphics produced CrystalEyes, a 3-D imaging software.

Royalties from the recording enabled Lipton, who has a background in physics, to start StereoGraphics and to work on a 3-D television system. CrystalEyes was the result. Wireless 3-ounce goggles equipped with liq-uid crystal lenses are used in conjunction with a television or computer monitor on which stereographically separated images are projected. This gives the viewer a very realistic view in three dimensions. One potential use for this technology is in endoscopy, an exploratory procedure in which a tiny video camera is inserted into a surgical incision. This is pending approval by the Food and Drug Administration. Currently only 2-D images are available.

Initially, Lipton offered his 3-D software to 2-D applications users free of charge to promote CrystalEyes. Because of this type of foresight, StereoGraphics is on its way to becoming the industry standard in 3-D imaging software.

Not bad for a "dragon" beginning!

Sound

All computers produce sounds. You hear beeps through the internal speaker of your computer when you first turn it on. This is not sound as it applies to multimedia. What sets multimedia apart is its ability to record, play, and alter sounds in a variety of ways. Sound in the form of music makes an ordinary program come to life. It informs in ways text or graphics alone cannot (see Figure 8-32). Hearing-impaired students and those who are learning English as a second language are using "Sounds of English" from Irvine Interactive, Inc. The student sees how the lips and tongue are positioned to form the words, hears a voice pronounce them properly, and learns by comparing their own recorded voice to the correct pronunciation.

FIGURE 8-32
Human anatomy is explained
with narrative sound accompa-
nying the pictures or animations.
(Courtesy of Interactive Ventures)

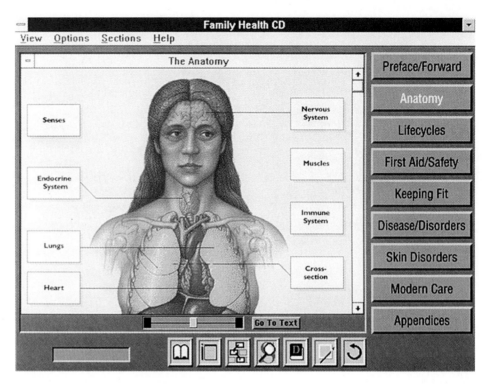

Multimedia audio is produced either by recording existing sounds or creating new sounds. There are two basic types of sounds: analog and digital. Your voice is an example of analog sound. The sounds must first be converted to digital form to be stored by the computer. Through a process called *sampling*, the sound is "grabbed" in small increments. A higher sampling rate means more parts of the analog signals are grabbed and the quality of the resulting digital sound is better. Once the sound is digitized, it can be manipulated just like any other computer digital data, that is, its volume adjusted, its pitch changed, and special effects added to the original recording. Audio editing software is used to alter the digitized audio files.

To hear the sound through a speaker, the digital audio must be converted back into analog form. To produce sound, you must have two other pieces of hardware: a sound board, or card, and speakers. Sound cards are the plug-in electronic circuits that enable your computer to generate audio signals. They are available in 8-bit, 16-bit, and 32-bit versions, with the last delivering better-quality sound.

Sounds initially generated by the computer are already in digital form called *synthesized* audio. A synthesizer is an electronic instrument that produces musical notes as well as an almost infinite array of sounds. **Musical instrument digital interface (MIDI)** is often a component of multimedia. Although mainly used for musical applications, it can be used in a variety of ways. MIDI is a communication protocol used to communicate between the computer and other peripheral devices, such as a MIDI-controlled synthesizer. A MIDI interface allows the user to compose, rearrange, and otherwise edit sounds into a complete composition with a computer, synthesizer, and sequencing software (see Figure 8-33).

With a multimedia system, you can also play standard audio CDs. You are able to listen to music in the background as you enter your term paper.

Money spent on high-quality equipment is wasted unless your system effectively reproduces the sound. Speakers are very important to this process. External computer speakers are different from home or car speakers. Because of close proximity to the computer, they must be shielded magnetically to protect them from interfer-

FIGURE 8-33
A musical instrument digital interface (MIDI) links computers to musical instruments to control and create sounds.

ence. Speaker systems are available in stereo and surround sound, which give multimedia applications a dramatic impact.

Video

Because multimedia applications use full motion, stills, graphics, and animation at the same time, some users consider video the most important part of a quality multimedia application.

To see a video image, you must be able to record that image. There are numerous ways to capture video, both full motion and still. As with sound, analog video must be converted into digital representation for use by the computer.

Multimedia presentations can be enhanced through devices such as videodisk players that are controlled by a computer. Videodisks store both still pictures and audio. They resemble CDs but are much larger, typically 12 inches in diameter. Photo compact disk players store images on disk for playing on the monitor. Compact disk-interactive (CD-I) players play back the images on a television screen instead of a monitor.

The next major change in multimedia is in digital video. Most television and broadcast video is in the form of analog signals. But a few systems are in place that send digital signals. Digital video, which can be treated as any other data file in a computer and thus be manipulated as such, will unite television and the computer as never before: interactive television, in which the user controls what is on the screen, has been undergoing test marketing. In addition, the Federal Communications Committee approved a video signal for telephones that allows you to receive digital video over phone lines. These developments will make multimedia a truly interactive medium.

One of the problems with sound and video is that it requires large amounts of storage. A one-minute audio file will be about 10MB, while video files such as animation or full-motion can be much larger. That is why most multimedia application clips are very short. Data compression technology like that used for text files reduces the storage demands for video and audio files. New technologies will further reduce the storage requirements. General Electric and RCA developed a compression technology (later purchased by Intel) called digital video interactive (DVI) that reduces a file to as little as 1 percent of its original size.

Images are also entered through scanners. Flatbed scanners are fairly inexpensive for midrange quality models and are available in both black-and-white and color. Slide scanners capture the images from 35mm films or slides.

OBJECTIVE 8.9
Define the concept of hypertext.

WHAT IS HYPERTEXT?

While reading an article on the history of aviation, your interest is piqued by the section on aircraft of World War II. You put that book down to find another on World War II aircraft. While reading this material, you wonder how gliders were used. Wasn't there more information on gliders in that recent magazine article? While reading about gliders, you want to know about aerodynamics, and so on.

Most of us read articles from beginning to end; hypertext lets you branch out and come back to the same point. **Hypertext** is graphic-oriented software that contains related data that are not stored in traditional files or records. They are stored as objects that can be arbitrarily linked together and accessed very rapidly in nonsequential ways. Imagine hypertext as a stack of index cards, each card containing one concept or idea. Those concepts may be in the form of text, graphics, or pictures, unlike a text database. You are able to move from one card to another, browsing through all the cards or moving to a specific card anywhere in the stack with the click of a mouse.

Hypertext software incorporates some components of a database and text and graphics editors, and employs a mouse to move through windows, click on icons, and access pull-down menus (see Figure 8-34).

Hypertext actually is a fairly recent implementation of a much older concept. In fact, visions of a hypertext system can be traced back to the 1940s. President Roosevelt's science advisor, Vannevar Bush, conceived a system that combined drawings, photographs, and notes in an on-line text and retrieval system. There would be links between any two points of data which could then be accessed and retrieved in his system. In the 1960s Douglas Englebart developed a system where stored infor-

FIGURE 8-34
Icon representation of features available in HyperCard.

mation could be shared on line. The mouse provided a means to increase the speed at which data could be input into the computer. Ted Nelson coined the term "hypertext" and developed a hypertext system, called Xanadu, that stored and cross-referenced all types of literary works. Popular hypertext programs today include HyperCard from Apple and ToolBook from Windows.

The term hypertext has been used commonly since early programs were mainly text oriented. But current programs also incorporate links between graphics, sound, and video. This type of program is often referred to as **hypermedia.** These two terms are sometimes used interchangeably, but they do have different meanings. Hypermedia combines all the features of linking data as in hypertext, but uses multimedia aspects as well.

Hypertext Applications

Hypertext applications fall into one of several categories. On-line browsers are those hypertext products whose main purpose is to permit the user to look through the information. They are used for products such as reference manuals where the contents are altered little, if ever, and provide the user with quick on-line information. Customizing is usually limited. Most microcomputer-oriented hypertext falls into the category of general-purpose or user-defined products in which the user defines the data and how they are linked together. Hypertext products can be combined with expert systems as part of a problem-solving process.

One of the more prominent areas for a hypertext application is in education. A hypertext product called "The Bone Box" teaches about the skeletal system and its terminology. The student chooses a particular bone from the skeletal system and sees different views of that same bone.

At the University of Southern California, music and text are integrated into a hypertext where scales and film scoring are taught. The application also provides for student improvisation.

Reference books and other voluminous manuals are suited for hypertext. For example, Ford Motor Company mechanics use a hypertext that provides easy access to their service and parts manuals.

Hypertext Basics

Organization is the key in creating a successful hypertext application. The data must be broken down into small, discrete units. These units of data usually fill one computer screen. HyperCard calls these units cards, while HyperPad calls them pages. The interface to ToolBook is designed more like a book rather than a stack of cards. Each unit (we'll refer to them as cards from here on) each unit contains text fields to store alphanumeric data. The cards may also contain graphics or pictures.

A collection of related cards under one name is called a stack; related pages are called a pad. (Notice the relationship of hypertext concepts to everyday objects: a stack of index cards, a pad of paper containing many pages.) All the cards in a stack may contain the same elements, or background. For example, if the stack were used for security identification, each card could contain an outline where a picture is placed or boxes where name and other fields of data are to be inserted. Each individual card contains data for one person. A background could be compared to a screen form in a text database.

To move from card to card in a stack, or page to page in a pad, the individual cards or pages must be linked together. Linking is the method by which the user moves about in a stack or pad. For the most part, the links established depend solely on the user. If you are creating the hypertext program, only you see how the data are related. Hypertext card arrangements take many forms—simple, straight-line links, simple or complex hierarchical structures, or random order.

To sort through the cards, you click on a "button." It can be a few descriptive words or an icon that describes the link. Buttons may be user- or program-defined icons (see Figure 8-35). Clicking on a button brings a new card immediately to the screen. Buttons can also be defined to perform functions such as activating a videodisk player or dialing a phone. For example, if you created a stack of cards on the birds of North America, the card might contain a button that activates a videodisk player with a map showing the range of the bird and provides an audio recording of the call that the bird gives.

The user has the option of working at various levels within the hypertext program. The level depends on what you are trying to accomplish. Some hypertext products contain all the levels; others do not. In general, the user-level options are browsing, typing, authoring, and scripting.

At the *browsing* level you move through individual cards or move from stack to stack. Browsing is usually limited to viewing and printing cards. Once the hypertext application is fully developed, the user spends most of the time at this level looking up information. Many systems contain a graphical browser that shows where you are in the stack with an on-screen map. It keeps you from getting lost in a complex card structure.

In addition to the capabilities of the browsing level, the *typing* level lets you edit text and add new cards to the stack. Higher levels usually contain the features of the preceding levels.

Cards are customized at the *painting* level. Here you alter the look of the card by adding or changing the images on each individual card or background. There are usually a number of paint tools available to create pictures, or art may be copied from another card.

At the *authoring* level the user acquires more control over the program. Here you can change the objects—move and redefine the buttons, change the placement and size of the text fields, and change the background graphics on a card. This level is where the applications are set up or authored and programming knowledge is not necessary.

Scripting provides the maximum in user control of the program. It involves programming in the hypertext language. HyperCard's script language is called HyperTalk.

FIGURE 8-35
HyperCard menu for creating a button.

Script languages must follow syntax rules just as programming languages do, but they are usually written more like English sentences. For example, if you wanted to insert the date in a card after a field called "date," the script could read: "put the date after field 'date'."

Advantages and Disadvantages

Hypertext is relatively easy to use once it is set up. Buttons simplify the process of moving between cards to access the right information. Hypertext has the potential to enhance learning by combining text, pictures (both still and motion), and sound into one complete presentation. Much of learning and understanding takes place visually. Could you describe da Vinci's *Mona Lisa* in words alone? It would be more effective to actually see the painting as you read about the artist than merely reading the text.

A potential problem with hypertext is created by the user who authored the application. If the developer devises obscure and meaningless links, the program is useless to future users. Jumping around in the program can be disorienting at times.

SUMMARY

Computer graphics are the images and pictures created by computers and people. Graphics software are the programs employed to create, edit, display, and print those images.

Computers create graphics in different ways: bit mapped or vector. Bit-mapped, or raster, graphics are comprised of individual pixels. Vector, or object-oriented, graphics are mathematically defined.

There are four basic types of graphics programs: paint and draw, design, chart and graph, presentation, and image editing. Graphic images aid in the areas of design, testing, simulating, training, analyzing, and modeling. Graphics allow visualization and understanding that might not otherwise be possible.

Well-designed presentation graphs should be simple, accurate, and easy to interpret and make a visual impact on the intended audience. Depending on the message you wish to convey, different methods of displaying those data are used. These include bar, line, and scatter graphs and pie, organizational, and flow charts.

Multimedia is the integration of high-quality sound, still and motion video, text, animation, and graphics in a complete system. Computers allow you to use all those media and control the presentation. This is called interactive multimedia.

Multimedia is used in education, resource materials, training, business, and home and entertainment markets. Multimedia, in addition to text and graphics, usually incorporates one or more of the following: animation, audio, or video.

Hypertext lets you branch out and come back to the same point in a document. Hypertext differs from most programs in that data are arbitrarily linked and accessed in nonsequential ways. Hypertext software incorporates components of a database and text and graphics editors and employs a mouse to move through windows, click on icons, and access pull-down menus.

Hypermedia combines all the features of linking information as in hypertext, but uses multimedia aspects as well.

Can you define the following?

animation (p. 228)
area graph (p. 235)
bar graph (p. 235)
bit-mapped graphics (p. 222)
chart/graph program (p. 225)
computer-aided design (CAD) (p. 225)
computer graphics (p. 221)
design program (p. 225)
draw program (p. 223)
flow chart (p. 239)
graphics software (p. 221)
high-low graphs (p. 238)
hypermedia (p. 249)
hypertext (p. 248)

image-editing program (p. 229)
line graph (p. 235)
morphing (p. 229)
multimedia (p. 240)
musical instrument digital interface (MIDI) (p. 246)
object-oriented graphic (p. 222)
organizational chart (p. 238)
paint program (p. 223)
pie chart (p. 238)
presentation graphics (p. 225)
raster graphics (p. 222)
scatter graph (p. 238)
simulation (p. 225)
slide show (p. 226)
vector graphics (p. 222)

REVIEW QUESTIONS

Multiple Choice

1. _____ graphics are generated by a computer as a series of dots.
   a. Presentation
   b. Raster
   c. Object oriented
   d. Vector

2. _____ are vector based, so the user is able to create illustrations and line art.
   a. Draw programs
   b. Paint programs
   c. Presentation graphics programs
   d. Chart programs

3. _____ programs are bit-mapped programs that let the user create images simulating the texture of a brush stroke.
   a. Draw
   b. Paint
   c. Film graphics
   d. CAD

4. _____ programs are employed by businesspeople for making formal presentations.
   a. Draw
   b. Paint
   c. Presentation graphics
   d. Design

5. As an architect, which program would you choose to draw plans for a client's new home?
   a. draw program
   b. paint program
   c. presentation graphics
   d. design program

6. Training an airline pilot in a device using computer graphics is an example of _____.
   a. animation
   b. simulation
   c. manipulation
   d. conditioning

7. The graphics program feature where a user specifies the sequence and timing of a series of graphics is known as _____.
   a. an undo
   b. a word chart
   c. simulation
   d. a slide show

8. The process of progressively transforming one image into another is called _____.
   a. digitizing
   b. morphing
   c. animating
   d. transmorgrafying

9. Which of the following is not important to a good presentation graph?
   a. be simple
   b. be three-dimensional
   c. be accurate
   d. make a visual impact

10. A(n) _____ shows the correlation between sets of data. These are also called X-Y graphs.
    a. area graph
    b. scatter graph
    c. pie chart
    d. high-low graph

Fill In

1. Images that are created as a set of lines are called _____ graphics. They are generated through mathematical formulas that determine the length, position, and orientation of the object.

2. Artificially creating an environment for testing products or processes is called _____.

3. The ability to simulate motion is called _____.

4. Simplicity, accuracy, and visual impact are qualities of a good _____.

5. Bar graphs are used to show _____.

6. A(n) _____ chart shows the relationship of the parts to a whole.

7. Hierarchy of data can be displayed with a _____ chart.

8. _____ is the integration of high-quality sound, still and motion video, text, animation, and graphics in a complete system.

9. The majority of multimedia software is used in the field of _____.

10. _____ is a communication protocol used to communicate between the computer and other peripheral devices, such as a synthesizer.

Short Answer

1. Define computer graphics and graphics software.

2. How do vector (object-oriented) programs differ from raster (bit-mapped) graphics?

3. List and contrast the four basic types of graphics programs.

4. Give examples, other than those in your book, where graphics play a role in design and testing.

5. Describe instances, other than those in your book, where graphics play a role in simulation and training?

6. A good presentation graph should conform to what three basic concepts?

7. List and briefly define the types of graphs and charts presented in this chapter.

8. Define what is meant by being interactive.

9. Contrast analog and digital sound and briefly describe how each is used in multimedia.

10. In your own words, describe and contrast hypertext and hypermedia.

Issues for Thought

1. What applications, in addition to those already discussed, could benefit from the graphic capabilities of microcomputers? Explain your answer.

2. Scanners and photocopy machines are capable of making realistic copies of documents, including money and other legal documents. What are some problems with this technology? What about copyright considerations? What ethical questions are posed by new technology?

DATA COMMUNICATION: LINKING A WORLD OF INFORMATION

OBJECTIVES

9.1 Define data communication and telecommunication, differentiate between analog and digital data transmissions, and describe how modems convert one to the other.

9.2 Describe the basic types of communication channels.

9.3 Define computer network and briefly describe wide area networks and local area networks.

9.4 Explain the purpose of communication software and describe its general functions; describe some of the parameters that must be set; define the terms log-on, log-off, command mode, data transfer mode, uploading, and downloading.

9.5 Describe various information resources available to the user through data communication.

9.6 Recognize some challenges presented by data communication.

PROFILE

Dennis Hayes

In 1977, Dennis Hayes and his partner, Dale Heatherington, started their business with corporate offices headquartered in Norcross, Georgia, in the Hayes's dining room. Their product was a PC modem. That's the device responsible for converting digital signals to analog signals and vice versa, allowing a computer to send data through telephone lines.

Modems had long been available for the larger computers. But, when Hayes saw personal computers coming on the market (the early Radio Shack and Apple models), he also foresaw the potential for a scaled-down modem. Hayes's vision led him to buy out his partner, leaving him as owner today of a business with estimated sales over $100 million a year. The Hayes modem, built in America, is well known for its high quality. In fact, it is considered the "standard" for personal computers to which competition devices are compared.

Hayes cannot rest on his laurels, though. The computer industry is highly competitive and rapidly changing, so these days Hayes Microcomputer Products, Inc., offers more in the way of communication software. Its Smartcom communication program, compatible with Microsoft Windows, configures the modem and allows you to begin communicating as quickly as possible.

Success brought the offices to Atlanta where we hope Hayes and his designers are hard at work on communication devices for the future. After all, their advertising motto is: "Hayes products have the computer world talking."

D ata communication technology contains solutions to the demand for more power and for data exchange and sharing. This chapter examines some basic concepts related to data communication and introduces computer networks, which enable computer systems to share data, hardware, and software. We'll also take a look at communication software. Finally, we'll present a number of ways in which you can put data communication to work in your personal and professional lives.

OBJECTIVE 9.1
Define data communication and telecommunication, differentiate between analog and digital data transmissions, and describe how modems convert one to the other.

WHAT IS DATA COMMUNICATION?

Data communication is the process of moving data electronically from one point to another. Linking computers and terminals to one another permits the power and resources of both to be shared. It also makes possible sharing and updating data in different locations.

Telecommunication is the technique of using communication facilities to send data.

Data communication allows users to send and receive data and information in a timely fashion to identify and solve problems and make decisions effectively. Even a slight delay in today's fast-paced electronic environment could mean a missed opportunity. Communication systems must also transmit the data accurately and in a form that can be understood and used by the receiving system.

Data communication is important for the home computer user too. It allows access to libraries, stock market quotations, on-line shopping services, and interactive game playing to name a few. Through data communication, individuals also link their home computers to office computers and share data, software, and hardware. Let's examine just how data are shared and transmitted.

Analog and Digital Data Transmissions

The two forms of data transmission are analog and digital. **Analog data transmission** is the transmission of data in continuous wave form (see Figure 9-1(a)). The telephone system is designed for analog data transmission in the form of sounds that change in frequency and volume.

Digital data transmission is the transmission of data using distinct on and off electrical states (see Figure 9-1(b)). Remember that data in digital form are represented as a sequence of 1's and 0's. Because computers work in digital form and because digital data communication is faster and more efficient, it would seem that all data communication between computers would be in digital form; however, that is not the case. A completely digital communication system is possible, but the analog telephone system is used for a great percentage because not only was it the largest and most widely used communication system; it was already in place.

Forms of data transmission

- Analog
- Digital

Modulation, Demodulation, and Modems

To avoid the expense of converting to a digital system or running a duplicate digital system over a wide geographic area, a method was devised to change digital signals into analog signals so they could be transmitted over analog telephone lines. After it travels over the telephone lines, the analog signal must then be reconverted to a digital signal so that the receiving computer can use it. The process of converting a digital signal to an analog signal is called **modulation** (see Figure 9-2(a)). **Demodulation** is the process of reconverting the analog signal back to a digital signal (see Figure 9-2(b)). The device that accomplishes both of these processes is a **modem,** short for *mo*dulator-*dem*odulator.

FIGURE 9-1
(a) Analog data transmission;
(b) Digital data transmission.

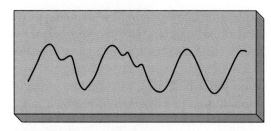

(a) Analog data transmission

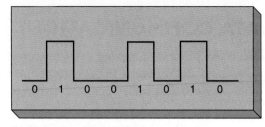

(b) Digital data transmission

FIGURE 9-2
(a) Modulation is the conversion of a digital signal to an analog signal; (b) demodulation is the conversion of an analog signal to a digital signal.

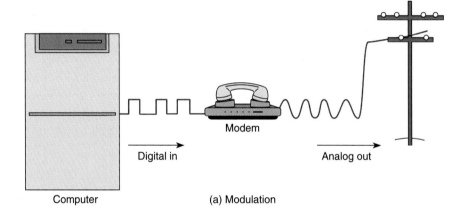

Computer   (a) Modulation

Digital in   Analog out

Modem

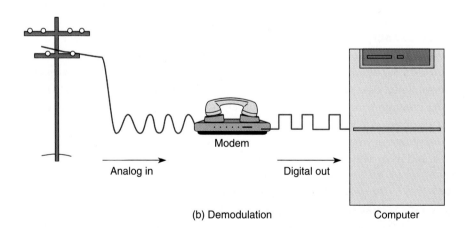

Analog in   Digital out

Modem

(b) Demodulation   Computer

Two types of modems

- External direct connect
- Internal direct connect

The two basic types of modems used with microcomputers are external direct connect and internal direct connect. An **external direct-connect modem** is outside the computer and connects directly to the telephone line with a modular phone jack (see Figure 9-3). An **internal direct-connect modem** has all of its communication circuitry on a plug-in board that fits into one of the expansion slots inside the computer case (see Figure 9-4). The Hayes Smartmodem is the industry standard modem used with microcomputers.

OBJECTIVE 9. 2
Describe the basic types of communication channels.

WHAT IS A COMMUNICATION CHANNEL?

A **communication channel** is the medium, or pathway, through which data are transmitted between devices. Communication channels fall into three basic types: wire cable, microwave and other wireless media, and fiber optics.

Wire cable comes in all sizes and designs, including twisted-pair and coaxial cables. **Twisted-pair** lines consist of a pair of wires, each wrapped in a protective coating and twisted around the other. Because it is used in telegraph and telephone lines, it is the most common type of data communication channel today. **Coaxial cable** consists of a single wire surrounded by both a layer of insulating material and a metal sheath or tube for protection (see Figure 9-5). Television cable is coaxial cable.

Because extensive wire-cable network channels already exist they are easier and cheaper to use than the other systems. Wire-cable is popular because the technology to transmit data is standardized, reducing compatibility problems.

A disadvantage of both twisted-pair and coaxial cables is that they are subject to electrical interferences that make them less reliable than other communication channels. In addition, it is difficult to create physical links when users are separated by long distances or by natural barriers, such as mountains or large bodies of water.

FIGURE 9-3
External direct-connect modems connect to a computer via a serial interface cable and to the telephone line via a modular phone jack.

(Photo by Larry Hamill)

FIGURE 9-4
Internal direct-connect modems contain the necessary serial interface circuitry and plug directly into the main circuit board of a computer.

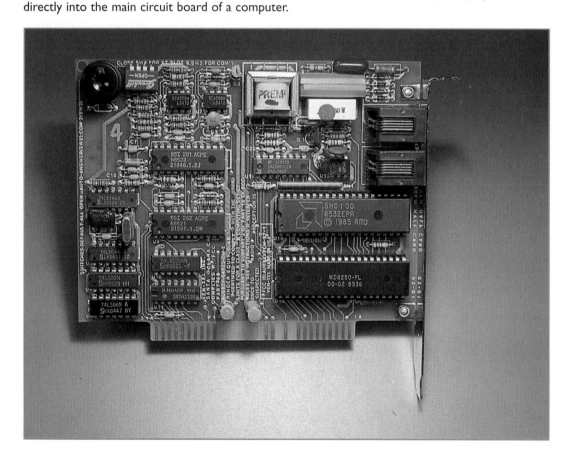

FIGURE 9-5
Types of communication channels.

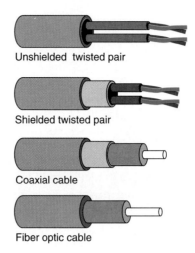

Unshielded twisted pair

Shielded twisted pair

Coaxial cable

Fiber optic cable

Types of communication channels

- Wire cable
  - Twisted-pair
  - Coaxial
- Microwave
- Fiber optic

Microwave is another type of analog communication channel. Microwave signals are transmitted through the atmosphere, like radio and television signals, rather than through wire cables. However, microwave signals must be sent in straight lines because they cannot bend around corners or follow the curvature of the earth. Microwave retransmitter stations are located about every 30 miles to redirect and boost the signals. You may have seen them along the roadside when you are driving.

Satellites direct microwaves over large, geographically dispersed areas too. A communication **satellite** is an electronic device placed in an orbit around the earth that receives, amplifies, and then retransmits signals. Microwave signals are sent from a transmitter station to an earth station, beamed to an orbiting satellite, and then retransmitted back to an earth station (see Figure 9-6).

The third type of communication channel is **fiber optics** (see Figure 9-7). A fiber optic channel transmits data in digital form. Light impulses travel through clear, flexible tubing, called fibers, thinner than a human hair. Hundreds of fibers fit in the space of a single wire cable.

FIGURE 9-6
Data communication is accomplished with the help of computers, satellites, and satellite dishes located at earth stations.

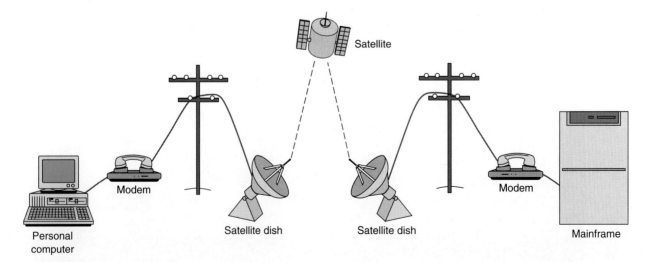

Satellite

Modem

Satellite dish

Satellite dish

Modem

Personal computer

Mainframe

FIGURE 9-7
Fiber optic cable.
(John Feingersh/Stock Boston)

Fiber optics are very reliable communication channels. In addition, they transmit data at very high speeds (several billions of bits per second) with few or no errors. Unlike wire cables, fiber optic cables are not subject to electrical interference. They also require repeaters to read and boost the light pulse signal strength over long distances. Technical developments are driving down the costs of installing, using, and manufacturing fiber optics so they are becoming competitive with traditional cabling. Sprint, a long-distance telephone company, has already converted to a fiber optic system, and others are in the process of converting.

OBJECTIVE 9.3
Define computer network and briefly describe wide area networks and local area networks.

WHAT IS A COMPUTER NETWORK?

A **computer network** is created when data communication channels link several computers and other devices, such as printers and secondary storage devices. The connections between computers on a network may be permanent, such as cables, or they may be temporary, made through telephone or other communication links. Computer networks may consist of only a few computers and related devices, or they may include many computers distributed over a wide geographic area. The purpose of a computer network is twofold. First, they provide users with a means of communicating and transferring information electronically. Second, they allow users to share hardware, data files, and programs. The two basic types of networks are wide area networks and local area networks.

Types of networks
• Wide area
• Local area

Wide Area Networks

A **wide area network (WAN)** consists of geographically dispersed computers and other devices that are linked by a communication channel such as the telephone system or microwave relay. For example, Chrysler Corporation supplies on-line information about a customer's car, including its complete maintenance history to its dealerships across the country. Devices are connected using satellites. The National Science

Foundation (NSF) in Washington, D.C., has connected six supercomputers in a WAN that links schools and research centers around the nation to the supercomputers.

Federal Express implemented a WAN to gain a strategic advantage over its competitors. Their on-line parcel tracking system, known as Cosmos (see Figure 9-8), handles inquiries from remote locations about the status of a parcel. In addition, it locates delayed shipments and automatically sends invoices to customers. The Federal Express delivery vans are equipped with on-board terminals, and through telecommunication, drivers make inquiries of the Cosmos system directly, thereby improving customer service. In fact, the global nature of many of today's businesses has increased the use of WANs to communicate internationally.

Local Area Networks

A **local area network (LAN)** is a data communication network that consists of one or more computers and other devices directly linked within a relatively small, well-

FIGURE 9-8
Federal Express processes over 700,000 packages a day. To make sure that deliveries and pickups are made quickly and accurately, each Federal Express delivery van is equipped with a small microcomputer. The office uses this to communicate with the driver about a package or to direct the driver to a pickup location. When a courier delivers a package, he or she scans the airbill number, adds information about the delivery, returns to the van, and feeds the delivery information into the computer. The information appears in the computers at the Federal Express headquarters in Memphis, Tennessee, within moments.

(Larry Hamill)

defined area, such as a room, building, or cluster of buildings. As personal computer use became widespread, the implementation of LANs provided an efficient way for users to connect them to share information and resources. Computer resources include hardware such as mass data storage devices, processors, printers, plotters, and software. LANs are privately owned and managed.

LANs have become very popular with businesses, educational institutions, and many other organizations where there is a desire to share data, programs, and expensive peripheral devices. Let's see what makes up a LAN.

COMPONENTS OF A LAN. A typical LAN consists of a number of components. These include workstations, one or more servers, the communication hardware that connects all the devices on the LAN, and the network operating system.

A **node** is any device, such as a workstation or printer, that is connected to and capable of communicating with other devices on a network. A **workstation** can be a personal computer or a terminal attached to the network. They interact with both the server and other workstations.

A **server** is the combination of hardware and software that provides access to the network and its resources for users. The computer can be a personal computer, minicomputer, mainframe, or specialized computer. A server can be configured in a number of ways. These include file, database, print, communication, or fax server. Depending on the load requirements of the network, one server may take care of all these tasks or there may be a separate server for each. A file server allows network users to share computer programs and data. A database server stores a database on disk so that it is accessible by multiple users. A print server provides network users with access to shared printers. A communication server allows all nodes on a network access to modems. It provides links to external data networks and to corporate minicomputers and mainframes. A fax server contains a fax board and the software that allows any user on the network to send or receive a fax at their workstation.

The hardware components of a network must all be connected. This is accomplished through a communication medium and network interface cards. Cable is a medium used in most networks to connect devices. Today, some networks are using fiber optics or wireless technologies such as infrared and microwave radio signals that are transmitted through the air. They are currently more expensive than cable alternatives. Infrared networks allow devices to be readily added or removed from their LANs without the hassles of running cable throughout the work area.

A **network interface card** is a circuit board that makes the physical connection to the network cable. It fits in an expansion slot inside a workstation. Its function is to move data from the workstation to the network, and vice versa.

LANs can also be connected to other networks using bridges and gateways. A **bridge** is an interface that connects LANs allowing communication between devices on each. A bridge passes data back and forth between the networks that use the same protocols. **Protocol** is the set of rules designed to enable computers to connect with one another and to exchange data with as few errors as possible. Since a bridge does no translation the computers on each network must use the same protocol.

Bridges allow the creation of numerous small, manageable networks that can be connected to form a larger network. This approach can be preferable to creating one large unwieldy network because it reduces traffic for individual computers and improves the performance of the network. It also enables a change from a LAN using one type of cable to a LAN using another type of cable.

A **gateway** is an interface that converts the protocol of one network into a form usable by another network or computer. LANs can be connected to WANs and an organization's minicomputers and mainframes through the use of gateways.

Components of a network

- Workstations
- Servers
  - File server
  - Database server
  - Print server
  - Communication server
  - Fax server
- Connections
  - Communication channels
  - Network interface cards
  - Bridges and gateways
- Network operating system

Just as stand-alone PCs have operating systems, so do networks. A **network operating system** is the software that controls the operations of a network.

WORKING ON A NETWORK.

Using a network is different from using a stand-alone computer. You must learn and remember your access code and password, and remember how to direct your output to the desired printer. Some equipment may not be on your desktop. In most organizations you'll learn the electronic mail (E-mail) application to communicate effectively with your coworkers. E-mail is described later in this chapter.

If you are involved in a work group where several individuals work on the same file simultaneously, you may use appropriate groupware applications. **Groupware** is a broad class of software that allows members of a group to work together without having all the participants in the same physical place or being available at the same time. For example, several users can revise the same document at the same time. Popular groupware applications include scheduling, document processing, time management, and conferencing.

BENEFITS OF USING A NETWORK.

Benefits of using a network

- Share information
- Share computer resources
- Improve communication
- Improve user productivity
- Provide access to wide variety of information sources

Drawbacks of using a network

- Expensive installation
- Training network administrator and users (learning curve)
- Maintaining the network
- Protecting data from system breaches, failures, or crashes
- Causing damage to information, hardware, or software
- Introducing virus programs

A network allows *sharing of information* and *sharing of computer resources* among its users. Because networks link users in work groups and departments throughout an organization as well as globally, they can *improve communication* among the members of the group. A network offers electronic mail to exchange messages and files with other users, even when they're not at their computer. Networks can also *increase user productivity* making it possible for users to do their jobs more quickly and efficiently. Because each user has access to the same files, less time is spent searching for the most up-to-date information. Many networks also store their files on redundant hard disks. If one should malfunction, the files are still accessible. This provides a level of data protection not found in single-user personal computers. A LAN can also be linked to other LANS, WANs, and larger computer systems to *provide access to a wide variety of information sources*. In many organizations LANs are linked to departmental minicomputers, corporate mainframes, and WANs to form a companywide information system.

DRAWBACKS OF USING A NETWORK.

Although there are some drawbacks to using a network, they are far outweighed by the benefits. Disadvantages include the fact that it may be expensive to install a network, train a network administrator and users, and maintain the network. There is also a learning curve that network administrators and users must go through to

Table 9-1 Hints on Choosing a Password
1. Choose a password that would not be easily guessed. For example, variations of your name, your date of birth, or any other well-known fact about you are NOT good choices.
2. Use a nonsense word. People who try to break into computers check against a dictionary of terms.
3. Use a combination of letters and numbers.
4. Keep your password a secret; don't write it down.
5. Use different passwords for different accounts.
6. Change your password often.

become comfortable and productive working on a network. In addition there is always the potential for system breaches, failures, or crashes. Although most networks have built-in safeguards, and access codes and passwords are installed to limit who reads or writes to network files, they may not always protect data. There is always the threat of people intent on causing damage through the introduction of virus programs or maliciously damaging information, hardware or software. Table 9-1 offers some ideas to consider when you are creating your own password.

OBJECTIVE 9. 7
Explain the purpose of communication software and describe its general functions; describe some of the parameters that must be set; define the terms log-on, log-off, command mode, data transfer mode, uploading, and downloading.

WHAT IS COMMUNICATION SOFTWARE?

In the past when a buyer purchased a microcomputer system, a modem and associated communication software were luxuries or extras. Today, communication hardware and software are important to a complete system. This section examines communication software.

Communication software are programs designed to control communication between two computers or devices. These programs

- Establish and maintain communication with a remote computer or device
- Tell the computer how to send data (i.e., set the communication parameters)
- Direct data from the keyboard, disks, or other devices through the communication port and into a modem and direct data from the communication port to the screen or disk

There are many communication programs with a wide variety of options. Popular microcomputer communication software includes Smartcom, Crosstalk, PC-Talk, and Qmodem. No matter how sophisticated or how basic the program, it must be able to set essential communication parameters.

Communication Parameters

Computers communicate as people do when making a telephone call. Someone initiates the call; the call must be received and answered. Once the connection is made, conversation must take place in the same language for the information exchange to be meaningful. If you do not understand what the other person has said, the message can be repeated. Similarly, the computer acknowledges an error in transmission and retransmits. Finally, when all is said and done, the communication link is broken by hanging up.

In most cases, the computer placing the call is responsible for matching the characteristics of the computer receiving the call. For communication software to work, your hardware must be "in sync" with the computer system with which you are trying to communicate. Configuring communication software involves setting **communication parameters** that synchronize it with your hardware and that of the **host computer**—the computer with which you want to communicate.

The necessary parameters are set from the setup screen. This screen varies from program to program. Some parameters that must be set include COM port, transmission speed, parity, word size and stop bit, emulation, duplex, and mode. Most offer a help function to guide in setting these. Many also offer preset communication parameters for various popular information services. The current values of the communication parameters can be viewed in a status screen (see Figure 9-9).

Communication parameters

- COM port
- Transmission speeds
- Parity, word size, and stop bit
- Emulation
- Duplex
- Mode

COM PORT. The COM port is the location where data both enter and exit your computer. This parameter must match the COM port on your computer. A computer typically has one to four COM ports, numbered 1 through 4. The computer needs to know which COM port is being used by the modem. Other COM ports can be used for a mouse and printer.

TRANSMISSION SPEEDS. The transmission speed defines how fast your modem will transmit or receive data. Hardware and software must agree on the transmission speed, which is measured in baud rates. The **baud rate** is the number of times per second that the signal being transmitted changes (modulates or demodulates). Baud is often equated with bits per second (bps); however, this comparison is not entirely accurate because a signal does not always carry one bit. Typical baud rates used by modems are 2400, 9600, and 14,400. The higher the baud rate, the faster the transmission of data. However, 14,400 bps is often as fast as conventional phone lines can transmit data without incurring many transmission errors. The modem baud rates for the two communicating computers must match.

PARITY, WORD SIZE, AND STOP BIT. The parity, word size, and stop bit settings refer to how individual bytes of data are interpreted. These settings must be agreed upon by the sending and receiving parties.

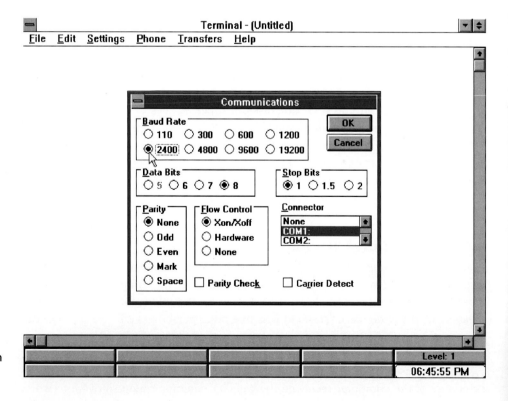

FIGURE 9-9
Screen showing communication parameters.

Parity is a type of error-checking procedure used in communication. The **parity bit** checks for transmission errors. Three parity-checking options are generally used with microcomputer communication: even, odd, or none. In even parity the number of 1's in each byte received must be an even number. In odd parity the number of 1's in each byte must be odd. When none is selected, no parity bit is used, and the data are not checked for accuracy.

If the parity count doesn't match the agreed-upon even or odd selection, the receiving computer is alerted that an error in data transmission has occurred. Many programs allow the user to choose how a parity error is handled. For example, the user may set the program to signal that an error has occurred or to ignore the error. Most programs automatically ask the sending computer to retransmit the data.

Parity checking is an elementary form of error checking. It cannot detect errors such as the loss of an entire character or larger block of data.

The **word size** refers to the number of data bits that make up a character. In microcomputer communication, characters are made up of either seven or eight bits. Both computers must be in agreement on the word size.

Each word contains one or two **stop bits** that allow the receiving terminal to synchronize itself with the transmitting terminal on a word-by-word basis. Most systems use one stop bit for speeds of 300 baud and above.

EMULATION. This parameter sets the type of terminal your communication software will emulate. Typically, this parameter is used if your personal computer acts as a terminal for a minicomputer or mainframe. This parameter is set to "none" for most commercial on-line services.

DUPLEX. In full-duplex mode there is simultaneous two-way communication between the participating computers. If a host computer is echoing the data you type, this parameter is set to full. If you are typing and do not see anything on your screen, the host computer is not echoing the data and this parameter should be set to half. Most dial-up computer systems require that the duplex be set to full. Typically, communication software defaults to full duplex when in a call mode and half duplex when in an answer mode.

MODE. The mode parameter tells your communication software whether it will be making a call or answering a call. You select the call mode to place a call and the answer mode to answer a call from another computer.

Log-on and Log-off Procedures

When you connect to another computer system, you'll hear a noise from your modem. This indicates that your modem is about to "shake hands" with the host modem. During this hand-shaking procedure, the modems exchange information about what parameters, among other things, they are using to ensure that they are in sync.

Once a connection is made, you hear another tone and then you can **log on** (also called log-in or sign-in). To log on you enter an access code and sometimes a password. Most programs let you automate the log-on procedure using a script. A **script** is a file your communication program uses to automatically enter information such as your log-on procedure. This saves time and long-distance telephone charges, since procedures like log-on can be performed quickly reducing the time you spend on the call. When you are done, you need to **log off** or disconnect from the host computer. This is typically done by selecting log-off, quit, bye, or hang up (see Figure 9-10).

FIGURE 9-10
Options such as a hangup button allow the user to log off.

(Courtesy of Norton-Lambert)

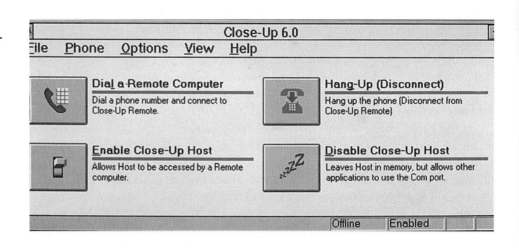

Command Mode and Data Transfer Mode

Most communication programs have at least two modes—command and data transfer (or conversation). In the **command mode,** whatever is entered is interpreted as a command. These commands vary among programs.

In the **data transfer mode,** communication actually occurs. Most programs automatically switch between the command and data transfer modes without disconnecting the communication link. The mode-switching feature allows you to leave the data transfer mode temporarily and enter the command mode (for example, to display a disk directory, delete a file, or activate a printer) and then to reenter the data transfer mode. To transfer data, however, one computer initiates the call, and the other computer receives it. Two submodes are available to indicate your choice. The computer that initiates the call must be in the **call mode** so that settings like entering the phone number and typing the command to initiate the dialing process can be made. To complete the connection, the receiving computer must be turned on and ready to receive the call. To receive a call, the computer must be in the **answer mode,** in which it is alerted to watch for an incoming signal from the modem.

File Transfer

Communication programs allow you to move files between computers. This procedure is called uploading and downloading. **Uploading** occurs when data are sent to another computer, and **downloading** occurs when data are received from another computer.

You can create a file on a disk before going on-line, and then upload it and send it from that disk. This procedure significantly reduces time spent on-line, thus lowering the cost of a communication session. Downloading lets you receive data and store it to a disk; the data can then be read or edited off line. This process dramatically reduces the cost of using information services where charges are based on actual on-line time.

OBJECTIVE 9. 5
Describe various information resources available to the user through data communication.

HOW CAN DATA COMMUNICATION WORK FOR YOU?

Equipping a computer with communication hardware and software opens a whole new world of information resources. Data communication has made the computer one of the most vital tools in our information-seeking society. It links one or more computers or terminals via communication channels and enables users to send and

Table 9-2 Hints on Using a Bulletin Board System

- Keep pencil and paper near your computer to write down names of files, list commands, and other instructions and note names of people or messages that are of interest.
- Write down the access code, if there is one, and keep it handy.
- Ask questions of the system operators and BBS users. These are usually people who like to share their experiences with others.
- Try early-morning hours, if the BBS line is always busy.
- Prepare messages before going on-line to save on phone charges, if calling long distance.
- Try local BBSs for public domain software. If the software is not available locally, then try long-distance BBSs.

Most BBSs use the remote bulletin board system (RBBS) or Hostcomm bulletin board system program. If the BBS you use requires a long-distance call, try to find out what program that BBS uses. Then find a local bulletin board that uses the same program to familiarize yourself with the operating environment. This saves money because you do not spend time on a long-distance phone connection, online, learning how that BBS operates.

receive electronic data with little regard for distance, schedule, or time zones. This section discusses some of the available options.

Bulletin Boards

One of the easiest and least expensive ways to begin exploring communication capabilities is by using a bulletin board system. Table 9-2 gives hints on using BBSs. A **bulletin board system (BBS)** is essentially the electronic equivalent of a conventional bulletin board. Many BBSs are established to let users exchange information about any topic. Others are set up for people who have a common interest. The first electronic BBS was created in 1978 by Ward Christensen and Randy Suess so members of the Chicago Area Computer Hobbyists Exchange could trade information.

Although features vary among BBSs, most provide users with the ability to

- post messages for other users to read
- read messages posted by other callers
- communicate with the system operator (sysop, the person who operates the bulletin board) to ask questions about the operation of the BBS, report problems, or make suggestions
- post notices of equipment or services for sale
- upload (transfer a file from your computer to the BBS) or download (transfer file from the BBS to your computer) programs

Many BBSs currently in operation are noncommercial and free of charge. The telephone company, however, charges for the long-distance phone time used when you communicate with a BBS that is outside your local calling area. A BBS provides an easy and inexpensive way to share information; however, there are some drawbacks.

Commercial On-Line Services

Have you ever asked yourself, "How am I ever going to find an answer to that question?" When you need information, on virtually any topic imaginable, a commercial on-line service probably has it. A **commercial on-line service** is a business that supplies information to subscribers electronically on numerous topics of interest by using powerful computer systems that store millions of pieces of data. These services offer numerous electronic databases and the opportunity to contact and talk electronically with experts in various fields, just "chat" with people who share a common interest, set up formal conferences, shop from your home, play games with a friend around the corner or across the country, or get the latest updates on news, weather, and sports.

The topics covered vary among the services (see Figure 9-11). Some allow you to electronically search millions of articles, abstracts, and bibliographic citations from thousands of books, periodicals, reports, and theses. Commercial on-line services have support in the form of printed catalogs and on-line indexes to help you select the appropriate database or service.

Commercial on-line services require a subscription and some require payment of hourly access charges; others require initial sign-on fees. Most provide access to the Internet. Although a few have limited hours, commercial on-line services usually operate 24 hours a day, 7 days a week. Charges are commonly lower for evening or weekend access. New subscribers are customarily issued a user number and a password to access the service and retrieve information.

Some commercial on-line services are geared toward general consumers and cover a wide range of topics and interests. These include, for example, CompuServe, Prodigy, America Online, Delphi, and GEnie.

Other commercial on-line services cater to special interests. These are subscribed to individually or in some cases accessed from the general consumer-oriented on-line services just listed.

Dialog Information Service is one of the largest commercial on-line services. It permits users to conduct research on topics such as agriculture, business and economics, chemistry, current affairs, education, energy and environment, law and government, medicine and biosciences, science and technology, and social sciences and humanities.

Dow Jones News/Retrieval offers financial, commodity, and stock information. In addition news and general information databases are offered.

Newsnet provides information from newspapers nationwide and full text access to industry newsletters highlighting products, technology, and trends.

Popular commercial on-line services

- General consumer
  - CompuServe
  - Prodigy
  - America Online
  - Delphi
  - GEnie
- Profession oriented
  - Dialog
  - Dow Jones News Retrieval
  - Newsnet
  - Lexis
  - Nexis

FIGURE 9-11
CompuServe basic services are listed in the Information Manager screen.

(Courtesy of CompuServe Inc.)

Lexis, a specialized database of legal information, is offered by Mead Data Central. Mead Data also offers Nexis, which provides full text (not just bibliographic citations or summary abstracts) of articles and news items covering a wide range of topics.

Electronic Mail

Electronic mail (E-mail) refers to the electronic transmission of correspondence over a computer network. It is an electronic version of the post office or interoffice mail, and it sends messages from one computer or terminal to another computer or terminal on a network (see Figure 9-12). E-mail is the most common use for the Internet with more than 4,000 messages being sent per second in early 1995. (See Infomodule III for a more in-depth look at the Internet and its services.) Many businesses use electronic mail systems to reduce paperwork and to reduce the time it takes messages to reach their destination. The same message can be addressed simultaneously to a list of recipients with "carbon" copies to others.

Electronic mail can be sent between subscribers to the same on-line service or between subscribers of different services. Many E-mail systems on different networks

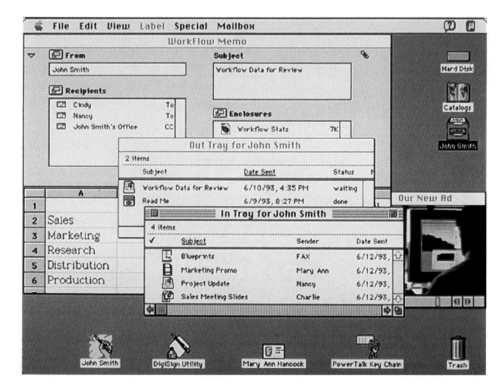

FIGURE 9-12
Interoffice mail can be sent electronically.
(Courtesy of Apple Computer, Inc.)

can be linked with the appropriate hardware and software, so that messages can be created locally and distributed globally.

E-mail systems differ in features offered. Some provide a text editor to create and edit messages. Many allow users to forward mail, request return receipts, and attach files to a message. Some remain active in the background while you work on other applications. They automatically inform you when new messages arrive and give you the option of viewing them immediately or reading later.

Messages can be sent to an individual recipient or to a larger group with one action. When messages are sent, they are stored in a file space called an electronic mailbox assigned to users on the network. The recipient can view, save, or delete a message at their convenience. You should assume that E-mail may be read by someone other than the addressee and avoid writing something that you may regret later.

Some of the benefits of electronic mail include the following:

- It is faster than traditional mail and less expensive to prepare and send.
- A single message can be sent simultaneously to multiple addresses.
- The recipient doesn't need to be on the line at the same time as the sender.
- A busy person isn't interrupted to receive the message.
- The message can be printed on paper.

Electronic mail has some drawbacks.

- There is no guarantee that systems will be compatible
- Privacy and security may be compromised; that is, incoming and outgoing mail may be read by others.
- You can be inundated by junk E-mail.
- E-mail cannot be retrieved after it is "sent."

Facsimile

Facsimile (fax) is the transmission of text or graphics in digital form over telephone lines (see Figure 9-13). A copy of an original document is electronically sent to and reproduced at another location. To send a fax using a conventional fax machine, you must insert the original document into the unit that is directly connected to the

FIGURE 9-13
A facsimile (fax) machine sends a document electronically to a branch office.

(Bob Dsammerich/Stock Boston)

phone lines. The machine scans the document and sends the text, graphics, photographs, even handwriting, over telephone lines. A fax machine at the receiving end gathers the electronic signals and converts them and produces a hard copy duplicate of the original document. Fax machines must be compatible to communicate with each other.

Microcomputers can also be equipped with fax boards and software to function as a fax machine. Documents created on the computer can be faxed, and if a scanner is connected, hard copy documents can be scanned into the computer and faxed, just as with a conventional fax machine. Fax/modem boards combine the functions of a fax machine and a modem on a single circuit board, taking up only one expansion slot in your computer. Cellular fax/modem boards are also available and are ideal for those who need to transfer documents using portable computers.

Voice Mail

The telephone is still the most frequently used device for communicating between individuals in business. It is simple, efficient, and easy to understand and use. **Voice mail** is a computer-supported system that allows voice messages to be received at a touch-tone telephone even if the recipient is unavailable to answer the call. Later, when it is convenient, the recipient dials his or her mailbox and hears the message. Voice mail has several advantages, including

- leaving messages for one or more persons
- cutting costs by avoiding multiple call backs when the recipient is not available
- using the convenience of touch-tone phones
- eliminating concern for schedules and time zones
- giving the personal touch by sending voice messages

Disadvantages include a caller becoming lost in a voice mail maze or needing to speak to someone personally because the particular call doesn't fit the menu choices.

Electronic Teleconferencing

Electronic teleconferencing allows participants in geographically dispersed locations to participate, sometimes interactively, in the same conference or meeting through a linked communication channel (see Figure 9-14). The audio and video signals are sent to the remote sites by satellite or through fiber optic lines because telephone lines are ineffective for transmitting video.

Businesses save money when their employees don't incur expenses for travel to distant sites to attend meetings. They are able to offer training seminars or continuing education to their employees. This saves the company both time and money, especially if there are no schools nearby that offer a particular subject. Universities share resources by conducting classes in this manner. The instructor is in one place while the students are in classrooms elsewhere.

Telecommuting

Telecommuting is an approach to working that some employers are implementing whereby an employee works at home or another remote location using computers, communication software, and modems to access the main office computers and information. For example, if the employee needs to refer to last year's budget in order to prepare next quarter's forecast for widget sales, he or she accesses the necessary information from the office computer via modem. The appropriate files can be downloaded onto the home computer, manipulated, and subsequently printed at the main office for the sales meeting.

FIGURE 9-14
Employees at different locations use video teleconferencing to hold a business meeting where the participants can see and converse with each other.

(Courtesy of PictureTel. Corp.)

Electronic Data Interchange

Today, many businesses use **electronic data interchange (EDI),** a method that automates and standardizes transactions between retailers and their suppliers. Users conduct transactions electronically, transferring information from a computer in one company to another computer in another company through a network. EDI reduces paperwork, human involvement, and time associated with processing orders manually. Some estimates indicate that turnaround time on orders has been reduced by as much as 50 percent.

Electronic Funds Transfer

Electronic funds transfer (EFT), the electronic movement of money among accounts, is a common data communication application. A large portion of money in the business and financial communities changes hands through EFT in the form of the automated teller machine. In fact, Society for Worldwide Interbank Financial Telecommunications (SWIFT), the most sophisticated private interbank system in the world, averages 1 million transactions daily for its member banks in numerous countries around the world. Nationally, the Cirrus banking network processes approximately 200 million transactions annually. The network provides services such as cash withdrawals and balance inquiries for checking, savings, and credit accounts and supports more than 6,500 automated teller machines.

Integrated Services Digital Network

When fully implemented, the **Integrated Services Digital Network (ISDN)** will provide a worldwide digital communication network service for computers and other devices to tap into through simple, standardized interfaces. Its goal is having the ability to transmit voice, data, music, and video in digital form over the same channel. It provides faster and more extensive communication services to users. ISDN facilitates electronic teleconferencing because it allows video signals to be sent over standard telephone lines.

Let's see how a college student uses some of these data communication methods on a daily basis. Sarah's campus, Future U, is part of a local area network and is also connected to the "backbone" of the Internet. A local BBS gives her a chance to contact other new student users with the same kind of computer she brought to campus. Many teachers, including the geography professor, insist that students get an E-mail address so that he can make assignments and keep in touch with students as necessary. In fact, at 5 A.M. he E-mailed all his students to cancel classes because freezing rain made it treacherous for people to be outdoors. Sarah sends E-mail to her friends at school in other cities. And her political science instructor conducts large classes via teleconference from a remote site back to the campus lecture hall. The Internet account helps Sarah search for historical citations for the term paper on Kafka that is due before the end of the semester.

While it is clear that Sarah is using many of the more obvious data communication applications available to her, she may be using data communication and not be aware of it. For example, the hospital where her brother was treated at the emergency room last week, used EDI to restock hospital supplies, and her routine banking required EFT from the remote teller on campus through the main office. If you are not using these technologies now, you soon will as you find jobs in an ever-changing workplace.

OBJECTIVE 9.6
Recognize some challenges presented by data communication.

WHAT CHALLENGES ARE PRESENTED BY DATA COMMUNICATION?

Using data communication has its challenges. Many computer systems are incompatible and cannot easily establish communication links. In addition, data sent over communication channels are subject to various kinds of interference that may alter or destroy some of the data. Besides the integrity of data, privacy of data must be protected. In this regard, passwords and access codes may be helpful. To prevent unauthorized access, data may have to be encrypted—or scrambled—before they are sent. Then, of course, they must be decoded—or unscrambled—as they are received.

SUMMARY

Data communication is the process of sending data electronically from one point to another. Using communication facilities such as the telephone system and microwave relays to send data between computers is a type of data communication often referred to as telecommunication. Transmission of data takes one of two forms: analog or digital. Modulation is the process of converting a digital signal into an analog signal. Demodulation is the process of converting the analog signal into a digital signal. A modem (*mo*dulator-*dem*odulator) is the device that converts the signals. Two basic types of modems are used with microcomputers: external direct connect and internal direct connect.

A communication channel is a pathway along which data are transmitted between devices. The three basic types of communication channels are wire cable, microwave, and fiber optic.

A computer network is created when several computers and other devices, such as printers and secondary storage devices, are linked together by data communication channels. A wide area network (WAN) consists of two or more computers that are geographically dispersed but are linked by communication facilities such as the telephone system or microwave relays.

A local area network (LAN) is a data communication network that consists of two or more computers directly linked within a relatively small, well-defined area, such as a room, building, or cluster of buildings. LAN users share information and computer resources; enjoy improved communication, user productivity, and security; have flexibility to expand on an as-needed basis; and provide access to a wide variety of information sources. A typical LAN includes the following components: workstations, server(s), the hardware to connect all the devices on the LAN, and the network operating system.

Communication software is a program designed to control communication between two computers. It must be configured to work with your hardware and the host computer system. This is accomplished by setting communication parameters, including setting the COM port, transmission speeds, parity, word size, and stop bit values; the type of emulation, if needed; the duplex mode; and the mode of operation (call or answer) of the software.

When connecting to a host computer, you need to enter a log-on sequence such as an access code and password to initiate a communication session with a host computer. A log-off command is required to end a session.

Most communication programs have a command mode in which characters typed are interpreted as commands and a data transfer mode in which the data communication process actually occurs.

Communication programs allow transmission and reception of files between computers. The files can be uploaded (data from a disk are sent to another computer) or downloaded (data are received from another computer and saved).

Equipping a personal computer with communication hardware and software opens a whole new world of information resources, including bulletin boards, commercial on-line services, electronic mail, facsimile, voice messaging, teleconferencing, telecommuting, electronic data interchange (EDI), electronic funds transfer (EFT), and Integrated Services Digital Network (ISDN).

Data communication challenges include hardware and software incompatibilities that make establishing communication linkages difficult; interference on communication channels, which may alter or destroy some of the data; and concerns about ensuring the integrity and privacy of the data transmitted.

Can you define the following?

analog data transmission (p. 257)

answer mode (p. 268)

baud rate (p. 266)

bridge (p. 263)

bulletin board system (BBS) (p. 269)

call mode (p. 268)

coaxial cable (p. 259)

command mode (p. 268)

commercial on-line service (p. 269)

communication channel (p. 259)

communication software (p. 265)

communication parameters (p. 266)

computer network (p. 261)

data communication (p. 257)

data transfer mode (p. 268)

demodulation (p. 257)

digital data transmission (p. 257)

downloading (p. 268)

electronic data interchange (EDI) (p. 274)

electronic funds transfer (EFT) (p. 274)

electronic mail (E-mail) (p. 271)

electronic teleconferencing (p. 273)

external direct-connect modem (p. 258)

facsimile (fax) (p. 272)

fiber optics (p. 260)

gateway (p. 263)

groupware (p. 264)

host computer (p. 266)

Integrated Services Digital Network (ISDN) (p. 274)

internal direct-connect modem (p. 258)

local area network (LAN) (p. 262)

log off (p. 267)

log on (p. 267)

microwave (p. 260)

modem (p. 257)

modulation (p. 257)

network interface card (p. 263)

network operating system (p. 264)

node (p. 264)

parity (p. 267)

parity bit (p. 267)

protocol (p. 263)

satellite (p. 260)

script (p. 267)

server (p. 263)

stop bits (p. 267)

telecommunication (p. 257)

telecommuting (p. 273)

twisted-pair (p. 259)

uploading (p. 268)

voice mail (p. 273)

wide area network (WAN) (p. 261)

word size (p. 267)

workstation (p. 263)

Multiple Choice

1. _____ is the process of using communication facilities to send data between computers.
   a. Telecommunication
   b. Modulation
   c. Analog data transmission
   d. Demodulation

2. A _____ is two or more computers directly linked within a small, well-defined area.
   a. wide area network
   b. local area network
   c. cellular network
   d. network topology

3. A _____ is a computer providing services to network users.
   a. workstation
   b. node
   c. bridge
   d. server

4. Which of the following parameters determines the rate at which the modem operates?
   a. emulation
   b. parity
   c. baud rate
   d. duplex

5. Sending a file from your computer to another computer is called _____.
   a. uploading
   b. downloading
   c. capturing
   d. pacing

6. Many businesses employ _____ which is the electronic transmission of correspondence over a computer network.
   a. bulletin boards
   b. commercial on-line services
   c. electronic mail
   d. electronic funds transfer

7. _____ electronically sends documents containing text, graphics, photographs, and handwriting over telephone lines and reproduces them at the receiving location.
   a. Voice mail
   b. Facsimile
   c. Bulletin boards
   d. Teleconferencing

8. _____ is a computer-supported system that allows a caller, using a touch-tone telephone, to leave a voice message even if the recipient is unavailable to answer the call.
   a. Voice mail
   b. A bulletin board
   c. Electronic mail
   d. Electronic data interchange

9. A(n) _____ specializes in supplying information on numerous topics of interest to subscribers.
   a. bulletin board
   b. commercial on-line service
   c. electronic mail system
   d. electronic teleconferencing system

10. _____ is a method that allows users to conduct business transactions electronically, transferring information from a computer in one company to another computer in another company through a network.
    a. Electronic funds transfer
    b. Telecommuting
    c. Integrated Services Digital Network
    d. Electronic data interchange

Fill In

1. The process of sending data electronically from one point to another is called _____.

2. A _____ is a device used to convert a digital signal into a analog signal and convert an analog signal into a digital signal.

3. _____ is a medium that transmits data at very high speeds and is not subject to electrical interference.

4. A _____ is created when data communication channels link one or more computers and other devices, such as printers and secondary storage devices.

5. A _____ is a data communication network that consists of two or more computers directly linked within a relatively small, well-defined area.

6. The _____ is the number of times per second that a signal being transmitted changes (modulates or demodulates).

7. _____ is the process of retrieving data from a remote computer and storing it in your computer's main memory or secondary storage.

8. An electronic version of the post office or interoffice mail in which messages are sent electronically over a computer network is called _____.

9. _____ involves the electronic movement of money among accounts.

10. _____ is an approach to working that some employers are implementing whereby an employee works at home or another remote location, using computers, communication software, and modems to access the main office computers and information.

Short Answer

1. How does data communication differ from telecommunication?

2. Describe the difference between analog and digital data transmission.

3. When is a modem needed? Why are two needed?

4. Define computer network and briefly describe wide area network and local area network.

5. Identify the purpose of communication software and describe three basic functions that all communication programs perform.

6. Describe the purpose of the communication parameters in a communication software package.

7. Describe some of the services you might find on a commercial on-line service and identify several popular commercial on-line services.

8. Discuss the benefits of using electronic mail.

9. How can the use of voice mail and electronic teleconferencing benefit a business?

10. Describe the purpose of electronic data interchange, electronic funds transfer, and Integrated Services Digital Network.

Issues for Thought

1. Computer networks allow users to take advantage of E-mail and easily send messages to coworkers. They also make it easy for management to secretly monitor and read messages sent between employees. While not illegal, do you think this is ethical? Does management have a right to know how its employees are using their time and company-provided equipment? If personal information is discovered in an E-mail message, such as an admission to a coworker of a dependency problem, should management be able to use this information?

2. If you were able to work from your home through communication channels connected to your place of employment, would you? What advantages and disadvantages do you foresee? Consider the discipline required for this type of work environment. Should employers monitor home workers' productivity? How?

INFOMODULE III
INTRODUCTION TO THE INTERNET

WHAT IS THE INTERNET?

The **Internet** consists of thousands of loosely connected networks, estimated at over 25,000 in mid-1995. Accessing the Internet puts all the information and data from each network at your fingertips. You can send E-mail to a friend, chat with others on virtually any topic, perform research, and hear and see audio and video presentations from across the world—all without leaving the chair in front of your computer.

The Internet can be compared to a library with holdings of books, music, videos, and so on. Using the library comparison, each book (network) has its own table of contents (structure) unrelated to other books (networks). The central card catalog is the Internet; it provides a means to locate any book (network). The library also contains many different rooms dedicated to different subject areas. Once you enter the building, you can browse anywhere you want that's open. The same is true for the Internet. One distinguishing difference is that there is no one physical location for the Internet; it is everywhere. It can be accessed from all seven continents. To be "on the Internet" means to be connected to it. To "surf" the Internet means to browse through the various services available.

No one knows exactly how many people are on the Internet at any one time. There are about 3 million host computers from which it is estimated that there are 10–20 million users.

WHO OWNS AND RUNS THE INTERNET?

No one person, company, organization, or government owns the Internet. However, each individual network may be owned or managed by a company, university, organization, or government. The hardware and software necessary to access the Internet must be purchased, and there are charges to connect to the Internet, although much of the actual information "flowing" on the Internet is free.

There is no official group or entity that runs the Internet on a day-to-day basis. But there have always been people interested in keeping the Internet going and running smoothly. A group of volunteers formed the Internet Society (ISOC), which is a coordinating group for all other groups interested in maintaining the Internet. They hold a conference each year on Internet issues. The Internet Engineering Task Force (IETF) is an all-volunteer group that oversees the technical standards of the Internet.

For more information, contact the Internet Society at

Internet Society
12020 Sunrise Valley Drive, Suite 270
Reston, VA 22091
(703) 648-9888
membership@isoc.org

HOW DID THE INTERNET START?

In 1969, the U.S. Department of Defense (DoD) was searching for a way to use computer networks while keeping the data on them secure in case of war. Their research led to the linking of four computers at universities in California and Utah. This project was developed under the Advanced Research Project Agency (ARPA), and the network was called ARPAnet. Over the next few years, many other universities and government agencies became linked with each other and became the Internet. Scientists around the world began using the Internet for research in the 1970s and 1980s. The DoD transferred much of the network authority to the National Science Foundation (NFSnet), which still runs many networks today. Beginning in the early 1990s the government opened access to the Internet. A group of Internet providers formed the Commercial Internet Exchange (CIX), which further linked services to allow traffic to enter and leave their networks. The CIX lobbies the government on Internet issues.

Currently there is no charge once you're on the Internet, but that could soon change. The problem lies in deciding just how to come up with a billing system, and how to collect fees and determining who should pay. One plan being considered was proposed by economists at the University of Michigan. It prioritizes transmission through a method of competitive bidding. Users could pay for the privilege of getting priority treatment. Those users choosing a lower priority would pay a lower fee.

HOW ARE INTERNET SERVICES ORGANIZED?

Once you are "on" the Internet, you are sure to ask some, if not all, of these questions: "Where do I go?" "How do I get there?" and "What can I find there?" In this section we'll look at some of the main services offered on the Internet. These fall into basic groups such as electronic mail, mailing lists, newsgroups, and various methods for searching for information contained in files and databases. There is no central location for finding information on the Internet.

Electronic Mail

Electronic mail, or E-mail, refers to electronic transmission of messages over a computer network and is the most used feature of the Internet. It's easy to see why—E-mail is cheap, and your message arrives at any E-mail address destination in the world within seconds, or at most a few minutes (see E-mail addressing later in this Infomodule). Some estimates indicate that 3,000 to 5,000 E-mail messages are sent per second. Just as you would send a letter, the key to getting your message there is entering the proper address. You can choose to read your messages immediately as they arrive at your E-mail box or you can read them later. Popular text-based E-mail programs include PINE, Mail, and ELM (see Figure IM3-1). Internet in a Box and Internet Chameleon are newer programs that offer a graphical interface for E-mail.

Mailing Lists

A **mailing list** is basically a discussion group that often pertains to one topic. The global mail system of the Internet lets a user send mail to all participants in that group at the same time. In turn, each member receives any response messages sent to and from other members in the same mailing list. Many mailing lists are moderated by a mailing list administrator from whom you ask permission to join. Others are not moderated. Some do not stick to one topic. Mailing list topics range from pure chit-chat to issues such as cancer support groups. Mailing lists may contain as few as two or three people or hundreds of subscribers. You can set up your own mailing list and become its administrator.

To get a list of some of the major Internet mailing lists, send an E-mail message addressed to *listserv@bitnic.bitnet*. Leave the "subject area" blank and enter *list global* in the body of your request. You should receive an E-mail response containing the requested list.

FIGURE IM3-I
An E-mail example on bgnet.

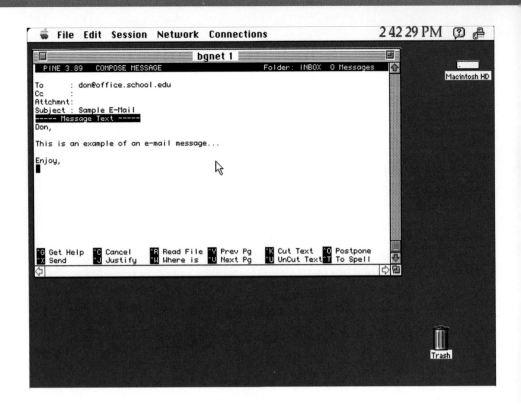

Newsgroups

Mailing lists serve smaller discussion groups best. For larger groups, often in the thousands, a newsgroup is more appropriate. A **newsgroup** is like a floating bulletin board on the Internet. A message is *posted* (similar to tacking a message on a physical bulletin board) rather than being sent directly to each member. In a newsgroup, which is generally not about news, multiple conversations can take place and can be more unstructured than a mailing list.

Usenet is the Internet service that organizes discussions into newsgroups. Names are based on hierarchies. There are about seven main topic groups, each of which is then subdivided into more specific topics under the main heading. For example; rec.sport.football.college would be a discussion group about college football. The general heading is found on the left, becoming more specific as you move right. Main topic areas are given below with some real examples of each.

Topic group	Example subtopics	Example addresses
rec	sports, games, pets, hobbies, etc.	rec.pets.cats
comp	computers and related topics	comp.security.misc
sci	science and health	sci.med.dentistry
soc	social issues and culture	soc.culture.soviet
talk	general chatting, debates	talk.politics.medicine
news	Usenet network	news.newusers.questions
k12	education	k12.ed.math
misc	topics not easily categorized	misc.jobs.misc
alt	you name it	alt.music.pearl-jam

Telnet

One of the older Internet services, **telnet** lets you tap into a remote computer and use yours as if it were a terminal for the remote computer. Although many Internet services are disallowing telnet access, library catalogs and bulletin boards continue to do so. A telnet access to library catalogs lets the user browse through both public and college library holdings, even the Library of Congress. Although easy to use, other interfaces, such as the World Wide Web (discussed later in this Infomodule) will probably be the access method of choice in the future.

The telnet site for LOCIS:Library of Congress Information System is locis.loc.gov (see Figure IM3-2). The choices available are shown in Figure IM3-2(b). The telnet site for the New York Public Library is nyplgate.nypl.org (at the login prompt, type nypl).

Gopher and Veronica

Gopher is a menu-based information service that allows you to search for the information you need. The service got its unusual name because it was originally created at the University of Minnesota, where students bear the nickname "Gophers." Gophers are located all over the world, but they are generally found at universities. A gopher screen contains a list of menus where you begin your search (see Figure IM3-3). A menu may contain another layer of menus (sometimes many layers deep) or lead you directly to a file. With a gopher you can access many types of information or open and read text files. The gopher searches any host computer that is currently connected to a gopher anywhere in the world.

Searching for the right information can be tedious if you don't know which Gopher has the information you need. **Veronica** provides an interface accessed through Gopher that makes it easier to narrow your search for information (see Figure IM3-4). It does not search within a file, however. Veronica is an acronym that stands for Very Easy Rodent-Oriented Netwide Index to Computer Archives. To use Veronica, you enter a search request, such as *camera,* and it gives you a list of all Gopher entries pertaining to this keyword. To limit your search, use multiple keywords, such as *camera background lighting.*

File Transfer Protocol and Archie

File Transfer Protocol (FTP) is an older Internet standard for the transfer of files from a host computer to your personal computer. FTP is an excellent way to download freeware and shareware programs for Macintosh, IBM, and IBM-compatible computers (see Figure IM3-5). Most host computers allow anyone to search and download files; it is often known by the name **anonymous FTP**. Some host computers contain confidential information and require a password to enter them. Although FTP is an efficient way to download files, it can be difficult to use.

Finding the right anonymous FTP site that contains the one file (out of 2 or 3 million files available on FTP) that you want can be complicated. As Gopher has Veronica, anonymous FTP has Archie. **Archie**, derived from the word "archive," lets the user narrow an anonymous FTP search by using keywords. For example, a search using the keywords *air transportation* returns a list of files pertaining to air transportation and the anonymous FTP sites where those files are located. One anonymous FTP site is the Smithsonian Institution. To search photograph archives, use photo.si.edu, which is found in the subdirectory /pub/multimedia/pictures/smithsonian.

FIGURE IM3-2

(a) "Visit" the Library of Congress; (b) choices at the LOCIS screen.

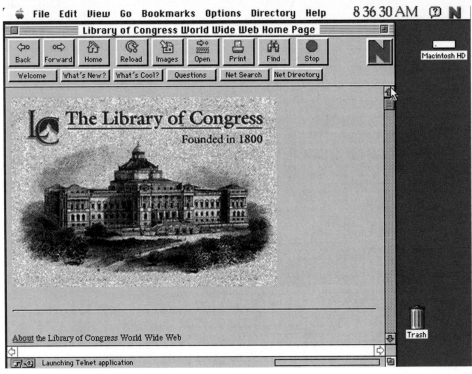

(a)

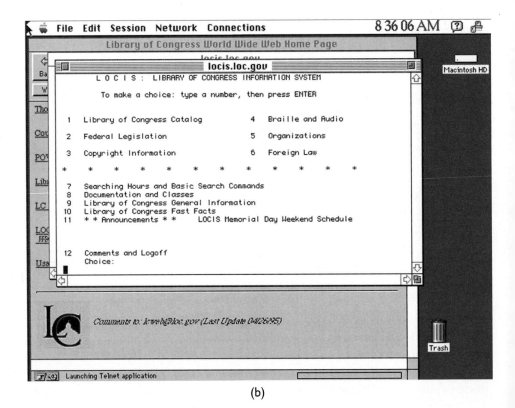

(b)

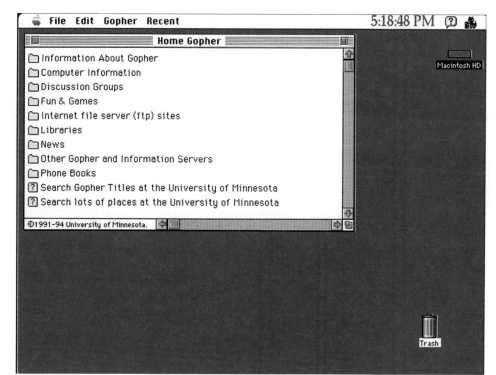

FIGURE IM3-3
Home Gopher screen.

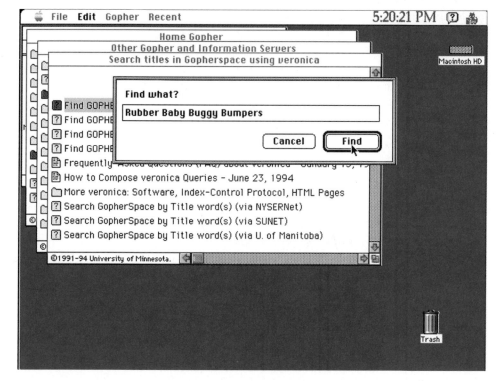

FIGURE IM3-4
Veronica screen search for
"Rubber Baby Buggy Bumpers."

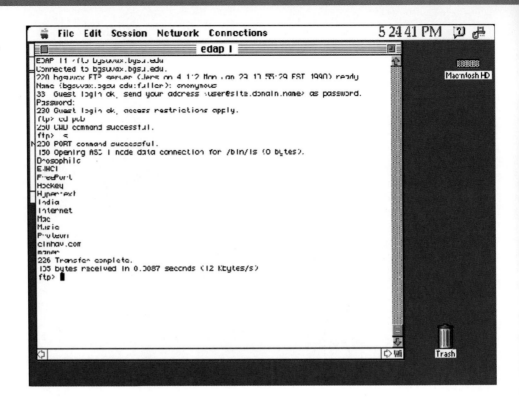

WAIS

Wide Area Information Service (WAIS) is another tool used to search for information on the Internet. It differs from an FTP or Gopher search in that you search through databases instead of menus or files. A particular site can use a WAIS to create a database of the files at their location. A user can specify which database or databases to search and let the WAIS search for the particular file (see Figure IM3-6). If you specify too many databases, the search can take a long time. Many Gopher and World Wide Web sites have built-in connections to WAIS. For WAIS sources, try *Directory-of-Servers.scr*.

World Wide Web and Web Browsers

The **World Wide Web (WWW)**, or **Web** for short, is one of the newest and hottest services for finding information on the Internet. The basic interface of the Internet is text based. The Web uses hypertext and hypermedia to link documents. You use a mouse to point and click on different parts of the document, which takes you to another document with related data (see Figure IM3-7). With the Web, you get an entire page of information, rather than a line of text. A Web page can contain text, graphics, and photographs. You can "visit" an art gallery and view paintings, shop on-line and actually see the product, or order from the menu in a restaurant.

To achieve the best results browsing the Web, a graphical user interface should be used. To use the graphical part of the Web or another graphical interface, you must have a direct connection (SLIP/PPP, described in the next section) to the Internet. Popular graphical interfaces (called Web browsers) include Netscape, Enhanced Mosaic, and WinWeb. These interfaces provide the user with the ability to receive multimedia information. Unlike a text-based interface, you can point and click on icons to receive text, sound, illustrations, and photographs. *Netscape Navigator* is one of the most popular Web browser on the market. In addition to Web access, you have access to E-mail, newsgroups, Gopher, and other Internet services (see Figure IM3-8). One advantage of using Netscape is that it initially downloads graphics in low resolution so that the user can immediately see the image. It then slowly improves the resolution. Most browsers try to download graphics directly in

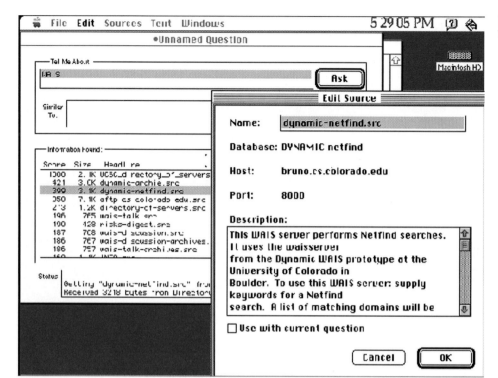

FIGURE IM3-6
WAIS search screen.

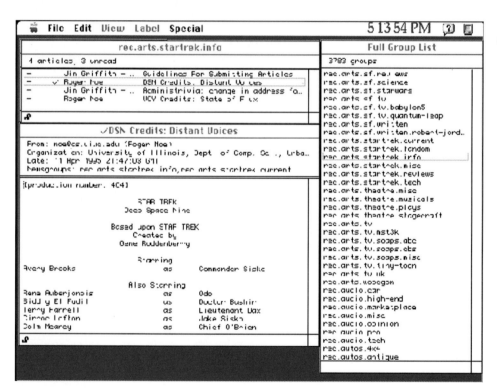

FIGURE IM3-7
a WWW search.

high resolution, which takes much longer. Another advantage is that it is free to noncommercial users. The E-mail address is *info@netscape.com*.

Through one of the graphical interfaces on the Web, you can create your own **home page** also called a Web site. You can customize your home page with pictures of yourself, family, pets, or any other personal touches if you have specialized hardware, such as scanners and video cameras and appropriate software (see Figure IM3-9).

FIGURE IM3-8
Netscape assistant screen.

FIGURE IM3-9
The Bowling Green State University, Bowling Green, Ohio, home page.

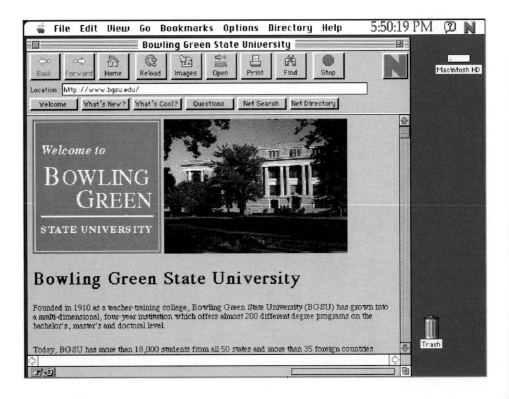

WWW uses HyperText Transport Protocol for data transfer, so you will see the initials *http:* before a WWW address. A few WWW sites are listed below by site, address, and general description of what it is.

EINet Galaxy	http://www.einet.net/ galaxy/html	Comprehensive directory of Internet resources.
Microsoft Corp.	http: //www.microsoft.com	About Microsoft and its products.
The White House	http: //www.whitehouse.gov	Get into the Executive Mansion and even sign the guestbook.
The Internet Plaza	http://plaza.xor.com/	On-line shopping.
Web Museum	http://mistral.enst.fr/	Download artwork from the Louvre.

So, how do you know when to use which? As a rule of thumb, use Archie for software or files on FTP; however, the service is overloaded and slow. Gopher helps you find something if you think there are gophers already created. WAIS searches by content. The Web subsumes all the others and is best to start with, if you don't know for sure what you are looking for.

Interacting in Real Time

Internet services, such as E-mail and newsgroups, allow the user to communicate with others; however, it is on a delayed basis. Internet Relay Chat and Multi-User Dimension are two Internet services that allow you to interact immediately.

INTERNET RELAY CHAT. Internet Relay Chat (IRC) is an Internet service where users communicate in real time. A user types a message at the keyboard and it is seen immediately by the person(s) at the receiving computer. IRC is similar to talking on the telephone in that the people in the conversation are in direct and immediate contact. An IRC is also like entering a room full of groups of people where each group carries on its own conversation. Some find this confusing while others enjoy chatting in multiple conversations. For a novice in an IRC, it is best to *lurk* first, that is "listen" to find out who is talking to whom and on what topics before contributing your own thoughts and opinions.

When you connect to an IRC you may type */list* to see a list of topics being talked about or */help* for on-line help with the IRC. Anything typed during an IRC conversation starting with a forward slash mark, "/," is assumed to be a command and not part of the conversation.

MULTI-USER DIMENSION. Multi-User Dimensions (MUDs) are programs that allow users to interact in real time within an environment with many other users. Some MUDs involve fantasy and sciece fiction type games and the surroundings can be anything imaginable. Once you become familiar with the basics of the MUD you may be able to design your own characters, weapons, and environments. Often the environment is based on a movie or book setting.

MUDs are normally accessed through telnet, and are location based, that is, the MUD is housed at a specific computer location. Logging in to a MUD, usually with a nickname, lauches the user into a virtual world of fantasy role playing. Typing the word *south* might give a response from the MUD such as "You have left the dark foyer and have entered the dank, musty-smelling main room. There is a trembling figure lurking in the corner, holding a shining object in its cold, knobby fingers." What happens next depends on your next typed entry.

IRCs and MUDs provide hours of fun, but be careful, they can be addicting!

HOW DO YOU INTERPRET AN INTERNET ADDRESS?

Imagine that a large piece of machinery is to be sent from Los Angeles to New York. First, it is broken down into manageable sections, sent on four different trucks, routed on four different highways, but scheduled to arrive at the destination at the same time where they are to be reassembled. As long as you give each section the correct address, it will arrive at its destination intact. Your E-mail message is broken down into packets (pieces), and each packet is sent to the destination, but not necessarily by the same route. All the packets will arrive at their destination and be reassembled into the original complete message. You don't have to know or care about how it travels, but the hardware on the Internet does. Because of this, each computer on the Internet has its own address of four numbers separated by periods, for example, 123.56.78.999. This doesn't convey much meaning to the users, but it is understood by the computer. The Internet computers use a mechanism called the Domain Name System, which lets you put the computer address in English words. The user does not have to be concerned with how this is accomplished; the computer translates it for you.

Computers and people have addresses on the Internet. For a person, an account name is specified along with the address, for example:

don@office.school.edu

The text to the left of the @ (at) symbol is the name of the sending or receiving person. The address naming scheme works using domains, or subsets. The domains increase in hierarchy as you move from left to right in the address. *Office* is a subdomain, or subset, of school. Office would be a specific location in the school. *School* is a subdomain of edu and specifies a specific system or network. In this address, *edu* is the highest domain. This consists of three letters and indicates the general type of system or organization. Not all the domains are necessary in an address. In the following list you will find some of the more common three-letter domain names in use in the United States:

.com—a commercial or business site
.edu—university or other educational site
.gov—a governmental site
.mil—a military site
.net—a network site
.org—private or nonprofit organization

HOW DO YOU CONNECT TO THE INTERNET?

There are four methods that allow the user to connect to the Internet. Some considerations that you need to take into account are the type of interface (text or graphical), the availability of all or part of the Internet services, and the expenses involved. Access to the Internet can be accomplished through indirect connection, direct connection, commercial gateway, or leased line.

Indirect Connection

Through an **indirect connection**, also called a **shell account**, you use your modem to dial a host computer that in turn provides access to the Internet. This is the oldest and most basic access method. Some companies provide this service for as little as $15 a month. The place where the provider's modems are located is called the point of presence (POP). Larger providers have POPs located throughout the country, while smaller ones may have them only in big cities. You may incur a long-distance telephone charge to access the Internet provider if there is no local access where you live. However, this type of connection enables you to access most of the services linked to the Internet. Shell accounts protect your computer from unwanted intrusions since another user cannot directly dial into it. The downside to indirect access is that it is merely a shell or text-based interface. This means that there are commands you must memorize and that you will view only the text of your file and not be able to see or hear audio and video components.

Direct Connection

A **direct connection** to the Internet is achieved through SLIP/PPP. **Serial Line Interface Protocol (SLIP)** and **Point-to-Point Protocol (PPP)** allow your computer to directly access the Internet without the need for an additional Internet provider. A PPP connection resends data if they arrive in error, while SLIP does not. SLIP/PPP connections are usually both offered by Internet service providers. In addition to direct access to the Internet, SLIP/PPP allows you to use graphical interfaces to "surf" the Internet so you'll be able to view and hear multimedia information.

This type of connection is more expensive than indirect connection. Also, to use SLIP/PPP your computer must be compatible with the Internet. Since there are many types of computers connected to the Internet, there must be a common "language" on the network. **Transmission Control Protocol over Internet Protocol (TCP/IP)** software is the common language and must be installed on your computer to use SLIP/PPP.

Basically, TCP assures that information arrives with no data loss or modifications, retransmits information that does not arrive correctly, and splits long messages into sections (packets) and then correctly reassembles them at the destination. IP defines how the information will look as it travels between computers, provides methods for identifying each computer on the Internet, and defines how Internet addresses work.

Commercial Gateway

Many of you already subscribe to commercial on-line services, such as CompuServe, Prodigy, America Online, GEnie, and Delphi. These services provide a gateway to the Internet. A gateway allows data to be transmitted between incompatible networks or applications. To get to the Internet through a commercial service, you dial the commercial on-line service and locate the gateway. This can be as easy as finding and clicking on an Internet icon. However, if you plan on spending much time surfing the Internet, it can be relatively expensive to explore this way since you must pay the hourly connect fees of the commercial service. Costs vary widely, and each gateway offers different levels of access to Internet services. All of the services have E-mail and local access numbers throughout the country.

Leased Lines

For most users, one of the foregoing three methods will provide you with the right combination of cost, access, and ease of use. For corporate users or any user needing to transfer very large amounts of data at high speed, a leased line may be beneficial. A **leased line** enables a direct, high-speed connection to the Internet while allowing multiple users to perform different tasks at the same time. A leased line can cost thousands of dollars a month.

If you need help determining which access is right for you or which one might be nearest to you, the *Internet Network Information Center (InterNIC)* can help. This volunteer-staffed hotline for information on the Internet can be reached at (619) 455-4600.

WHAT KIND OF INFORMATION IS ON THE INTERNET?

Although sending and receiving E-mail is the most popular service on the Internet, searching, finding, and downloading files on many topics is another of the many uses.

PC users have a large selection of files through Simtel PC archives at Oakland University in Rochester, Michigan (oak.oakland.edu). Macintosh users can find an archive of files on the Internet in InfoMac at Stanford University (sumex-aim.stanford.edu). Mailing lists and other discussion groups are extremely popular Internet activities. Here are some interesting topics that can be found on the Internet.

Weather—nothing but weather, from the local forecast to detailed information from the National Oceanic and Atmospheric Administration to satellite pictures of a hurricane.

News—read on-line news magazines; view the latest Dow-Jones financial reports and other hard-core news topics.

Education—devoted to educational issues. Teachers can access AskERIC, an Internet site funded by the U.S. Department of Education for resources for elementary and secondary school teachers (through Gopher, ericir.syr.edu). School children interact with other children via the Internet.

College libraries—an outstanding wealth of information. All college catalogs are available by telnet access through a program called Hytelnet. This is a database of all known public library catalogs.

Jobs and careers—job postings by many private companies and nonprofit services such as the Online Career Center. Here you find information on writing resumes, getting career assistance, and women and minority career issues.

Government information—local, state, and federal information. Laws such as the Freedom of Information Act mean that previously unseen data are becoming available, much of them on the Internet.

Travel—information on locations, maps, and other related topics.

Games, sports, and hobbies—name the sport, and there are people who want to talk about it. Popular fantasy games and chess can be played through E-mail.

WHAT IS NETIQUETTE?

Netiquette is the etiquette, or code of behavior, on a network. Remember, when you communicate with someone, unless they tell you, there is no way of knowing where they live. You have no idea of their local customs because the Internet is international, so more than common courtesy is a must.

New users on the Internet are commonly referred to as **newbies**; that is, they are generally unfamiliar with procedures for communicating on line. One thing that many newbies do is ask the same questions that have been asked many times before. There are files that address this very issue. **Frequently Asked Questions (FAQs)** are files that provide the answers. By first consulting these files, you can avoid the ire of longtime users.

When communicating, be brief, clear, and courteous. Often, shorthand symbols are used in place of common phrases, such as BTW for By The Way, OTOH for On The Other Hand, and TTFN for Ta Ta For Now. You will probably learn or develop others. Since there is no way on-line to "show" facial expression and emotions, many users spice up their communication with emoticons. To view these "smiley" symbols that are created from your keyboard, tilt your head to the left. Some emoticon examples are :-) (smile), :-((frown), and ;-) (wink). Because sarcasm and irony may be unclear when read from the screen, using an emoticon can help make your point.

Shouting is indicated when you type in all capital letters, which is considered by most to be a rude display. Spamming occurs when someone posts the same messages in multiple areas. Users waste time and money and incur aggravation when they find they've downloaded the same message many times. Flaming is making inappropriate or offensive comments.

By using common sense and following a few basic rules of netiquette, your time on the Internet will be more enjoyable for both you and those on line with you.

Can you define the following?

anonymous FTP (p. 283)
Archie (p. 283)
direct connection (p. 290)
file transfer protocol (FTP) (p. 283)
frequently asked questions (FAQs) (p. 292)
gopher (p. 283)
home page (p. 287)
indirect connection (p. 290)
Internet (p. 280)
Internet relay chat (IRC) (p. 289)
leased line (p. 291)
mailing list (p. 281)
multi-user dimensions (MUDs) (p. 289)

netiquette (p. 292)
newbies (p. 292)
newsgroup (p. 282)
point-to-point protocol (PPP) (p. 291)
serial line interface protocol (SLIP) (p. 291)
shell account (p. 290)
telnet (p. 283)
transmission control protocol over
  Internet protocol (TCP/IP) (p. 291)
Usenet (p. 282)
Veronica (p. 283)
web (p. 286)
wide area information service (WAIS) (p. 286)
world wide web (WWW) (p. 286)

REVIEW QUESTIONS

Multiple Choice

1. The Internet is _____.
    a. a single network
    b. over 25,000 loosely connected networks
    c. an online commercial service
    d. a government-owned database

2. A _____ is a discussion group usually pertaining to one given topic.
    a. gateway
    b. telnet
    c. Gopher
    d. mailing list

3. _____ is a menu-based information service, created at the University of Minnesota.
    a. Veronica
    b. FTP
    c. Archie
    d. Gopher

4. Serial Line Interface Protocol and Point-to-Point Protocol are required to connect to the Internet through a(n) _____ .
    a. indirect connection
    b. direct connection
    c. commercial gateway
    d. leased line

5. Flaming, newbies, and FAQs are all concepts dealing with on-line _____.
    a. protocols
    b. federal laws
    c. file transfers
    d. netiquette

Fill In

1. _____ is the most used feature of the Internet.

2. _____ is an Internet service that organizes discussions into newsgroups.

3. _____ allows you to search through databases on the Internet.

4. _____ is an interface that makes File Transfer Protocol easier to use.

5. An Internet service for finding information through hypertext and hypermedia is called _____ .

Short Answer

1. Who owns and runs the Internet?

2. Describe the relationship between Gopher and Veronica, and FTP and Archie.

3. A user can connect to the Internet in four basic ways. Briefly describe them.

4. What is the Domain Name System? Describe how the address sue@salesdept.widgetcorp.com is interpreted.

5. Describe six topic areas of information that can be found on the Internet0.

CHAPTER

10

TRENDS IN TECHNOLOGY

OBJECTIVES

10.1 Describe several emerging directions in technology and speculate on the impact you think they will have in the future.

10.2 Explain how green computing affects the environment.

10.3 Recognize how computers are changing careers.

PROFILE

Alan M. Turing

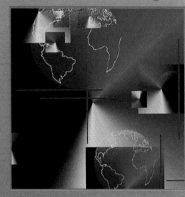

"Can machines think?" Alan Turing spent much of his life being intrigued by this question.

Turing, a brilliant mathematician who was born in London in 1912, received his education at Cambridge University and later Princeton. He and his colleagues were responsible for developing the first (arguably) operational computer, in 1940. The machine, known as Robinson, was instrumental in breaking the codes used by the German government in World War II. Turing's decryption methods have remained secret. For all we know, they may still be in use somewhere.

After the war, Turing authored papers entitled "Intelligent Machinery" and "Computing Machinery and Intelligence." Because his theory compared the human brain to a machine, he wondered if the machine could also "think." He is responsible for creating the Turing test as a model to determine whether a machine is intelligent. Turing hypothesized that if a person *thought* a machine was intelligent; then it *was*. With reference to machine intelligence, Turing said ". . . it is possible that one man would consider it as intelligent and another would not." Turing would most likely be highly involved in the study of what is known today as "artificial intelligence."

You might have heard or read about the Turing test that was conducted at the Boston Computer Museum as part of the first Loebner Prize Competition in November 1991. Ten human judges using only keyboards were charged with determining whether they were interacting with a terminal (there were eight) or a human (one of two). Each judge had to decide whether a program or a person was answering their inquiries. Judges were restricted to preselected topics, among them women's apparel, Shakespeare, and martini making. Turing most likely would not have liked the idea of these restrictions. However, several programs were identified as "human," or having human intelligence. In other words, they passed the Turing test. The winning program, **PC Therapist**, lets users vent their emotions.

Such a program might have been helpful to Turing, who in spite of all his scientific success apparently committed suicide at home. Evidence that the 41-year-old mathematical marvel may have ingested cyanide was found near his body.

O ngoing technological developments continuously alter and improve the way we manipulate and communicate information. In this chapter you will read about aspects of computing that are moving from the "gee whiz" realm into everyday applications. You will also read how environmental concerns affect computing and how computers and computing affect careers.

OBJECTIVE 10.1
Describe several emerging directions in technology and speculate on the impact you think they will have in the future.

WHAT ARE THE EMERGING DIRECTIONS IN TECHNOLOGY?

Although predicting the future is difficult, some technological advances and trends are recognizable. It is easy to predict that computers and related equipment will get faster, smaller, and cheaper (see Figure 10-1). Manufacturers will strive to make hardware and software easier to use and computer technology will find new applications. This section discusses recent advancements and speculates about what is expected for the future.

FIGURE 10-1
(a) The HP LX series of palmtop computers and HP OmniBook series of notebook computers from Hewlett-Packard Company utilize a standard PC architecture with built-in leading-edge applications to access or create information wherever it is needed. (b) The HP LX series of palmtop computers is a complete hand-held solution for mobile professionals. It features built-in financial management, personal organization, and communications capabilities.

(Courtesy of Hewlett-Packard)

(a)

(b)

Multimedia

Multimedia systems containing sound boards, speakers, CD-ROM drives, and high-resolution monitors have become the system of choice for most new computer buyers (see Figure 10-2). The performance of these devices continues to increase while their costs decrease. More and more applications will take advantage of multimedia, incorporating sound, animation, and full-motion video.

Television and computers are expected to merge into one device offering a wide range of interactive services to the consumer, including entertainment, shopping, and financial services. Just as the telephone system can reach every home in the United States today, every home may soon have the ability to tap into a vast array of information and services directly from the television.

Storage Technology

New disk-drive technologies are being developed to reduce the physical size of the drives and increase the storage capacities of the disks. Two of these are the wet disk and the glass disk. The wet disk uses liquid instead of air to separate the disk drive heads from the rotating disk; the glass disk uses glass platters instead of aluminum. These methods allow data to be written more densely, thereby increasing the storage capacity. However, both are more expensive than currently available technology.

Reading to and writing from magnetic hard disks may take a giant leap soon with developments from IBM's Adstar subsidiary. They are making practical use of giant magnetoresistance (a discovery by French scientists in 1988) in new read/write heads. It is predicted that by the year 2000 densities of 10 billion bits per inch will be possible. A 3 ½-inch disk could contain the equivalent of 10,000, 300-page books.

AT&T Bell Laboratories developed new ways of storing data at much higher densities than are currently available on magnetic storage. The AT&T technology uses lasers and fiber optics and allows storage of 2 billion bits per inch—about 300 times more than magnetic storage and 100 times more than CD-ROM storage. Applications for this technology include high-definition television and multimedia.

Another new storage option is flash memory. **Flash memory** is a type of silicon chip or card that retains its memory even when the power is turned off. Flash memory cards can be used as removable hard disks, but they are more durable. They are currently more expensive than hard disks. Flash memory is lightweight and requires less power than traditional magnetic disks. Because of their low power consumption,

Computers have been important in scientific research since they were invented. But those early computers were never fast enough to solve many of the more complex scientific problems. Science is entering a new era—digital science—taking problems that can be stated in mathematical formulas and presenting them as images on a computer screen. Some problems become more clear when depicted graphically.

Scientists use the new supercomputers to solve the so-called "grand challenges." These are projects that are generally beyond the scope or capability of a single researcher or group of researchers. Some involve developing software that simulates biological structures that will offer understanding of human systems and modeling global climate; another is development of fusion energy reactors; yet another creates techniques to discover new materials.

Other discoveries are waiting to be found. For example, astrophysicists look to a computer model to study stars. It was impossible to study the billions of years in the life of a star from cosmic dust to supernova status until that life could be played out in minutes via computer. Meanwhile at the other end of the spectrum, a researcher at the Scripps Institute of Oceanography examines the protein action in a body by studying the blink of an eye. A blink, which normally lasts 1 or 2 billionths of a second, has been stretched into 7 hours generating approximately 750,000 separate computer images.

Where this computerized science research takes us is anyone's guess. Don't blink!

flash memory cards are becoming popular with notebook computers to increase the time between battery recharging. The Fujitsu FMR-Card notebook computer weighs only 2 pounds and runs for 100 hours using flash memory.

Superconductors

A **superconductor** offers little resistance to electricity. Current superconductor materials work at low temperatures—near absolute zero (-473°F). This lack of resistance means that on and off switching operations occur about 1,000 times faster than with silicon transistors. However, because of the low temperatures involved, producing this switch is costly. If materials that become superconductors at higher temperature could be used, this type of computing would be more feasible. Research is being conducted to find these materials. If such a superconducting material is found, it may provide a cost-effective way to dramatically improve the speed of computers.

Parallel Processing

Another promising technique for increasing computer speed and power is a combination of hardware and software. **Massive parallel processing (MPP)** links many processors so that greater volumes of data are processed simultaneously instead of in sequence, as with single-processor computers. Mobil Oil creates 3-D seismic images to locate energy reserves in the ocean using this technology. The computer contains 128 processors and reduces the time needed for certain seismic applications from 30 weeks to 10 days. Applications for MPP are limited by available software and are found mostly in commercial data processing and scientific and engineering fields. Some people believe that a computer with the ability to simulate human thinking could be built using millions of processors all communicating with one another.

Optical Computing

Some experts think that the next generation of computers will be found in new designs to increase speed, power, and memory, rather than squeezing more circuitry into smaller spaces. One option is found in optics (using light energy) instead of electricity for processing and storing data. An **optical computer** uses laser beams instead of electrical signals to perform the ON/OFF switching. Photons, or light particles, move at ten times the speed of electrons and light beams can cross each other without causing interference—a common problem with electrical signals. A working model, called a bit serial optical computer, was developed at the University of Colorado's Optoelectronic Computing Systems Center. The relatively simple machine gave credence to the feasibility of more complex parallel optical computers. Future optical computers will contain millions of switches connected by light using mirrors and holograms. Holographic technology, which stores bits of data at the molecular level, is being developed by IBM.

Biochips

Some scientists employ biomolecular technology with the hope of creating a biochip. **Biochips** are tiny circuits grown from the proteins and enzymes of living material. The circuits would use oxygen and send signals similar to those sent and received by the human brain. One can only speculate whether the successful development and implementation of biochips could lead to a truly intelligent computer.

Interoperability

Interoperability refers to using hardware and software from different vendors interchangeably. For end users, it means not having to learn machine-specific operating system commands. Application programs would "look and feel" the same on any system, and data from one application could be readily linked to the next. Interoperability should lead to increased productivity and competitiveness for businesses.

Visualization

Visualization software allows data to be analyzed graphically, which makes it easier to comprehend complex information and allows viewing data multidimensionally (see Figure 10-3). In part because of advances in microprocessor speed and power and availability of large amounts of memory, visualization software is finding more applications on microcomputers. Some applications, such as heat mapping, where large amounts of numerical data are gathered, is best interpreted in graphical form.

FIGURE 10-3
Atmospheric ozone density profiles. Left image is original layer structure. Data are gridded geographically to preserve the original layering. Right image shows results spherically warped, registered with a topographic globe and volume, rendered over the valid spatial regime. The volume is cut open to reveal the internal 3-D structure.

(Data courtesy of NASA Goddard Space Flight Center, Greenbelt, Maryland. Photo courtesy of IBM Visualization Systems.)

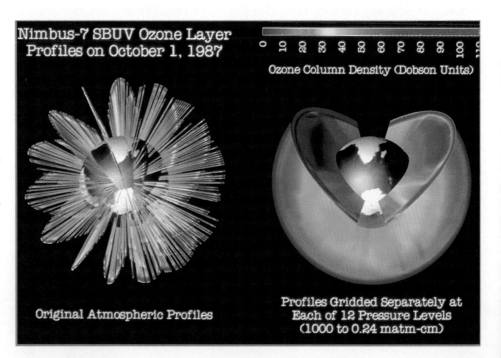

1998, 1999, 2000! "I expect there will be some who aren't going to notice until it happens." What Peter Weinberger, director of software and system research at AT&T Bell Laboratories, is referring to is how computers will be prepared to handle the change of dates from 1999 to 2000.

When computers, especially mainframes, were first used, memory conservation was very important. One area where conservation was thought to be appropriate was excluding the first two numbers of the year; that is, 1950 simply became 50. The possible ramifications for the year 2000 didn't enter into many people's minds. After all, it was a long time in the future. But now the time's arrived and there may be big problems for many businesses.

Software written for computers that use two digits instead of four for the date take the larger number to be the later date. This means many programs will interpret 99, or 1999, as a later date than 00, or 2000. This could have disastrous outcomes, for example, in compounding bank account interest, sorting data by dates, and computing ages by deducting the year of birth (a smaller number) from this year (a larger number). In the year 2000, your age will register as a negative number! And imagine the problems created by a check written in 1999; the bank could read the date and assume that it was 99 years old.

Some companies sell software to test your computer system to see how it handles the change of dates. It may sound trivial, but changing a database or other program everywhere a date is used is not an easy task. It won't be done overnight, and the costs worldwide, including design, could approach $75 billion.

Torrington Co., a division of Ingersoll-Rand Co., has been working on the century date change issue since 1991. An internal group discovered that 30 percent of its programs and 25 percent of its files and databases would be affected. Correction costs could range from as little as $35,000 to as much as $3.5 million

A Brooklyn, New York, newsletter "Tick, Tick, Tick," makes subscribers aware of many of these problems. It even ran a contest seeking the worst case scenario. It is hoped that won't be the case when the millennium approaches. Tick. Tick. Tick.

Three-dimensional representations aid in understanding and diagnosing many kinds of problems. In Canada, doctors at the University of Saskatchewan use three-dimensional visualizations of ovarian follicles to study ovarian cancer. The computer analysis of a tumor structure allows them to determine if it is malignant or benign. Visualization applications extend beyond science and medicine. For example, foreign exchange traders at Chemical Bank determine the relative strength of foreign currencies quickly through visualization. With the power and speed of microcomputers, continually increasing data visualization will find more applications in the business world.

Pen-Based Computing

Pen-based computers allow users to enter data by writing on the screen rather than using a keyboard (see Figure 10-4). As the technology to read and accurately convert handwriting into digital form is perfected, this type of computing will likely see greater use. Pen-based computers are small enough to carry, and some are equipped with screens of embedded intelligence called **smart paper.** The user enters "2 × 5 =" and the answer "10" appears on the smart paper. Spelling is checked and corrected as it is entered, and a rough sketch of a square object is converted into a perfect square. Further developments in pen-based user interfaces for computers along with voice-based interfaces will make computing more intuitive and bring the power of the computer to almost anyone.

Voice Recognition

Voice input gives the greatest freedom for computer users. Kurzweil and Dragon Systems are two popular makers of devices that recognize thousands of words. These systems are being used by physically challenged individuals and by professionals in the field of medicine. The ability to recognize the voice of the speaker using ordinary conversational speech has proved to be a major stumbling block, but greater advances in speech recognition systems are expected as technology continues to expand.

FIGURE 10-4
(a) Pen-based computing allows the user to compute on the go without the need for a power cord or keyboard; (b) complementary additions of a portable keyboard, wireless pager, telephone headset, and memory cards enhance the computer.

(Courtesy of Sony Electronics)

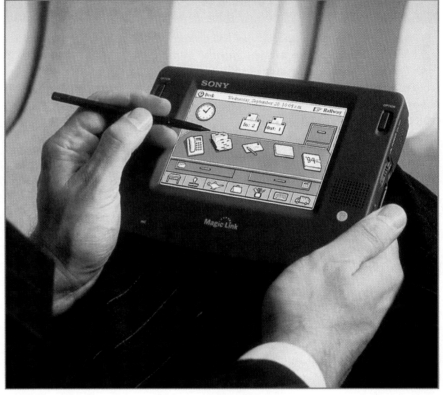

(a)

(b)

Major companies like IBM and Microsoft are introducing sophisticated voice recognition software and hardware for personal computers. IBM's Speech Server Series allows a user to enter data and control the PC by voice. Developments in digital signal processing will create new applications in areas where dictation plays a large part, such as medicine, law, and police work.

FIGURE 10-5
Virtual reality headset and gloves.
(Peter Menzel/Virtual Reality Autodesk, Inc./Stock Boston)

In an effort to make computers available to all who want to use them, researchers at Carnegie-Mellon University developed a prototype application where a person wearing a data glove makes American Sign Language hand signals and arm movements that are subsequently translated, synthesized, and spoken through computer equipment.

Virtual Reality

Applications in virtual reality are also on the horizon. **Virtual reality** is the integration of color, sound, and animation in a "wraparound" environment that offers the capability of three-dimensional applications. Virtual reality systems allow the user to "step into" the animated environment and to sense the position of an object (X, Y, and Z coordinates) and its orientation (pitch, roll, and yaw) in relation to the position of the user's head. Virtual reality devices include goggles through which the user can see in 3-D (see Figure 10-5) and a glove that is used to manipulate the 3-D entities.

Some systems add virtual sound as an enhancement of the experience. Sounds seem to emanate from a stable point. In other words, if you turn your head to the right the sound doesn't move as it does when you wear a headset. Instead, the sound appears to be coming from the same point as when you were facing it. You get the feeling of moving away from the sound.

Experiments using virtual reality can be conducted without encountering the costly or destructive trial-and-error process that occurs in real-life situations. A common example is the flight simulator where pilots learn to deal with conditions such as fuel loss, engine failure, low visibility, insufficient runway space, or other potential calamities. Everything looks terrifyingly real. The pilot works the controls properly and "saves" the craft or improperly and "loses" it. Happily, none of the mistakes are fatal—or expensive. Applications for virtual reality are seen in the fields of finance, science, education, architecture, and aviation, to name a few. NASA used virtual reality to train the astronauts who repaired the *Hubble Space Telescope.*

Virtual reality is moving from the realm of video games to everyday applications. Most business applications are found in architecture, design, and training. A virtual reality application called Wheelchair VR from Prairie Virtual Systems allows architects to visualize how individuals in wheelchairs will move around in a new building before it is constructed.

BioControl Systems in California developed a device called the Biomuse, which permits interface in a virtual environment through use of eye, muscle, and brain signals rather than a traditional mouse or joystick. One young quadriplegic used the Biomuse to "fly" in the virtual environment by puffing his checks and twitching his forehead. Hospitals are exploring the Biomuse for applications such as medical rehabilitation and minimally invasive surgery.

Surgeons from Brigham and Women's Hospital in Boston and General Electric Scientists are developing 3-D images that can be consulted during surgery to aid in diagnosis by providing data on the size and weight of a tumor. The 3-D images are developed from magnetic resonance images and can be rotated, pivoted, and layered to expose various parts of the brain.

Wireless Computing

The ability of a computer to communicate is one of its most powerful characteristics. One of the most exciting developments is wireless computing. **Wireless computing** implements the technologies of cellular, infrared, and radio frequencies so that computers communicate without a conducting medium such as copper wire. Although cellular is the most popular, radio frequency (RF) modems will become more prevalent with the FCC standardization of frequencies for data communication. Portable computers are most likely to use wireless communication. A portable system from GO Corp. recognizes the presence of a wireless LAN and transmits messages to the pen-based computer that you hold in your hand as you walk into the room. Rearranging an office would be easier if the devices in it did not require rewiring. By the end of this century, it is estimated that there will be over 15 million users on wireless computing networks.

Global Communication

Corporations in the United States and abroad are becoming multinational. Increasingly, businesses recognize the necessity of competing in a global market. Much of this global shift is due to increased competition. This competition fuels the importance of information technology and global networking through telecommunication. International corporate telecommunication is increasing by 15–20 percent per year.

To be competitive in the global marketplace, information systems and the technology to implement them must take high priority. Organizations operating in world markets must be prepared to do business on a 24-hour basis, to mesh with working schedules in different time zones.

By some estimates over 60 percent of all jobs in the industrialized countries of the world will be related to computers and the exchange of information by the turn of the century (see Figure 10-6). Computers and computing influence international monetary transactions, information gathering, strategic communication, and the way that information reaches individuals—even those under less than democratic governments. For example, the Berlin Wall and the Iron Curtain began to disintegrate when the governments behind them could no longer keep their citizens in the dark about what was happening in the world outside. Telecommunication was more than a channel for conveying political news; it became an actual part of the political

FIGURE 10-6
These students are preparing for a global society where careers will rely heavily on their ability to use computers and information. Early introduction to these technologies will help them be at ease with the tools needed for a future in the information age. Elementary students learn to (a) read, (b) perform math drills, and (c) tell time using computers.
(Courtesy of International Business Machines Corp.)

(a)

(b)

(c)

process. Computer technology and communication kept people informed during the breakup of the former Soviet Union in the early 1990s.

The global economy is gradually shifting toward more reliance on information systems to provide the continuing development of nations. Telecommunication and information networks help developing countries operate in the global community by providing them a means to coordinate development projects, pursue scientific study, and conduct business. Accessibility, accountability, and democracy can benefit from connecting to information technology.

There are, however, several hurdles to be overcome when going on line with an information network in a global environment. They include language and cultural barriers, different standards, software piracy, and finding skilled labor. Global organizations will have to meet international standards and integrate foreign language and cultural differences (see Figure 10-7).

FIGURE 10-7
A Chinese phonetic keyboard.
(Courtesy of International Business Machines Corp.)

Information Superhighway

While not yet fully implemented, the term "information superhighway" refers to a proposed wide array of high-speed, state-of-the-art telecommunication links (see Figure 10-8). These links are being designed to carry very large amounts of data, voice, and video communications globally. The goal is to eventually converge telephone, television, and computer technologies to allow interactive two-way communication. Video-on-demand and interactive TV are two commonly talked about applications for the information superhighway. Video-on-demand will provide a user with access to programs stored digitally on a video server connected to the information superhighway. Movies, television shows, or other programming can be viewed at the user's convenience. Interactive TV will provide a two-way communication between the broadcaster and viewer. This will open a whole host of possible applications from telemedicine (see Figure 10-9) and home banking to interactive game shows and advertising.

Artificial Intelligence

Artificial intelligence (AI) refers to the capability of computers to simulate functions usually associated with human intelligence, such as speech recognition, image understanding, deduction, inference, reasoning, judgment, perception, insight, intuition, common sense, evaluation, learning, and self-improvement. Computer scientists are attempting to build computers with these characteristics that can "think," "reason," "make decisions," and "learn from their mistakes" like humans. The task of developing hardware and software to reproduce and imitate the complexities of human intelligence is an ambitious project. In part, this is because there is no universal agreement on what constitutes human intelligence. Even where there is agreement, scientists have not determined exactly how the mind accomplishes these tasks. Scientists are only scratching the surface of what constitutes human intelligence and determining how it works.

While some are asking, "Can a machine really possess human intelligence?" a more important question might be, "Do we really want machines that think like humans?" Humans are prone to mistakes, misjudgments, and miscalculations. If a computer can be made to think like a human, can we trust the decisions it would make?

FIGURE 10-8

The tiny fibers of transparent glass in fiber optic cables transmit data at the speed of light. The beam of light sent through these fibers can be turned on or off at about 1 billion times per second. The cables are replacing traditional telephone lines and are used to connect computers in telecommunication systems. A fiber optic network will provide the backbone for the information superhighway.

(Courtesy of United Telecommunications.)

FIGURE 10-9

Dr. William A. Speir, Jr., pulmonologist, consulting with Dr. George S. Walker, internist, at Dodge County Hospital.

(This picture was shot from the Medical College of Georgia Telemedicine Center. Courtesy of The Medical College of Georgia.)

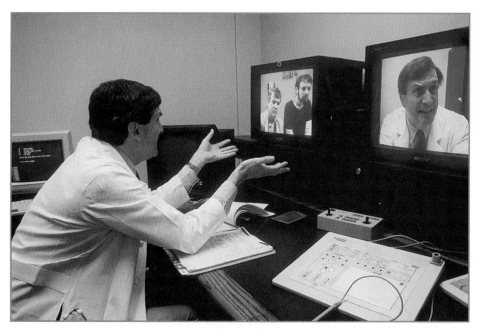

Perhaps machine intelligence will be something quite different from human intelligence. After all, humans learned to fly, but it wasn't accomplished by a plane that mimics the flapping of a bird's wings.

Although research in AI started in the mid-1950s, it remains in the early stages of development. Several areas being pursued in current research are expert systems, natural language processing, voice recognition, and computer vision.

EXPERT SYSTEMS. An **expert system,** also called a **knowledge-based system,** is software that uses knowledge and inference procedures acquired by human expertise to solve problems in a particular field such as finance or medicine.

Expert systems are considered one of the most practical applications of AI research so far. The popularity of expert systems has grown significantly in recent years. Once solely topics among AI researchers, expert systems are now seen in offices, hospitals, research laboratories of various types, industrial plants, manufacturing shops, repair shops, oil wells, and the like (see Figure 10-10). A few well-known expert systems found in diverse organizations include

- DENDRAL, an expert system that examines the spectroscopic analysis of an unknown chemical compound and predicts its molecular structure
- MYCIN, a landmark expert system used to diagnose infectious diseases and suggest possible therapies
- PROSPECTOR, a geological expert system to help find valuable mineral deposits
- DELTA, (diesel-electric locomotive troubleshooting aid), an expert system used to help maintenance people repair diesel-electric locomotives

Two major components of an expert system are a knowledge base and an inference engine. A **knowledge-base** contains the knowledge of an expert; it is the most important component of an expert system. The performance of an expert system is a function of the size and quality of its knowledge base. A knowledge base resembles a database; however, in addition to data, it contains rules that are applied to the data. The knowledge of an expert is transformed into rules and associations that are stored in the knowledge base. An **inference engine,** an integral part of every expert sys-

FIGURE 10-10
An expert system enables Ford plant electricians to maintain robots without undergoing lengthy and expensive training. Pictures and instructions on a computer screen (shown in the center of the photo) lead plant personnel to robot problems. At the left is a robot arm lifting three 40-pound automatic transmission torque converters.
(Courtesy of Ford Motor Company.)

tem, is software that applies the rules from a knowledge base to the data provided by a user to draw a conclusion.

The process by which the knowledge of an expert is transformed into a knowledge base is called **knowledge engineering.** Special skills are required to capture the knowledge of an expert and put it into programmable form. A new group of professionals, known as **knowledge engineers,** are trained to perform that role.

Several commercial tools are available to help build expert systems. They make it unnecessary to start from scratch. The tools are known in the industry as **expert system shells,** or shells. Most shells contain all of the components of an expert system except the knowledge base. Thus, buyers need to add only a knowledge base to create their own expert systems.

NATURAL LANGUAGE PROCESSING. Natural language processing is the ability of a computer to "understand" ordinary human language. This ability allows a user to type input in a normal conversational fashion rather than using a specific set of commands or syntax. For example, you could request a list of customers from a database by typing, "Print a list of customers with an outstanding balance greater than $500." Current natural language processing systems recognize and interpret only limited vocabularies relating to very specific topics. In addition to allowing users to interface with computer applications, one of the most notable and important uses of natural language processing will be to understand input in one language and translate it into any other language.

SPEECH RECOGNITION. Probably the easiest and most natural way to input commands and data into a computer would be to speak them. The ability of a computer to recognize the speech of a user and take action based on the words spoken is called **speech recognition** or **voice recognition.** A user typically uses a microphone to input the speech (see Figure 10-11). The computer matches the spoken words against stored speech patterns to determine what was said. Once speech is recognized it can then be used directly in applications, such as to input commands or dictate text, or it may be further processed by a natural language processor that enables normal human speech to be understood.

Speech recognition speeds the input of data. It also frees the hands and eyes of the user allowing other tasks to be performed while data are input. For example, physicians performing surgery could receive information from the computer by simply ask-

FIGURE 10-11
With a speech recognition data entry system, an operator's hands are free to write while the operator speaks commands to the computer.
(Courtesy of Texas Instruments.)

ing. Speech recognition input is also valuable for individuals who have lost some or all of their eyesight or functional use of their hands. Voice recognition may ultimately become the method for giving instructions to computers or commands to robots.

COMPUTER VISION. To be truly intelligent, a computer will have to be able to recognize its surrounding environment and adapt to changes in it. To do this, it must be able to "see" what's going on. **Computer vision** is the capability of a computer to mimic the ways that the human brain processes and interprets light waves. Major applications of computer vision include applications such as military weapons guidance systems, industrial machines to replace people or improve the manufacturing process, and robotics.

Robotics

A **robot** is defined by the Robotics Institute of America as ". . . a reprogrammable, multifunctional manipulator designed to move material, parts, tools, or specialized devices through variable programmed motions for the performance of a variety of tasks." More simply put, a robot is a machine that can be programmed to do a variety of useful tasks (see Figure 10-12). The field that involves the design, construction, and operation of robots is called **robotics.**

FIGURE 10-12
NBC News robot cameras.

(Courtesy of NBC News.)

While some experimental robots are made in humanlike forms, most industrial robots resemble nothing of the sort, and it would be impractical to make them so. Far from being intelligent, robots are capable of completing only preprogrammed instructions. However, robots can be programmed to do complicated tasks, and they can turn out products in a factory with unsurpassed precision.

The first industrial robot was installed in 1961. Early industrial robots were simply computer-controlled mechanical arms performing single, simple tasks. Industrial robots are used mainly for individual assembly-line tasks, but some can do multiple tasks, moving along on wheels or a track or belt system. Today, robots are still used in manufacturing mainly for simple, repetitive tasks on factory assembly lines to reduce costs and to increase productivity. Robots never tire; they are excellent at repetitive tasks that humans find boring. Robots are ideal replacements for humans on many jobs that are hazardous such as bomb disposal, ocean exploration, outer-space probes, coal mining, and cleanup of chemical or nuclear accidents.

COMMON ROBOT TASKS. Generally, robots are delegated to three types of jobs: (1) operating tools, (2) lifting and handling materials or parts, and (3) assembling parts. The most common application of robots is in the operation of tools, that is, spot welding, arc welding, and spray painting automobile parts are typical tasks (see Figure 10-13). The robots at Fey Manufacturing in California weld bumpers for small trucks. Drilling the hundreds or thousands of rivet holes in aircraft components is a natural task to assign to robots, and General Dynamics does just that. At the University of California at Davis, physicians and computer technicians are perfecting a robot to assist doctors in hip-joint replacement operations. The robot designs the artificial joint implant and then drills a hole in the thigh bone for the replacement. It does so with far more precision than a human hand.

Lifting and handling materials are fairly uncomplicated tasks for robots of the "pick and place" variety (see Figure 10-14). Such robots simply pick up objects and place them somewhere else. For example, a robot might pick up a piece of metal and place it in a stamping machine. Metal Casings, in Worcester, England, makes aluminum

FIGURE 10-13
Robots are used for welding automobile parts at this Honda plant.
(Courtesy of Honda America. Marysville, Ohio.)

FIGURE 10-14
"Pick and place" robot.
(Courtesy of Martin Marietta.)

cast parts for car and consumer goods industries. Its robots are precisely timed to ladle specific volumes of molten aluminum into machines and then remove the hardened components and place them in cool-water baths.

Assembly is still difficult for robots; however, some companies use robots to insert electrical components of standard shapes into printed circuit boards intended for many types of electrical equipment. IBM not only sells robots that handle this type of assembly task but also uses them to assemble products in its computer and terminal plants.

ROBOTICS RESEARCH. MIT, Stanford University, Carnegie-Mellon University, and several other institutions and private companies are heavily involved in robotics research. Four areas of great interest are vision, touch, mobility, and miniaturization.

Robots can be adapted with sensors that, together with a computer, help robots "see" and "feel" their way around the workplace. An elementary sense of sight is accomplished with digital-imaging cameras or by bouncing infrared or microwave signals off an object. The robot computer receives these signals and uses pattern recognition technology to match them with previously stored images for identification and inspection.

Tactile sensing, the sense of touch, while still in the early stages of development, allow robots to distinguish many different shapes, handle each appropriately, and perform various operations. Robots can be programmed to pick up heavy objects or objects as delicate and lightweight as an egg without damaging either. These tasks are possible because the robot's "hands," called end effectors, are designed in many varieties and are often interchangeable (see Figure 10-15). The robot hand is constantly undergoing refinement to enable it to grasp objects more delicately and move them with greater accuracy. A researcher at the University of Utah has perfected a four-finger robot hand that grasps and picks a flower without crushing the stem or picks up and replaces pieces on a chess board.

Researchers want to increase the usefulness and range of applications for robots by making them more mobile and giving them the ability to negotiate a wide range of terrains such as stairs, rocks, mountains, and the ocean floor. To create effective

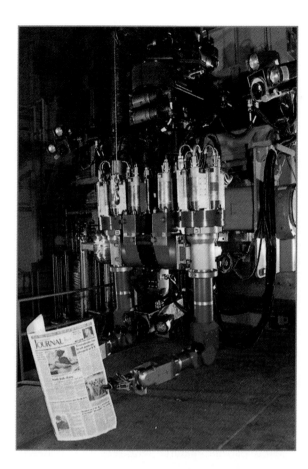

FIGURE 10-15
Robotics hand (end effector.)
(Courtesy of Martin Marietta.)

walking robots, scientists at Oregon State University created their designs by watching, studying, and filming the movement of spiders over difficult terrain. The actions were digitized and computer analyzed to see how spider motions could be adapted to the much heavier robot machines.

A robot firefighter, developed in Japan, is equipped with two television cameras and a camera that "sees" infrared, or heat, waves (instead of light waves). This mobile, remote-controlled "firefighter" goes up and down stairs in a building to report poisonous gas or smoke. In other efforts to improve robot mobility and stability, an MIT team mounted a robot on four legs that were agile enough to let it "bound" around the room. A company in Anaheim, California, has nearly perfected a six-legged maintenance robot that moves on its own. The same firm, in conjunction with the University of Florida, built a snakelike robot to work in areas containing mazes of pipe. The 30-foot "snake" front 10-foot section is designed to work as an arm and the remainder is divided into 2-foot segments mounted on wheels and equipped to carry tools.

Extreme miniaturization is a new area of robotics. Because some of these new devices are too small for the eye to see, they are called "microbots." Their moving parts are too tiny to be built as the elements of a regular robot are. Instead, their design is printed on material such as polysilicon, which is then bathed in plasma or acid. These substances dissolve the material that is not a part of the printed design, leaving the microscopic parts of the robot. Scientists hope that microbots will work on small, delicate machines or even be inserted into the human bloodstream to remove cholesterol deposits or eradicate viruses.

Researchers at the Robotics Institute at Carnegie-Mellon University believe that for many years robots will continue to function simply as "enhanced power tools." They see the newer robots in service industry jobs as being assistants to humans rather than replacements.

OBJECTIVE 10.2
Explain how green computing affects the environment.

WHAT IS GREEN COMPUTING AND HOW DOES THE COMPUTER AFFECT THE ENVIRONMENT?

After April 1993, the federal government was directed to buy only "green" computers. **Green computers** are those computers and related equipment that fit an ecological profile set by the Environmental Protection Agency (EPA) Energy Star Computers Program. Some of the guidelines follow. Computers and monitors cannot use more than 30 watts of power each when idle. The equipment must "power down" or automatically go into an idle or low-power mode when not being used. These computers would have no fans and lower-power microprocessors, and be equipped with power management software, thus requiring less demand for power. Computers without fans are less noisy, and monitors with low emissions reduce radiation risks. Since the U.S. government is the largest purchaser of computers in the world, manufacturers have a real incentive to produce green computers.

The EPA estimates that computers use about 5 percent of commercially consumed power. Use of green computers could cut energy consumption by half, according to their estimates—enough to power Maine, Vermont, and New Hampshire annually. The EPA also estimates that the equivalent carbon dioxide emissions of 5 million cars could be saved because of the reduced production of electricity. Green computers are identifiable by the Energy Star logo—a star with the word "energy" written in script partway through it (see Figure 10-16). The greening of the computer industry includes replacing nonbiodegradable packing material with recyclable materials and printing manuals on recycled paper. Although green computers may cost more money, saving the environment is worthwhile.

Peripheral equipment is going green. Kyocera Electronics, Inc., substituted the laser printer toner cartridge with a silicon drum. Because the drum never needs replacing, waste deposited in landfills is reduced. A company called Greendisk recycles old floppy diskettes. Software firms such as Autodesk, Inc., which previously threw out hundreds of thousands of floppy diskettes that contained old versions of their software, are sending them to Greendisk, where they are reformatted and sold as recycled diskettes. The environment wins because of less trash, and consumers win with lower diskette prices.

FIGURE 10-16
The Energy Star logo identifies a "green" computer.

(Courtesy of IPC Technologies)

OBJECTIVE 10.3
Recognize how computers are changing careers.

HOW ARE COMPUTERS AFFECTING CAREERS?

No matter what your chosen career, it will likely involve computers. Even if you are not a system analyst, programmer, or other computer specialist, your job will probably require that you use a computer. The information age has made advances to help the physically challenged participate in careers that were previously not available to them (see Figure 10-17). This section describes computer occupations as well as

(a)

(b)

FIGURE 10-17
(a) Here, a VersaBraille II information center lets the blind user word process documents by touching a braille keyboard; the entry is indicated on the braille display. This system also communicates with other computer systems and printers.
(b) The VersaPoint Printer creates hard copy in braille for this user.

([b] Courtesy of Telesensory Systems, Inc.)

other professions in which computers play an important role. In fact, you may start out using a computer, on-line service, and software to find a job.

Computer Professional Careers

Computer professional careers are directly involved with computers. Most of these occupations require higher education with a minimum of a bachelor's degree.

System analysts are strategists and planners who design and improve information systems. They analyze the problems of the current system, decide how to solve them, determine which data to collect, and ascertain the processing steps required to get the information to the user. This process results in the criteria for an algorithm.

A **programmer** codes the instructions that tell the computer how to solve a problem. Programmers code the algorithm, designed by the system analyst to solve a problem, into a programming language making sure that it all works. In a small organization, the jobs of programmer and system analyst are sometimes combined and called programmer/analyst. Application programmers write programs for users to solve problems; system programmers write programs that run the computer.

The increase in the number and size of databases in government and business creates a need for someone to coordinate all the elements. A **database administrator** designs, implements, and maintains the database. They monitor users and data security and direct and plan all the elements required to maintain a database. The database administrator consults with others in the organization to determine each one's information needs and decide the best ways to access that information. They also help other managers plan the collection, storage, and organization of the data.

The **information system manager** plans and oversees all the information resources in an organization. This title may vary depending on the size and structure of the enterprise; it is usually one of the higher-level computer positions. The title might be management information system (MIS) director, information system manager, or data processing manager. This person needs technical knowledge about the system development process as well as managerial and leadership skills to oversee and motivate the programmers, system analysts, and computer operators in a data processing or MIS department. This person must be familiar with the overall goals and information needs of the business.

Other jobs that developed from and relate to the computer industry include
- Service technicians who install and repair computers and equipment, for example, damaged disk drives, tape drives, keyboards, and circuit boards.
- Sales representatives who sell computer equipment and software.
- Technical writers with experience in a particular specialized area who explain in nontechnical terms how to use the equipment and software. They write user manuals, operator manuals, and software documentation.
- Security personnel who specialize in techniques to protect the computer room, hardware, programs, and the stored data and information.
- Electronic data processing (EDP) auditors who monitor and evaluate computer operations to ensure that there are no incidents of fraud or misuse of the system.
- Hardware developers who formulate new ideas using the latest technology to design computer hardware and chip circuitry.
- Software engineers who create and write new system programs (e.g., operating systems) and new application programs for business (e.g., word processors, spreadsheets, database management software) or for entertainment (e.g., video games).
- Network designers, or telecommunication specialists, who design and improve computer networks.

How Computers Affect Other Jobs

It is likely that using computers or handling information will be necessary to perform your job. Here are some of the ways computers affect noncomputer careers.

- A graphic artist designs logos for television programs or art for music videos with computers and graphics software. Movie and television producers and special-effects creators produce scenes with computer images and simulations (see Figure 10-18).
- Journalists enter news stories from computer terminals or PCs. Copy editors revise text on a computer and transmit it via telecommunication to publishing personnel, who typeset it electronically and print the final story on computer-controlled presses.
- Physicians prescribe diagnostic tests for their patients by computer-controlled tools, and most coordinate their office management by computer.
- Technicians in hospital laboratories operate computerized testing equipment, store the results in a computer, and retrieve them upon request.
- Employees use computers for word processing; some also implement financial applications to handle budgets and keep expense records.
- Automobile mechanics employ computer diagnostics to pinpoint engine troubles.
- Teachers use computers to expedite research, design learning materials, keep student records, and also encourage students to use computers as study aids.
- Managers retrieve information from a database in the form of reports; they send messages and schedule appointments using computers (see Figure 10-19).

Opportunities to use computers abound in all careers. Almost every occupation needs specialists with expertise in that particular field, and the skills and knowledge to employ computers to enhance their positions.

Using Computers to Find a Job

Computers can help you find a job. Job-hunting software falls into two major categories: those that help you advance, such as resume preparation, and on-line services that advertise career positions.

FIGURE 10-18
Special effects as shown in *Jurassic Park*.
(Universal City Studios and Amblin/Photofest)

FIGURE 10-19

With the revolutionary Timex Data Link communications technology, you can transfer scheduling and personal information from a PC to this Timex watch, without the use of wires or cables. In seconds, the sensor on the face of the watch reads flashing bars of light (the data) on a desktop monitor.

(Courtesy of Timex)

Some software packages contain various templates for cover letters, eliminating the problem of formatting it yourself. Resume-writing software often includes different resume templates designed for specific jobs, e.g., in engineering or business. Programs such as Career Directions by Cambridge Career Products help determine where your professional interests lie. Many programs analyze specific career objectives.

Job hunts can be conducted using on-line computer services and bulletin boards like the Career Network, an on-line employment service. These services are used by people looking for work, employers, and college placement offices. In addition to specialized services, CompuServe and Prodigy allow users to post a version of a help wanted ad. Operated by the Professional Association of Resume Writers, the National Resume Bank is a service where subscribers electronically post their resumes.

It's clear that this introduction to computers is just the beginning. You will see that computers are widespread in your school, your country, and throughout your world.

SUMMARY

We can expect that computers and related equipment will get faster, smaller, cheaper, and easier to use. Some emerging directions in technology include multimedia, storage technology advances, development of superconductors, massive parallel processing, optical computing, research into the development of biochips, interoperability, visualization, pen-based computing, voice recognition, virtual reality, wireless computing, global communication, efforts to develop an information superhighway, artificial intelligence, and robotics.

Green computing focuses on environmental issues. Using less electricity and producing less waste are goals toward which computer manufacturers strive.

Many jobs are directly related to and in fact came about because of computers. Most other jobs are dependent on the computer.

Job applicants use computers to search for a job through software programs designed to help the applicant write a cover letter or a resume. On-line computer services provide a method for electronically posting and looking through resumes or help wanted ads.

Can you define the following?

artificial intelligence (AI) (p. 306)
biochip (p. 300)
computer vision (p. 310)
database administrator (p. 316)
expert system (p. 307)
expert system shell (p. 308)
flash memory (p. 298)
green computers (p. 314)
inference engine (p. 308)
information system manager (p. 316)
interoperability (p. 300)
knowledge-base (p. 308)
knowledge-based system (p. 308)
knowledge engineering (p. 309)

knowledge engineer (p. 309)
massive parallel processing (MPP) (p. 299)
natural language processing (p. 309)
optical computer (p. 299)
programmer (p. 316)
robot (p. 310)
robotics (p. 310)
smart paper (p. 301)
speech recognition (p. 309)
superconductor (p. 299)
system analyst (p. 316)
virtual reality (p. 303)
visualization software (p. 300)
voice recognition (p. 309)
wireless computing (p. 304)

REVIEW QUESTIONS

Multiple Choice

1. _____ uses laser beams instead of electrical signals to perform the ON/OFF switching.
   a. A wireless computing system
   b. Virtual reality
   c. An optical computer
   d. Pen-based computing

2. Tiny circuits grown from living matter are called _____.
   a. superconductors
   b. ceramics
   c. biochips
   d. glass disks

3. _____ refers to the ability to use hardware and software from different vendors interchangeably.
   a. Operability
   b. Robotics
   c. Interoperability
   d. Flexibility

4. The integration of color, sound, and animation in a "wraparound environment" is called _____.
   a. virtual reality
   b. pen-based computing
   c. artificial intelligence
   d. visualization

5. The capability of computers to "think" like humans is called _____.
   a. visualization
   b. parallel processing
   c. artificial intelligence
   d. robotics

6. A(n) _____ is software that uses data along with knowledge and inference procedures acquired by human expertise to solve problems in a particular field.
   a. expert system
   b. inference engine
   c. knowledge base
   d. natural language processor

7. A(n) _____ is a commercially available tool for building expert systems.
   a. knowledge-based management system
   b. knowledge-acquisition subsystem
   c. knowledge base
   d. expert system shell

8. A _____ is a professional trained to acquire knowledge from an expert.
   a. database administrator
   b. knowledge engineer
   c. system analyst
   d. programmer

9. The ability of the computer to understand and translate ordinary human languages is called _____.
   a. voice recognition
   b. artificial intelligence
   c. parallel processing
   d. natural language processing

10. The field that involves the design, construction, and operation of robots is called _____.
    a. artificial intelligence
    b. natural language processing
    c. neural network processing
    d. robotics

Fill In

1. Silicon memory that retains its contents when the power is turned off is called _____.

2. A material that offers little resistance to electricity is called a _____.

3. _____ links multiple processors to process data and instructions faster.

4. A(n) _____ uses laser beams instead of electrical signals to perform the ON/OFF switching in a computer.

5. _____ refers to using hardware and software from different vendors interchangeably.

6. The integration of color, sound, and animation in a "wraparound" environment that offers the capability of three-dimensional applications is called _____.

7. _____ refers to the technology that enables computers to communicate without a conducting medium such as copper wire.

8. The ability of a computer to recognize the speech of a user and take some action based on the words spoken is called _____.

9. _____ are those computers and related equipment that fit an ecological profile set by the Environmental Protection Agency (EPA) Energy Star Computers Program.

10. A _____ is a machine that can be programmed to do a variety of useful tasks.

Short Answer

1. What impact do you think user interface technologies such as pen-based computing, voice recognition, and virtual reality will have on how computers are used and the types of applications they will be used for?

2. What is wireless computing and how, in your opinion, might it affect the use of computer networks?

3. What are the three obstacles that may hinder global computing?

4. Tell what the term information superhighway refers to and suggest some possible uses for it.

5. Define artificial intelligence and discuss some of the implications you think its development might have on society.

6. Define expert system, expert system shell, and knowledge engineering and identify the role of a knowledge engineer.

7. What is speech recognition, and how does it differ from natural language processing?

8. Define robot and describe three common tasks for which they are generally used for.

9. Briefly relate what is meant by green computing.

10. Describe how the use of computers might affect the career you wish to pursue.

Issues for Thought

1. Of the emerging technologies presented in the chapter discuss the impact you think each will have on computing in the future. Why?

2. How could it be determined if a computer has intelligence? What questions might you ask or what tasks might you expect it to accomplish? What types of problems do you foresee, if any, if computers can be made to think like humans?

GLOSSARY

Absolute cell reference   A method of copying in which the exact formula is repeated, using the same cell references; used with spreadsheets.

Accounting information system   An information system using primarily transaction-processing systems to record transactions that affect the financial status of an organization. It maintains a historical record of transactions and produces reports that give a financial picture of the organization.

Accounting software   Application software that is designed specifically to manage more complex financial transactions in greater volume than ordinary spreadsheet software.

Active cell   A cell in a spreadsheet that is currently being used for data entry or data manipulation; usually indicated by the cell pointer.

Active window   In a word processor, the window in which the cursor currently resides.

Analog data transmission   The transmission of data in continuous wave form.

Animation   A feature of some graphics packages that rapidly displays drawings that progressively change slightly, thereby simulating motion.

Anonymous FTP   A file transfer protocol in which a host computer allows any user to search and download files from it without access codes and passwords.

Answer mode   In communication software, the operational mode in which a computer watches for an incoming signal from the modem and answers it when received.

Application generator   A program that simplifies the coding of an entire custom application by generating much of the program code automatically.

Application software   Software that allows the user to accomplish a specific task or set of tasks such as preparing documents, managing data, and creating graphics.

Archie   Internet software that lets a user narrow an anonymous File Transfer Protocol (FTP) search by using keywords.

Area graph   Line graph in which the areas between sets of data are filled in or shaded.

Arithmetic-logic unit (ALU)   The part of the central processing unit (CPU) that performs arithmetic operations, logic operations, and related operations.

Artificial intelligence (AI)   The capability of computers to simulate functions usually associated with human intelligence, such as speech recognition, image understanding, deduction, inference, reasoning, judgment, perception, insight, intuition, common sense, evaluation, learning, and self-improvement.

Assembler   The language-translator program used to translate assembly language code into machine language.

Assembly language   A low-level programming language that uses mnemonics in place of 1's and 0's to represent instructions.

Attributes   The set of characteristics used to describe a data entry field or the appearance of output. These are often set by a user to fit a particular situation.

Audit trail   A software feature that shows deletions, changes, or additions to a file; tells when an action was taken and by whom.

Automatic page numbering   An application software feature that prints the page number on each page.

Automatic recalculation   A spreadsheet option that automatically recalculates the entire worksheet after a new figure is entered.

Automatic spillover   A spreadsheet option in which a cell label continues, or spills over, into the next cell.

Background recalculation mode   A spreadsheet option where recalculation occurs while other operations are in process.

Bar graph   A graph using a fixed scale to compare data in simple and compound relationships. Data may be represented as either vertical or horizontal bars.

Baud rate   The number of times per second that a transmitted signal changes (modulates or demodulates).

Binary system   The base-2 numbering system using the digits 0 and 1. Computer data are represented by this numbering system.

Biochip   A technology for designing integrated circuits; uses living protein and enzymes to grow circuits; exists in theory only.

Bit   A binary digit; the smallest piece of data that a computer can process.

Bit-mapped graphics   Graphics created with pixel-oriented images.

Block design   A method of spreadsheet design that involves defining and positioning a number of blocks of cells, each with a specific purpose, within the limits of the spreadsheet.

Block editing   An application software feature that permits units, or blocks, of text—characters, words, sentences, paragraphs, sections, or even pages—to be moved, copied, deleted, saved, or altered as a unit.

Boot   Loading the operating system, which prepares the computer for operation.

Bridge   An interface that connects different LANs allowing communication between devices on each.

Browse mode   A database management system feature that shows an entire screen full of records and permits you to edit each field.

Built-in functions   A function contained within an application program that automatically performs a mathematical or logic function without manually entering a formula.

Bulletin board system (BBS)   Electronic equivalent of a conventional bulletin board. A BBS is part of a communication network where users post messages, read those posted by other users, communicate with the system operator, and upload and download programs.

Bus   An electrical path for signals to flow from point to point in a circuit.

Byte   A grouping of bits (typically 8 bits) that represents a character. The basic unit used to measure the size of memory.

Cache memory   A special type of buffer memory that holds a copy of data or instructions in main memory if they are likely to be needed next by the processor. Generally increases the speed at which data and instructions are accessed and thus at which a task is completed.

Calculation block   A block of cells of a spreadsheet that contains formulas and fixed data.

Call mode   In communication software, the operational mode in which a computer initiates a call to another computer.

Cartridge tape   A form of magnetic tape similar to cassette tape but with a much greater storage density; generally used for backing up the contents of a hard disk.

Cassette tape   A form of magnetic tape about one-fourth inch wide; generally used for backing up the contents of a hard disk.

Cathode ray tube (CRT)   A type of display that uses an electron beam to illuminate a phosphor-coated screen to form characters.

Cell   A data entry point in a spreadsheet, defined by its row and column coordinates.

Cell pointer   A highlighted box in a spreadsheet that shows the active cell.

Cellular network   A network in which transmitters are placed in a checkerboard pattern throughout the system service area to enable mobile communication.

Centering   An application software feature that places a heading or other text in the center of the line.

Central processing unit (CPU)   The name given to the processing unit of a computer that interprets and executes instructions and controls and communicates with the other parts of the computer. It is composed of the arithmetic-logic unit and the control unit.

Character enhancements   An application software feature that permits specific emphasis to the text such as boldface, italics, underlining, or a combination.

Chart/graph program   Software used to create charts and graphs; used for pictorial representation of data.

Chip   A complete electronic semiconductor circuit contained on a piece of silicon; used for logic and memory circuitry. Also called an integrated circuit (IC) or microchip.

Client/server architecture   The processing of an application is split between the client's, or user's, computer, and a separate server.

Clip art   Predrawn art available on separate disks or built into a program; the user selects individual images to bring into a document or publication to enhance its appearance or to illustrate a point.

Coaxial cable   A communication channel that consists of a single wire surrounded by both a layer of insulating material and a metal sheath or tube for protection.

Column   In a worksheet, the alphabetic ordering from left to right that, along with the numeric row designation, locates the position of a cell.

Command-line interface   An interface that requires a user to type the desired response at a prompt using a special command language.

Command mode   (1) A mode of operation in which application program commands are selected. (2) In communication, when typed characters are interpreted as commands and not data.

Commercial on-line service   A business that supplies information electronically to subscribers on numerous topics of interest by using powerful computer systems that store millions of pieces of data.

Communication channel   The medium, or pathway, through which data are transmitted between devices; may be wire cable, microwave, or fiber optics.

Communication parameters   Communication software settings to synchronize a user's computer hardware with the computer system with which the user is trying to communicate. These include COM port, transmission speeds, parity, word size and stop bit, emulation, duplex, and mode.

Communication software   An application program designed to control communication between two computers; software that allows a computer to "talk" to other computers.

Compiler   The language translator program used to translate a whole program into machine language all at one time before the program is executed.

Computer   An electronic device that accepts input, processes it in a prescribed manner, outputs the results, and stores the results for later use; a tool used to process data into information.

Computer-aided design (CAD)   The integration of computers and graphics to aid in the design and drafting processes.

Computer-aided manufacturing (CAM)   The use of computers to control machines in the manufacturing process.

Computer crime   A crime in which computers and software are used with illegal intentions.

Computer ethics   A set of rules that govern the standards or conduct of computer users; principles used with computers and the information they produce.

Computer graphics   Images and pictures generated by a computer, software, and the person using them.

Computer-integrated manufacturing (CIM)   An information system that automates and integrates the entire manufacturing enterprise.

Computer literacy   Having an understanding of computers and information systems and the ability to use them.

Computer network   The use of data communication channels to link two or more computers and other devices, such as printers and secondary storage devices to provide a means of communicating and transferring data and information electronically as well as sharing hardware, data files, and programs.

Computer program   The instructions that cause hardware to work. Also called software.

Computer programming   Involves designing, writing, modifying, and testing the instructions that are given to the computer to complete a task.

Computer vision   The capability of a computer to mimic the ways that the human brain processes and interprets light waves.

Computer word   The number of adjacent bits that are manipulated as a unit.

Control panel   An area in an electronic spreadsheet that provides valuable information about activity on the worksheet.

Control unit   The part of the processor (CPU) that retrieves and interprets instructions and directs the ALU and other parts of the computer in response to these interpretations.

Coordinate   The intersection of a row and a column in a spreadsheet; defines the position of a cell in a spreadsheet.

Coprocessor   A chip used along with the main microprocessor dedicated to speed large number-crunching activities.

Copyright infringement   What occurs when the appropriate royalty payment is not made for use of the protected work.

Cursor   An on-screen indicator, such as a blinking underline or rectangle, that shows where the next keystroke will appear when typed.

Daisy-wheel printer   A type of printer that uses a print wheel resembling a daisy. At the end of each "petal" is a fully formed character.

Data   Numbers, letters, special characters, or combinations thereof (raw facts) that convey little meaning by themselves.

Database   A cross-referenced collection of files designed to minimize repetition of data.

Database administrator   An individual who designs, implements, and maintains a database.

Database design screen The portion of a database management system where names, types, width, and other factors for each field in a database file are defined.

Database management system (DBMS) Software developed to store, organize, manipulate, retrieve, display, and print data from a database; the interface among programs, users, and data in the database.

Database programming language A language specific to the database management system that allows the creation of customized applications. Its commands permit a user to create and control how data are entered, processed, and retrieved from the database.

Database query language A language used in conjunction with a database; acts as an interface between a user and a database management system to facilitate access to data, manipulation, analysis, and report creation without use of complex programming code.

Data communication The process of sending data electronically from one point to another.

Data entry The act of entering data and instructions into a computer.

Data manipulation In a computer crime, refers to a user improperly altering data without proper authorization.

Data processing The steps associated with converting data into information: input, processing, output, and storage. Also called information processing.

Data stealing What occurs when data gathered for a legitimate purpose are used for another purpose.

Data-transfer mode In communication software, the operational mode in which actual data transfer takes place between communicating devices.

Decision support system (DSS) An information system designed to allow managers to interact directly with a computer for assistance with semistructured or unstructured decisions.

Default settings In application software, values used by a program unless the user gives other instructions.

Demodulation The process of reconverting an analog signal into a digital signal. Contrast with modulation.

Design program A graphics program used as a design tool to create and/or alter the image of an object.

Desktop computer A microcomputer designed to fit conveniently on a standard business desk.

Desktop publishing A concept that combines the use of microcomputers with word processing, page composition software, and high-quality laser printers.

Device driver The software that allows peripheral devices to communicate with the computer and other peripheral devices.

Digital data transmission The transmission of data using distinct on and off electrical states.

Direct connection An Internet access method that allows a user direct access to the Internet without the need for an additional Internet provider through SLIP/PPP connections.

Disaster recovery team A team of experts who help recover data destroyed by criminal damage, fire, flood, electrical surges, or virus attack.

Disk pack A removable, hard disk storage device containing multiple hard disks in a plastic case; provides increased storage capabilities for large computer systems.

Documentation (1) The written or graphic record of the steps involved in developing or maintaining an information system. (2) Written or graphic descriptions detailing the purpose and the operation of software.

Documentation block A block of cells that does not contain actual data, but rather supplies information about a spreadsheet.

Document design The methodology that combines text and artwork or graphics into a final product.

Dot-matrix printer An impact printer that uses a print head containing pins, usually 9 or 24; produces characters by printing patterns of dots.

Downloading The process of receiving a file from another computer. Contrast with uploading.

Draw program A vector-based graphics program displaying high-quality dots and lines. Users also draw, fill in shapes, and change color while creating illustrations.

Edit mode In a database management system a feature that shows the contents of an individual record and allows editing each field.

Edit window In a word processor, the work area for entering and editing a document.

Electronic data interchange (EDI) An application of data communication that automates and standardizes transactions between retailers and their suppliers; allows them to conduct business transactions electronically.

Electronic funds transfer (EFT) An application of data communication that involves movement of money among accounts electronically.

Electronic mail (E-mail) Electronic transmission of messages over a computer network.

Electronic teleconferencing A method of communicating via computers connected through a telephone system. Each user or group of users participates by keying in their conversations.

Electronic work monitoring   The process in which software permits an employer to monitor an employee's work at a computer. It can count keystrokes, track data entry errors, record the length and frequency of breaks, determine what files have been accessed and for how long, and read a user's electronic mail.

Embedded processor   A special-purpose computer that is part of a larger system whose primary purpose is not computational.

Encoding system   A system whereby alphanumeric characters are represented by patterns of 1's and 0's so they can be recognized and used by a computer. The two most widely used encoding systems are ASCII (American Standard Code for Information Interchange) developed by several computer manufacturers and EBCDIC (Extended Binary Coded Decimal Interchange Code) developed by IBM.

Encryption   A data coding scheme that converts data into unintelligible characters that cannot be read or used by unauthorized persons.

End user   A person who uses computer hardware and software to perform a task. Also referred to as a user.

Executive support system (ESS)   An information system that caters to an executive's special information needs in managerial planning, monitoring, and analysis.

Expansion ports   Pluglike connectors found either at the back or on the side of a computer that allow a computer to physically connect to and communicate with peripheral devices. Also called input/output (I/O) ports.

Expansion slots   Receptacles on the motherboard into which circuit boards can be plugged.

Expert system   Software that uses knowledge and inference procedures acquired by human expertise to solve problems in a particular field. Also called a knowledge-based system.

Expert system shell   A general-purpose inference engine and a skeleton of the knowledge base into which users add their own special data.

Explanation subsystem   The component of an expert system that can respond to user requests and inquiries while the system is executing.

External direct-connect modem   A type of modem external to a computer, connected directly to a telephone line.

Eye trackers   A pointing device that uses video cameras to track the position of the pupils of the user's eyes and translate these data into a screen coordinate, thus enabling the eye to point to and select items on the screen.

Facsimile (fax)   The electronic transmission of text or graphics in digital form over telephone lines.

Fiber optics   A communication channel that transmits data in digital form using light impulses that travel through clear, flexible tubing.

Field   A name given to each data item contained in a record in a database.

Fifth-generation computer   The next generation of computers, which will incorporate artificial intelligence.

Fifth-generation language   One of the next generation of programming languages that will include natural languages.

File   A collection of related records in a database in which each record contains related data fields.

File-locking   A procedure used by multiuser database management systems that permits only one user to access a file at a time.

File Transfer Protocol (FTP)   An Internet standard for the transfer of files from a host computer to a user's computer.

Financial information system   An information system designed to provide management with information concerning the acquisition of funds to finance a business and the allocation and control of the organization's financial resources.

Firmware   Silicon chips that contain instructions permanently etched into them.

First-generation computer   Computers developed and used before 1960; they employ vacuum tube technology.

Flash memory   Silicon memory that retains data even when its power supply is turned off.

Flatbed scanner   A scanner that resembles a photocopy machine; suited to scanning full-page documents.

Flat-panel display   A display that does not use a picture tube to present characters; includes liquid crystal (LCD) and gas plasma.

Floppy diskette   A flexible, mylar magnetic diskette commonly used with microcomputers for magnetic storage of data.

Flow chart   A chart that displays how events are sequenced by time or order.

Footer   Text that appears at the bottom of a page, often a page number or chapter title; sometimes repeats on every page, on odd pages only, or on even pages only.

Font   A set of alphanumeric characters that shares the same characteristics, for example, 12-point Times

Roman, 12-point bold Courier, and 10-point italic Times Roman.

Format   The setting of parameters such as margins or tabs that control the appearance of text or the setting of attributes to describe how data are to be displayed.

Formulas   The mathematical equations entered into a spreadsheet program to perform calculations.

Fourth-generation computer   Computers developed and in use from 1971 to the present which use large scale integration (LSI) and very large scale integration (VLSI).

Fourth-generation language   One of a variety of programming languages that requires much less effort creating programs than high-level languages. The objectives are to increase the speed of developing programs, minimize end-user effort to obtain information from a computer, decrease the skill level required of users, and minimize maintenance by reducing errors and making programs easy to change.

Free-form approach   A method of worksheet design in which values, labels, and formulas are entered without any preplanned structure.

Frequently Asked Questions (FAQs)   Files with answers to often asked questions; new users should consult before participating in a discussion group.

Fuzzy logic   A form of logic using approximate rules of inference in which variables have degrees of truthfulness or falsehood represented by a range of values between 1 (true) and 0 (false); provides the ability for a computer to deal with uncertainty and make "decisions" based on varying degrees of probability.

Garbage-in, garbage-out (GIGO)   A situation in which incorrect input produces incorrect output.

Gas plasma display   A flat-panel monitor used in portable computers; contains an ionized gas (plasma) between two glass plates.

Gateway   An interface that converts the protocol of one network into a form usable by another network or computer.

Generalized application software   Application software that is applied to a variety of tasks.

General-purpose computer   A computer capable of performing a variety of tasks. It can be put to different uses by changing the software.

Global ethics   A category of ethics that deals with the flow, impact, production, dispersal, and utilization of information among nations.

Gopher   A menu-based service of the Internet that allows a user to search for information.

Grammar and style checker   An application software feature that points out potential problems with

punctuation, grammar, sentence structure, and writing style.

Graphical user interface (GUI)   A user interface operating in a graphics mode using pointing devices, on-screen pull-down menus, windows, icons, and other graphical devices.

Graphics software   An application program that allows a user to create, edit, display, and print graphic images; may be a separate software program or integrated into another software program.

Graphics tablet   An input device (also called a digitizing tablet) that consists of a flat plastic rectangle that contains electronic circuitry below its surface to detect when an object makes contact with the tablet. It is used in conjunction with pointing devices such as the stylus and the puck.

Green computers   Computers and related computer equipment that fit an ecological profile set by the Environmental Protection Agency Energy Star Program.

Groupware   A broad class of software that allows members of a group of users to work together without all the participants being in the same place or available at the same time.

Handheld scanners   A type of scanner that is held in the hand. They are best suited for scanning small images such as photos.

Hand-tracking device   A special-purpose input device that converts hand movements into digital signals to control various functions such as the movement of a graphically produced hand displayed on the screen.

Hard copy   Output that can be read immediately or stored and read later, such as paper. It is a relatively stable and permanent form of output.

Hard disk   A hard metallic disk used for magnetically storing data. Its rigid construction permits higher storage densities, allowing more data to be stored; data are accessed faster than with a floppy diskette.

Hard-disk drive   The input/output device that transfers data to and from a hard disk.

Hard page break   An application software feature that lets the user specify exactly where text stops on one page and begins on another.

Hardware   The physical equipment that makes up a computer and information system such as the system unit, input devices, output devices, secondary storage devices, and communication equipment.

Head position trackers   A pointing device that uses a headset to emulate a mouse and a control unit that sits on top of the computer that measures the change in the headset's angular position and translates this change into cursor movements. The headset also contains an attached mouth tube into which the user lightly puffs to select an item, such as a letter to be entered into a word processing document, from a keyboard that is displayed on the screen.

Header   Text that appears at the top of a page, often a title; sometimes repeats on every page, on odd pages only, or on even pages only.

High-level language   A programming language that contains instructions that closely resemble human language and mathematical notation and does not require that a programmer have detailed knowledge about the internal operation of a computer.

High-low graphs   A special type of line graphs that plot minimum and maximum values over time.

Home page   A Web site that can be created and personalized by users of the Internet.

Host computer   The computer with which you establish communication.

Human resources information system   A system designed to provide management with information involving the recruitment, placement, evaluation, compensation, and development of employees.

Hypermedia   A name given to hypertext programs that link text and create links between graphics, sound, and video.

Hypertext   Graphically oriented software in which data are stored as objects that can be arbitrarily linked and accessed. Hypertext software incorporates components of a database, text editor, and graphics editor and uses a mouse to move through windows, click on icons, and pull down menus.

Image database   Database software that allows storage of both pictures and text in a database.

Image-editing program   Programs that allow the user to modify a graphic or photographic image.

Impact printer   A type of printer that produces characters by using a hammer or pins to strike an ink ribbon against a sheet of paper.

Indexing   The process of creating a file which contains the user's sorted-data conditions. The index file is saved separately, allowing the original database to be left unchanged.

Indirect connection   A method in which a user accesses a host computer that provides access to the Internet.

Inference engine   The component of an expert system that applies the rules from a knowledge base to the data provided by a user to draw a conclusion.

Information   Processed data that appears in context and conveys meaning to people.

Information literacy   The ability to judge the value of and use the information wisely.

Information processing   The steps associated with converting data into information: input, processing, output, and storage. Also called data processing.

Information system   A set of components (hardware, software, people, data, and procedures) that work together to manage the acquisition, storage, manipulation, and distribution of information.

Information system manager   An individual who plans and oversees all the information resources in an organization.

Ink-jet printer   A type of nonimpact printer that forms characters on paper by spraying ink particles in character forms.

Input   Refers to data and instructions entered into a computer for processing and also describes the act of entering data and instructions.

Input block   A block of cells set up in a spreadsheet to contain variable data used in formulas.

Input device   A peripheral device that allows instructions and data to be entered into the computer for processing, for example, keyboard and mouse.

Input/output (I/O) ports   Pluglike connectors either at the back or on the side of a computer that allow a computer to connect physically to and communicate with peripheral devices. Also called expansion ports.

Insert mode   A mode in an application package in which adding new text results in all text being moved to the right to make room for the new text.

Install   Preparing a program to work with a computer.

Installation   The second task in the implementation phase of the system development life cycle, during which an information system is made operational by puting it to work for the users.

Installation program   A program that is responsible for getting an application up and running, guiding a user through the installation process by presenting a screen menu of setup options.

Integrated circuit (IC)   A complete electronic semiconductor circuit contained on a piece of silicon; used for logic and memory circuitry. Also called a microchip or just chip.

Integrated Services Digital Network (ISDN)   Worldwide digital communication network using standardized interfaces. This communication will be entirely digital when fully implemented.

Integrated software   A category of application software that combines a number of applications, such as word processing, database management, spreadsheet, graphics, and communication, into a single package.

It allows data to be easily transferred from one application to another and provides a consistent interface.

Intelligent recalculation　A spreadsheet option in which only cells affected by a change are recalculated.

Interactive system　A system that allows a user to communicate with a computer through dialog.

Interface　The joining of two parts so that they can work together.

Interface cable　The cable that connects a peripheral device to the computer.

Internal direct-connect modem　Similar in function to the external direct-connect modem; has all the circuitry on one circuit board, which fits into an expansion slot inside the computer.

Interoperability　The ability to use hardware and software from different vendors interchangeably.

Interpreter　The language-translator program used to translate a program into machine language one line at a time, executing each line after it is translated.

Interprocessing　A method of processing, also called dynamic linking, that allows any change made in one application to be automatically reflected in any related, linked applications.

Justification　The application software feature that aligns the text flush with the left margin (i.e., left justified) or flush with the right margin (i.e., right justified), or spreads the text to fill to both margins (i.e., full justified).

Kerning　In document design, a method for adjusting the space between characters.

Keyboard　An input device that resembles a typewriter keyboard in which individual keys or combinations of keys are pressed to send data to the computer for processing.

Key fields　A field that uniquely identifies a record.

Knowledge-acquisition subsystem　The component of an expert system that accomplishes the transfer of the knowledge acquired from a human expert to the knowledge base.

Knowledge base　The component of an expert system that contains a collection of facts and the rules by which those facts are related.

Knowledge-based system　Software that uses knowledge and inference procedures acquired by human expertise to solve problems in a particular field. Also called an expert system.

Knowledge engineer　Professionals trained to capture the knowledge of an expert and put it into programmable form.

Knowledge engineering　The process by which the knowledge of an expert is transformed into a knowledge base.

Knowledge worker　A person who creates, processes, and distributes information.

Label　Text that identifies some aspect of a spreadsheet, such as its title or contents of a cell.

Language translator program　A system program that converts programming language code into machine language.

Laptop computer　A microcomputer that runs on both AC and batteries and weighs between 10 and 15 pounds.

Large scale integration (LSI)　The process of putting several thousand complete circuits on a single chip.

Laser printer　A nonimpact printer that is capable of printing typeset-quality images using a technology similar to a photocopier.

Leading　In document design, refers to the amount of space between lines.

Leased line　An Internet access method that enables a direct, high-speed connection to be made while allowing multiple users to perform different tasks at the same time.

Line graph　A graph that represents data as a series of points connected by straight or curved lines; used to show trends and emphasize movement and direction of change over time.

Liquid crystal display (LCD)　A flat-panel display commonly used in portable computers; produces images by aligning molecular crystals when voltage is applied.

Load　Refers to bringing a program into main memory so it can be executed.

Local area network (LAN)　A data communication network that consists of two or more computers directly linked within a relatively small, well-defined area, such as a room, building, or cluster of buildings.

Logical system design　The phase of system design that shows the flow of data through an information system. It can be thought of as the information system blueprint.

Log off　The process of disconnecting from the host computer.

Log on　The process of connecting to a host computer by entering an account number followed by a password to control user access.

Low-level language　A programming language that requires programmers to have detailed knowledge of how computers work, since every detail of an operation must be specified.

Machine language　A binary code made up of 1's and 0's, the only language that a computer understands.

Macro   A file that contains a series of previously recorded keystrokes or commands that are quickly executed with one or two keystrokes.

Macro block   The part of the spreadsheet where macros are located.

Magnetic disk   A mylar (floppy diskette) or metallic (hard disk) platter on which electronic data are stored; allows direct access to those data.

Magnetic ink character recognition (MICR)   The method by which a computer recognizes characters written in special magnetic ink. The computer determines the shape by sensing the magnetic charge in the ink.

Magnetic strips   Thin bands of magnetically encoded data found on the backs of many credit cards and automated teller cards.

Magnetic tape   A ½- or ¼-inch ribbon of mylar (a plastic material) coated with a thin layer of iron oxide on which data are recorded.

Mail merge   The process of combining two documents into one. For example, merging a form letter with a file containing names and addresses, to generate a personalized letter.

Mailing list   A discussion group on the Internet that often pertains to one topic. A user can send mail directly to all participants in a group at the same time and receive any message sent to others in the same group.

Main circuit board   Contains the microprocessor and other support chips and circuitry of a microcomputer. Often called the motherboard or system board.

Main memory   The internal storage of a computer where instructions and data are stored while waiting to be processed. Main memory consists of both RAM and ROM. Also called primary storage.

Mainframe computer   A large-scale computer with processing capabilities greater than those of a minicomputer but less than those of a supercomputer.

Maintenance programmer   A programmer responsible for the maintenance of an information system.

Management information system (MIS)   A system that supplies managers with information to aid in problem solving, control, and decision making.

Manager   A person responsible for using available resources—people, materials/equipment, land, information, money—to achieve the goals of an organization.

Margin settings   Specifications that describe the blank spaces at the left, right, top, and bottom of a document.

Marketing information system   An information system that involves gathering details about day-to-day sales transactions, managing and controlling marketing operations, and planning sales and strategies for the future.

Massive parallel processing (MPP)   A link of many processors so that greater volumes of data are processed simultaneously instead of in sequence, as with single-processor computers.

Menu-driven interface   A type of user interface that allows the user to select commands from a list (menu) using the keyboard or a pointing device such as a mouse.

Microchip   An integrated circuit.

Microcomputer   A computer that is built around a single-chip processor called the microprocessor; relatively small in size.

Microprocessor   A single chip that contains both the arithmetic and logic unit (ALU) and the control unit.

Microwave   A type of data communication channel in which data are transmitted through the air as analog signals for reception by satellites or microwave transmitting stations.

Minicomputer   A computer in the large-scale category that has less processing capability than a mainframe computer but more than a desktop computer. Minis are designed to accept input from and produce output to a large number of users, supporting from 10 to 100 terminals.

Mixed cell reference   A method of copying a formula in a spreadsheet; requires that each cell reference be specified as either absolute or relative.

Mnemonic   An alphabetic abbreviation used as a memory aid.

Model   To use mathematics to describe a situation or a physical object. For example, spreadsheet programs are used to model financial and other business-related data.

Modem   Acronym for modulator-demodulator; the device that converts signals from analog to digital and from digital to analog.

Modulation   The process of converting a digital signal to an analog signal. Contrast with demodulation.

Monitor   A televisionlike device that displays data or information.

Morphing   The process of transforming one image into another.

Mouse   A popular pointing device that controls the cursor position on the screen. It is designed to be easily gripped and contains one or more buttons on top that select items and choose commands.

Multidimensional spreadsheet   An electronic spreadsheet capable of showing ranges of cells as solids (three-dimensional objects). This form allows for organization of complex worksheets.

Multimedia The integration of high-quality sound, still and motion video, text, animation, and graphics in a complete system.

Multiprocessing An operating system capability that allows the simultaneous execution of programs by a computer that has two or more CPUs.

Multitasking An operating system capability that allows a single CPU to execute what appears to be more than one program at a time.

Multiuser information system An information system designed to be used by many users.

Multiuser operating system An operating system that allows two or more users to access a computer at the same time.

Musical Instrument Digital Interface (MIDI) A component of multimedia. A communication protocol used to communicate between the computer and other peripheral devices that are MIDI controlled, such as a synthesizer. With a MIDI interface, computer, synthesizer, and sequencing software, a user can compose, rearrange, and otherwise edit sounds into a complete composition.

Natural language processing The ability of a computer to understand and translate a natural language, such as English, into commands to perform a specific operation.

Netiquette The code of behavior on a network.

Network interface card A circuit board that makes the physical connection to the LAN cable.

Network operating system The software that controls the operation and the functions of a LAN.

Neural-expert system A combination of neural and expert systems that "learns" new rules or adapts old rules based on experience and modifies its knowledge bases appropriately.

Neural network A system modeled after the neurons in the human nervous system and designed to simulate the way the human brain processes information, learns, and remembers.

Newbies New users on the Internet.

Newsgroup A floating bulletin board on the Internet to which members of discussion groups can post and read messages concerning the topic(s) of the newsgroup.

Node Each computer or device in a computer network system.

Nonimpact printer A type of printer that produces characters without physically striking the paper.

Nonremovable hard disk drive A drive in which the hard disk(s) is enclosed permanently in a sealed case.

Nonvolatile When applied to computer memory, it means the contents of memory are not lost when the electric current is turned off.

Notebook computer A microcomputer that is about the size of an 8 ½ × 11-inch notebook, uses both AC and battery options, weighs around 6 to 8 pounds, has a display screen from 7 to 10 inches, and a keyboard that is smaller than desktop microcomputers.

Object-oriented graphics See vector graphics.

Office information system (OIS) An information system that helps knowledge workers manage the preparation, storage, retrieval, reproduction, and communication of information within and among business offices.

Operating environment Software that enhances the function of an operating system and improves its user interface.

Operating system (OS) A core set of programs that gives the computer the instructions to operate, telling it how to interact with hardware, other software, and the user.

Operational information system An information system that records and helps manage a transaction. Also transaction processing system (TPS).

Operational (low-level) managers Managers directly involved with the day-to-day operation of business.

Optical bar recognition (OBR) A data input method that involves scanning and translating a bar code into digital signals to be used by a computer.

Optical bar reader An input device that scans and interprets the pattern of lines printed on products.

Optical card Also, laser card, the size of a credit card with an optical laser-encoded strip capable of storing approximately 4 megabytes of data.

Optical character recognition (OCR) software Software that translates images captured with a scanner into text files to be used by programs capable of manipulating text.

Optical computer A computer that uses laser beams instead of electrical signals to perform ON/OFF switching.

Optical laser disk A type of storage medium on which data are stored and read by a laser. Metal disks ranging in size from 3.5 inches to 14 inches.

Optical mark reader An input device that scans a form and identifies the positions of marks rather than their shapes.

Optical mark recognition (OMR) A data input method in which a series of pen or pencil marks on a special form is scanned and their position is translated into computer-readable code, for example, computer-scored test answer sheets.

Optical recognition   The process of using light-sensing equipment to scan paper or other sources and translate the pattern of light and dark, or color, into a digital signal that can be used by the computer.

Optical scanner   An input device that uses light to sense the patterns of black and white (or color) on paper or other medium and converts them into a digital signal. Often, simply called a scanner.

Optical tape   A storage medium similar to magnetic tape in that it is read sequentially, but stores data with optical-laser techniques.

Optical technology   The technology that uses lasers as a means of storing and retrieving data.

Organizational chart   A chart that displays a hierarchy of data.

Orientation   In word processing, the direction in which the letters print on the paper.

Orphan line   The first line of a new paragraph that stands alone at the bottom of a page.

Output   (1) The process of retrieving stored information, converting it into human-readable form and displaying it in a form understandable to a user. (2) The result of processing.

Output block   The part of the spreadsheet where results of calculation are displayed.

Output device   A peripheral device that receives information from the computer, for example, monitor or printer. Hardware that enables a computer to communicate information to humans or other machines so that it may be used.

Page composition software   Graphic-oriented software used in positioning and aligning text, graphics, and other elements of a document page on the screen.

Paint program   A microcomputer graphics program that allows a user to "paint" an image using an input device, such as a mouse, as a brush. The user also draws, fills in shapes, and changes the color and texture of a painting. Paint programs handle graphics as rasters.

Palmtop computer   A microcomputer that weighs less than one pound and fits easily into your pocket; provides quick access to the data wherever you need it.

Parallel processing   A system that allows several processes to be performed simultaneously, using multiple CPUs; much faster than serial processing techniques.

Parity   A type of error-checking procedure used in communication.

Parity bit   The bit used to check for error in a transmitted signal. It may be even, odd, or none.

Password   A unique combination of characters that a user enters as an identification code. Passwords protect entire programs or selected parts.

Pen-based computer   A microcomputer that uses a penlike device to input data. Ideal for mobile workers.

Peripheral devices   Hardware that is attached externally to the system unit.

Personal computer (PC)   A microcomputer designed to be used primarily by one individual.

Personal financial managers   Programs that offer computerized checkbook, savings account, and loan account in addition to other specialized programs.

Personal information managers (PIMs)   Specialized programs that include address and phone number lists, appointment schedules, and to-do lists.

Personal information system   An information system designed for use by an individual user.

Physical system design   A stage of the system development life cycle, converts the system blueprint into specific hardware and computer programs that transform the logical design into a working information system.

Pie chart   A graph that uses a circle (pie) divided into segments to show the relationship of data to the whole.

Pixel   The smallest part of a display screen that can be individually controlled.

Plotter   An output device that reproduces graphic images on paper using a pen attached to a movable arm.

Point   In printing, a measurement of a font's size.

Point-to-Point Protocol (PPP)   A protocol used for direct Internet connection that resends data if they arrive in error.

Pointing device   An input device that controls an on-screen cursor or creates drawings or graphical shapes. Often used for actions such as choosing menu items, "pressing" on-screen "buttons" in dialog boxes, and selecting text or other values.

Presentation graphics   Graphics suitable for a formal presentation.

Primary storage   The storage where instructions of a computer program and the data on which they work must be found in order to be executed. Also called main memory.

Printer   An output device that produces hard copy, consisting of text or graphics.

Printer driver   Software that informs the computer what type of printer is connected and its capabilities.

Procedures   The instructions that tell a user how to operate and use an information system.

Processing   Involves performing calculations and logical operations on data to achieve a desired outcome.

Processor   See central processing unit.

Production/operations information system   An information system that gathers and processes data about the activities involved in producing goods and services.

Programmer   An individual who translates the tasks a user wants a computer to accomplish into a form the computer understands, that is, codes the instructions in a programming language for a computer to solve the problem.

Programming language   A set of written symbols that tells the computer hardware how to perform specified operations.

Project management   The structured coordination and monitoring of all activities involved in a one-time endeavor or project.

Protocol   A set of rules and procedures for transmitting and receiving data so that different devices can communicate with each other.

Puck   A pointing device, often used with a graphics tablet, that has a mouselike shape with buttons for selecting items or choosing commands and a clear plastic piece extends out from the body with crosshairs printed on it for locating the entry point.

Query   The process of extracting data from a database and presenting it in a requested format. Queries are accomplished through a database query language.

Query by example   A query language style in which the user inputs query conditions in the desired fields.

Random-access memory (RAM)   The part of main memory in which you enter (write) data and instructions and then retrieve them (read) in a random (nonsequential) manner. Data in RAM are erased when power is off—it is volatile memory.

Range of cells   In a spreadsheet, a method of selecting specific contiguous cells; permits large blocks of cells to be manipulated together.

Raster graphic   Graphic image drawn from a collection of dots.

Readability   A measure of the appropriateness and understandability of a document.

Read-only memory (ROM)   Part of main memory from which data and instructions can only be retrieved (read). The contents of ROM are generally unchangeable and permanent. ROM is nonvolatile.

Ready mode   A mode of operation in which a spreadsheet program indicates that it is ready to receive information. When a character is entered, the program automatically switches to the entry mode.

Real-time processing   An operating system capability that allows a computer to control or monitor the performance of other machines and people by responding to input data in a specified amount of time.

Record   A collection of related data items in a database.

Record locking   A procedure used by multiuser database management systems that permits more than one user to access a file at one time but only one user to access a record at a time.

Reel-to-reel tape   Magnetic tape placed on open reels typically 10 ½ inches in diameter, about 2,400 feet long and ½-inch wide. Reel-to-reel tapes are relatively inexpensive and durable, and hold a large quantity of data.

Relational database   A database composed of many tables having unique rows, in which data are stored.

Relational database management system (RDBMS)   The database management system that allows data to be readily created, maintained, manipulated, and retrieved from a relational database.

Relative cell reference   A method of copying cells in a spreadsheet where the formula is the same but the cells referenced in that formula are different.

Removable hard disk drive   A drive in which the hard disk(s) is contained in a removable cartridge that offers hard disk advantages with portability.

Report generator   In addition to customizing the placement of fields, most report generators allow you to incorporate headers, footers, formatting, and mathematical and statistical functions.

Resolution   On a monitor screen, the image quality is measured by the number of pixels the screen contains.

Robot   A machine programmed to do a variety of useful tasks.

Robotics   The area of study dealing with design, construction, and operation of robots.

Row   In a spreadsheet, the numeric ordering from top to bottom that, along with the column designation, locates the position of a cell.

Satellite   An electronic device placed in orbit around the Earth to receive, amplify, and transmit signals.

Scatter graph   A graph in which two sets of data points are plotted; shows the correlation (if any) between the data sets.

Screen form   A form that describes the layout for entering data into a record in a data manager. Fields are positioned according to user preference and serve as an output screen where field alignment is determined for printing.

Script   A file used by a communication program to automatically enter information such as the log-on procedure.

Search and replace   An application software feature that lets a user look for a word or phrase in a file and determine whether it should be replaced. One option permits automatic replacement.

Second-generation computer   Computers developed and used between 1959 and 1965 that contained transistors to control internal operations.

Secondary storage   The external storage of a computer; preserves programs and data permanently or relatively permanently. It is nonvolatile.

Secondary storage device   Hardware that provides permanent or relatively permanent storage of data and instructions, for example, hard disk drives and floppy disk drives.

Serial Line Interface Protocol (SLIP)   A protocol used for direct Internet connection that does not resend data if they arrive in error.

Serial processing   A processing method in which a single CPU finishes executing one instruction before starting the next.

Server   A computer that services a local area network.

Shell account   See indirect connection.

Simulation   The ability to imitate an object or process and make it respond to different situations as if it were a real object or process.

Single tasking   An operating system capability that allows only one program to execute at a time; it must finish executing completely before the next program begins.

Single-user operating system   An operating system that allows only one user at a time to access a computer.

Slide show   In a graphics program, a feature that allows individual graphics files to be displayed in a predetermined order for a predetermined amount of time, similar to a slide projector and slides.

Smart paper   Embedded intelligence in a computer screen.

Soft copy   A form of volatile output, usually a screen display.

Soft page break   An application software feature that indicates the end of one page and the beginning of another. Contrast with hard page break.

Software   Instructions, written in a programming language, that cause the hardware to do the work.

Software piracy   The unauthorized duplication of copyrighted computer programs.

Sorting   The process of arranging data in numeric or alphabetic sequence, either in ascending or descending order.

Specialized application software   Application software that performs a specific task; it cannot be changed or programmed for a different task. For

example, a payroll application program is designed exclusively for payroll.

Special-purpose computer   Computer designed to work on a limited scope of problems.

Speech coding   A type of voice output. The computer uses stored sounds to build sentences or phrases to be spoken.

Speech recognition   The ability of a computer to recognize speech and take action based on the words spoken. Also voice recognition.

Spelling checker   A program to locate misspelled words and typographical errors.

Spreadsheet   A paper form, divided into rows and columns, used to keep track of and manipulate numeric data. The computerized version is called an electronic spreadsheet.

Spreadsheet design   The arrangement of values, labels, and formulas in rows and columns of a spreadsheet.

Spreadsheet software   Computerized spreadsheet program that instructs the computer to manipulate rows and columns of numbers, make calculations, and evaluate algebraic formulas. Also called electronic spreadsheet.

Status line   One or more lines at the top or the bottom of a display screen; provides information about the current file or operation in progress.

Stop bit   In communication, the bit used to synchronize the receiving and transmitting terminals on a word-by-word basis.

Storage   The ability of the computer to maintain data or information for use at a later time. Two key means of storage are internal (called main memory, or primary storage) and external (called secondary storage).

Strategic (top-level) managers   Managers who make decisions involving the long-range, or strategic, goals of organizations.

Structured-block design approach   The preplanned layout method which improves the design, understandability, and usefulness of a spreadsheet.

Structured query language (SQL)   The standard database query language used with relational databases.

Style sheet   A blueprint or master plan for a document; it sets out specifications, such as typeface and point size, to be used; spacing to be inserted between letters, lines, and paragraphs; margins and paragraph indentation to be set, for example. A style sheet maintains continuity for your document(s).

Stylus   A pointing device used with a graphics tablet or pen-based computer. It is pressed against the graphics tablet or computer screen to draw, point, or enter data. Also called a pen.

Supercomputer   The most powerful type of computer; used primarily by organizations that process vast quantities of data.

Superconductor   Material that offers little resistance to electricity. Current superconductor materials perform at temperatures near absolute zero (-473° F).

System analysis   The process of identifying a system problem or new opportunity, analyzing the current system in light of the problem or new opportunity, and justifying the development of a new system or modification of an old system to meet the needs of users.

System analyst   Person who determines the information processing needs of the users.

System clock   Device that generates electrical timing signals that regulate operations of the processor and other parts of the computer.

System design   A phase of the system development life cycle that is comprised of two stages: (1) the logical design and (2) the physical design.

System designer   A specialist who designs a system to fulfill the users' information needs.

System development life cycle (SDLC)   A structured sequence of operations required to conceive, develop, and make operational a new information system; includes a system analysis phase, a design phase, and an implementation phase.

System implementation   The phase of the system development life cycle during which a completely new system or replacement system is introduced into the workplace; includes testing, installation, and training.

System maintenance   The fourth phase in the system development life cycle, during which an information system is continually modified to meet the changing requirements of its users.

System operator (sysop)   In an electronic network, the person in charge of operating a bulletin board system.

System software   Software that directly controls and monitors the operation of computer hardware and determines how application programs will run.

System unit   The housing that contains the major components and controls of the computer.

Tab settings   An application software feature that sets indentations in a file and aligns columns and decimal numbers.

Tactical (middle-level) managers   Managers concerned with short-term, tactical decisions directed toward accomplishing the organizational goals established by the top-level managers.

Tape drive   The input/output device that reads, writes, and erases data on tape.

Telecommunication   Also called teleprocessing, the process of using communication facilities, such as a telephone system or microwave relays, to send data to and from devices.

Telecommuting   A method of working whereby a person uses a computer and a communication channel to establish a link with a remote office computer. With a personal computer (or terminal) connected to a company's computer, an off-site employee communicates with the office.

Telnet   An Internet service that lets a user tap into a remote computer and treat their computer as if it were a terminal for the remote computer.

Template   In an application program, a screen form that contains only entries that do not change. A template may be used as an input form as well as an output form.

Testing   The activity through which a new information system is checked to ensure that it is correct.

Thesaurus   A software program that provides alternative words (synonyms) for a given word in a document.

Third-generation computer   Computers developed and used between 1965 and 1971 that first implemented integrated circuits (ICs).

Time bomb   A program put into a computer that is set to disrupt operations and destroy data either at a certain time or after a specified number of times the program is run.

Time-sharing operating system   An operating system that allows many users to access a single computer; typically found on large computer operating systems where many users need access at the same time.

Titles   A feature in a spreadsheet program that freezes row and column titles so that they remain stationary as the spreadsheet is scrolled.

Touch screen   An input device that allows a user to enter data or show position by touching the screen with a finger or other object through a built-in grid of sensing lines or a grid of infrared beams and sensors.

Trackball   A pointing device that uses the movement of a hand-rotated stationary sphere to control the movement of the pointer.

Training   The third task in the implementation phase of the system development life cycle; intended to familiarize users and others with a system so they are able to work with it.

Transaction   A business activity or event, for example, the receipt of an order or the sale of a product.

Transaction processing system (TPS)   An information system that processes data about transactions or other events that affect the operation of a business. Also, operational information system.

Transistor   Device made from a semiconducting material, such as silicon, to control the flow of electricity through circuits.

Transmission Control Protocol over Internet Protocol (TCP/IP)   Software that provides the common language of the Internet; allows the different types of computers to communicate with each other.

Trojan horse   A program that disguises itself as a legitimate program, but once installed, the rogue program does its damage—garbling data, destroying indexes, or erasing all the data in the computer.

Twisted-pair   Communication channel consisting of a pair of wires, each wrapped in a protective coating and twisted around the other.

Typeface   The design of a set of print characters.

Typeover mode   A mode in application software; as new text is entered, it takes the place of—overwrites—any existing text occupying that space.

Updating   The process of modifying data that are stored in a computer through adding, deleting, or changing.

Uploading   The process of sending a file from one computer to another.

Usenet   The Internet service that organizes discussions into groups, called newsgroups.

User   A person who uses computer hardware and software to perform a task. Also end user.

User interface   The portion of a program that users interact with—entering commands and data and viewing the results of those commands.

Utility program   A program that performs a wide range of functions in support of the OS. Utility programs perform functions such as copying data from one storage device to another, converting data from one format to another, restoring damaged or accidentally erased data, and diagnosing (detecting, locating, and describing) problems with hardware and software, to name a few.

Vacuum tube   Device used to control the flow of electricity through circuits in early computers.

Validating   The process of checking data for appropriateness and accuracy as they are entered.

Value   A constant that can be entered into a spreadsheet cell by itself or as part of a formula.

Value of information   A determination of how meaningful and useful information is, determined by each user on a case-by-case basis; should be reevaluated periodically and viewed in terms of its incremental value and user benefit.

Vector graphics   Images that are created as a set of lines. They are generated through mathematical formulas that determine the length, position and orien-

tation of an object. A vector graphic, such as a circle is handled as a single entity.

Veronica   On the Internet an interface used with Gopher; makes it easier to narrow down your search for information.

Very large scale integration (VLSI)   The process of putting several hundred thousand complete circuits on a single chip.

Virtual reality   The integration of sound, color, and animation in a wrap-around environment. It gives the illusion of computing in three dimensions.

Virus   A program that can enter a computer to destroy or alter data and spread itself to other computers.

Visualization software   Software that allows numeric data to be analyzed graphically—makes it easier to comprehend complex information and allows viewing data multidimensionally.

Voice messaging systems   Computer-supported systems that allow human voice messages to be sent without requiring the recipients to be present to accept the messages sent and received from standard push-button telephones.

Voice output   Soft copy output in which the computer mimics the human voice.

Voice recognition   The ability of a computer to recognize the speech of a user and take action based on the words spoken. Also speech recognition.

Voice synthesis   The capability of a computer to electronically reproduce a human voice in recognizable patterns.

Volatile   When applied to computer memory, it means that the contents of memory are lost when power is turned off.

Web   See World Wide Web (WWW).

Weight   A reference to the width of a character.

What-if analysis   In spreadsheets, involves changing data entries in a worksheet to show how the change affects other entries.

White space   In word processing, an area of the document containing no text or graphics.

Wide Area Information Service (WAIS)   A method used on the Internet to search for information in databases.

Wide area network (WAN)   Consists of two or more geographically dispersed computers linked by communication facilities such as a telephone system or microwave relays.

Widow line   The last line of a paragraph that stands alone at the top of a page.

Window   Separate, defined areas on a computer screen used to display data, menus, or other software packages.

Wire cable   A type of data communication channel; includes twisted-pair and coaxial cables.

Wireless computing   The use of cellular, infrared, or radio frequencies to transmit and receive data without a conducting medium such as copper wire.

Word processing   The activity of entering, viewing, storing, retrieving, editing, rearranging, and printing text material using a computer and a word processor.

Word processor   An application program that creates, edits, manipulates, and prints text; generally used for writing documents such as letters and reports.

Word size   In communication, the number of bits that make up a character.

Wordwrap   A word processor feature; automatically continues a sentence to the next line without the user pressing return at the end of the line. Any words that extend past the right margin are moved down to the next line.

Working memory   In an expert system, the part of computer memory in which appropriate rules and data are stored for an instant during execution; also known as short-term memory or dynamic knowledge base.

Worksheet   The blank spreadsheet form used to enter and organize numeric data.

Workstation   (1) A category of powerful stand-alone computer whose base price includes a high end processor, very large main memory, considerable calculating and graphics capability; (2) a personal computer or a terminal attached to a LAN. A workstation is an input/output device at which a user works.

World Wide Web (WWW)   Software used to find information on the Internet. It uses hypertext and hypermedia to link documents together. The user moves to another document with related data by pointing and clicking on different parts of the initial document.

Worm   A surreptitious program that issues false or misleading commands. Occupies computer memory and spreads quickly as does a virus—stopping normal computer operation.

Write-once, read-many (WORM) optical disk   An optical disk that is written to once and read many times. Data on WORM disks cannot be erased and are thus suitable for long-term storage.

WYSIWYG (What You See Is What You Get)   This capability means that the printed output looks exactly like what is seen on the display screen.

INDEX

Bulletin board system (BBS), 269
  defined, 269, 322
  features of, 269
  tips for use, 269
Bus
  defined, 77, 322
  and speed of computer, 77
Bush, Vannevar, 56
Business information systems, 131–33
  accounting information system, 132
  financial information system, 132
  human resources information
    system, 133
  marketing information systems, 132
  production/operations information
    system, 133
Business Software Alliance (BSA), 39
Byte, defined, 74, 322

C language, 61, 120, 121
Cable Communication Policy Act of
    1986, 41
Cache memory
  defined, 77, 322
  operation of, 77
Calculation block, defined, 209, 322
Call mode, defined, 268, 322
Careers in computers
  database administrator, 316
  information system manager, 316
  programmer, 316
  system analyst, 316
Cartridge tape, defined, 92, 322
Cassette tape, defined, 92, 322
Categories of computers
  main frame, 24
  microcomputer, 19–22
  minicomputer, 23
  supercomputer, 24
Cathode ray tube (CRT)
  defined, 89, 322
  features of, 89
CD-ROM
  applications for, 97, 156
  and multimedia, 244
  storage capacity, 97
Cell
  active cell, 195
  defined, 195, 322
Cell pointer, defined, 195, 322
Cell reference, 200
  absolute, 206
  mixed, 206
  relative, 206
Cellular network, defined, 322
Censorship, on networks, 39
Centering, defined, 153, 322
Central processing unit (CPU), 14,
    74–77
  defined, 74–75, 322

main memory, 77–78
microprocessor, 75
parts of, 75
and serial and parallel processing, 77
and software compatibility, 75–76
speed of, 76–77
Character enhancements
  defined, 153, 322
  types of, 153
Chart program, defined, 225, 322
Charts, 238–39
  flow chart, 239
  organizational chart, 238, 239
  pie chart, 238, 239
Chip
  defined, 75, 322
  and development of computers, 60,
    61, 67, 72
  future developments, 300
  See also Integrated circuit
Christensen, Ward, 269
Cirrus, 274
Client/server architecture
  components of, 182
  defined, 182, 322
Clip art
  defined, 159, 322
  in desktop applications, 159
Clipper chip, 49
Coaxial cable, 260
  defined, 259, 323
COBOL, 61, 120, 121
Codd, E.F. profile of, 170
Color, in document design, 161
Column, 197, 198, 199
  defined, 323
  inserting and deleting, 204–5
COM port, 266
Command mode, defined, 268, 323
Command-line interface, defined, 112, 323
Commercial Internet Exchange
    (CIX), 281
Commercial on-line service, 269–70
  defined, 269, 323
  features of, 269–70
  gateway from Internet to, 291
  types of services, 270
Commodore computers, 62
Communication channel, 259–61
  cable, types of, 259
  defined, 259, 323
  fiber optics, 260–61
  microwave, 260
  satellite, 260
Communication parameters, 265–68
  answer mode, 268
  call mode, 268
  COM port, 266
  command mode, 268
  data transfer mode, 267

defined, 265, 323
duplex, 267
file transfer procedures, 268
log on and log off, 267
mode, 267
parity, 266–67
stop bits, 267
terminal emulation, 267
transmission speed, 266
word size, 267
Communication software
  defined, 265, 323
  functions of, 265
  types of programs, 265
Compact-disk interactive (CD-I), 247
Compaq, personal computers, 63, 65
Compiler, defined, 120, 323
Completeness, of information, 11
Complex Number Calculator, 57
CompuServe, 38, 39
Computer crime, 43–50
  criminals, types of, 44
  data stealing, 44
  defined, 43, 323
  detection of, 46
  and disaster recovery, 49
  legislation related to, 50
  prevention of, 47–49
  software piracy, 43
  time bombs, 44
  Trojan horse, 44
  viruses, 43
  worms, 44
Computer Crime Unit, 50
Computer Emergency Response Team
    (CERT), 38
Computer ethics
  of Association for Computing
    Machinery (ACM), 34–35
  computer crime, 43–50
  defined, 12, 323
  and electronic work monitoring,
    35–36
  global ethics, 39–40
  government ethics, 36–37
  individual ethics, 36
  issues difficult to solve, 42
  liability and incorrect information,
    41
  misuse of information, 40–41
  and networks, 37–39
  piracy of software, 39, 43
  privacy issues, 38, 41, 42, 50
  professional ethics, 34–36
  software mishaps, 42
  Ten Commandments of, 34, 35
  See also Computer crime
Computer Fraud and Abuse Act of 1986,
    41, 50
Computer graphics. *See* Graphics

Digital data transmission, 258
  defined, 257, 324
Digital Equipment Corporation, 60, 61, 66
Digital video, in multimedia, 247–48
Direct connection
  defined, 291, 324
  on Internet, 291
Directories, 111
Disabled persons, computer technology
  for, 11, 158, 301, 308–9
Disaster recovery, 49, 99
  disaster recovery team, defined, 49, 324
  software for, 49
Disk pack, defined, 95, 324
Docking station, 21
Document design, 160–63
  color enhancement, 161
  defined, 160
  graphics enhancement, 162
  readability, 163
  style sheet, 160
  typefaces/fonts, 161–62
  white space, use of, 161
Documentation, defined, 324
Documentation block, defined, 209, 324
DOS, features of, 114
Dot-matrix printer
  defined, 88, 324
  operation of, 88
Downloading, defined, 268, 324
Dragon System, 301
Draw programs, 223
  defined, 223, 324
  types of, 223
Duplex, data communication mode, 267

E-mail. *See* Electronic mail (E-mail)
Eckert, J. Presper, 58, 59, 64, 65
Edit mode, defined, 177, 324
Edit window, defined, 145, 324
Editing, in word processor, 147–48
Education, use of computers, 9–10, 241
Electronic books, 6
Electronic Communications Privacy Act
  of 1986, 41
Electronic Community Citizenship
  Examination, 39
Electronic data interchange (EDI), 274
  benefits of, 274
  defined, 274, 324
Electronic Delay Storage Automatic
  Computer (EDSAC), 59
Electronic Discrete Variable Automatic
  Computer (EDVAC), 58–59
Electronic funds transfer (EFT), 135, 274
  defined, 274, 324
Electronic Integrator and Computer
  (ENIAC), 58, 220
Electronic mail (E-mail), 271–72
  benefits of, 272
  defined, 271–72, 324

employer monitoring of, 38
  features of, 271–72
  on Internet, 281
  types of programs, 281
Electronic monitoring of criminals, 44, 46
Electronic teleconferencing
  benefits of, 273
  defined, 273, 324
Electronic work monitoring
  defined, 35, 325
  ethical issue, 35–36
Embedded processor, defined, 325
Emulation, terminal, 267
Encoding system
  defined, 74, 325
  types of, 74
Encryption
  defined, 49, 325
  by government agencies, 49
End user, 12, 17
  defined, 12, 325
Engelbart, Douglas, 61
Enigma, 57
Entertainment applications, 6–7, 117
Environment, and green computers, 314
Epson dot-matrix printer, 63
Erasable optical disks, 97–98
Ergonomics, taking breaks, 25
Ethics
  defined, 34
  See also Computer ethics
Executive support system (ESS)
  defined, 130, 325
  functions of, 130–31
Expansion ports, defined, 92, 325
Expansion slots, defined, 325
Expert system, 308–10
  components of, 308–9
  defined, 308, 325
  knowledge engineering, 309
  types of, 308
Expert system shell, defined, 309, 325
Explanation subsystem, defined, 325
Extended Binary Coded Decimal
  Interchange Code (EBCDIC), 74
External direct-connect modem,
  defined, 258, 325
Eye trackers
  defined, 82, 325
  operation of, 82

Facsimile (fax), 272–73
  defined, 272, 325
  in microcomputers, 272–73
Fair Credit Reporting Act of 1970, 41
Federal Bureau of Investigation (FBI),
  fingerprint identification system, 37, 44
Federal Electronic Communications
  Privacy Act, 38
Federal government, use of computers,
  5–6

Fiber optics, 260–61, 306
  advantages of, 261
  defined, 260, 325
Field
  in creating database, 175–76
  defined, 172, 325
Fifth-generation computers
  defined, 67, 122, 325
  types of, 67, 68
Fifth-generation language
  defined, 325
  nature of, 122
File, defined, 171, 325
File transfer protocol (FTP)
  anonymous FTP, 283
  defined, 283, 325
  on Internet, 283
File-locking
  defined, 47, 325
  methods of, 47–49
Financial information system
  defined, 132, 325
  functions of, 132
Fingerprint identification system,
  37, 44
Firmware, defined, 325
First-generation computers
  defined, 65, 325
  types of, 65, 66
First-generation language, 122
Flash memory, 298–99
  defined, 298, 325
Flat-panel display
  defined, 90, 325
  features of, 90
Flatbed scanners
  defined, 86, 325
  operation of, 86
Floppy disk drive, 14
Floppy diskette, 93–94
  capacities, 93, 94
  defined, 93, 325
  formatting, 111
Flopticals, 93
Flow chart, 239
  defined, 239, 325
Font, defined, 162, 325
Footer
  of database, 180
  defined, 153, 325
Format, defined, 148, 326
Formatting document, 148, 150–52
  of database, 180–81
  example document, 151
  formatting features, 148, 150–52
  of spreadsheet, 204–5
Formulas, defined, 199, 326
Forrester, Jay, 59, 64
FORTRAN, 61, 120, 121
Fourth-generation computers, types of,
  66, 67

Olsen, Ken, 60, 61, 65
Operating environment, defined, 114, 330
Operating system (OS), 109–16
  common uses of, 110–11
  defined, 109, 330
  DOS, 114
  functions of, 110
  Macintosh OS (the System), 115
  OS/2, 115
  processing methods, 112
  for single and multiple users, 111
  single and multitasking, 112
  Unix, 115–16
  user interaction with, 112, 114
  Windows95, 114–15
Operational information system, defined, 330
Operational (low-level) managers
  defined, 128, 330
  role of, 128
Optical card, defined, 97, 330
Optical character recognition (OCR) software
  defined, 86, 330
  operation of, 86
Optical computer
  defined, 299–300, 330
  future development, 299–300
Optical laser disk
  CD-ROM, 96
  defined, 96, 330
  erasable disks, 96
  write-once, read-many (WORM), 97
Optical mark reader, defined, 85, 330
Optical mark recognition (OMR)
  defined, 85, 330
  operation of, 85
Optical recognition, 85–87
  defined, 331
  optical bar recognition (OBR), 86
  optical mark recognition (OMR), 85
  optical scanners, 86
Optical scanners
  defined, 86, 331
  flatbed scanners, 86
  handheld scanners, 86
  operation of, 86
Optical storage, 96–97
  optical card, 97
  optical laser disk, 96
  optical tape, 98
Optical tape, defined, 98, 331
Optical technology, defined, 96, 331
Optical-bar reader, defined, 86, 330
Optical-bar recognition (OBR)
  defined, 86, 330
  operation of, 86
Organizational chart, defined, 238, 239, 331

Orientation, defined, 162, 331
Orphan line, defined, 164, 331
OS/2, 63
  features of, 115
Osborne, Adam, 63
Output
  categories of, 87
  defined, 87, 331
  in information processing, 16, 17
Output block, defined, 209, 331
Output devices, 14, 87–91
  defined, 87, 331
  monitors, 89, 90–91
  plotters, 88
  printers, 87–88
  speech coding, 91
  voice output, 90

Page composition software, defined, 159, 331
Page-layout, in word processor, 157
PageMaker, 63, 157
Paint programs, 223–24
  defined, 223, 331
  types of, 224
Palmtop computers, 23, 297
  characteristics of, 21
  defined, 331
Paradox, 173
Parallel processing
  defined, 77, 331
  functions of, 77
  future developments, 299
Parity, defined, 266, 331
Parity bit, defined, 267, 331
Parity checking, in data communications, 267
Pascal, 61, 120, 121
Pascal, Blaise, 54, 121
Pascaline, 54, 64
Password, 48–49
  and database, 184
  defined, 48, 331
  effectiveness of, 49
  guidelines for choice of, 265
PC-DOS, 62
PDP-I, 61, 67
PDP-8, 61
Pen-based computers, 21, 64
  characteristics of, 21
  defined, 21, 331
  future developments, 301
  stylus, 80, 82
Pentium, 75
Peripheral devices, 14
  defined, 331
Personal communication system, 264
Personal computer (PC), defined, 331
Personal Electronic Transactor (PET), 62

Personal financial managers
  defined, 211, 331
  functions of, 211
  types of programs, 211
Personal Information Managers (PIM), defined, 186, 331
Personal information system, 12–13
  defined, 331
Physical system design, defined, 127, 331
Pie chart, defined, 238, 239, 331
Piracy. See Software piracy
Pixel, defined, 89, 331
Plotter
  defined, 88, 331
  operation of, 88
Point, defined, 163, 331
Point of presence (POP), 290
Point-of-sale (POS) system, 136
Point-to-point protocol (PPP)
  defined, 291, 331
  on Internet, 291
Pointing devices, 80–82
  defined, 80, 331
  eye trackers, 82
  graphics tablet, 82
  head position trackers, 82
  mouse, 80, 81
  puck, 82
  stylus, 80, 82
  trackball, 80, 81
Portable computers
  characteristics of, 20
  screen of, 90
  types of, 20–21
Ports
  COM port, 266
  purpose of, 92
Presentation graphics, 225–26, 228
  defined, 225, 331
  features of, 225–26
  programs for, 228
Primary storage
  defined, 77, 331
  See also Main memory
Printer driver, defined, 91, 331
Printers, 87–88
  defined, 87, 332
  development of, 63
  dot-matrix printer, 88
  impact printer, 88
  ink-jet printer, 88
  laser printer, 88
  nonimpact printer, 88
Printing
  document, 153
  spreadsheet, 207
Privacy, ethical issue, 38, 41, 42, 50
Privacy Act of 1974, 41
Privacy for Consumers and Workers Act of 1993, 38, 41

Privacy Protection Act of 1980, 41
Procedures, defined, 331
Processing
    defined, 16, 332
    in information processing, 16, 17
    types of, 112
Processing speed, measurement of, 19
Prodigy, 38
Product design, and computers, 17
Production/operations information
        system
    defined, 133, 332
    functions of, 133
Programmer, defined, 119, 127, 314, 332
Programming language
    assembly language, 120
    defined, 119, 332
    development of, 61, 62, 65
    fifth-generation language, 122
    fourth-generation language, 122
    high-level language, 120
    machine language, 120
PROSPECTOR, 307
Protocol, defined, 263, 332
Puck
    defined, 82, 332
    operation of, 82
Punched-card data processing machine,
        55, 56

Query, defined, 179, 332
Query by example, defined, 182, 332

Random-access memory (RAM)
    defined, 77, 332
    operation of, 77
Range of cells
    defined, 200, 332
    spreadsheet, 200, 202
Raster graphic, defined, 222, 332
Read-only memory (ROM)
    defined, 77, 332
    operation of, 77
Readability, defined, 164, 332
Ready mode, defined, 332
Real-time processing, defined, 112, 332
Record
    defined, 171, 332
    deleting, 178-79
    updating, 176-77
Reel-to-reel tape, defined, 92, 332
Reference materials, multimedia,
        241-42
Relational database, defined, 182, 332
Relational database management system
        (RDMS)
    defined, 182, 332
    functions of, 182
Relative cell reference, defined, 206, 332
Relevance, of information, 11

Reliability, of information, 12
Removable hard disk drive, defined,
        94, 332
Repetitive stress injuries, 25
Report generator
    of database, 179-81
    defined, 179, 332
Rescue, 49
Resolution, defined, 89, 332
Retail sales, computerized operations,
        135-36
Roberts, Ed, 61, 65
Robot, defined, 310, 332
Robotics, 310-13
    defined, 310, 332
    development of, 311
    future developments, 313
    tasks performed, 311-13
Row, defined, 332
SABRE, 7
Sachs, Jonathan, 192
Sampling, 246
Satellite
    as communication channel, 260
    defined, 260, 332
Saving. *See* Backup
Scanners. *See* Optical scanners
Scatter graph, 238
    defined, 238, 332
Screen form, defined, 332
Script, defined, 250, 267, 332
Search and replace, defined, 148, 333
Second-generation computers
    defined, 66, 333
    types of, 66
Second-generation language, 122
Secondary storage, 14, 92-95
    defined, 92, 333
    floppy diskette, 93-94
    hard disk, 94-95
    magnetic disk, 93
    magnetic tape, 92
    optical storage, 96-98
Secondary storage problems, 99-100
    limited storage capacity, 100
    lost data, 99-100
    slow data access, 100
Security
    computer, 46-49
    database, 184
    lock up of system, 47
    password, 48-49
Semiconductor Chip Protection Act of
        1984, 41
Serial Line Interface Protocol (SLIP)
    defined, 291, 333
    on Internet, 291
Serial processing
    defined, 77, 333
    process of, 77

Server, defined, 263, 333
Shell account
    defined, 290
    on Internet, 290-91
Simulation, 213-14
    defined, 213, 225, 333
    uses for, 213-14, 231
Single tasking, defined, 112, 333
Single-user operating system
    defined, 111, 333
    types of, 114, 115
Slide show, defined, 226, 333
Smart homes, 8-9
Smart paper, defined, 301, 333
Society for Worldwide Interbank
        Financial Telecommunications
        (SWIFT), 274
Socrates, 9
Soft copy, defined, 87, 333
Soft page break, defined, 149, 333
Software, 12, 15, 109
    application software, 109, 116-19
    interaction with, 15
    interoperability, 300
    operating system, 109-16
    as product versus service, 33
    system software, 109
    tasks performed by, 15
    utility programs, 116
    workability versus mishaps, 42
Software piracy, 39, 43
    defined, 333
    prevention of, 43
Sorting
    defined, 179, 333
    in spreadsheet, 207
Sound, 245-47
    multimedia audio, 246
    musical instrument digital interface
        (MIDI), 246
    sampling, 246
Special-purpose computers
    defined, 18, 333
    functions of, 18-19
Specialized application software, 116-17
    defined, 116, 333
Speech coding, defined, 91, 333
Speech recognition, 83, 309-310
    defined, 83, 309, 333
    future developments, 309-310
    operation of, 83
Spelling checker, defined, 154, 333
Spinrite, 100
Spreadsheet, 116
    benefits of, 194-95
    blocks of, 209-10
    built-in functions, 200, 202
    common uses of, 195
    data entry, 199-200
    data manipulation, 205-7

Spreadsheet, *continued*
database in, 208
defaults, 199
defined, 193, 333
desktop publishing in, 208
development of, 62
editing, 203-4
formatting, 204-5
formulas, 200
graphing function, 208
labels, 199
order of calculation, 202
printing, 207
range of cells, 200, 202
saving data, 202-3
values, 199
worksheet, 195-99
Spreadsheet design, defined, 209, 333
Spreadsheet software, defined, 193, 333
Status line, defined, 146, 196, 333
Stibitz, George, 57
Stop bit, defined, 267, 333
Storage, 14
defined, 77, 333
future developments, 298-99
in information processing, 16
main memory, 77-78
secondary storage, 92-95
Strategic (top-level) managers
defined, 128, 333
role of, 128
Structured query language (SQL),
defined, 183, 333
Structured-block design approach,
defined, 209, 333
Style sheet, defined, 160, 333
Stylus
defined, 80, 333
operation of, 80
Suess, Randy, 269
Supercomputer
characteristics of, 24
defined, 24, 334
development of, 61
Superconductor
defined, 299, 334
future developments, 299
SuperVGA graphics adapter card, 90, 91
Surge protector, 99
Synthesized audio, 246
System, nature of, 12
System analysis
defined, 127, 334
process of, 127
System analyst, defined, 127, 315, 334
System clock
defined, 76, 334
and speed of computer, 76
System design
defined, 127, 334
process of, 17

System designer, defined, 334
System development life cycle (SDLC),
defined, 126, 334
System implementation
defined, 127, 334
process of, 127-28
System maintenance
defined, 128, 334
process of, 128
System operator (sysop), defined,
334
System software, defined, 109, 334
System unit, 14
defined, 334

Tab settings, defined, 149, 334
Tactical (middle-level) managers
defined, 128, 334
role of, 128
Tandy TRS-80 Model I, 61
Tape drive, defined, 92, 334
Tax preparation software, 211
Tax Reform Act of 1976, 41
Telecommunications
defined, 257, 334
See also Data communications
Telecommuting, defined, 273, 334
Telnet
defined, 283, 334
on Internet, 283
Template, defined, 194, 334
Ten Commandments of Computer
Ethics, 34
Terabyte, 98
Testing, defined, 127, 334
Thesaurus, defined, 154, 334
Third generation language, 122
Third-generation computers
defined, 66, 334
types of, 67
Three-dimensional graphics,
245, 301
Three-dimensional spreadsheet, 207
Time bomb, defined, 44, 334
Time-sharing operating system, defined,
111, 334
Timeliness, of information, 11-12
Titles
defined, 204, 334
of spreadsheet, 204
Touch screens, 82-83
defined, 82, 334
operation of, 82-83
Trackball
defined, 80, 334
operation of, 80, 81
Training
defined, 128, 334
and multimedia system, 241
and simulation programs, 231
Transaction, defined, 334

Transaction processing system (TPS)
defined, 128, 334
functions of, 130
Transistor
defined, 335
and development of computers, 66
Transmission Control Protocol over
Internet Protocol (TCP/IP), defined,
291, 335
Transportables, characteristics of, 20
Trojan horse, 44
defined, 44, 335
Turing, Alan, 57, 64, 65
profile of, 296
Turing test, 296
Tweening, 244
Twisted-pair, 260
defined, 259, 335
Typeface
characteristics of, 162
defined, 162, 335
types of, 162
Typeover mode, defined, 147, 335

Uninterruptable power supply, 100
UNIVAC I, 59, 65
Unix, features of, 115-16
Updating, defined, 176, 335
Uploading, defined, 268, 335
USENET, 39
Usenet, defined, 335
User, defined, 126, 335
User interface, defined, 112, 335
Utility programs
defined, 116, 335
functions of, 116

Vacuum tube
defined, 335
and development of computers, 57,
58, 60
Validating, defined, 335
Value, defined, 199, 335
Value of information, defined, 335
Vector graphics, defined, 222, 335
Ventura Publisher, 157
Veronica
defined, 283, 335
on Internet, 283
Very large scale integration (VLSI)
defined, 67, 335
and development of computers,
67
VGA graphics adapter card, 90, 91
Video, 247-48
in multimedia systems, 247-48
Videodisks, 247
Virtual reality
defined, 303, 335
systems in use, 303
uses of, 303

Virus, 43
  defined, 43, 335
  prevention of, 49
VisiCalc, 62, 193
Visualization software
  defined, 214, 300, 335
  future developments, 300-301
Voice mail
  advantages of, 273
  limitations of, 273
  voice-messaging systems, defined, 273, 335
Voice output, defined, 91, 335
Voice recognition, 309-10
  defined, 301, 308, 335
  future developments, 301-3, 309-10
  operation of, 83
Voice synthesis, defined, 91, 335
Volatile
  defined, 77, 335
  RAM, 77

Wang, An, 59, 64
Watson, Thomas J., 57
Web. *See* World Wide Web (WWW)
Weight, defined, 162, 335
Wet disk, 298
What-if analysis
  defined, 203, 335
  process of, 203-4
Whirlwind computer, 60
White space
  defined, 161, 335
  use in document, 161

Wide Area Information Service (WAIS)
  defined, 286, 335
  on Internet, 286
Wide area networks (WAN), 261-62
  defined, 261, 335
  example of system, 262
Widow line, defined, 164, 335
Wilkes, Maurice V., 59, 64
Williams, Samuel, 57
Window, defined, 196, 335
Windows95, features of, 114-15
Windows 3.0, 64
Wire cable, defined, 336
Wireless computing
  defined, 304, 336
  future developments, 304
Wirth, Niklaus, 121
Word, 63
Word processing
  defined, 143, 336
  compared to desktop publishing, 159
  early programs, 63
Word processor, 143-57
  advantages to use, 144-45
  CD-ROM reference materials, 156
  defined, 143, 336
  editing information, 147-48
  entering information, 146
  formatting document, 148-49, 150-52
  grammar and style checker, 156
  mail merge, 156
  math function, 156-57
  page-layout, 154
  printing document, 153
  saving information, 147

spelling checker, 154
  thesaurus, 154
  work area, 145-46
Word size, defined, 267, 336
WordPerfect, 63
  development of, 142
WordStar, 63
Wordwrap, defined, 146, 336
Working Group on Intellectual Property, 50
Working memory, defined, 336
Worksheet
  components of, 195-99
  defined, 195, 336
  entering data, 199-200
  moving in, 199
Workstation
  characteristics of, 20
  defined, 263, 336
World Wide Web (WWW), 286-89
  connecting to, 286-87
  defined, 286, 336
  graphical interfaces for, 286
  home page, 287
  organization of information, 286
  sites, examples of, 289
Worm, 44, 64
  defined, 44, 336
Wozniak, Stephen, 62, 65
Write-once-read-many (WORM)
  optical disk, defined, 97, 336
WYSIWYG (What You See Is What You Get), defined, 149, 336

Zuse, Konrad, 57